Social Structure and Forms of Consciousness

Volume 1
The Social Determination of Method

István Mészáros

AF652908

AAKAR

SOCIAL STRUCTURE AND FORMS OF CONSCIOUSNESS
István Mészáros

© Monthly Review Press 2010
© Aakar Books for South Asia 2010

Published in agreement with Monthly Review Press, New York for publication and sale only in the Indian Subcontinent (India, Pakistan, Bangladesh, Nepal, Maldives, Bhutan & Sri Lanka)

All rights reserved. No part of this book may be reproduced or transmitted, in any form or by any means, without prior permission of the publisher.

First Published in India, 2010

ISBN 978-93-5002-078-4 (Pb)

Published by
AAKAR BOOKS
28 E Pocket IV, Mayur Vihar Phase I, Delhi 110 091
Phone : 011 2279 5505 Telefax : 011 2279 5641
aakarbooks@gmail.com; www.aakarbooks.com

Printed at
Mudrak, 30 A, Patparganj, Delhi 110 091

Social Structure and Forms of Consciousness

Volume 1

The Social Determination of Method

Contents

For Donatella

INTRODUCTION

As we all know, the social formation dominated by the power of capital extends over a long historical epoch, with no end in sight as yet. However, beyond the far-reaching material changes which mark the intellectual physiognomy of the particular phases of development of the capital system, there are some major continuities as well.

It is precisely the latter that circumscribe the broad methodological parameters of capital's epoch as a whole, with clearly identifiable characteristics. They are shared by the most diverse thinkers who are situated on the same social ground, as we shall see in the chapters that follow.

Understandably, the particular phases of socioeconomic development are marked by significant theoretical and methodological innovations, in accordance with the changing circumstances. It is important to stress, however, that all such methodological shifts and theoretical transformations must accommodate themselves within the constraining limits of the common structural framework that defines the epoch in its entirety.

The class basis of the dominant theories of capital's epoch as a whole is and remains, in Marx's words, "the personification of capital." For several centuries this is coextensive with the bourgeoisie, both in its ascending phases of development and under the conditions of its historical retrogression. In our own age, however, this relationship becomes much more complicated, as we shall see in chapter 8, dealing with the problems of method in a historical epoch of transition.

But returning to the classical phase of capitalist developments, what defines from the outset the fundamental methodological characteristics of the theories which arise on the class basis of the bourgeoisie is precisely the historical situation of this class as the entrenched hegemonic force of the social formation under the rule of capital, together with the structural imperatives inseparable from that rule.

Accordingly, the methodological parameters of the various theories which coherently articulate the fundamental interests of this class basis, notwithstanding the differences of the particular thinkers—differences which arise on the ground of the given national setting; the locally prevailing relation of forces and conditions of social interaction; the historically changing role of the class with regard to the productive potentialities of capital's social formation and the ensuing intensification of the social antagonisms on a global scale; etc.—are set for the epoch in its entirety, embracing not only all of its phases up to the present but, *mutatis mutandis*, also what lies beyond. They extend as far ahead, in fact, as capital can successfully assert and reassert itself—also in the most complex epoch of transition to a new social order—as the significant controlling force of the social metabolism. For the fundamental methodological parameters of historical epochs are circumscribed by the *ultimate structural limits* of its dominant force of social metabolic control, and as such they are defined in terms of the potentialities (and, of course, also the limitations) inherent in the prevailing mode of productive activity and corresponding distribution of the total social product.

This is why the representative figures of capital's social horizon must conceptualize everything in a determinate way, and not otherwise. And since the limits in question are *structurally untranscendable*—in that their supersession would require the institution of a *radically* different mode of production and distribution—the principal methodological characteristics of the synthesizing theories which originate within their framework cannot be significantly altered. For a radical alteration of the limits in question would be tantamount to completely abandoning capital's "standpoint of political economy" (corresponding to capital's self-serving vantage point more or less consciously adopted by the major thinkers), as Marx himself actually did.

Indeed, as we know from past history, the methodological boundaries of capital's social formation cannot be fundamentally altered even when some exceptional thinkers, under quite extraordinary historical circumstances, become aware of the contradictions which they are called upon to defend, and try to devise some form of theoretical "reconciliation." An outstanding example in this respect is Hegel, as we shall see below in a number of very different contexts.

THE METHODOLOGICAL CHARACTERISTICS of the various systems of thought, which emerge within the historical framework and in support of capital's social formation, constitute a closely interlocking set of conceptual determinations.

Understandably, all such characteristics are also crucial with regard to defining these systems of thought as specific forms of ideology. Furthermore, they are clearly discernible across the particular phases of development of capital's social formation as a whole.

We must concentrate in the present study on some of the most important of these methodological characteristics, which may be summed up as follows:

1. *Programmatic orientation towards science* and the key methodological/theoretical as well as practical role assigned to natural science.

2. General tendency to *formalism*.

3. The standpoint of *isolated individuality* and its enduring methodological equivalent, capital's "*standpoint of political economy*," as seen from the established system's necessarily prejudged and structurally limiting vantage point.

4. *Negative determination* of philosophy and social theory.

5. The increasingly more evident and ultimately quite devastating *suppression of historical temporality*.

6. The imposition of a *dualistic* and *dichotomous* categorial matrix

on philosophy and social theory, significantly prevailing even when some of the greatest thinkers of all times, like Hegel, attempt to distance themselves from it.

7. The *abstract postulates* of "unity" and "universality" as the wishful transcendence of the persistent dichotomies—in place of real *mediations*—and the purely speculative supersession of the major social contradictions without altering in the slightest their causal foundations in the actually existing world.

As we shall see, all of these characteristics are firmly anchored to the need to articulate and defend determinate social interests by the leading intellectual personifications of capital. It is for this reason that they cannot help being inseparably methodological and ideological in their innermost determination.

NATURALLY, IT IS IMPORTANT TO UNDERLINE here that stressing the social determination of method does not—and cannot—mean anything *mechanical,* as the thinkers who nowadays align themselves with the material and ideological vested interests of the established social reproductive order try to misrepresent it. There can be nothing one-sided and mechanical in these relations. On the contrary, the complex dynamics of historical development can only be properly understood on the basis of *dialectical reciprocity*. This is precisely how Marx characterized, already in one of his early works, *The German Ideology*—in a forceful critique of the idealist approach dominant at the time in philosophical debates—his view of the "*reciprocal action*" in evidence among the various factors and forces which constitute the overall social complex. Talking about his own assessment of the irrepressible historical transformation he insisted that

> This conception of history relies on expounding the real process of production—starting from the material production of life itself—and comprehending the form of intercourse connected with and created by this mode of production, i.e., civil society in its various stages, as the basis of all history; describing it in its action as the state, and also explaining how all the different theoretical products and forms of consciousness, reli-

> gion, philosophy, morality, etc., etc., arise from it, and tracing the process of their *formation* from that basis; thus the whole thing can, of course, be depicted in its totality (and therefore, too, the *reciprocal action* of these various sides on one another). It has not, like the idealist view of history, to look for a *category* in every period, but remains constantly on the real ground of history; it does not explain practice from the idea but explains the *formation* of ideas from material practice, and accordingly it comes to the conclusion that all forms and products of consciousness cannot be dissolved by *mental criticism,* by resolution into 'self-consciousness' or transformation into 'apparitions,' 'spectres,' 'whimsies,' etc., but only by the *practical overthrow* of the actual social relations which gave rise to this idealistic humbug; that not criticism but *revolution* is the driving force of history, *also of religion, of philosophy and all other kinds of theory*. It shows that history does not end by being resolved into 'self-consciousness' as 'spirit of the spirit,' but that each stage contains a material result, a sum of productive forces, a *historically created* relation to nature and of individuals to one another, which is handed down to each generation from its predecessor; a mass of productive forces, capital funds and circumstances, which on the one hand is indeed *modified* by the new generation, but on the other also *prescribes* for it its conditions of life and gives it a definite development, a special character. It shows that *circumstances make men* just as much as *men make circumstances.*[1]

It would be very difficult to spell out these matters with greater clarity than it was done by Marx in the quoted lines. But that seems to make no difference at all when the material and ideological vested interests must prevail in the all too eagerly adopted enterprise of "refuting" Marx and Marxism at whatever cost. Also, it goes without saying that the same fundamental points of criticism which were addressed by Marx in *The German Ideology* to the idealist varieties of philosophy applied with equal justification to the materialist failure to grasp the dialectical complexity of the actual historical process. This was made amply clear by Marx in his well known "Theses on Feuerbach," written in the same period as *The German Ideology*. It is all the more revealing, therefore, that the general rule is always a systematic distortion of the position of *historical materialism*—not to mention the idea of *dialectical materialism* which must be treated and dismissed with the profundity of swearwords only— whether such refutation is offered by Marx's speculative idealist adversaries or by the representatives of positivistic materialism.

However, the real issue is that the vantage point of capital which is adopted by the major thinkers of the historical epoch under discussion *is* in a proper sense truly *adopted* by them, through their most active involvement in this matter of ultimately overwhelming importance. The social determination of method does not—and cannot—mean that the methodological and ideological position corresponding to capital's vantage point is *imposed* on the thinkers concerned, including the outstanding figures of bourgeois political economy and philosophy. They actively *make it their own* in the course of—and through the creative process of—*articulating* the position which embodies the fundamental *interests*, as well as the *values*, of a social reproductive order with which they identify themselves. They are *conscious participants* in an enterprise which always involves conflict and confrontation with the advocates of potentially rival sets of values, even if the corresponding social interests are not (or cannot be, because of the historical immaturity of the relevant social forces) rendered quite explicit by their adversaries. For even the most firmly entrenched *ruling ideology* can never be *absolutely ruling*. In other words, it cannot be so totally dominant that it should be able to ignore altogether some, at least potentially far-reaching, alternative position. Not even when the dominant ideology unhesitatingly claims for itself the privilege of representing the one and only tenable outlook which in its view wholly agrees with *nature itself*, in one such version,[2] or in the same sense of exclusiveness it is said to correspond to the fully realized "rational actuality" of the "World Spirit," in another approach, as we shall see below.

Thus, without the slightest doubt, the major thinkers of the historical epoch discussed in this book not only adopt but *actively* and in its genuine meaning *consciously shape*—both when they originally *articulate* and when they subsequently *renew*—the position corresponding to the vital interests of the capital system. For without constant renewal and reassertion of its basic tenets the ruling order could not properly sustain itself. The most important thinkers in question, as we shall have the opportunity to see in the development of their conceptions, pursue such work of renewal with great coherence and determination under the changing conditions and circumstances of their society, and doing that well within the overall horizon—which offers to them in determinate historical periods (when their class finds itself in the ascendant, but less and less so as we approach our own time) significant margin for creative intervention in the social process, despite the ultimately prevailing structural limitations—of capital's interests and controlling power.

THE *CONSCIOUS* CHARACTER OF THE INVOLVEMENT, and the corresponding historical *responsibility*, of the major intellectual representatives of capital is not diminished (and even less can it be minimized) by the circumstance that they also adopt and constantly reproduce the *illusion* that in their conception of the right and proper social order they are articulating the *universal interest* of society, and not only of its structurally dominant force. For, again, we are talking about a process whereby the thinkers concerned *actively make their own* such illusions, which happen to be *ideologically most convenient* illusions, corresponding to the vantage point of capital's social metabolic order.

This is how we end up being offered even by the greatest figures of the bourgeois intellectual tradition a view of the world in which an *obvious historical formation*, the established order of society which, moreover, is also dense with insoluble *antagonistic contradictions*, is transfigured into something not just *tenable*, presented without any reference whatsoever to historical time, but also as *the only viable mode of societal interchange* conceivable at all. And this is also the way in which the great dialectical thinker, Hegel, violates his own principle of dialectics—indeed in methodological and ideological terms even more revealingly in the name of a postulated "dialectical advance"[3]—so as to be able to transubstantiate the real *compulsion* inseparable from the given reproductive system, and explicitly acknowledged by Hegel himself, into the *universal enjoyment* of each "self-seeking individual" subsumed under capital's structurally entrenched hierarchical mode of social control.[4]

According to all available evidence the insurmountable problem is that the major intellectual representatives of capital's epoch which we are concerned with, no matter how great they might be as thinkers, take for granted the *fundamental practical premises* of the given social order in their combined totality, as a *set of deeply interconnected determinations.*

These practical premises—like the radical divorce of the means of production from labour; the assignment of all of the important directing and decision making functions in the established productive and reproductive order to the personifications of capital; the regulation of the social metabolic interchange between human beings and nature and among the individuals themselves (unalterably and ever more dangerously) on the basis of capital's second order mediations; the determination and management of the all-embracing political command structure of society in the form of the capitalist state—are so crucial to this particular mode of societal control that it could not function at all for any length of time without even one of them. For they set the *structural limits of viability* of a historically produced mode of production and distribution which has been firmly rooted now for centuries and resists with all means at its disposal all meaningful change.

As noted before in past discussions, the actuality of the historical movement and change was at times acknowledged also by some great intellectual figures who viewed the world from capital's vantage point, like Hegel. However, whenever historical development happened to be acknowledged in that way, it was always done with reference to the past. Transformatory historical movement and societal change was admissible by those who viewed the world from the standpoint of political economy only in the form of, and to the extent to which, they could fit into the strictly circumscribed framework of capital's fundamental practical premises. The importance of radical, structurally evident, historical change could be underlined by the major thinkers of the enlightened bourgeoisie as regards the *feudal past* but denied at the same time in the direction of the future.

To be sure, what makes it extremely difficult to envisage abandoning capital's vantage point even by the greatest thinkers who share the standpoint of political economy is precisely the fact that the practical premises mentioned above constitute a set of deeply interconnected—and indeed, as mentioned before, *closely interlocking*—determinations, as the all-important defining characteristics of capital's organic system. Thus they cannot be abandoned *selectively*, so as to put thereby under question mark the whole system, by the thinkers who define their own position in tune with the standpoint of capital. Nor can they be, for the same reason, practically transcended by a rival force *partially*—as has been proved with painful conclusiveness by the historical failure of social democracy—without radically superseding capital's *structurally dominant* order in its entirety by a sustainable *hegemonic alternative.* Thus, when some great thinkers express their misgivings about the negative impact of some ongoing social developments, as Adam Smith did when he deplored the dehumanizing neglect of education which he saw arising from the division and fragmentation of labour, or when he eloquently acknowledged that "*the people who clothe the world are in rags themselves*,"[5] such misgivings never could amount to more than a marginal critique of the given social order, coupled with the great Scottish thinker's wholesale enthusiasm for capital as "*the natural system of perfect liberty and justice.*"[6]

The vital practical premises of the established reproductive order had to be *actively internalized* by even the greatest thinkers of the bourgeoisie in the ascendant, and turned into the essential methodological and ideological conceptions of a whole historical epoch, most powerfully contributing thereby at the same time to the full development and long continued viability of the capital system itself. This is how the frequently unmentioned (or unmentionable) but absolutely necessary *practical premises*—and, in other words, *systemic* as well as *structural determinations*—of by far the most dynamic social metabolic order in all human history became *actively embodied* in the most important *theoretical systems* of the bourgeoisie, deeply affecting the way of thinking of the great majority of the people even in our time.

THE HISTORICAL DIMENSION OF THESE MATTERS is fundamental. For a number of reasons the importance of this fact cannot be stressed strongly and frequently enough.

First, because the ruling ideology cannot sustain its claims to universal validity without systematically denying the inescapability of historical determinations, by *eternalizing* its own position, no matter how much distortion—and in our time even a constant violation of the facts—is needed in order to make plausible its anti-historical view of the allegedly unalterable system of societal reproductive interchange. Hayek's idealization of the capitalist exchange relations—despite the historical specificity of their deep-seated and ultimately explosive antagonisms—as the eternalized "extended economic order," presented by him in completely unthinking positive terms, and at the same time his vituperative depiction of the grossly misrepresented socialist alternative as "The Road to Serfdom," offer a graphic illustration of such wanton disregard for even the most obvious historical facts.

Second, because the meaning of the dynamic historical determinations is often misunderstood as some kind of fatalistic necessity also by those who have no vested interest in adopting the standpoint of capital. And it makes no real difference in this regard that the people concerned might assume a positive attitude towards such misconceived "necessity." For also in that way the actual historical process is significantly distorted and can only generate resentment and even hostility towards the idea of the necessary historical transformation. What really decides the issue is that in the dialectical interactive process of dynamic historical determinations nothing can be taken as rigid and absolutely final, whether you approve of it for the time being or not. *Historical necessity* is truly historical not simply because it emerges with undeniable firmness from highly complex dialectical determinations in the course of its unfolding, but also because it becomes in due course a "*disappearing necessity*"—"eine verschwindende Notwendigkeit"—in Marx's words. Voluntaristically ignoring this vital aspect of historical necessity can produce devastating socioeconomic and political consequences, as we had to learn it in the twentieth century from the tragic failure of some major strategies pursued in the socialist movement.

Third, because the contrast between the views of the great thinkers of the more remote past and some twentieth century conceptualizations of the same problems is most revealing. Let it suffice to take here only the example of the *Discourse on Method* by Descartes. As we know, Descartes was much concerned with the question of *methodological doubt* and with the need for *self-evident certainty,* saying at the same time: "Not that in this I imitated the *sceptics*, who doubt only that they may doubt and seek nothing beyond *uncertainty* itself; for on the contrary, *my design was singly to find ground of assurance*, and cast aside the loose earth and sand that I might reach the rock or the clay."[7] In complete contrast we find in the celebrated work of a twentieth century historian nothing but boundless scepticism and pessimism when he tries to make us believe that "there is no more sense in human history than in the changes of the seasons or the movements of the stars; or if sense there be, it escapes our perception."[8]

When he was looking for philosophical certainty, Descartes insisted on the importance of making knowledge practical and useful in the great enterprise of the envisaged human control of nature by putting into relief that "I perceived it to be possible to arrive at *knowledge highly useful in life;* and in room of the speculative philosophy usually taught in the schools, to discover a *practical* [philosophy] by means of which . . . we might also apply them to all the uses to which they are adapted, and thus *render ourselves the lords and possessors of nature.*"[9] By contrast, we find in the work of even a major twentieth century philosopher, Edmund Husserl, the most rigid opposition between "the theoretical attitude" and "the practical" when he asserts that "The *theoretical attitude*, even though it too is a professional attitude, is *thoroughly unpractical.* Thus it is based on a deliberate *epoché* [bracketing] from *all practical interests,* and consequently even those of a higher level, that serve natural needs within the framework of a life's occupation governed by such practical interests."[10] No wonder, therefore, that by setting himself a methodological trap of this kind Husserl could only postulate a totally unreal appeal to the "*heroism of Reason*"[11] as the wishfully predicated counter-force to Nazi barbarism.[12]

And finally, in contrast to self-enclosed, "monadologically" oriented philosophy in the twentieth century, Descartes was fully conscious of the importance of carrying on the work of intellectual creation as a genuine collective enterprise: ". . . so that, by the last beginning where those before them had left off, and thus *connecting the lives and labours of many*, we might *collectively* proceed much farther."[13] Only by reviving such ethos, and meaningfully enhancing it in accordance with the urgent requirements of our own time, can we really face up to the issues we must confront.

THE RELATIONSHIP BETWEEN SOCIAL STRUCTURE and forms of consciousness is seminally important. This is because the actually given social structure constitutes the overall framework and horizon in which the particular thinkers, in all fields of social and philosophical study, are situated and in relation to which they have to define their conception of the world.[14]

As mentioned before, the fundamental methodological and ideological parameters of the particular historical epochs, including the age of capital, are firmly circumscribed by the *ultimate structural limits* of their dominant social force, matching the prevailing type of productive activity and the corresponding modality of distribution. Any theoretical attempt to escape from such determinations, in the misconceived pursuit of some evasive "meta-theories," can only damage the philosophical enterprise. In fact the more comprehensive and the more mediated the chosen subject matter might be, the more obvious must be its link to the "totalizing" structural determinations of the relevant historical epoch. This must be the case in view of the fact that a proper conception of *mediation* in any field of analysis is unthinkable without a *comprehensive* grasp of the field of study in question, whether we think of "meta-ethics" or indeed of methodology in general. The legitimate analysis of the various *discourses*—e.g., the moral, the political and the aesthetic discourse—is inconceivable without being dialectically inserted into the proper structural framework of overall determinations. For the particular discourses are not intelligible at all without being grasped as *specific forms of social consciousness.* That is, as forms of consciousness which are historically constituted and likewise historically transformed in close conjunction with the overall determinations of the *social structure* from which they cannot be speculatively abstracted. Moreover, the fact that there is an essential *trans*-historical[15]—but decidedly not *supra*-historical—dimension to all such discourses, as there is also to the analysis of methodology in general, in that their study can be legitimately pursued *across* human history as a whole, such, frequently ignored, fact can only underline the importance of always inserting them, no matter how mediated they might be (as the analysis of methodology inevitably has to be) into their appropriately comprehensive and historically defined structural framework.

Despite the unavoidably mediated character of the problems at stake it is necessary for us to engage in the discussion of the issues arising from the methodological and ideological determinations of capital's epoch. This is so because they happen to be most relevant to our own concerns not only theoretically but also in practical terms. For no matter how strongly we may, and indeed must, disagree with the methodological and ideological tenets of the theoretical tradition inseparable from capital's standpoint, it is an essential condition of a proper historical understanding—which is itself vital for the elaboration of long term sustainable social and political strategies—to be fully aware of the *connecting links* and persistent continuities as well, instead of noticing the sharp *discontinuities* only. This means that it is indispensable to focus also on those elements of the theories in question which must be and can only be "aufgehoben"; that is, dialectically superseded/preserved by being raised to a historically more advanced level, so as to be put to a socially positive use.

This is particularly important in a period of *transition* toward a historically viable social order. In other words, properly engaging with the problems at stake constitutes a contribution to a much needed transition to what Marx called "the new historic form" which happens to be a literally vital defining characteristic of our own time. To be sure, the solutions conceived from capital's vantage point conformed at the time of their formulation to some fundamental, structurally determined social interests, in accordance with capital's vantage point, and thus they obviously cannot fit into the framework of the necessary hegemonic alternative. Nevertheless the fact remains that the solutions in question have been produced in response to very real historical challenges and objective social determinations which, in an important sense, are still part of our own predicament. For the objective historical challenges do not cease to exist, nor lose their power, by receiving from a structurally biased standpoint—matching capital's unreformable practical premises—the kind of answers which turn out to be socially untenable in the longer run. The questions constantly reproduced by social reality itself, despite receiving extremely problematical solutions even by the greatest bourgeois thinkers of the past, can only accentuate the weight and continued relevance of the underlying problems themselves. Thus, if anything, the long persistent objective challenges calling for historically viable answers are more pressing today than ever before. That is the true measure of the task for the future.

NOTES

1. Karl Marx and Frederick Engels, *Collected Works*, Vol. 5, Lawrence and Wishart, London, 1975, pp. 53–4.

2. For instance in the seminal work of the great Scottish representative of the Enlightenment, Adam Smith.
3. See Hegel's *Philosophy of Right*, Clarendon Press, Oxford, 1942, pp. 139–30.
4. See chapter 7.5 below.
5. Adam Smith, *Lectures on Justice, Police, Revenue, and Arms*, in Herbert W. Schneider (ed.), *Adam Smith's Moral and Political Philosophy*, Hafner Publishing Company, New York, 1948, p. 320.
6. Adam Smith, *The Wealth of Nations,* Adam and Charles Black, Edinburgh, 1863, p. 273.
7. Descartes, *A Discourse on Method,* Everyman Edition, Dent and Sons, London, 1957, p. XVI.
8. Sir Lewis Namier, *Vanished Supremacies: Essays on European History, 1812–1918,* Penguin Books, Harmondsworth, 1962, p. 203.
9. Descartes, *ibid.,* p. 49.
10. *Philosophy and the Crisis of European Man,* in Husserl, *Phenomenology and the Crisis of Philosophy,* Harper & Row, New York, 1965, p. 168.
11. Ibid., p. 192. See the discussion of these problems in chapter 7.1 below.
12. Lukács used to recall that when Max Scheler was talking to him with great enthusiasm about Husserl's novel approach to philosophy centered on phenomenological reduction, saying that with the help of such method it was possible to analyse even the devil and hell by putting them into the proper "methodological bracket," the Hungarian philosopher's ironical answer was that "yes, you do that, and when you open the bracket you will have to face the devil himself." And that is precisely what happened to Husserl in 1935, when he was groping, in vain, for answers to Nazi barbarism in his Prague lecture on *Philosophy and the Crisis of European Man.*
13. Descartes, *A Discourse on Method*, p. 50.
14. Although he does not use the expression "social structure," Hegel is willing to acknowledge in some way the determining role of the given historical conditions when he writes: "It is just as absurd to fancy that a philosophy can transcend its contemporary world as it is to fancy that an individual can overleap his own age, jump over Rhodes." (*The Philosophy of Right*, p. 11.) But he uses such insight reconciliatorily in the service of the *closure* of history in the present "rational actuality," idealizing it through the "World Spirit" as the "eternal present."

15. Plato and Aristotle are great examples of how far concern with some major issues of the moral, political and aesthetic discourses goes back in history, underlining at the same time the importance of both the *transhistorical* dimension and the inescapable, historically confined, *specificity* of the views elaborated by them.

CHAPTER ONE

The Programmatic Orientation toward Science

1.1 "The Mastery of Man over Nature"

The key methodological and practical role assigned to natural science by the general orienting principle that envisages "The Mastery of Man over Nature" is not simply a question of the way in which "Descartes, in defining animals as mere machines, saw with eyes of the manufacturing period, while to eyes of the middle ages, animals were assistants to man."[1]

Nor does it consist merely in the use to which science is put as the *model* for philosophical activity when Kant, for instance, insists that:

> What the *chemist* does in the analysis of substances, what the *mathematician* in pure mathematics, is, in a still higher degree, the *duty of the philosopher*, that the value of each different kind of cognition, and the part it takes in the operations of the mind, may be clearly defined.[2]

For no matter how telling all such uses might be in their own—rather limited—context, they do not apply to the epoch as a whole. Indeed, it would be rather difficult to treat animals on the model of machines in the light of contemporary knowledge. Equally, it would be extremely restrictive in relation to the complexities of modern philosophy to model the "duty of philosophers" on chemistry and pure mathematics.

What is centrally important right from the beginning, and remains so to our own days—indeed, in its vital ideological functions it becomes even more important, as the diffusion of the "scientific" ideology of "social engineering/little by little" shows—is the expectation to solve the problems of humankind through the advancement of science and productive technology alone. An expectation, that is, to solve the identified problems without any need for a major intervention on the plane of the antagonistically contested social structure itself.

In this sense it is by no means accidental that ever since Descartes the question of how to accomplish the "mastery of man over *nature*" should be pursued with unrelenting intensity and one-sidedness. Accordingly, the task of philosophy must be defined as wedded to the realization of this objective. As Marx argued:

> That Descartes, like Bacon, anticipated an alteration in the form of production, and the practical subjugation of nature by Man, as a result of the altered methods of thought, is plain from his *Discours de la méthode*. He there says: 'It is possible' (by the methods he introduced in philosophy) 'to attain knowledge very useful in life and, in place of the speculative philosophy taught in the schools, one can find a *practical philosophy* by which, given that we know the various trades of our craftsmen, we shall be able to employ them in the same manner as the latter to all those uses to which they are adapted, and thus as it were *make ourselves the masters and the possessors of nature*,' thereby contributing 'to the *perfection of human life*.' In the preface to Sir Dudley North's *Discourse upon Trade* (1691) it is stated, that Descartes' method had begun to free Political Economy from the old fables and superstitious notions of gold, trade, &c. On the whole, however, the early English economists sided with Bacon and Hobbes as their philosopher; while, at a later period, the philosopher *par excellence* of Political Economy in England, France, and Italy, was Locke.[3]

At the same time, the closely related question of how it might be possible for humankind to achieve the *conscious mastery over the material and human conditions of social reproduction* (in other words: "the mastery of men over themselves," i.e., over their *social* conditions of existence and *human* interchange with one another)—which inevitably affect, frustrate, and ultimately even nullify the realization of the more limited task of "mastery of man over nature," too—is either completely ignored, or more or less mechanically subordinated to that of how to secure the self-development of science and material production, which in the given social reality is equivalent to blindly obeying the imperatives of self-expanding exchange-value.

Within this perspective, the legitimately feasible objectives of human activity *must* be conceptualized in terms of material advancement through the agency of the natural sciences, remaining blind to the *social dimension* of human existence in other than essentially functional/operative and manipulative terms. For an alternative view would necessitate abandoning the "standpoint of political economy," equivalent to the vantage point of capital, which must see even in living labour nothing but a "material factor of production."

No wonder, thus, that we are constantly presented, across the span of several centuries, with the same science-oriented ideology, in so many different versions, from the Cartesian conception of "practical philosophy" and its object to the recent postulates of the "second and third industrial revolution," the "technological revolution," the "electronic revolution," and the "information revolution," as discussed in Part One of my book on *The Power of Ideology*.[4] For the common denominator of all such diversity is the desire to find solutions to the identified problems and deficiencies of social life—which are subject to rival interpretations and irreconcilable conflict in strategic perspectives—strictly within the confines of science and technology.

The "self-evident rationality" of the latter is supposed to speak for itself, and its stipulated remedies by definition (in virtue of their eminently uncontentious "technical" or "technological rationality") exclude the possibility of antagonistic confrontations and the danger of fundamental—structural societal—change.

1.2 Behaviourists and Weberians

The nearer we come to the present, and the more sharply the basic social contradictions erupt into the open, the more accentuated becomes the apologetic character of the theories which remain identified with capital's self-serving vantage point that circumscribes the orientation of bourgeois political economy. Their principal concern assumes ever more *manipulative* and *technocratic* forms. As a result, the very idea of human choice becomes extremely problematical, to the point of almost complete meaninglessness, whatever the much disputed but in reality rather superficial differences among the various thinkers.

Admittedly, a behaviourist, like B. F. Skinner, does not hesitate to dismiss the idea of human *choice* itself as an illusion, in favour of his own manipulative concept, arguing that:

> An organism can be reinforced by—can be made to 'choose'—almost any given state of affairs. . . . The decision I am to make used to be assigned to the province of *ethics*. But we are now studying similar combinations of positive and negative consequences, as well as collateral conditions which affect the result, in the *laboratory*. Even a *pigeon* can be taught some measure of *self-control!* And this work helps us to understand the *operation of certain formulas*—among them *value-judgments*—which folk-wisdom, religion, and psychoterapy have advanced in the interest of *self-discipline*. The observable effect of any statement of value is to alter the relative *effectiveness of reinforcers*. . . . *Inner control* is no more a goal than *external*. . . if we value the achievements and goals of democracy we must not refuse to *apply science to the design and construction of cultural patterns*, even though we may then find ourselves in some sense in the position of [Orwell's] *controllers*.[5]

However, the fact that "choice" is put in sceptical inverted commas while the notion of the *pigeon's self-discipline* is entertained in all seriousness, should not hide from us the fundamental identity of Skinner's views with those who are anxious to enlist some abstract moral imperatives in the service of the desired technological manipulation.

The Weberian Robert Nisbet, for instance, takes for granted the concern "with the rational and calculated achievement of ends which, more and more in our society, are autonomous and self-justifying ends," rhetorically opposing to it a vacuous and impotent wish for "individual responsibility." What is telling about the whole enterprise is that even if such "individual responsibility" could be envisaged as marginally operative—though it decidedly cannot be, since the whole notion, totally devoid of any real foundation, is sustained only by the power of an impotent "ought"—it would in no way alter the dominant social practices which are uncritically accepted by the author. For, according to him:

> The very progress of *modern administrative techniques* has created a problem in the maintenance and nurture of individual thought and action. . . . By its *triumph of rationality, scientific administration* has reduced much of the elbow room, much of the intellectual and moral friction which *ethical individuality must have if it is to flourish*. . . . Such administration, and all that it implies, can too often take away the informal and challenging *atmosphere* that *creative people need.*

The apologetic determinations behind Nisbet's hollow "ought-to-be" of "individual responsibility" and elitistic "creativity" become clear when he touches upon some vital social factors, but only in order to exempt them from their very real responsibility. As he puts it: "Admittedly, *military defence* is the context of a great deal of present-day technology, but I would argue[6] that *technological imperatives* have attained a degree of *primacy* not likely to be offset by any changes in the international scene. *Modern technology* has *its own* characteristic structures, *its* built-in drives, *its* moral codes."

Nisbet deals in the same way with the grave material problems and social contradictions of the countries emerging from the former colonial Empires, described by him with customary vacuity as "non-Western cultures." He sees in their plight—in reality the predicament of continued exploitation of staggering proportions—nothing but "symbolic dislocation," with "deep moral consequences." Quoting Susanne Langer about the dangers of suddenly plowing up "the field of our unconscious symbolic orientation," he adds: "This plainly is what is happening to large parts of the non-Western world at the present time, and the results are frequently to be seen in *cultural disorganization and moral confusion.*"

Thus the function of his discourse is no more than to focus on some empty moral postulates and to leave the actual, highly exploitative power relations from which the "non-Western cultures" continue to suffer completely out of sight.[7]

In all these respects, Nisbet's neo-Weberian equation has the "triumph of rationality," "scientific administration," the "rational and calculated achievement of autonomous and self-justifying ends" and the "technological imperatives" of the military/industrial complex on one side, and the vague desiderata of "individual responsibility" and "informal and challenging atmosphere" for the benefit of the "creative people" on the other. No one in their right mind should expect from such a contest even the slightest, let alone significant, social change. Indeed, just as Galbraith's "*technostructure*," which transubstantiates the antagonistic material determinations of capital into a reified pseudo-scientific construct, with its own "technological imperatives" and self-justifying claims to rationality, Nisbet's fetishistic conception, too, makes real conflictuality disappear behind the façade of a frozen science and technology, inextricably locked into the vicious circle of their allegedly autonomous imperatives and inalterable "primacy."

1.3 Mannheim's "Scientific Sociology of Culture"

But even if we think of an avowedly very different approach—Mannheim's advocacy of "democratic planning" and "social reform"—a closer examination reveals that the substance of his theory not only does not match but directly contradicts the author's claims. For while he is willing to talk about the need for "focusing responsibility on some visible social agent,"[8] he accepts, just as uncritically as Nisbet does, the material foundations of the established order, defining the tasks in terms of "building up a new social order *under competent leadership*" which he identifies with the "wealthy and educated few."[9]

Since the established order is taken for granted by Mannheim, his primary concern is confined to "the development of the method of democratic value guidance, as it is *gradually* being worked out in the *Anglo-Saxon democracies*."[10] And the cynically *manipulative* substance of his "scientific" educational strategy comes into the open when he advocates one kind of enlightenment for those who are destined to fulfil the role of "competent leadership," and a radically different one for the "simple man":

> if our present-day democracy comes to the conclusion that this frame of mind [i.e., the socially vacuous postulate he earlier advocated for 'strengthening the intellectual powers of the ego'[11]] is undesirable, or that it is impracticable or not yet feasible where great *masses* are concerned, we ought to have the *courage* to build this fact into our educational strategy. In this case we ought, in certain spheres, to admit and foster those values which appeal directly to the *emotions* and *irrational powers* in man, and at the same time to concentrate our efforts on *education for rational insight* where this is *within our reach*. [i.e., we continue to favour the 'wealthy few'.] . . . The solution seems to me to lie in a kind of *gradualism* in education, which acknowledges stages of training where both the *irrational* approach and the *rational* find their *proper place*. There was something of that vision in the *planned system of the Catholic Church,* which tried to present the truth to the *simple man* through *images* and the dramatic processes of the *ritual,* and invited the *educated* to face the very same truth on the level of theological *argument*.[12]

Thus, again, the sociologist's "scientific" enterprise aims at the production of "the necessary consensus and compromise" and at the "reconciliation of antagonistic valuations"[13] by "devising a *technique* for coming to an agreement about basic valuations"[14] and a "*machinery* of co-ordination and value mediation."[15] The possibility that social antagonisms are not merely differences in "valuation" (suspended in thin air)—to be brought under control by the institutionalization of irrational "images and rituals" on one side, and the self-perpetuating "rationality" of manipulative "techniques," "instruments" and "machinery" of the "competent leaders" on the other—but the manifestations of fundamental differences of interest, hence calling for a *radical alternative* to the established social order as their only viable condition of solution, cannot conceivably enter the horizon of Mannheim's apologetic wisdom.

From the point of view of his "scientific sociology of knowledge" and "sociology of culture," Mannheim is unable to perceive the intractable conflictual character of weighty social problems (including "unemployment, malnutrition or lack of education"), preferring to see them instead as merely "environmental obstacles"[16] whose removal—and thereby the successful implementation of the desired "process of group adjustment and value reconciliation"—is predicated on the basis of the "*empirical methods* of investigation which in so many other fields pointed out *remedies for institutional deterioration.*"[17]

As to the possibility of not adopting his recipe for "democratic planning" and "social reform"—which leaves the structural framework of the established order *exactly* as it is, making only "scientifically" more effective its manipulative instrumentality for the control of the masses (hence its curious claims of "democratic planning" and "social reform")—we are presented by Mannheim with the starkest warning:

> If this does not happen, the enslavement of mankind by some totalitarian or dictatorial system of planning will follow, and once it is established it is hard to see how it could ever be removed, or wither away by itself.[18]

1.4 The Structural Links of Science-Oriented Ideology

However, the most important aspect of the problem here discussed is not the apologetic and manipulative uses to which science and technology can be put in contemporary bourgeois ideology. Rather, it concerns the untranscendable *structural limitations* of this science-oriented horizon itself across the different phases of capital's historical development. For what is necessarily ruled out from the very beginning of this development is the possibility of radical social changes that might undermine capital's spontaneously enforced material dictates.

Every legitimate improvement must be containable well *within* the structural parameters of such dictates, and everything that lies outside them, or points beyond them, *ipso facto* remains conceptually hidden from the bourgeois intellectual horizon, since it cannot be fitted into the vital *material premises* of the given society. And since the dominant productive practices are indissolubly wedded to the practices of the natural sciences under the rule of capital's logic, the material interests of self-expanding exchange-value and the ideological interests of defining "social improvement" in its terms necessarily coincide, reducing the all-important concept of *social control* to *conformity* to the structural presuppositions and imperatives of the established order.

It is precisely this *coincidence* of the two fundamental interests of productive expansion through science on the one hand, and ideological conformity to the requirements of envisaging "social improvement" only in such materially predetermined and socially containable terms on the other—with its powerful impact on helping to perpetuate the rule of capital—that makes the "standpoint of political economy" science-oriented throughout its long history.

NOTES

1. Marx, *Capital,* Vol. 1, Foreign Languages Publishing House, Moscow, 1959, p. 390.
2. Kant, *Critique of Pure Reason*, Everyman's Library, p. 476.
3. Marx, *Capital,* Vol. 1, p. 390.
4. See István Mészáros, *The Power of Ideology*, Harvester/Wheatsheaf, London, and New York University Press, 1988, pp. 3–174.
5. Carl R. Rogers and B. F. Skinner, "Some Issues Concerning the Control of Human Behavior: A Symposium," *Science*, No. 124 (Nov. 30, 1956), reprinted in Jack D. Douglas, ed., *The Technological Threat*, New Jersey, 1971, pp. 146–9.
6. Without any attempt at offering even the slightest proof, of course.
7. All quotations are from "The Impact of Technology on Ethical Decision-Making," in Robert Lee and M. E. Merty, eds., *Religion and Social Conflict*, Oxford University Press, New York, 1964, pp. 185–200.
8. Karl Mannheim, *Diagnosis of Our Time: Wartime Essays of a Sociologist*, Routledge & Kegan Paul, London, 1943, p. 21.
9. Ibid., p. 14.
10. Ibid., p. 26.
11. Ibid., p. 23.
12. Ibid., pp. 23–4.
13. Ibid., p. 27.

14. Ibid., p. 30.
15. Ibid., p. 29.
16. Ibid., p. 28.
17. Ibid.
18. Ibid., p. 30.

CHAPTER TWO

The General Tendency to Formalism

2.1 Formalism and Conflictuality

On the face of it, this tendency is all the more surprising since it is coupled, as we have just seen, with the "standpoint of political economy" in its programmatic orientation toward the material/expansionary aims of (technologically defined) productive accomplishments.

And yet, we encounter the most varied manifestations of formalism, from the axiomatic foundations (modelled on "analytical geometry") which Descartes wants to give to his "practical philosophy," through the Enlightenment postulate of "conformity to the formal laws of reason," all the way down to Husserl's "rigorous phenomenological reductionism," not to mention the arbitrary categorizations of thought by "logical positivism."

To make things more baffling still, we are at times even presented with *politically* genuine efforts to escape from the strait-jacket of the standpoint of political economy and isolated individuality, motivated by a deeply felt commitment in the face of crying injustice and human suffering that remain, nevertheless, *philosophically* trapped by the abstract formalism of the overall horizon within which the thought of the thinkers concerned was originally constituted. It is enough to think in this respect of the particularly telling example of Jean-Paul Sartre's monumental attempt to make intelligible the process of totalization in *real history*, in his "Marxisant" *Critique of Dialectical Reason*. For, notwithstanding the author's conscious efforts, his work remains blocked at the level of "the *formal* structures of history" (Sartre's expression), and cannot get to grips with the *substantive* issues of the historical dynamics.

The explanation of this paradoxical conjunction between capitalist material determinations and philosophical formalism is, again, unthinkable without putting into relief the historically specific ideological functions of the numerous theoretical systems which share, and in their own way actively support—even if by no means always consciously—capital's inherently antagonistic social ground. For the primary function of the (socially determined and materially anchored) formalism which we encounter in the most varied bourgeois conceptualizations of the world is to accomplish a major conceptual shift. The ideological corollary of this shift is to transfer the problems and contradictions of real life from their painfully real social plane to the legislative sphere of formally omnipotent reason, thereby ideally "transcending," in terms of universally valid formal postulates, *real conflictuality*; or, when the earlier envisaged general supersession of contradictions and antagonisms is no longer plausible, to transform them into the formalistically dichotomized and "ontologically untranscendable" conflicts of "being as such," as in the case of modern existentialism.

TO UNDERSTAND THE MEANING of these mystifying conceptual transformations of real conflictuality, we must relate them to their historically specific material ground. For at the roots of the formalistic theorizations and ideological rationalizations of the world of capital we find the perverse practical formalism of the capitalist mode of production, with its structural imperatives and abstract/reductive value-determinations that assert themselves "universally," on all planes of social and intellectual life.

Moreover, what is important to bear in mind is that the practically enforced formal tendency to "universality," which is one of the principal defining characteristics of this mode of production, directly underpins on the plane of social consciousness three vital ideological interests:

1. The *abstract/reductive* transformation of direct human relations into *reified material and formal connections*, simultaneously

mediated and obfuscated by the formally hierarchized and legally protected second order mediations of the capitalist productive and distributive system. The practical diremptions and formal separations of generalized commodity production, with its inexorable tendency to "universality"—equivalent in the last analysis to its being a historically unique mode of domination which no society can escape on this planet—can be identified:

a) in the alienation of the conditions of purposeful productive activity from living labour, and their conversion into reified or "dead labour" as capital;

b) the expropriation and conversion of land into alienable (or saleable) commodity, and the formal determination of its "rightful" share, as rent, in the overall system of capitalist production; and

c) the universal extension of the dehumanizing material imperatives of self-expanding commodity-production and exchange over all areas of human interchange, including the traditional "spiritual" regulators of the social metabolism. All this is surrounded, sanctioned, in their formal separateness protected, and more or less directly controlled by a formally codified system of law, as exercised by the various organs of the capitalist state, so as to match and reinforce the underlying practical formalism of the productive system itself.

2. The formally consistent articulation and general diffusion of "*equalities*" (or "*equalizations*"), required:

a) for the practical functioning of capital's productive and distributive mechanism;

b) for the global development of the capital system through the assertion of its irresistible "universality" (which is, of course, a pseudo-universality in that it is a strictly determined and limited historical formation which must claim for itself the status of forever untranscendable validity); and

c) the ideological legitimation of generalized commodity production and exchange as the one and only unobjectionable social system, on the claimed ground that it regulates the interchange of all individuals on the basis of "equality," in accordance with the "Rights of Man." (And, of course, conformity to the latter is commended on the basis of the doubly fortunate and convenient claim that the capitalist codification of the "Rights of Man" is not only directly derived from the formal rules of Reason itself, but that it is also perfectly in tune with the innermost determinations of "human nature" as such.)

3. The elimination of the *historical dimension* of socioeconomic life from view—in the direction of the past as well as of the future—thanks to the perverse categorial metamorphoses resulting from the abstract/reductive, and only in a *formal* sense equalizing, practices that prevail in the material interchanges themselves and, at the same time, find their mystifying conceptual equivalences at the level of philosophical and social theory.

- Consequently—in view of the fact that the concept of radical social change (especially if formulated with reference to a global scale, carrying with it the necessity to confront the great complexities and "unevenness of development" of many different, but deeply interconnected, societies) is simply inconceivable without the dynamic openness of the future—the reduction of temporality into the immediacy of the present *ipso facto* extinguishes in these theories the possibility of fundamental structural transformations.

- What we are offered, instead, as the only viable perspective, are the partial or "piecemeal" measures of manipulative adjustments and "fine-tuning correctives" within capital's overall framework, in conformity to the one-dimensional "presentification" of temporality as the "eternal present."

- Accordingly, any action that cannot be accomplished within the atemporal horizons of such conveniently manipulative immediacy, but appeals, instead, to the historical perspective of a progressively unfolding structural change, with all of its necessary *mediations* and their corresponding *time-scale,* is a priori disqualified on the ground of the "formal rationality" stipulated by the central functional characteristics of the established socioeconomic framework.

The apologetic social intent of the ideological objections formulated in this spirit, backed up by primitive formal categorizations (like the undialectical opposition between "partial" or "piecemeal" and "holistic" or "wholesale"), is revealed by their refusal to acknowledge the fairly obvious. Namely, that radical comprehensiveness by itself cannot undermine the viability of a social strategy. Only if there is a *contradiction* between its stated *objectives*, on the one hand, and the necessary practical *mediations* as well as their appropriate *time-scale*, on the other, only that can constitute the ground for a justifiable critique. For *any* programme of action whatsoever, even the most limited one, must be considered hopelessly "holistic" unless it is adequately defined both in terms of its time-scale and the mediatory steps and means required for its realization.

NATURALLY, THE COMBINED EFFECT of these three sets of material and ideological determinations cannot be other than the understating of real conflictuality in the domain of social thought. One can really say that the baffling theoretical alignment of the highly transposed and mediated terms of the dominant ideological discourse is, in a way, not even a "battle of books," but a veritable "battle of book-bindings" in which the contestants themselves remain quite indifferent as to what is being inserted between the front and back covers. For the various systems of abstract/reductive categorization, which at the same time successfully dispensed with the historical dimension of the debated issues as well, can have no interest at all in actual human relations; interest is confined to their logical skeleton and to the concomitant requirement of "formal consistency."

Indeed, the latter is supposed to constitute the fundamental orienting principle and the common ground of evaluation of the contending sets of disembodied categories. At the same time, those aspects of experience which cannot be handled in this way, are dismissed as irrelevant to philosophy proper, thereupon exempted from the rules of rationality and logical consistency, and formally transferred to the separate realm of "emotivism" (under a variety of similar names) with the same solipsistic self-confidence with which Fichte answered the objections according to which the facts contradicted his theory by saying: "umso schlimmer es für die Tatsachen."[1]

As a result, once the "Enlightenment-illusions" are historically left behind and buried as mere illusions by the adherents of the selfsame philosophical tradition which originally propounded them, we are presented with truly astonishing developments. For in the twentieth century even the most gruesome contents can be readily accommodated within the "neutral" categorial framework of such philosophy, provided that the substantive inhumanity of the advocated propositions is handled with suitable "formal consistency."

The examples to recall in this respect are legion, from the neo-positivist and "ethical emotivist" Bertrand Russell's recommendation to attack the Soviet Union with nuclear weapons "while we can do it without the danger of self-destruction" (which he lived to regret and, to his honour, denounce with great passion), to the anaesthetizing ("collateral damage"-type) concepts, the neatly formalized military "theatre" analogies, and the arbitrarily stipulated "escalatory" symmetries of war-mongering "games-theory."

To be sure, given certain presuppositions it "makes sense," at the level of formal consistency, to suggest that it is "better" to exterminate only a tenth of humankind than all of it. However, what is left out of consideration in such recommendations is the monstrosity of the *material presuppositions* themselves which are being taken for granted—i.e., the *acceptability* of the destruction of hundreds of millions of human beings, as if it was an unavoidable natural calamity, instead of concentrating on how to *remove the causes* of the envisaged disaster—but remain hidden behind the façade of "eminently sensible" formal proportionality. In truth, though, any system of thought that can abstract in the course of its elaborate formal deductions from its own—necessary, even if inexplicit—material presuppositions, or claim to be able to transfer them to a separate "realm of emotions," can only lead to total arbitrariness in matters of such, literally vital, importance.

The problem is that the material or substantive presuppositions in question—concerned with *human* objectives—are inherently *qualitative* in their determinations. The absurd attempt of "*utilitarianism*" to reduce these concrete human qualities to abstract *quantities*, so as to be able to apply to them its formal measure of proportionality as the basis of value-judgement, is modelled on capital's universally asserted formal/reductive value-relations. With a significant difference, though. For capital has in quantifiable labour-power an objective basis for the successful operation of its measure, practically resolving the problem of "*incommensurability*" by bringing everything to a common denominator within the structural framework of a legally safeguarded system of material domination and subordination.

By contrast, the utilitarian application of capital's reductive and quantifying procedure to the philosophical sphere of value-judgements is devoid of an objective foundation. For while it presents no difficulty for commodity society to regulate on an abstract quantitative basis the qualitatively incommensurable varieties of "pleasure" that one can buy in an art gallery (or in a brothel), to which the same practical rules of reification and exploitation apply as to everything else, it is quite another matter when one tries to turn such transactions into the model of "moral discourse."

Consequently, arbitrariness is a salient feature of this approach from the moment of its inception. All it can offer is an ideological rationalization of the established material power relations, even if in its earlier versions still wedded to some liberal illusions. Its vague rhetoric about "the greatest happiness of the greatest number" is, of course, thoroughly vacuous as a criterion for evaluating actions, notwithstanding the virtues of "scientific exactitude" claimed for it at times.

However, what is ideologically more significant is the very nature of the utilitarian orientation itself. For the application of its abstract/quantifying criterion of evaluation can only hide from view the fundamental—

inescapably *substantive* and *qualitative*—modality of human interchange (and corresponding "distribution of happiness") in capitalist society, namely: the dynamics of *domination* and *subordination*.

Of necessity, the competing sets of values arise, and the social groups which uphold them, fight out their rival claims within the practical, hierarchical, substantive, and qualitative framework of such domination and subordination. But it is precisely this historically specific and tangible structural articulation of the socioeconomic conditions of moral discourse that disappears under the abstract quantitativeness of (no matter how large or small) utilitarian *numbers* to which rulers and exploited alike can be conveniently reduced as mere individuals.

THE DIRECT INFLUENCE OF UTILITARIANISM on neo-positivism is here of secondary importance, since our primary concern lies with the abstract/reductive socioeconomic processes themselves which the various philosophical trends reflect in one way or another.

Put in general terms, what really matters is that their abstraction from qualitative/substantive determinations opens the gates to even the most extreme form of arbitrariness, since the material ground to which the formal rules could be anchored has been abandoned. The rules themselves are often enunciated *ad hoc*, as expediency requires, and their claimed consistency and autonomy is "demonstrated" with the help of mere *analogies*, in the absence of an openly undertaken substantive grounding that could be put to the test.

The nearer we get to the present, the more perverse the manifestations of this trend become. At the end of the road, the obscenity of "strategic thinking" that treats the question of human survival in terms of some "game" (whose formal rules are exhibited, with self-recommending "cool matter-of-factness," in the "European theatre of war," or in whichever other "theatre"), graphically illustrates the moral and intellectual disintegration of a mode of reasoning which is sustained by nothing but circular deductions and arbitrarily stipulated analogies.[2]

Thus, the pronounced (and, *mutatis mutandis*, throughout the long history of the bourgeois philosophical tradition recognizable) tendency to formally divorce the categories from their social ground, and to convert them into self-referential "discourses," governed by formal rules which allow the greatest arbitrariness with regard to the categorial contents themselves, is brought into being and continues to be reproduced in more and more extreme form by clearly identifiable ideological interests.

2.2 The Structural Affinity of Practical and Intellectual Inversions

Nevertheless, it is important to stress here that the material and ideological determinations which we are concerned with affect not only the more or less systematic intellectual articulations of the established social relations, but the totality of social consciousness. The "formal rationality" which is idealized (and fetishized) in the dominant theoretical discourse as if it was a "self-generating" intellectual advancement closely matches, in fact, the *practical* processes of abstraction, reduction, compartmentalization, formal equalization and "dehistorization" which characterize the establishment and consolidation of the capitalistic socioeconomic metabolism in its entirety.

Thus, the philosophers who try to deduce the social structure and institutional/administrative machinery of modern capitalism from the "spirit" of "rational calculation," etc., put the cart before the horse and represent the world of capital upside-down, in accordance with the standpoint of political economy. For the methodology of the latter must treat the successfully accomplished historical *outcome* (that is, labour's "self-alienation" and conversion into capital) as the self-evident and unalterable (i.e., characteristically "dehistorized") point of *departure.*

In this sense, the various theoretical transformations and inversions which we encounter in the course of bourgeois philosophical development, no matter how bewildering at first sight, are perfectly in accord with their socioeconomic ground. In other words, however paradoxical this may sound, the contradictory characteristics of this development must be grasped and explained in terms of the peculiar rationality of their objective contradictoriness, as arising from their sociohistorically determined real ground, instead of being "explained away" and "dissolved" as formal/theoretical "inconsistencies" from the imaginary height of a timeless, self-complacent, and completely circular "pure rationality." After all, the reason why Hegel's magisterial attempt to elucidate the profound interconnection between "rationality" and "actuality" had run into insurmountable difficulties was not because in reality the relationship itself does not exist. Hegel had to fail on account of grossly violating his own principle of historicity when he *congealed* the dynamic rationality of unfolding actuality into the static pseudo-rationality of a structurally closed present. And he did this in accordance with capital's standpoint of political economy which makes the "rationality of the actual" synonymous with the antagonistically divided (hence by its very nature inherently unstable), yet in a baffling way unproblematically eternalized actuality of the established order.

In the various theories which conceptualize the world from the "standpoint of political economy," the material determinations and historical genesis of capitalistic rationality are totally ignored, not to mention the wanton disregard for the devastating irrationality of capital's reified rationality under many of its self-contradictory, destructive, and ultimately even self-destructive practical aspects. It is therefore quite absurd to misrepresent the end-result of ubiquitous "rational calculation" as a *self-generating "principle,"* so as to be able to treat it both as a quasi-theological *causa sui* (i.e. *its own cause)* and as the inner cause of all subsequent development. The idealist ideological bias that locates the determinants of fundamental social change in mysteriously emerging "spirits of the age" and in self-generating "formal principles," etc., can only serve to undermine (and ultimately to disqualify) belief in the viability of radical intervention in the socioeconomic sphere for the purpose of instituting a meaningful alternative to the given order.

And yet, all these socially specific irrationalities, notwithstanding the subjective bias of their originators, are in their own rather peculiar way both rational and representative. This is because they necessarily arise from a socioeconomic ground whose fundamental structural determinations are shared, and perceived in a characteristically—but by no means capriciously—distorted form, by all concerned, be they leading philosophers, economists, "political scientists," and other intellectuals, or only spontaneous participants in the prevailing "common sense" of capitalist everyday-life.

Indeed, the "hegemony" of the ruling ideology cannot be made intelligible at all in terms of its claimed "autonomous power." Not even if one is willing to ascribe to it a materially unlimited and diabolically perfected range of instruments. Rather, the normally preponderant rule of the dominant ideology can only be explained in terms of the *shared existential ground* just referred to. For the constantly reproduced practical *inversions* generated by the given socioeconomic system—to which the various theoretical and instrumental manifestations of the ruling ideology actively contribute at the appropriate level—constitute, in the paralyzing immediacy of their inescapable materiality, the most fundamental determination in this respect.

In truth, only the profound *structural affinity* between the practical and intellectual/ideological inversions can make intelligible the massive impact of the ruling ideology on social life. An impact which in the real world is incomparably more extensive than what could be expected from the relative size of its directly controlled resources, displaying the dominant ideology's unimpeded influence on the broad masses of the people in the form of an ability to "preach to the converted," as it were, under normal circumstances. And likewise, the historically more than once experienced (though by no means necessarily permanent or even long-lasting) "sudden collapse" of formerly dominant ideological forms and institutional practices, under the circumstances of a major crisis, can only find its explanation in the effective paralysis of the otherwise materially sustained and spontaneously reproduced practical *inversions*, as a result of the crisis in question.

2.3 Reconciliation of Irrational Forms

In order to better understand this intricate relationship between the mystifying practical inversions, abstract/reductive transformations, and absurd formal equations, on the one hand, and their conceptualizations both by "ordinary common sense" and by sophisticated theoretical/ideological syntheses, on the other, let us consider some of the principal regulators of the capitalistic socioeconomic metabolism.

In this respect, perhaps nowhere is the irrationality which we are concerned with more striking than in the establishment of spurious connections of formal equality between qualitatively different entities that, *prima facie*, have absolutely nothing to do with one another. As Marx puts it in a rather difficult but very important part of *Capital:*

> The relation of a portion of the surplus-value, of money-rent . . . to the land is in *itself absurd* and *irrational*; for the magnitudes which are here measured by one another are *incommensurable*—a particular *use-value*, a piece of land of so many and so many square feet, on the one hand, and *value*, especially *surplus-value*, on the other. This expresses in fact nothing more than that, under the given conditions, the ownership of so many square feet of land enables the landowner to wrest a certain quantity of unpaid labour, which the capital wallowing in these square feet, like a hog in potatoes, has realized. But prima facie the expression is the same as if one desired to speak of the relation of a five-pound note to the diameter of the earth.
>
> However, the *reconciliation of irrational forms* in which certain economic relations appear and *assert themselves in practice* does not concern the active agents of these relations in their *everyday life*. And since they are *accustomed* to move about in such relations, they find nothing strange therein. A *complete contradiction* offers not the *least mystery* to them. They feel as much at *home* as a fish in water among manifestations which are separated from their internal connections and *absurd* when isolated by themselves. What Hegel says with reference to certain mathematical formulas applies here: that which *seems irrational* to ordinary common sense is rational. and that which *seems rational* to it is itself irrational.[3]

Thus, the irrationality of "common sense," to which systematic ideological mystifications can readily attach themselves, grows out of the same soil as the "sophisticated" conceptualizations which constantly reinforce everyday consciousness in its "absurd" prejudices. More important still, in the present context, is to stress that the *practical absurdity*—which constitutes their common ground—simultaneously also corresponds to the only feasible "rationality" and "normality" of the given order, as manifest in the most vital regulators of its socioeconomic metabolism as a whole.

Of necessity, the practical irrationality of separating manifestations from their internal connections is an important aspect of this system of societal reproduction. But key material factors cannot and do not remain for long suspended in their irrational separateness. For if they did so, it would be quite impossible to exercise society's essential metabolic functions, and therefore the whole structure erected on them would collapse.

This is why the successful "*reconciliation of irrational forms*" mentioned by Marx is an elementary requirement of the capital system from the very beginning, and it remains so throughout its long history. To put it in another way, capital's dynamic but inherently problematical and irrational regulatory system remains viable only as long as its "irrational forms" can be *successfully reconciled* with one another in the practicality of the social reproduction process itself.

Ultimately, it is the practical efficacy of *total social capital* which reconciles the irrational forms and operationally overcomes their separateness. "Total social capital," contrary to some misconceptions, is not a "theoretical abstraction" (or "ideal type"), but a very real social substance. It manifests and objectively asserts itself, as the ultimate regulator of the socioeconomic metabolism, through a multiplicity of coherently articulated—though, of course, under many of its aspects immanently antagonistic—productive, distributive and administrative practices and corresponding instrumentalities. Moreover, as we shall see in a moment, the *totality of labour* as well is incorporated into "total social capital," even if in a necessarily reified form.

The same considerations concerning the objectively grounded reconciliatory imperative apply to the assessment of the various theories as well. For a closer inspection reveals that the clearly identifiable "reconciliatory" aspects of all philosophies conceived from capital's standpoint of political economy—whether we think of the Hegelian system, or of some twentieth century theories—are not, more or less extensive, "aberrations" of the thinkers in question. On the contrary, they constitute the ultimate and *absolutely incorrigible* ideological parameters of the entire philosophical tradition, as marked out by the objective boundaries and insurmountable structural imperatives of the established socioeconomic order itself.

- Naturally, these structural imperatives become "internalized" and conceptually transformed by the thinkers who adopt them as the "natural" (at any rate unmentioned) premises which constitute the ground of their synthesis and evaluation of the given social totality.

- Given the nature of the objective premises on the basis of which the totalizing theoretical conceptualizations arise, what we find here, again, is a functional equivalent to the homogenizing generality of total social capital, although in philosophy it is translated, of course, into the abstract universality of "reason" under which everything must be subsumed, or else be excluded from "rational discourse" as such.

IT MUST BE EMPHASIZED, however, that the basic requirement emanating from the social soil vis-à-vis philosophical theory need not be more restrictive than the demand to produce a suitable reconciliation of the *irrational forms* themselves, and to do that in a way which happens to be feasible under the prevailing circumstances. The realization of this task does not necessarily imply the conscious positive self-identification of the philosophers concerned, at all times, with the narrow class interests embodied in such forms. What the intellectuals *directly* have to face is the imperative actively to contribute to the reconciliation of the forms in terms of which one can make sense at all of the practical regulatory principles of capital's social metabolism.

Since such regulatory principles "assert themselves in practice" whether the particular philosophers like them or not, and since the theoretical enterprise of making sense of the irrational forms does not *ipso facto* carry with it the enthusiastic acceptance of their dehumanizing substance, a considerable degree of criticism with regard to detail—recognizable, among others, in all "romantic anti-capitalism" so called—can subjectively coexist in the representative figures of this approach with their "uncritical positivism" as far as the overall task of "the reconciliation of irrational forms" is concerned.

In this respect the formalistic separation of the categories from their social ground is a paradoxical ally of partial criticism, in that it strengthens the illusions of intellectual "autonomy" and "independence" vis-à-vis the "perverted actuality" of the real world.

Only in situations of intense class confrontation is the margin of such criticism practically wiped out, transforming the originally *highly medi-*

ated connection between the philosophical reconciliation of irrational forms and corresponding class interests into *direct* (at times even openly professed) manifestations of social apologetics.

2.4 Formal/Reductive Homogenization and Universal Value-Equation

This is where we can really appreciate the importance of capital's formalizing determinations, both in the immediacy of socioeconomic interchanges and in their complex rationalizations on the plane of philosophy and social theory.

From the point of view of capital as the overall regulator of the social metabolism, the primary issue is the reductive transformation of the potentially infinite variety of *use-values* into uniformly manipulable *value*, without which the ubiquitous *exchange-relations* of generalized commodity-production could not be established and reproduced.

Significantly, therefore, until the practical process of reductive abstraction and formal equalization becomes generally diffused in the course of capitalist development, embracing living labour as a commodity no less than all other commodities with which labour is—*prima facie* absurdly—equated, the rational meaning of this practice of generalized value-equation remains totally unintelligible to those who try to make sense of it, no matter how penetrating their vision in other respects.

The difficulties inherent in the problems here referred to defeat even such giants of philosophy as Aristotle, who was "the first to analyze so many forms, whether of thought, society, or nature, and amongst them also the form of value."[4]

Aristotle's situation itself is rather paradoxical. For, on the one hand, his philosophical predicament does not impose on him the "reconciliation of irrational forms" which no one who shares capital's "standpoint of political economy" can escape. On the other hand, however, neither does it offer him the vantage point from which he could gauge the immense dynamic potential of ubiquitously prevailing value-relations; not even in a one-sided and characteristically distorted form, as the political economists succeed in doing it at a much later stage of development.

Thus, instead of attempting the theoretical reconciliation of the contradictions which he perceives, Aristotle concludes his reflections on the mystifying problem of value by somewhat naively insisting that it is

> in reality impossible that such unlike things can be *commensurable*, i.e., qualitatively equal. Such an equalization can only be something foreign to their real nature, consequently only 'a makeshift for practical purposes.'[5]

At the same time, though, on the positive side, Aristotle's "age of innocence," as far as the rule of capital—still minimal—is concerned, enables him to grasp the many forms which he analyses as inseparably conjoined with *substance*, his basic category, whereas the fundamental tendency of bourgeois philosophy is, on the contrary, the reductive transformation of *substantive relations*—with all their qualitative determinations, no matter how varied—into *formal* categorial connections.

In actuality the perverse but very real socioeconomic practice of reductive formal metamorphoses, which produces *universal commensurability*—not as a more or less haphazard "makeshift for practical purposes," but, on the contrary, as the inescapable and all-embracing law of material and intellectual interchanges—simultaneously also makes people become *accustomed to function,* with normally undisturbed *operational efficacy,* within the framework of "equivalences" which truly match the absurdity of correlating five-pound notes with the diameter of the earth. The only rationality that capital needs—and, of course, also dictates and successfully enforces—is precisely the "strictly economic" and *operational rationality* of the individuals engaged in the process of its enlarged reproduction irrespective of the consequences.

In the course of historical development the vital practical rules of such operational (or "functional") rationality assert themselves through the *substantive irrationality* of the direct subsumption of use-values under (and their domination by) exchange-value. Moreover, the untranscendable contradictions involved in this relationship need not produce any complications or misgivings at all, thanks to the practical framework of ubiquitous formal equivalences into which the suitably reduced particular individuals themselves are inserted, as commodities or exchange-values of a kind. A framework which accomplishes the formal "homogenization" and abstract "equalization" of the greatest diversity, including the commodification of human labour, desires, aspirations, etc. A universal framework of formally consistent reification which the individuals not only *can* but indeed *must* take for granted.

Thus, "the reconciliation of irrational forms"—by hiding their *substantive irrationality* and incommensurability under the practically preponderant operational efficacy of "*formal rationality*," which radically abstracts from all "irrelevant" (i.e., *substantive/qualitative/unequalizable*) aspects of the instituted correlations—is in the first place the spontaneous tendency of the reductive and homogenizing socioeconomic processes themselves.

The special reconciliatory contribution of the various philosophies which systematically articulate the standpoint of political economy arises on the ground of such material processes. The important ideological function which the philosophies and social theories must fulfil consists in elevating the already accomplished practical diremption of formal rationality from its substantive ground to the level of timeless categorial determinations.

To accomplish this, they have to construct sophisticated—and from Kant to Max Weber noticeably different—networks of "eternalizing" rationalization, in accordance with the changing historical conditions of capital's ever-expanding self-reproduction. What remains constant is the eternalizing tendency itself, on the one hand, and the transubstantiation of capital's operational rationality into "formal rationality" or "rationality as such," on the other. And, of course, the characteristic methodological formalism of this philosophical tradition provides an ideologically suitable underpinning to both.

2.5 The Social Substance of Operational Rationality

The relationship between the formal compartmentalization of socioeconomic practice, on the one hand, and the conceptualizations of this process by "common sense" and theory, on the other, is extremely complicated. Talking of the triadic articulation of the capitalist regulatory mechanism—and of the corresponding "trinity formula" in which it is theorized by political economy—this is how Marx describes the impact of the mystifying formal transformations (which take place in the material world itself) on social consciousness:

> even the best spokesmen of classical economy remain more or less in the grip of the world of illusion which their criticism had dissolved as can not be otherwise from a bourgeois standpoint, and thus they all fall more or less into *inconsistencies, half-truths and unsolved contradictions.* On the other hand, it is just as natural for the actual agents of production to feel completely at home in these *estranged and irrational forms* of CAPITAL—INTEREST, LAND—RENT, LABOUR—WAGES, since these are precisely the *forms of illusion* in which they move about and find their *daily occupation.* It is therefore just as natural that vulgar economy, which is no more than a didactic, more or less *dogmatic, translation of everyday conceptions* of the actual agents of production, and which arranges them in a certain rational order, should see precisely in this trinity, which is *devoid of all inner connection,* the *natural* and indubitable lofty basis for its shallow pompousness. This formula simultaneously corresponds to the interests of the ruling classes by proclaiming the *physical necessity and eternal justification* of their sources of revenue and elevating them to a dogma.[6]

Thus, the "inconsistencies, half-truths and unresolved contradictions" of political economy cannot be explained on their own, as—in principle corrigible—departures from the timeless rules of "rationality" itself. Instead, they must be inserted into the social horizon of their originators in terms of which they make very good sense indeed.

Equally, the formalist tendency of such theory, however problematical, is not arbitrary; it is not so in the sense that it reflects the practical separation and independence of identifiable structures. At the same time, it must be also recognized that the "*formal rationality*," which codifies and elevates to a quasi-theological dogma the practice of reifying compartmentalization, hides a "*substantive irrationality*." For the formula, CAPITAL—INTEREST (PROFIT), LAND—RENT, LABOUR—WAGES, represents, in fact, "*a uniform and symmetrical incongruity*."[7]

The irrationality, then, is an immanent characteristic of the given socioeconomic reality itself. However, the process of mystification does not end there. For the formal separation of the constituent parts of value, and their transformation, in their absurd separateness, into the necessary point of departure of all social interchange that could be conceived on the practical premises of their (formally secured and legally safeguarded) diremption, simultaneously also establishes them as the absolutely necessary conceptual matrix of rationality as such.

Moreover, the *formal* transformations that have appeared and become consolidated in reality—and are now necessarily taken for granted as the self-evident framework of rational action—are also very effective in hiding the change of *substance* at their roots. At the same time they turn out to be also very effective in hiding the *specific social character* (or substance) of the ruling "operational rationality." Besides, together with the specific social substance of this problematical "rationality," its *historical specificity,* too, completely disappears from sight.

In reality, the ongoing process of capital's historical unfolding produces—through the alienation of labour and land—new substantive relations, together with their rather absurd, but universally stipulated and accepted, equations.

Thus, the alienation of labour and the expropriation of the material conditions of labour produce CAPITAL, bringing with it at the *end* of this conversion-process—which becomes from then onwards the eternalized *beginning* of the metabolic cycle of social reproduction as a whole—the absurd equation: MEANS OF LABOUR equals CAPITAL.

Similarly, land is alienated from the community of men and turned into the private property of the privileged few, imprinting on the minds of all members of society the even more absurd equation: LAND equals MONOPOLIZED LAND.

And finally, since the means of labour have been successfully alienated from living labour, the established conditions of production practically assert and prove every day (both in industry and in the sphere of agricultural production) the most absurd equation of all, namely that LABOUR itself equals WAGE-LABOUR. And the latter, in its turn, can be further reduced, of course, into VARIABLE CAPITAL, so as to be incorporated into, and subsumed under, TOTAL SOCIAL CAPITAL in this formally homogenized and reified form. Thus living labour is successfully deprived of its character as the subject of the social reproduction process. Instead, it can be treated from now on as a mere "means of the means": in its doubly alienated capacity of "material factor of production" and self-producing "means of reproduction" of itself as a subordinate part of the means of production.

In this way, the system that takes pride in its claimed "rationality," in reality functions on the basis of the (operationally successful) *violation* of the most elementary rules and categories of reason: by making the historically and socially limited *specific form* (i.e., CAPITAL, MONOPOLIZED LAND, and WAGE-LABOUR) usurp the place of the—sociohistorically untranscendable—*general form* (i.e., MEANS OF LABOUR, LAND, and LABOUR as productive activity in general, which together represent the absolute conditions of production and social reproduction as such).

2.6 The Concept of Nature as a Dehistoricized Formal Abstraction

The fetishistic practical irrationalities of the capitalist system appear with particular intensity in the context of the formal separation, compartmentalization and division of wealth. As Marx puts it, with reference to the peculiar but highly revealing position of rent among the component parts of value:

> Since here a part of the surplus-value seems to be bound up directly with a natural element, the land, rather than with social relations, the form of *mutual estrangement and ossification* of the various parts of surplus-value is completed, the *inner connection* completely disrupted, and its *source entirely buried*, precisely because the relations of production, which are bound to the various material elements of the production process, have been rendered *mutually independent*.
>
> In CAPITAL—PROFIT, or still better CAPITAL—INTEREST, LAND—RENT, LABOUR—WAGES, in this *economic trinity* represented as the connection between the component parts of value and wealth in general and its sources, we have the *complete mystification* of the capitalist mode of production, the *conversion of social relations into things*, the direct coalescence of the material production relations with their historical and social determination. It is an enchanted and perverted, topsy-turvy

> world, in which Monsieur le Capital and Madame la Terre do their ghost-walking as social characters and at the same time directly as mere things.[8]

Thus, thanks to the formal metamorphoses that go with the practical unfolding and consolidation of generalized commodity production, both the specific social substance and the unique historical character of capital's mode of social control disappear under the thick crust of reification. At the same time, the powerful apologetic function of this fetishism of capital remains hidden from the individuals. For, in Marx's words, through the—not only prima facie absurd but also pernicious—conversion of social relations into things: "Capital becomes a very mystic being, since all of *labour's* social productive forces *appear to be due to capital,* rather than labour as such, and seem to issue from the womb of capital itself. Then the process of circulation intervenes, with its *changes of substance and form,* on which all parts of capital, even agricultural capital, devolve to the same degree that the specifically capitalist mode of production develops."[9]

Significantly, the same philosophical tradition that operates with the help of formalistic reductions also displays its great predilection for the concept of "nature."

On the face of it, this may seem surprising, or even contradictory. Yet, there is no contradiction involved in this curious conjunction, since both predilections arise from the same determinations. Indeed, a closer look at the concept of "nature" as employed by this philosophical tradition discloses that the "nature" referred to is often a *dehistorized formal abstraction*, produced by the *stipulative generalization* of determinate given characteristics which must be *assumed*, in accordance with the necessary limitations of the philosophers' social horizon, as *absolute* and a priori *untranscendable.*

As an example, we may think of the use to which they put the concept of "human nature," directly elevating the *limited immediacy* of capital's determinations to the level of a claimed "universality." In other words, what we witness here is, again, a *formal* operation, fulfilling the same ideological functions as the general tendency to formalism. For it makes the concepts of "nature" and "natural" synonymous with *universal* and *necessary*, so as to exempt from historical qualifications the phenomena so described, simultaneously also removing them through such categorization from the sphere of social conflict.

THIS IS CLEARLY VISIBLE in the way in which the question of formal metamorphosis is handled.

Again, it is important to recall that the theoretical mystifications arise on the material ground of corresponding practical absurdities, consolidated by the social reproduction process itself into which the particular individuals—including the philosophers and political economists—are inserted and which they all take for granted. As we have seen earlier, the historically unfolding socioeconomic process produces the practical irrationality of three fundamental equations:

MEANS OF PRODUCTION = CAPITAL;
LAND = MONOPOLIZED LAND;
LABOUR = WAGE LABOUR.

However, as the social reproduction process practically consolidates these absurd formal conversions and equations, *a second conversion* takes place and asserts itself with apparently "natural" and "absolute" finality. As a result, what the particular individuals are now confronted with is the doubly mystifying socioeconomic absurdity according to which:

CAPITAL = MEANS OF PRODUCTION;
MONOPOLIZED LAND (OR LANDED PROPERTY) = LAND;
WAGE-LABOUR = LABOUR.

The reason why this practical reversal of the two sides of the original equations is so mystifying is because the historical dimension of the relations expressed in them is now completely obliterated. In the case of the earlier set of equations, it was still possible to grasp the first side as the primary member of a historical sequence. Accordingly, one could still adopt with regard to the practically stipulated and enforced relations of interchange a critical posture, by explaining their relative merits as well as major socioeconomic limitations in terms of determinate historical forces. Now, however, CAPITAL, MONOPOLIZED LAND and WAGE-LABOUR constitute the *absolute* point of departure, radically divorced from their historical genesis. Thus the contradictory but nonetheless objectively prevailing *unity* of the established system of social reproduction appears as a *natural organism.* As a result, the historically limited immediacy of the given order is fallaciouslv elevated to the status of unchallengeable "universality," on account of its claimed direct correspondence to the "*natural*" conditions of human existence in general.

This is the situation that confronts just as much the participants in the "common sense" of everyday-life as the intellectuals who share the standpoint of political economy. Thanks to the successful consolidation of capital's socioeconomic framework, the formal/reductive and material/substantive determinations seem to coincide and constitute a natural form which, in its turn, can be assumed as the orienting frame of reference of theory itself. Moreover, the "uncritical positivism" of the latter appears equally "natural," since the conclusions of theory can be derived with the greatest ease and formal rigour from the direct adoption of the structural parameters of the given order—which is by now completely divorced from its historical dimension—as the "self-evident" substantive points of departure of theoretical discourse.

These points of departure are indeed self-evident in their practically given immediacy. The "uncritical positivism" is therefore unavoidable if the timeless immediacy itself is not challenged from a radical historical perspective. For

> It is clear that capital presupposes labour as wage-labour. But it is just as clear that if labour as *wage-labour* is taken as the *point of departure*, so that the identity of labour in general with wage-labour appears to be self-evident, then capital and monopolized land must also appear as the *natural form* of the conditions of labour in relation to *labour in general.* To be capital, then, appears as the *natural form* of the means of labour and thereby as the purely real character arising from their function in the labour-process in general.[10]

In this sense, a viable theoretical solution for these problems would require both the critical transcendence of the seemingly "*natural forms*," in the direction of their intrinsic social determinations, and the radical questioning of the practically given *formal* reductions and equations in the context of their simultaneously substantive and historical processes, instead of maintaining them as the fixed presuppositions of a closed system.

As we have seen, however, the ideological interests associated with capital's standpoint of political economy push their adherents in the opposite direction. They push them toward the adoption of formal schemes—including the "formal universality of the natural law" (in Kant's words)—through which the self-sustaining stability of the existent can be more readily conveyed.

The connections of this tendency with the interest of weakening social conflictuality are not too difficult to see. With regard to capital's consolidated pseudo-natural forms and their alleged "universality" it is enough to remember that:

> Labour as such, in its simple capacity as purposive productive activity, relates to the means of production, not in their social determinate form but rather in their concrete substance, as material and means of labour; . . . If then, labour coincides with *wage-labour*, so does the *particular social form* in which the conditions of labour confront labour coincide with their *material existence.* The means of labour as such are then capital, and the land as such is landed property. The *formal independence* of these conditions of labour in relation to labour, the *unique form* of this independence with respect to wage-labour, is then a property *inseparable from them as things*, as material conditions of production, an inherent, immanent, intrinsic character of them as elements of production. Their *definite social character* in the process of capitalist production bearing the stamp of a definite historical epoch is a *natural*, and intrinsic substantive character belonging to them, as it were, from *time immemorial*, as elements of the production process.[11]

Naturally, so long as the semblance of timeless universality and untranscendable natural necessity is maintained, any attempt to question the viability of the established order finds itself in a most uncomfortable position within theoretical discourse. For it is very difficult to quarrel with Nature itself; especially when the latter finds on its side the authority of Reason as such, armed with the inexhaustible arsenal of its circularly constituted and multipliable formal rules.

2.7 "Formal Rationality" and Substantive Irrationality

As we can see, then, what generates this tendency to stipulative formalism is the need to do away with conflicts on the plane of theory, leaving their material constituents untouched in the practical world. Accordingly, throughout the history of this philosophical tradition we are offered solutions which deny the rationality of conflicts of value, so as to "outlaw" them on the unchallengeable authority of reason itself (the Kantian philosophy, for instance); or to "dissolve" contradictions as "confusions" with the help of formal conceptual schemes; or indeed, as mentioned already with reference to modern existentialism, to declare the identified conflicts and antagonisms to be "ontologically insurmountable," thereby rendering them strangely "non-existent" from the point of view of practically feasible strategies for attacking the social roots of historically determinate conflict.

The philosophical impact of this orientation on the weakening of social conflictuality is, of course, far from marginal. Indeed, it tends to affect the structuring core of the various philosophies, at times with rather strange and even unintended consequences. Thus, Kant uses formal "universalization" (characteristically derived from a formalist conception of nature whose relevance to philosophical judgement is reduced to supplying the analogy of "the form of the natural law") in order to categorically banish conflict from the world of morality under the rule of his "Practical Reason." This speaks loud enough for itself, paradoxically carrying with its postulated solutions insoluble dilemmas and dichotomies.

However, Hegel's case is even more revealing in this respect. For he explicitly rejects Kantian formalism and apriorism, and consciously endeavours to give an objective foundation to his own categories. And yet, no matter how great a philosopher and pathbreaker of a dialectical system of logic he is, he ends up, against his original intentions, with a logically highly suspect conception of "mediation," in the service of conceptual "reconciliation," as he himself acknowledges this intent. Thus

Hegel ends up with a veritable "reconciliation of irrational forms," which is devised to resolve the clearly perceived class contradictions of "civil society" by means of the formalistic, often tautological, and vacuously stipulative definitions of the Hegelian State, with its fictitiously "universal class" of disinterested civil servants.

FORCEFULLY OPPOSING THIS KIND OF APPROACH, Marx observes in his critique of the Hegelian conception of the mediatory relationship between the classes of civil society and the institutions of the state: "If civil classes as such are political classes, then the mediation is not needed; and if this mediation is needed, then the civil class is not political, and thus also not this mediation. . . . Here, then, we find one of Hegel's inconsistencies within his own way of reviewing things: and such *inconsistency* is an *accommodation.*"[12]

Thus, what vitiates Hegel's position is the apologetic character of the envisaged "mediation." For the latter reveals itself as a sophisticated reconstruction of the assumed dualistic reality (the necessary circular complementarity of "civil society" and the state)—and eternalized as such—within the Hegelian discourse, and no real mediation at all.

As Marx puts it: "In general, Hegel conceives of the syllogism as middle term, a *mixtum compositum.* We can say that in his development of the rational syllogism all of the transcendence and mystical dualism of his system becomes apparent. The middle term is the wooden sword, the concealed opposition between Universality and Singularity."[13]

The aprioristic pseudo-mediatory character and logical fallaciousness of the whole scheme is graphically brought out by Marx in the following passages of his *Critique:*

> The sovereign, then, had to be the *middle* term in the legislature between the executive and the Estates, and the Estates between him and civil society. How is he to mediate between what he himself needs as a mean lest his own existence becomes a one-sided extreme? Now the complete absurdity of these extremes, which interchangeably play now the part of the extreme and now the part of the mean, becomes apparent. . . .
>
> This is a kind of *mutual reconciliation society.* . . . It is like the lion in *A Midsummer Night's Dream* who exclaims: 'I am the lion, and I am not

> the lion, but Snug.' So here each extreme is sometimes the lion *of opposition* and sometimes the Snug *of mediation*. . . .Hegel, who reduces this absurdity of mediation to its *abstract logical*, and hence pure and irreducible, expression, calls it at the same time the speculative mystery of logic, the rational relationship, the *rational syllogism*. Actual extremes *cannot be mediated* with each other precisely because they are *actual extremes*. But neither are they in need of mediation, because they are opposed in essence. They have nothing in common with one another; they neither need nor complement one another.[14]

Significantly, this dubious formalistic reduction of the real—antagonistic—constituents of the situation surveyed is undertaken by Hegel precisely in order to be able to do away (by means of twisting empirical facts into logico-metaphysical axioms) with the structural contradictions of the social order which determine his own conceptual horizon, in accordance with capital's standpoint of political economy.

WHAT IS PARTICULARLY RELEVANT here is that the formalistic methodological remedies are meant to facilitate the philosophers' escape from the inherent contradictions of capital's conceptual framework. Since no practically viable solution can be envisaged to the problems encountered in the actuality of social existence (or "civil society") within the horizon of bourgeois political economy, the "reconciliation of irrational forms" must be attempted in the postulated domain of formal structures and self-referential categorial edifices. It is therefore by no means surprising that modern philosophical development, parallel to the eruption and intensification of society's contradictions, should produce so many attempts to evade the difficulties of finding *substantive* solutions to substantive issues. The cult of methodology for the sake of methodology finds its real meaning precisely in this context.

Similarly, the great popularity of Weber's concept of "rationalization" and "ideal types" is incomprehensible without being inserted into this persistent and ideologically motivated trend.

Ultimately, the Weberian notion of "*formal rationality*" itself is a convenient way of rationalizing and legitimating capital's *substantive irrationality*. For, in accordance with the untranscendable structural limitations of the bourgeois horizon, this Weberian category ascribes "irrationality" and "emotionalism"—in an upside-down and circular/definitional fashion—to all those who dare to question, and practically challenge, the capitalist state's "formal and rational" rule, which happens to be in reality imposed on the individuals with ruthless material efficacy. In Weber's eyes, however, those who come into conflict in a substantive way with the modern state's "in principle rational" system of "rule-bound" law-enforcement, must be dismissed on account of their "emotionalism," on the ground that no less an authority than *reason* itself *"demands"* the acceptance of such rule.

This is how Weber argues his case in his celebrated discussion of "Bureaucracy and Law":

> The only decisive point for us is that in principle a system of rationally debatable 'reasons' stands behind every act of bureaucratic administration, that is, either subsumption under norms or a weighing of ends and means. . . . If, however, an 'ethos'—not to speak of instincts—takes hold of the masses on some individual question, it postulates *substantive* justice oriented toward some concrete instance and person; and such an 'ethos' will unavoidably collide with the *formalism* and the *rule-bound* and *cool 'matter-of factness'* of bureaucratic administration. For this reason, the ethos must *emotionally* reject what *reason demands.*[15]

As to why the practical pursuit of their substantive objectives by the subordinate classes should not be allowed to qualify for rationality, at least under the heading of "weighing of ends and means" (not to mention other criteria of rationality which Weber must ignore), is a mystery to which only Weber himself knows the answer.

However, we can gain an insight into the apologetic ideological function of the Weberian categorization of rationality from another passage. It reads as follows:

> One must, above all, distinguish between the *substantive* rationalization of administration and of judiciary by a patrimonial prince, and the *formal* rationalization carried out by trained jurists. . . . However fluid the difference has been . . . in the final analysis, the difference between *substantive*

> *and formal rationality* has persisted. And, in the main, *it has been the work of jurists to give birth to the modern Occidental state.*[16]

Thus, the Weberian category of "formal rationality"—as opposed to "substantive rationalization"—and the identification of the former with the "rationality" of modern bureaucracy enable the author to bypass, systematically, the embarrassing question which concerns the relationship between the material imperatives of capital's socioeconomic order and its state formation, *circularly deducing* the latter from "the work of the jurists" and from the advancement of reason itself.

But irrespective of Weber's particular circumstances and ideological motivations, the general methodological significance of this tendency to formalism consists in the attempt associated with it to transcend within its terms of reference some important material contradictions—whether we think of that between the inherently social character of morality and the Kantian "Individualethik," or the objective material determinations of capital's substantive irrationality in the realm of "civil society" and their abstract Hegelian logico-metaphysical reconciliation in the "rationality of the state," not forgetting, of course, their Weberian equivalent—which are not amenable to any other solution within the conceptual horizons of the thinkers concerned.

NOTES

1. "It is all the worse for the facts themselves."
2. It is not surprising that this mode of "strategic thinking"—with its pernicious set of hidden assumptions—can "accept the unthinkable" as the future to plan for.
3. Marx, *Capital,* Vol. 3, Foreign Languages Publishing House, Moscow, 1959, pp.759–60.
4. Ibid., Vol. 1, p.59.
5. Quoted by Marx, *ibid.*
6. Ibid., Vol. 3, pp. 809–10.
7. Ibid., p. 803.
8. Ibid., p. 809.

9. Ibid., p. 806.
10. Ibid., p. 804.
11. Ibid., pp. 804–5.
12. Marx, *Critique of Hegel's Philosophy of Right*, Cambridge University Press, Cambridge, 1970, p. 96.
13. Ibid., p. 85.
14. Ibid., pp. 88–9.
15. H.H. Gerth and C. Wright Mills, eds., *From Weber: Essays in Sociology*, Routledge & Kegan Paul, London, 1948, pp. 220–1.
16. Ibid., pp. 298–9.

CHAPTER THREE

The Standpoint of Isolated Individuality

3.1 Individualistic Conceptions of Conflict and Human Nature

The explicit glorification of "methodological individualism," for the sake of turning it into a self-justifying and universally accepted programme, is a relatively recent phenomenon. But whatever we may think of the wild claims and grave structural deficiencies of "methodological individualism," the issue itself is of the greatest importance. For ultimately it is the paradoxical social standpoint of *isolated subjectivity* that sets untranscendable limits to the particular philosophical conceptions throughout the developments under review, no matter how great the differences among the individual thinkers in subjectively conceptualizing their own situation.

In his *Theses on Feuerbach* Marx defined the irreconcilable opposition between his own approach and that of his materialist predecessors by saying that: "The highest point reached by contemplative materialism, that is, materialism which does not comprehend sensuousness as practical activity, is the contemplation of single individuals and of civil society. The standpoint of the old materialism is *civil society;* the standpoint of the new is human society, or *social humanity*."

Whatever might their differences amount to in other respects, as far as the question of social standpoint is concerned Marx's considerations can be applied to *all* philosophies which originate on capital's material foundations, including the *idealist* ones. Leibniz, Berkeley, Kant, Fichte and Hegel are in this sense by no means less subject to the problematical determinations of the standpoint of isolated individuality than Holbach, Helvetius, Feuerbach and others who were the immediate targets of Marx's critique of materialism. Indeed, Marx himself referred to Hegel in one of his early works as someone who shares "the standpoint of political economy."[1] A standpoint which is essentially the same in all its vital methodological aspects as "the standpoint of civil society," corresponding to capital's vantage point, contrasted by Marx to the standpoint of "social humanity" (i.e., to that of "socialized" or socialist humanity).

What is at issue here is the way in which philosophers conceptualize the conflicts to which they have to bear witness, under the circumstances of an inherently antagonistic social system of production which sustains them, and which they themselves actively sustain, even if they do not consciously set out to do so.

As we know, the possible forms of conceptualizing conflict are manifold, according to the specificities of the individuals' social predicament and the changing historical circumstances, from Hobbes's *bellum omnium contra omnes* to Kant's unique transformation of Adam Smith's concept of the "commercial spirit" into a moralistic philosophy of history, not to speak of the "sado-masochistic" drive which is supposed to characterize the "project" towards the "other" in Sartrean existentialism. Yet, surprising as this may appear at first sight, there is a fundamental structural affinity in all such diversity. This affinity consists in the *individualistic* representation—and misrepresentation—of the nature of the objectively grounded conflicts and antagonisms that can be perceived under the circumstances of the established social formation at all levels of interpersonal relations. Marx rightly insists on the important point that

> The bourgeois mode of production is . . . antagonistic not in the sense of *individual* antagonism but of an antagonism that emanates from the *individual's social conditions of existence.*[2]

However, what we witness throughout the history of these developments, from their earliest phases to the present time, is a socially motivated *systematic* distortion of the antagonisms of "civil society" as if they were essentially or primarily *individualistic* in character. They are treated as if they emanated not from the individuals' social conditions of existence, but from their alleged constitution by nature itself as "egotistic individuals."

Accordingly, a fictitious "*human nature*" is projected upon them, in tune with the subjective/individualistic definition of objective/social conflictuality. And, of course, this stipulated "human nature" is conceptualized as a "mute generality" which the multiplicity of isolated individuals necessarily partake in as *separate* and incurably self-oriented individuals. They are pictured as *directly* linked (i.e., in their fictitious *monadic* separateness) to their *species* precisely in virtue of their *abstract*—socially undefined—and *generic* individuality.

It must be also emphasized, again, that the view of individuals as "genus-individuals" noted by Marx in relation to Feuerbach is by no means confined to materialist philosophy. Hegel, too, speaks of a totality of determinations in human life in which "the process of the *genus* with the individual"[3] is the overriding moment. The constraining horizon of "civil society" which they share establishes the fundamental identity of materialist and idealist conceptions also in this respect.

Ironically, though, this "solution" of the difficulties which the thinkers—who more or less consciously identify themselves with capital's social interests—are objectively compelled to adopt creates more problems than it can solve, as we shall see below in the discussion of other key methodological characteristics of their conceptual framework. What happens, in fact, is that their assumption of the stipulated direct relationship between the egotistic/isolated individual and the human species merely *displaces* the original difficulty to other sets of relationships.

As a result, the thinkers who share the standpoint of isolated individuality are presented with *mysteries* of their own making—with regard to the nature of knowledge itself, the determinations of historical development, the relationship between "subject" and "object," the "particular" and the "universal," etc.—whose solution remains of necessity beyond their reach. And just how ironical all this is, can be appreciated if we remember that the problems involved were supposed to have been satisfactorily and permanently settled by the stipulative assumption of the isolated individuals' generic "human nature" which was meant to transfer all such problems *outside* the sphere of legitimate enquiry, in an aprioristic fashion.

3.2 The Elevation of Particularity to the Status of Universality

In the end, all attempts to escape from the objective contradictions of the social situation itself *must* be frustrated and defeated, even if at times some outstanding intellectual figures try to devise solutions on the plane of ingenious and complicated conceptual schemes. And they must be defeated primarily because of the restrictive horizon of the standpoint of isolated individuality as such within which the solutions themselves are attempted. For the contradictions themselves are constitutive of this very standpoint, inasmuch as the latter imposes itself as the *only possible* framework of a solution associated with its conflict-torn social ground, although in view of its inherent characteristics it cannot possibly offer any *real solution* to the underlying objective conflicts of interest and corresponding conceptual difficulties.

Indeed, normally—that is, with the exception of periods of extreme crisis—the standpoint of isolated individuality imposes itself on the thinkers concerned in such a way that it *precludes* even the perception of the objective difficulties themselves, with a tendency to transfigure their *social ontological* determinations into *subjective epistemological* concerns. In other words, the intrinsic difficulties of social practice (concerned with the realization of tangible objectives) are transubstantiated into the mystifying, and at the level of isolated subjectivity absolutely insoluble problems of "how can the immanence of consciousness"—conceived as the self-referential inwardness of the *ego*—"reach its object"; without violating, that is, its self-imposed scholastic rule of accomplishing such task "rigorously within the sphere of immanence."

At the methodological centre of the bourgeois philosophical tradition—from Descartes and Pascal to Kant, Fichte, Kierkegaard, Husserl, Sartre and beyond—we find this self-oriented (and necessarily self-defeating) "*ego*," named and defined in a multiplicity of different ways, according to the changing sociohistorical circumstances and the corresponding ideological requirements of the particular systems concerned.

Inevitably, any methodological orientation which has at its structuring core the standpoint of isolated individuality, goes with a tendency to *inflate* the individual—to whom, in virtue of its being the central supporting pillar of the whole system, so much has to be *ascribed*—into some kind of pseudo-universal entity. This is why the dubious conceptions of "human nature"—which constitute one of the most important hallmarks of the whole philosophical tradition, with their thoroughly unsubstantiated claims—are not only the aprioristic corollaries of determinate ideological interests, but simultaneously also the realization of an inherent *methodological imperative* to elevate mere *particularity* to the status of *universality*. The other side of the same coin is, of course, the necessary absence of a viable concept of—socially articulated—*mediation* through which the dialectical relationship between *particularity* and *universality* could be grasped in its dynamic complexity.[4] Its place must be taken by the abstract *postulates* of "unity" and "universality," as we shall see in chapter 7.

This stubborn persistence of conceptualizing everything from the standpoint of isolated individuality across centuries of philosophical development can only be explained through the continued practical reproduction of the underlying ideological interests themselves. Naturally, the forms in which such interests can be reproduced vary enormously, according to the historically changing intensity of the social antagonisms and the prevailing relation of forces. There are times when the antagonisms violently erupt into the open, calling for conceptualizations like Hobbes's *bellum omnium contra omnes*, whereas under very different historical circumstances they are successfully displaced and remain latent for relatively long periods of time, generating the various theories of "*consensus*" and the celebrated ideologies of "the end of ideology." But whatever might be the immediate ideological message of these theories, their shared methodological objective is the production of conceptual schemes through which one can come to terms with the *manifestations* of conflict without seriously addressing oneself to their underlying *causes*.

In this sense, Hobbes's pseudo-causal explanation of what he calls *bellum omnium contra omnes*—in terms of an allegedly egotistic "human nature" directly manifest in every particular individual as "genus-individual"—is no explanation at all. It is merely a *springboard* for the required leap towards the rationalizing "solution" of the identified problem through the absolute power of *Leviathan.* And even Rousseau, whose critical intent (on the eve of the French Revolution) succeeds in diagnosing some very real problems and contradictions of the given society, is led astray by his individualistic/anthropological approach and the formal/universalistic postulates that go with it. For he conceptualizes the "body politic" on the model of the abstract "self," and ends up with the glorification of the former as a hypostatized "moral being," deriving from it the apologetic as well as circular rationalization of "everything ordained by the law" as "lawful."

This is how Rousseau argues in favour of such a position in his important but neglected *Discourse on Political Economy:*

> The *body politic*, taken individually, may be considered as an organized, *living body*, resembling that of *man*. The sovereign power represents the head; the laws and customs are the brain, the source of the nerves and the seat of the understanding, will, and senses, of which the Judges and Magistrates are the organs: commerce, industry, and agriculture are the mouth and stomach which prepare the common subsistence; the public income is the blood, which a prudent economy, in performing the functions of the heart, causes to distribute through the whole body nutriments and life: the citizens are the body and the members, which make the *machine live*, move and work; and no part of this machine can be damaged without the painful impression being at once conveyed to the brain, if the *animal* is in a state of health. The life of *both bodies* is the *self* common to the whole, the reciprocal sensibility and internal correspondence of all the parts. Where this communication ceases, where the *formal unity* disappears, and the contiguous parts belong to one another only by juxtaposition, the *man is dead*, or the *State is dissolved*. The body politic, therefore, is also a *moral being* possessed of a *will*; *and this general will*, which tends always to the preservation and welfare of the *whole* and of *every part*, and is the source of the laws, constitutes for all the members of the State, in their relations to one another and to it, the rule of what is *just or unjust*: a truth which shows, by the way, how idly some

> writers have treated as theft the subtlety prescribed to children at Sparta for obtaining their frugal repasts, *as if everything ordained by the law were not lawful.*[5]

As we can see, the standpoint of isolated individuality—which turns the individual self into the model of the "body politic" as an "organic machine": a model that hypostatizes the "reciprocal sensibility" of all the parts for the State's functioning—can only lead to the moralistic reaffirmation of the internal necessity of the established structural framework. The projection of the individualistic/anthropological model onto the social complex as a whole conceptually "transcends" the inherent antagonisms of the established order and substitutes for them the mere postulate of a "*moral being*" which, by definition (and only by unsustainable definition), "tends to the preservation and welfare of the whole and of every part," and thereby rightfully decides "what is just or unjust." Thus, it is by no means surprising that the circular definitional assumptions of isolated individuality—which necessarily obliterate the vital material mediation of *class* interests, misrepresenting *class rule* as the (morally postulated) harmony of "*every part*" with the *whole*—should culminate in the apologetic circularity which stipulates that "everything ordained by the law is lawful."

It is equally relevant to note in the present context that the standpoint of isolated individuality brings with it not only a whole series of abstract moral postulates with regard to the practical functioning of the whole construct, but also that as its own sustaining ground it can only refer to the concept of a "*formal* unity." In other words, the tendency toward formalism noted above applies to Rousseau no less than to many other outstanding figures of the philosophical tradition under review. As to the postulate of *unity* itself, we must have a closer look at the problems intrinsic to it in chapter 7.

3.3 The Inversion of Objective Structural Relationships

The crucial ideological function of the standpoint of isolated individuality is the radical *inversion* of the objective structural relationship between different types of conflict and antagonism. Given its immanent constitution and orientation, it must focus attention on the *secondary* and subjective/individualistic aspects of contradiction, relegating at the same time the *primary* antagonisms of society to the periphery, if recognizing them at all.

- Thus, only "competition among individuals" can be acknowledged as being rooted in "objective"—i.e., generically "natural"—determinations, while the difficulties of "group conflict" and "group interest" must be dissolved into the vacuous concept of "aggregative individual interaction."

- Similarly, at the level of the material structures of society, it is the sphere of *distribution* and *circulation* that counts, with its secondary conflicts and individualistically competitive vicissitudes, while the objective *presuppositions* of the whole *productive system* are simply taken for granted. For recognizing that the fundamental material premise of the capitalist social formation consists in the *exclusive* "distribution" of the means of production in favour of capital and of "its personification: the capitalist"—which defines this social order in terms of capital's unalterable *monopoly* of control over the production process in its entirety—would carry with it explosive, hence totally inadmissible, implications. It would amount, in fact, to acknowledging that the only contest that really counts in the end is the one which concerns the structural foundations of the productive system itself. A contest conceivable only as a *class* confrontation in which one of the contending parties must envisage a radically different social order as the only feasible solution to the conflict, in contrast to the more or less marginal competitive clashes which are allowed to take place *within* the already prejudged and a priori safeguarded structural parameters of the established system.

- Understandably, the standpoint of isolated individuality cannot contemplate such confrontations and alternatives. Viewed from its vantage point, the objectively given types and relations of conflict must be inverted and transubstantiated into essentially individualistic forms of competition over strictly limited and capitalistically manageable objectives. And this is where we can see both the inseparability of the method in question from its ideological ground, and the fundamental identity between the *standpoint of isolated individuality*—concerned with individualistic conflictuality only—and the *standpoint of political economy* which cannot help being oriented toward the sphere of the *structurally prejudged* "competitiveness" of capital's *self-expansive circulation.*

- The ahistorical and idealistic hypostatization of the categories; the methodological inversion of their objective interconnections (as, for instance, in the case of the relationship between production and consumption); the tendency toward one-sided, mechanical explanations, conveying a fetishistic belief in the natural determination and absolute permanence of the social relations reflected in the categorial inversions; the liquidation of the dialectical results obtained in ideologically less sensitive contexts; and the ultimate triumph of circularity even in the conceptual schemes of such towering figures as Hegel—all these are ideologically revealing methodological characteristics of the philosophical tradition here surveyed which often assert themselves against the subjective intentions of the philosophers concerned. All these characteristics display in a bewildering form the internal contradictions and structural limitations of the standpoint of political economy—in its methodological equivalence to the standpoint of isolated individuality—which cannot be transcended even by the greatest of individual accomplishments emanating from capital's social ground and material premises.

SIGNIFICANTLY, THE LINE OF DEMARCATION in this respect between varieties of idealism and materialism which share the standpoint of "civil society" and political economy is virtually non-existent. As a graphic illustration, we may recall the way in which Ricardo defines the difference between fixed and circulating capital: "Depending on whether the capital is more or less perishable, hence must be more or less frequently reproduced in a given time, it is called circulating or fixed capital."[6] As Marx rightly comments:

> According to this, a coffee-pot would be fixed capital, but coffee circulating capital. The *crude materialism* of the economists who regard as the *natural properties* of things what are *social relations* of production among people, and qualities which things obtain because they are subsumed under these relations, is at the same time *just as crude an idealism*, even *fetishism*, since it *imputes social relations to things* as inherent characteristics, and thus *mystifies them*.[7]

On a different plane, in the work of Adam Smith—who greatly influenced not only Kant but Hegel as well—ideologically motivated circularity dominates. For:

> Capital appears to him . . . not as that which contains wage labour as its *internal contradiction* from its *origin*, but rather in the form in which it emerges from circulation, as money, and is therefore *created out of circulation*, by saving. Thus capital does not originally realize itself — precisely because the *appropriation of alien labour* is not itself included in its concept. Capital appears only afterwards, after already having been *presupposed* as capital—a *vicious circle*—as command over alien labour. Thus, according to Adam Smith, labour should actually have its own product for wages, wages should be equal to the product, hence labour should not be wage labour and capital not capital. Therefore, in order to introduce *profit* and *rent* as *original* elements of the cost of production, i.e. in order to get a *surplus value* out of the capitalist production process, he *presupposes* them, in the clumsiest fashion. The capitalist *does not want* to give the use of his capital for nothing; the landowner, similarly, *does not want* to give land and soil over to production for nothing. They want something in return. This is the way in which they are *introduced*, with their *demands*, as historical fact, but not *explained*.[8]

Thus, the "clumsy" behaviour of a great thinker—the blatantly circular presupposition of what must be historically traced and explained—produces the ideologically welcome result of transforming the specific conditions of the capitalistic labour process into the timeless *natural* conditions of the production of wealth in general. At the same time, a determinate *sociohistorical necessity*—together with the historical temporality appropriate to it—is turned into a *natural necessity* and into an *absolute condition* of social life as such.

Furthermore, since the question of capital's *origin* is circularly avoided—i.e., the exploitative dimension of its genesis from the "appropriation of alien labour," in permanent *antithesis* to labour, is pushed out of focus—the inherently *contradictory,* indeed ultimately explosive, character of this mode of producing wealth remains conveniently hidden from sight. Accordingly, the bourgeois conceptualization of the capitalist labour process, predicating the absolute permanence of the given "natural" conditions, cannot be disturbed by the thought of the historical dynamics and its objective contradictions.

The Hegelian conceptualization of the world from the standpoint of political economy is by no means radically different in its substance from what we find in the writings of his great Scottish and English predecessors. It is true that in Hegel there is no trace of Adam Smith's "clumsy" openness and somewhat naive circularity. However, the same determinations and contradictions of capital's constraining horizon are reproduced in his philosophy at the highest level of abstraction. Indeed, the selfsame contradictions and the concomitant circularity are reproduced perhaps more strikingly than anywhere else precisely in the sublimated and transubstantiated realm of the Hegelian Logic. Thus, as a result of Hegel's ingenious philosophical transformations, the socially unavoidable circularity of the standpoint of political economy is elevated to the status of the most sublime methodological principle of "science" and consciously adopted as the pivotal point of the whole system. In Hegel's own words:

> The Absolute Idea is the only object and content of philosophy. As it contains every determinateness, and *its essence is to return to itself* through its self-determination or particularization, it has various phases. . . . *mediation* takes its course through determinateness; it goes through a content as through an *apparent Other* back to its *beginning* in such a manner that it not only reconstitutes the beginning (as determinate, however), but that the result equally is *transcended determinateness,* and

> therefore is the reconstitution of the first indeterminateness with which the method began. . . . By reason of the nature of the *method* which has been demonstrated the science is seen to be a *circle* which returns upon itself, for *mediation bends back its end into its beginning* or simple ground. Further, *this circle is a circle of circles*; for each member, being inspired by the method, is *intro-Reflection* which, returning to the beginning, is at the same time the beginning of a new member. . . . Thus the Logic too in the Absolute Idea has returned to this simple unity which is its *beginning*.[9]

NOTES

1. See Marx, *Economic and Philosophic Manuscripts of 1844*, Lawrence & Wishart, London, 1959, p. 152.
2. Marx, *A Contribution to the Critique of Political Economy*, Lawrence & Wishart, London, 1971, p. 21.
3. Hegel, *Philosophy of Mind*, Clarendon Press, Oxford, 1971, p. 64.
4. For a penetrating history of the concept of "particularity" from Kant and Schiller to the mid 1950s, see Lukács, *Über die Besonderheit als Kategorie der Aesthetik*, Luchterhand, Neuwied, 1967.
5. Rousseau, "A Discourse on Political Economy," in Rousseau, *The Social Contract and Discourses*, Dent & Sons, London, 1958, pp. 236–7.
6. Ricardo, *On the Principles of Political Economy*, Everyman's Library, p. 26.
7. Marx, *Grundrisse*, Penguin Books, Harmondsworth, 1973, p. 687.
8. Ibid., p. 330.
9. Hegel, *Science of Logic*, Allen & Unwin, London, 1929, Vol. 2, pp. 466–85.

CHAPTER FOUR

Negative Determination of Philosophy and Social Theory

4.1 Substance, Subjectivity and Freedom

Spinoza sums up in a most striking fashion the inescapable negativity of the philosophical conceptions which are representative of capital's social formation by insisting that *omnis determinatio est negatio*: "all determination is negation." It is by no means surprising, therefore, that Hegel voices his enthusiastic adhesion to this principle and praises Spinoza's assertion as "a proposition of *infinite importance.*"[1]

In some respects Spinoza's general approach is, of course, anathema to Hegel. Situated at a much earlier phase of historical development—with its temptations for envisaging more naive solutions than what seems to be acceptable to Hegel in view of the great social turmoil of the French Revolution and its dramatic aftermath—Spinoza must be criticised from the point of view of the proposed Hegelian transcendence of "inert objectivity." For, according to Hegel:

> with Spinoza, Substance and its absolute unity, have the form of an inert, that is, of a not self-mediating, unity,—of a rigidity wherein the concept of the *negative unity of the self (Subjectivity)* has not yet found a place.[2]

What Hegel is trying to do, therefore, is radically to extend Spinoza's "infinitely important" principle of negativity both in the direction of the "absolute," and toward "subjectivity," "personality," and "individuation." He insists that "Spinoza does not pass on beyond *negation as determinateness or quality* to a recognition of it as *absolute*, that is, *self-negating negation*," and, moreover, that in Spinoza's philosophy "Substance lacks the principle of *personality*."[3]

Accordingly, Hegel wants to remedy what he considers to be the defects of Spinoza's system by pushing Leibniz's concept of the *monad* to its absolute limits, defining it in a radically negative way, in order to be able to derive from it the equally negative "principle of individuation." And he wants to do this in such a way that both the negatively defined monad and the principle of individuation are "raised to the rank of speculative concepts."[4]

At the roots of the Hegelian criticism of Spinoza we find Hegel's preoccupation with "transcendence" in the spirit of his "circle of circles" which stipulates a "return to the beginning," as we have seen in note 9 of the previous chapter. This is why Spinoza's solution must be found defective. As Hegel puts it:

> Spinoza's exposition of the Absolute is complete in so far as it begins with the Absolute, follows up with the Attribute, and ends with the Mode; but these three are only enumerated one after the other without any inner sequence of development, and the third term is not *negation as negation*, not *negatively self-relating negation*—if it were, it would of itself be *return to the first identity*, and this identity would be veritable identity. Hence the necessity of the progress of the Absolute to unessentiality is lacking, as well as its dissolution in and for itself into identity.[5]

The "inner sequence of development" postulated by Hegel is one that produces, through its "negatively self-negating negation," the "supersession" of Substance (and therewith the transcendence of the contradictions of content as manifest in the "darkness of causality") through "something higher—the Notion, the Subject."[6] Thus, the Hegelian "consummation of Substance"[7] in the "genesis of the Notion"[8] claims to refute Spinoza's system and transcend the "inert objectivity" and "rigidity" of Substance (the world of necessity in terms of the Hegelian philosophy) by opening up "the realm of Freedom":

> The Relation of Substantiality, considered solely in and for itself, *leads over to its opposite, the Notion*. . . . The oneness of Substance is its relation of *Necessity;* but thus it is only inner Necessity; and positing itself through the moment of *absolute negativity*, it becomes manifested or posited identity and consequently *Freedom*, which is the identity of the Notion. . . . In the Notion, accordingly, the *realm of Freedom* has opened. The Notion is the free because it is the identity which is in and for itself and which constitutes the *necessity of Substance*; simultaneously it exists as *transcended* or as positedness, and this positedness, as *self-relating*, is precisely that identity. The darkness in which each of the substances which are in the Relation of Causality stands to the other, has vanished, for the originality of their individual persistence has passed over into positedness, and has thereby become *self-transparent clarity*. The original fact is this in being only its own cause, and this is Substance which, having *achieved Freedom*, has become *Notion*.[9]

In this way, Substance—and the "necessity of Substance"—are transubstantiated into Freedom, thanks to the "recognition of negation as absolute negation" and to conceiving the "third term" as "negatively self-negating negation." And as the abstract negativity of speculative pseudo-mediation "bends back its end into its beginning" (so as to accomplish its "circle of circles"), we are offered a system which idealistically "sublates" the contradictions of the real world in the fictitious "realm of freedom" of the Notion, while leaving everything in actuality as before. A system which legitimates the established order by preaching that "what is rational is actual and what is actual is rational"[10] and that the false positivity squeezed out of the "negation of the negation," with its openly advocated principle of "reconciliation with the present," represents the one and only valid synthesis of "comprehended" substantiveness, subjective freedom, universality (as opposed to "particularity"), necessity (in opposition to "accidentality"), and the "existing absolute."[11]

4.2 The Positive Aspect of Critical Negation

And yet, it is of no minor importance that many representatives of the philosophical tradition under discussion self-consciously define their own position as *critical*. Nor should one conclude that such claims—in view of the contradictions and ideological interests associated with them—should not be taken seriously.

Indeed, the negative orientation of their enterprise—from the critical intent of the Cartesian methodic doubt and from Bacon's struggle against the "Idols," through the programmatic "Copernican revolution" of Kant's "critical philosophy" and Hegel's "negatively self-relating negation," all the way down to "critical theory" in the recent past—contains a genuinely critical *moment* that aims at transforming the object of its criticism, even if only within the well marked conceptual and ideological horizons of the theories concerned. For, in accordance with the dynamic of complex dialectical determinations at the roots of representative theoretical conceptions, the negative *limits* of all approaches, no matter how pronounced, are simultaneously also their positive *boundaries* (i.e., their objectively circumscribed margins for action) within which determinate accomplishments become feasible.

Thus, even the negative—and *ultimately* apologetic/eternalizing—definition of "human nature" as "egotistic," has a limited positive function in its *original* context. For in its historically specific social setting such a conception of human nature promotes the formulation of various theories of "rational egotism," with their liberating potential as opposed to the paralyzing "irrationality" of the religiously consecrated old order. (Characteristically, however, the situation is completely reversed at a later stage of historical development, and the claimed determinations of "human nature" are used in philosophy and social theory so as to rule out all substantive criticism of the established order.)

Similarly, while the "Rights of Man" in their abstract negativity[12] turn out to be not much more than hollow rhetorics in the fully realized bourgeois society—and as such they are graphically pilloried by Anatole France's characterization according to which they "equally forbid to everyone to sleep under the bridges," irrespective of who actually needs to indulge in such luxuries—with regard to their postulated universal validity they represent something potentially most significant, well beyond their original concern and limited frame of reference.

Naturally, it is by no means accidental that the Rights of Man are emptied of their original meaning as capital's "reign of Reason" is practically implemented. For "universality" as their claimed guiding principle, even if only negatively defined, is quite incompatible with the incurable *partiality* of the exploitative relationships on which the established social order is built.

Nevertheless, there is a positive dimension to this conception too, even though it must assume an extremely paradoxical form under the circumstances. For precisely in their postulated (even if never implemented) universality—which they can neither abandon, nor fulfil within the framework of the given social system, with reference to a legal sphere strictly dependent on its perverse material foundation—the Rights of Man objectively envisage as their condition of realization the necessity to go beyond both their restrictive material ground and their correspondingly narrow state-institutional frame of reference. And just as the truly critical dimension of the Hegelian dialectic can be extricated by Marx from its conservative integument and turned to emancipatory use, likewise, the socialist conception of human rights remains a necessary feature of the entire period of transition. It remains so for as long a period, in fact, as the constraining framework and predominantly negative "formal universality" of *legality as such* is not progressively superseded by the *substantive* and inherently *positive* processes of consciously regulated social life itself.

4.3 The Quantification of Quality and the Law of Measure

In the end, however, the boundaries of critical negativity and "negation of the negation" do not reach very far. For they simultaneously also represent the untranscendable limits of the social horizon shared by the thinkers we are concerned with.

Hegel's subtle yet ultimately failed attempt at decyphering the meaning of "Measure" well illustrates this point. His point of departure is the assertion that:

> When more fully developed and reflected, Measure becomes Necessity; . . . 'The Absolute, or God, is the Measure of all things' is a definition not more strongly pantheistic but infinitely more true than 'the Absolute, or God, is Being.' Measure is indeed an external way or manner, a more or less, but it is also reflected into itself, and is a determinateness not merely indifferent and external, but existing in itself. It is thus *the concrete truth of Being* [Hegel's italics]; and, therefore, mankind has revered in Measure something inviolable and holy. The idea of Essence is already contained in Measure, namely that it is identical with itself in the immediacy of determinateness, so that this self-identity *reduces* the immediacy to a *mediate*; and also this mediate is mediated only through this externality, but is *self-mediation*; it is the reflection whose determinations *are*, but, thus being, exist only as moments of their *negative unity*. The *qualitative* is *quantitative* in Measure: determinateness or *difference is indifferent*, and, therefore, the difference is no difference, it is *transcended*: and this *quantitativity*, a *return upon self*, where it exists as the *qualitative*, constitutes the *Being-in-and-for-Self* which is *Essence*.[13]

Significantly, however, in a society as dominated by the quantifying commodification of all qualities (even the most unlikely ones, including fresh air and unique works of art)—and thus by the absolute tyranny of the "general standard" and "external Measure" of everything (money)—as capitalist society is, Hegel is unable to grasp the underlying determinations and the objective laws at work. He ends up, instead, with sceptical, superficial, and arbitrarily stipulated pseudo-explanations as "solutions" which fall far below the level of his penetrating diagnosis of the problem itself:

> It is . . . foolish to speak of a natural standard of things. Moreover, a *general standard* is designed to serve only for *external comparison*; and in this most superficial meaning, where it is taken as *General Measure*, it is quite *indifferent* what is used as measure. It is not meant to be a fundamental Measure, which would mean that in it the natural Measures of particular things would be represented and would hence, according to a Rule, be recognized as specifications of a universal Measure, the Measure of their universal body. But without this meaning an absolute standard is

> interesting and significant only as being common to all; and such a common element is *universal not in itself*, but only by *convention*.[14]

As to why the convention in question arises on the material foundation of capital and rules the social metabolism with its "iron law," despite being apparently only a "convention," remains a complete mystery; as indeed it must to all those who view the world from the standpoint of political economy and isolated individuality. The mythically self-explanatory power of "convention" is merely *assumed* as the absolute limit at which all further questioning must stop, just as the "Cunning of Reason" is assumed in other key places as the mysterious explanatory device whose function is to make intelligible how the chaotic multiplicity and "infinite variety" of individual interactions might and must result in the strictly lawful unfolding of historical development.[15]

Thus, the stipulated limits of philosophical intelligibility—misrepresented as the ultimate limits of human reason itself—are, in fact, the uncritically accepted *practical premises* of capitalist "civil society," conceived as the depository of aggregative individual interchanges. Inevitably, such a model of an intrinsically—and unalterably—individualistic "civil society" turns the objective determinations of social interaction into hopelessly elusive problems. This is why even the great dialectician Hegel must opt for the circular pseudo-explanation of measure as "convention," maintaining—in accordance with capital's standpoint of political economy which cannot conceivably acknowledge the explosive dynamics of antagonistic class relations, let alone contemplate them as the general explanatory framework of sociohistorical development—that:

> in *developed* civil society *aggregates of individuals* belonging to different trades are in a certain relation to one another; but this *yields neither laws of Measure nor peculiar forms of it*.[16]

To be sure, if society were really constituted on the more or less accidental foundation of "aggregates of individuals belonging to different trades" (which they could, in keeping with the legend, freely join and abandon), there could be no objective law of measure in terms of which their productive and distributive practices would be regulated.

In that case the only solution that might be envisaged would have to be the conscious planning of social life as a whole by the individuals concerned. This in turn, however, is a priori ruled out by the individualistic presuppositions of the theory which stipulates the necessary fragmentation of "civil society" by the centrifugal force of its incorrigibly self-oriented members. (Hence the conceptual necessity in the Hegelian—and by no means only in the Hegelian—system for the bewildering intervention of the "cunning of Reason." For the latter providentially supplies from the back of the historical stage the required totalizing overview, foresight, and global rationality, while preserving the system of bourgeois "civil society" in its given state—with all its anarchy, irrationality, fragmentation, and contradictions—as mysteriously corresponding to its own hidden design, thereby conveniently complementing and remedying the gratuitous suggestion of "convention" as regards the regulatory measure.)

However, what is of necessity missing from all such conceptions is precisely an adequate account of the *structural determinations* of the established order. A specific sociohistorical order which unceremoniously *assigns* the totality of individuals, not simply to "different trades," but to materially articulated and legally safeguarded positions of super- and sub-ordination—i.e., to closely interlocking *class-relations* of domination and dependency—in the prevailing social hierarchy.

Moreover, since in reality the individuals are assigned from the moment of their birth to particular classes—whereupon they are necessarily subjected to *dual* class determinations: on the one hand, to the objective requirements implicit in the membership of their own class, and on the other, to the unavoidable constraints which arise from the antagonistic interactions of the competing classes among themselves—the heavy-handed *practical apriorism* that regulates these processes, on the basis of historically constituted material power relations, stands in the sharpest possible contrast to the individualistic conception of "civil society" and its idealized state in which merit alone assigns the guardians of the ruling order to their rightful place in the fictitious "universal class," destined to safeguard the "universal interests" of society.

Furthermore, while such political-economist conception of "developed" civil society—which is expected to remain with us forever, since it is said to constitute civil society as "developed to its full adequacy with its concept"—cannot *yield,* indeed, "laws of measure nor peculiar forms of it," the real society in which we happen to live, erected on the material ground of labour's structural subordination to capital, operates, not through some imaginary "convention" of aggregates of isolated individuals, but on the *presupposition* of, and in accordance with, the objective determinations of the *law of value*. And the latter regulates by means of its ubiquitous reificatory measure, with utmost efficacy, not only the broad structural parameters of domination and subordination, but even the most minute details of the social metabolism.

WHAT NEEDS TO BE EQUALLY STRESSED here is that the "Enlightenment illusion" concerning the Reason-determined and contract-based social interchanges of the idealized social order, as manifest in the most implausible explanations of centuries of bourgeois thought—from Locke's "tacit consent" to Kant's conception of the social contract as the "regulative idea of Reason," and from Rousseau's "General Will" to the Hegelian characterization of measure as "convention": all totally devoid of recognizable contracting parties to the philosophically hypostatized "agreement"—is not the *cause* of such conceptual derailments but, rather, the necessary *consequence* of the underlying ideological determinations. For the absolute, even if unconscious, taboo, which must prevail against all possibility of acknowledging the *incorrigibly* exploitative and inhuman character of the idealized sets of social relations, finds its fitting rationalization in the abstract postulates of a totally powerless "Reason."

The inherent *negativity* of this rationalizing device often assumes the *pseudo-positive* form of some "*ought-to-be*." And even if it is clearly demonstrated by the actual mode of functioning of the idealized "civil society" that the abstract negativity of the envisaged "corrective ought" of Reason is quite impotent with regard to the tasks which it is called upon to accomplish, its rationalizing function is by no means undermined by that. For now the methodological postulates of *isolated individuality* come to the rescue, blaming only the monadic/atomistic *individuals* on account of their *subjective failure* to "heed the voice of Reason," thereby a priori exempting from all conceivable blame the *objective structural determinations* of the existing social order.

4.4 Second Order "Mediations of the Mediation" and the Triumph of Negativity

It is a measure of Hegel's genius that he attempts to unravel the entangled problem of measure both in terms of its *reductive* character and as inseparably linked to the complexities of *mediation*, as we have seen above. However, he flounders as a result of his own—ideologically conditioned—reductionism. For, precisely because the objective laws of internally divided commodity society cannot be identified in their sociohistorical specificity by someone who shares capital's standpoint of political economy, only the abstract logical skeleton of mediation remains visible to Hegel.

The ideological determination (and usefulness) of this way of conceptualizing the problems at stake becomes clear in that, thanks to the reduction of the great material complexities of mediation (as they manifest in real life) to their abstract logical skeleton, Hegel is able to transubstantiate empirical facts—and irreconcilable social contradictions—into logico-metaphysical axioms, thereby a priori depriving the latter of their objective power and ultimate explosiveness.

What we are directly concerned with in this context is the fact that capitalistic mediations—which operate in conjunction with the objective law of value and its reifying measure—are not simply reciprocally convenient "mediations," corresponding to some socially neutral content. Let alone could they be ideally subsumed under the logico-metaphysical axioms of an abstract syllogism.

In reality the prosaic facticity of capitalist mediations could not be further removed from the ideological constructs offered in Hegel's philosophy. For in their overpowering facticity they happen to constitute the practically/materially dominant *second order mediations* of CAPITAL, EXCHANGE, and the structural/hierarchical SOCIAL DIVISION OF LABOUR.

And that makes all the difference. For as such, these second order mediations fatefully superimpose themselves in terms of their self-propelling determinations and alienated imperatives on the primary mediation between human beings and nature that takes place through essential productive activity.

It is the necessary conceptual evasion of this perverse, and ultimately self-destructive, practical "*mediation of the mediation*" that brings with it the Hegelian reductivism and abstraction from the non-eternalizable determinateness of the given historical form, notwithstanding its painfully obvious lawfulness (compared by Marx to the "inexorability of a natural law"). Hence the false polarity of "natural measure" on the one hand, and "convention arising out of the free deliberations of aggregates of individuals in civil society" on the other (which Hegel himself opts for), while in reality the far from natural, yet highly objective, second order "mediations of the mediation" impose *their own* standard and measure on all members of commodity society.

DUE TO THE *NECESSARY* EVASION of the insoluble contradictions of capitalist second order mediations, as well as to the ensuing deficiencies of the concept of mediation in general (shared by this whole philosophical tradition), negativity prevails at all levels and underneath the most diverse forms of alleged "positivity." Indeed, since the unquestioning acceptance of the inherently negative, dehumanizing, and destructive second order mediations constitutes the fundamental premise and structuring core of all such thought, the actual relations of negativity and positivity can be readily *reversed* in the philosophical deductions whose conscious or unconscious ideological assumptions remain deeply hidden from sight.

Thus, we are presented not only with the pseudo-positivity of impotent "ought" mentioned above; nor indeed simply with the positive claims of the "little by little" of "piecemeal social engineering" (whose real substance is nothing but the aprioristic, and all too eager, negation of the possibility of major changes that might undermine the given structural framework of second order mediations); but even with the strangest conceptual *inversions* which, ironically, tend to obfuscate and obliterate the real theoretical achievements of the philosophers concerned.

It is enough to think in this respect of Hegel again who "sees only the *positive,* not the *negative* side of labour."[17] And, of course, he cannot see the dehumanizing negativity of labour under the rule of capital precisely because the second order mediations of the established social system constitute for him the absolute horizon of human life as such. Accordingly, the abstract logical skeleton of timeless "mediation" must replace in his vision the tangible—and potentially alterable—historical specificity of alienated second order mediations, with serious consequences for his monumental theoretical enterprise as a whole. For the idealist abstraction from the real determinations (which also helps to produce the radical *inversion* of the positive and the negative) carries with it:

a) that the ongoing historical dynamic is arbitrarily locked into the eternal prison of metaphysically defined alienation in his scheme of things; and

b) that his own achievement in identifying the crucial role of labour as the key to understanding human development in general—one of the most fundamental insights in the entire history of philosophy—is greatly diminished thereby.

Thus, labour must be conceptualized by Hegel in an extremely one-sided fashion, so as to fit the "positive" preconception, losing at the same time most of its explanatory power by the apologetic inversion and by being confined to the realm of philosophical abstraction. This is why in the Hegelian universe of discourse:

> Labour is man's coming to be for himself within alienation, or as alienated man. The only labour which Hegel knows and recognizes is abstractly mental labour. Therefore, that which constitutes the essence of philosophy—the alienation of man in his knowing of himself, or alienated science thinking itself—Hegel grasps as its essence.[18]

As a result, an idea of the greatest practical implications is restricted to a narrow contemplative sphere. At the same time, a potentially emancipatory conception is turned into opaque self-referentiality and utter mystification.

4.5 Reconciliatory Function of "Negativity as Self-Transcending Contradiction"

As we can see, then, at the roots of the—by now for centuries generally prevailing—negative determination of philosophy and social theory we find the more or less conscious identification of the thinkers concerned with the fundamental structural parameters and second order mediations of class-divided "civil society" and its state formation.

Since the overall framework of the ruling order is assumed as the necessary foundation of social life in general, and "eternalized" as such, the inherently positive vision of building a new and qualitatively different social order cannot conceivably arise. The only admissible criticism is the formulation of *partial correctives,* both with regard to the material operations of market society and the "interfering"—or, on the contrary, in relation to the subordinate class not sufficiently and not effectively enough interfering—exercise of state power. Accordingly, as mentioned already, there can be no real positivity in this framework of thought, since within the confines of its general presuppositions it can only offer either the pseudo-positivity of apologetic inversion—e.g., the Hegelian "uncritical positivism" vis-à-vis the "rationality" of the ruling order, whatever its contradictions—or the definition of positivity as the "*negation of the negation*": a formula problematically extended far beyond its validity.

We can clearly identify these interconnections in an important passage of Hegel's *Science of Logic.* In it Hegel addresses himself to some of the most thorny issues of modern philosophy in the following terms:

> The *self-relation of the negative* must be considered as the second premise of the whole syllogism. . . . The first premise is the moment of universality and communication; the second is determined by individuality, which at first is in an exclusive relation to the Other, as existing for itself and as different. The *negative* appears as *mediator,* since it includes both itself and the immediate term of which it is the negation. In so far as these two determinations are taken as externally related in any manner, the negative moment is merely the formal mediating element; but as *absolute negativity* the negative moment of *absolute mediation* is the unity which is subjectivity and soul.
>
> At this turning point the course of cognition also turns back upon itself. This *negativity,* as self-transcending contradiction, is the reconstitution of the first immediacy, of simple universality; for, immediately, the *Other of the Other* and the *negative of the negative* is the *positive* identical, and universal. . . . For us the Notion itself is (1) the universal which is *in itself,* (2) the negative which is *for itself,* and (3) the third term, which is

> *in and for itself*, the universal which runs through all the moments of the syllogism. But the third term is the conclusion, in which it *mediates itself with itself through its negativity*, and is thus posited for itself as the universal and the *identity* of its moments.[19]

Thus, the "self-relation of the negative" dominates the whole conception. First, because it must define "individuality" in totally vacuous negative terms, since its feasible positive definition—the *social individual* who is both made of, and is the active co-maker of, a multiplicity of tangible social/interpersonal determinations—is radically incompatible with the standpoint of isolated individuality. And second, because it must ascribe to this "moment of individuality"—i.e., for Hegel the second premise or "for-itself," in its abstract negation of the first premise of universality or "in-itself"—the mystical power to "include" in the nothingness of its "self" both itself and the object of its negation, thereby assuming the key role of "mediator" which is simultaneously also the "conclusion." As a result, we are presented with the mere *semblance* of a concluding positivity in the form of the assertion according to which the "Other of the Other and the negative of the negative is the positive identical, and universal."

TO UNDERSTAND THE HIDDEN MEANING of this opaque syllogism, we have to listen to what is being left unsaid in the course of constructing the Hegelian "circle of circles." For the negative as "mediator" is condemned in fact right from the beginning to the futility of pursuing a hopeless task in the sense that—as Marx rightly stressed—real extremes and opposites cannot be mediated and brought to a common denominator, in view of their innermost determinations which set their mutually exclusive claims dead against one another. Consequently, in relation to real extremes the programme of mediation can amount to no more than the empty ceremoniality of some imaginary postulate.

In truth, however, Hegel is not interested in the *removal* of contradictions but, on the contrary, in their reconciliatory *preservation*. And since the contradictions of the present (with which he explicitly wants to make his peace, elevating the "ought" of resignatory reconciliation to the dignity of the highest philosophical principles, as we have already seen) are *inseparable* from the evaded second order mediations of the given social reality, a radical *inversion* of the actual sets of relations must take place in the Hegelian system. As a result, the real world of reified mediations must be reduced by Hegel to its timeless logical skeleton and presented as the magic mediator of all contradictions, thanks to the hypostatization of its abstract negativity "as self-transcending contradiction and reconstitution of the first immediacy."

Thus, by subordinating the very perception of the problem itself to its amenability (or non-amenability) to the stipulated logico-metaphysical mediation and "*reconstitutive* negation," the intrinsically contradictory second order mediations of the established social order completely disappear from sight. For the regulatory centre and anticipated solution in terms of which everything must be assessed cannot critically question at the same time its own credentials. It acts, instead, as the refractory prism through which the world is viewed and evaluated while it itself a priori escapes all scrutiny, no matter how distorting its operation. In this way, the perverse "rational actuality" of the prevailing system of mediations not only cannot be subjected to critical examination but, in its abstractly transubstantiated form, becomes the necessary presupposition of all feasible questioning.

Inevitably, the reduction of historically specific real mediations (dense with the social contradictions of capital's second order mediations) to their contentless and timeless logical skeleton also means that the "negative moment" of mediation cannot be other than "merely the *formal* mediating element." To extricate himself from the total vacuity of such formalism, Hegel offers an ingenious but purely *semantic* solution—setting the trend even in this respect for modern philosophy—by renaming his key terms of reference as "*absolute* negativity" and "*absolute* mediation." Since, however, such categories cannot be derived from the original constitution of his Absolute, they must be ascribed to "subjectivity and soul," so as to produce with their help both "the progress of the Absolute to unessentiality" and its "return to the first identity as veritable identity," claiming to overcome thereby Spinoza's alleged failure.

In this way, the formalistic reduction of mediation—which produced the negative moment as "merely the formal mediating element"—is reversed, so to speak, in the sense that "content" reappears in the picture as the redefined substantiveness and new modality of "absolute mediation," inherent in the postulated unity of the Subject.

However, there is no danger of historical contamination (let alone of the implications of a potential social destabilization) in such determination of the concept, since it bears no relation to the identifiable second order mediations of the real world. The "absolute mediation" of the Subject can only yield what is expected of it, namely: the "progress of the Absolute to unessentiality" and its "return to veritable identity with itself" through the establishment of the "identity of its moments," thanks to the "reconstitutive negation" of "absolute negation" as "negatively self-relating negation."

WE CAN SEE, thus, that the claimed "concluding positivity" is a false appearance. For it is *assumed* right from the beginning as the absolute end to which one must return in order to complete the "circle of circles."

The formalistic reduction of real mediations to their logical skeleton; the stipulative transubstantiation of the latter into "absolute mediation"; the key role assigned to the concepts of "absolute negation" and "negatively self-relating negation"; the mystificatory problematic of identical Subject and Object through which the "progress of the Absolute to unessentiality" and its subsequent "return to veritable self-identity" can be accomplished; and the postulates of "unity and universality" which imaginarily transcend partiality—all these are vital aspects of a conception that produces "*concluding* positivity" on the ground of its aprioristic *presupposition*.

It even offers the "transcendence of alienation" by presenting the vision of a—purely imaginary—"second alienation of alienated existence" (through religious experience) which, however, simultaneously decrees the absolute permanence of *actual* alienation in virtue of the stipulated identity of the concepts of *alienation* and *objectification*.

Thus the claimed concluding positivity of the "Other of the Other" and the "negative of the negative"—to be accomplished, according to the great German philosopher, through the "absolute mediation" and "absolute negation" of the Subject—turns out to be the *circular presupposition* and glorification of the false positivity of the existent. This is why the negative determination of the philosophical categories—and, above all, of the category of mediation—must assume such an important methodological function in the Hegelian conceptual framework.

4.6 Negativity in Sartre and Marcuse: Dependency on the Ideologically Dominant Discourse

The last century and a half of philosophical development did not change these determinations for the better. Rather, it made them even more extreme in their negativity.

Heidegger's philosophy, with the boundlessness of its "nihilating negation," is a representative example in this respect. What makes things worse, however, is that often even philosophers who try to oppose the established order—and not just in matters of marginal importance—remain trapped within the overwhelming negativity of the ideologically dominant discourse.

This is true not only of the existentialist but also of the "Marxisant" Sartre, as he later describes himself. In this sense, the existentialist synthesis of *Being and Nothingness,* in Merleau-Ponty's at the time still highly sympathetic account, "is first of all a demonstration that the subject is freedom, absence and negativity."[20] But even if we consider Sartre's most positive phase of development—the years of writing the *Critique of Dialectical Reason*—we find that negativity remains the central orienting principle of his philosophy.

This is all the more remarkable since in *The Problems of Method* Sartre clearly recognizes that, throughout its history, the role of Cartesianism was primarily *negative.*[21] And yet, when it comes to articulating his new philosophical synthesis, Sartre himself is unable to escape the same predicament. For while the "fused group" of the *Critique* represents an essentially positive "formal structure of history" on account of its great cohesion, this positivity is subsumed under two inescapable orders of negativity. On the one hand, the "fused group" only emerges in response to a mortal threat which its members must counter or perish. And on the other hand—which happens to be in the present context the more important consideration—it is condemned to a strictly transient existence, since it cannot sustain itself as a socially viable structure. On the contrary, under the pressure of its internal tendency to relapse into "seriality," it is progressively undermined, and even its highly questionable countermeasures, enacted in order to prolong its own life, cannot prevent the ultimate disintegration.

MARCUSE'S CASE IS EVEN MORE PARADOXICAL and revealing. For he is very far from being satisfied with Adorno's "negative dialectic." Not only in the sense that he is much better disposed toward Hegel than his Frankfurt School comrade in arms but, above all, in that he defiantly tries to reassert the validity of "utopia" as the radical counter-image to the established social order which he condemns in the most passionate terms.

In this way Marcuse insists that the "historical imperative" and the "moral imperative" advocated by him, together with the categorical rejection of complicitous positivity and "affirmation," constitute subversion and negation: "not for the sake of negation, but for 'saving' human values invalidated by the affirmation."[22]

At the same time Marcuse claims that the "moral imperative" of his "revolutionary imperative"—opposed to the prevailing "technological imperative"[23] of society—is an "*empirical postulate* derived from the very banal (and quite 'unscientific') experience of unnecessary suffering."[24]

However, even if we disregard his—sometimes direct and sometimes indirect—dependency on the dominant "anti-ideological" discourse,[25] Marcuse's solution is extremely problematical. For his utopian rejection of the present—what he calls "The Great Refusal"[26]—turns out to be a "correction" to Hegel from an explicitly Kantian position, asserting the validity of "an 'ought' which imposes itself on the individual *against* inclination [Marcuse's italics], personal need, interest."[27]

Given Marcuse's false diagnosis which takes for granted the fateful "integration" of "probably the majority of the population,"[28] nothing but the abstract imperative of "the emergence of a new Subject"[29] remains as the orienting principle of his philosophy. In this spirit he decrees in the name of the hypostatized new Subject:

> the priority of the subjective factor, dislocation of the revolutionary potential from the old working classes to minoritarian groups of the intelligentsia and white collar workers.[30]

Thus, we are offered as a solution a postulated synthesis which is said to be:

> the work of a *supra-individual* historical Subjectivity in the individual—just as the Kantian categories are the syntheses of a *transcendental Ego* in the empirical Ego.[31]

Indeed, a few lines further on it is stated that "Kant's *transcendental construction* of experience may well furnish the *model* for the *historical construction* of experience."[32]

THIS IS WHAT WE END UP WITH ALREADY at the time when Marcuse, still in an optimistic mood, praises the "positive" future of his utopia whose horizons are defined by him in terms of "non-repressive sublimation," expected to arise from the processes of, and akin to, "desublimating art and anti-art." It is no wonder, therefore, that the disappointed expectations with regard to the "new Subject," as embodied "in the militant youth of today,"[33] lead to the utter despair and pessimism of Marcuse's last years—when, according to him, "in reality *evil triumphs*," leaving to the individual nothing but the "islands of good to which one can *escape* for short periods of time."[34] For the paralyzing negativity of the dominant theoretical discourse cannot be broken by strategies modelled on the pseudo-positivity of Kantian imperatives and transcendental constructs, but only by redefining in inherently positive—as well as practically viable—terms both the direction of the journey and the social agency of the advocated radical transformation.

Such a redefinition concerns above all the question of mediation. It is understandable, therefore, that critics of the ruling order, like Sartre and Marcuse, should reject the false positivity of which the Hegelian conception of mediation is a characteristic example. However, the return to Kant which we find in the writings of both Sartre and Marcuse cannot solve the problems at stake. On the contrary, their reliance on Kantian "ought" only makes their negation more abstract and generic, with a tendency to disregard the key role of socially effective mediation in bringing about the necessary structural change.

NOTES

1. Hegel, *Science of Logic*, Vol. 1, Allen & Unwin, London, 1929, p. 125.
2. Ibid., p. 266.
3. Ibid., Vol. 2, p. 168.
4. Ibid., p. 171. Hegel argues that: "The lack of intro-Reflection which is common to Spinoza's exposition of the Absolute and to the theory of emanation is made good in the concept of the *monad* in Leibniz." (Ibid., p.170.) He praises Leibniz inasmuch as the latter "ascribes to the monads a certain self-completeness, a kind of independence; . . . It is an extremely important concept that the changes of the monad are imagined as actions having no passivity, or as self-manifestations, and that the principle of *intro-Reflection or individuation* clearly emerges as essential." (Ibid., p.171.) However, he wants to go beyond Leibniz in the sense indicated above: "But now the task would be to find in the concept of the *absolute monad* not only this absolute unity of form and content, but also the nature of Reflection as *self-relating negativity* which is *self-repulsion,* by means of which it exists as positing and creating." (Ibid.)

   We shall see presently the connection between this conception of "positing and creating" as "self-relating negativity" and "self-repulsion," and the insoluble mysteries of "measure" arising from the Hegelian standpoint of isolated individuality, with its focus on "aggregates of individuals" in "developed civil society."
5. Ibid., p. 170.
6. Ibid., p. 214.
7. Ibid.
8. Ibid., p. 215.
9. Ibid., pp. 215–6.
10. Hegel, *Philosophy of Right*, Clarendon Press, Oxford, 1942, p. 10.
11. "To recognize reason as the rose in the cross of the present and thereby to enjoy the present, this is the *rational insight* which *reconciles* us to the *actual,* the reconciliation which philosophy affords to those in whom there has once arisen an inner voice bidding them to *comprehend*, not only to dwell in what is *substantive* while still retaining subjective freedom, but also to possess *subjective freedom* while standing not in anything *particular* and *accidental* but in what *exists absolutely*." (Ibid., p. 12.)

12. It has been rightly argued that in the liberal tradition "The defence of liberty consists in the 'negative' goal of warding off interference. . . . This is liberty as it has been conceived by liberals in the modern world from the days of Erasmus (some would say of Occam) to our own." (Isaiah Berlin, *Two Concepts of Liberty*, Clarendon Press, Oxford, 1958, p. 12.)

    But even the "positive" concept containable within such horizons turns out to be fundamentally *negative*. "The essence of the notion of liberty, both in the 'positive' and the 'negative' senses, is the holding off of something or someone—of others, who trespass on my field or assert their authority over me, . . . intruders and despots of one kind or another." (Ibid., p. 43.)

13. Hegel, *Science of Logic*, Vol. 1, pp. 347–8.
14. Ibid., p. 352.
15. Kant has, of course, his own version of the "Cunning of Reason." For a detailed discussion of these problems see my essay on "Kant, Hegel, Marx: Historical Necessity and the Standpoint of Political Economy," first published in *Philosophy, Ideology and Social Science*, Harvester/Wheatsheaf, 1986.
16. Hegel, *Science of Logic*, Vol. 1, p. 350.
17. Marx, *Economic and Philosophic Manuscripts of 1844*, Lawrence & Wishart, London, 1959, p. 152.
18. Ibid.
19. Hegel, *Science of Logic*, Vol. 2, pp. 478–80.
20. Merleau-Ponty, "The Battle over Existentialism," in: *Sense and Non-Sense*, Northwestern University Press, 1964, pp. 72–3. (Originally published in *Les Temps Modernes*, No. 2, November 1945.)
21. "The analytical, critical rationalism of the great Cartesians has survived them; born from conflict, it looked back to clarify the conflict. At the time when the bourgeoisie sought to undermine the institutions of the Ancien Régime, it attacked the outworn significations which tried to justify them. Later it gave service to liberalism, and provided a doctrine for procedures that attempted to realize the 'atomization' of the Proletariat. . . . In the case of Cartesianism, the action of 'philosophy' remains *negative;* it clears the ground, it destroys, and it enables men, across the infinite complexities and particularisms of the feudal system, to *catch a glimpse of the abstract universality of bourgeois property*." Sartre, *The Problem of Method*, Methuen &

Co., London, 1963, p. 5.

22. Marcuse, "Freedom and the Historical Imperative" (a lecture delivered at the Rencontre Internationale de Genève in 1969), in: Marcuse, *Studies in Critical Philosophy*, N.L.B., London, 1972, p. 216.

23. Ibid., p. 215.

24. Ibid., p. 216.

25. Marcuse, curiously, aims at an "*unideological* discussion of freedom" (ibid., p.212), and a little later he uses the term with the same generic anti-ideological connotation when he asks the question: "Does this mean that the imperatives of history preclude the realization of freedom in any other than a partial, repressive, *ideological* form?" (Ibid., p. 213.)

26. Ibid., p. 221.

27. Ibid., p. 219.

28. Ibid., p. 217.

29. Ibid., p. 222.

30. Ibid., pp. 222–3.

31. Ibid., p. 217.

32. Ibid., p. 218.

33. "I believe that, in the militant youth of today, the radical political synthesis of experience is taking place—perhaps the first step toward liberation." (Ibid., p. 223.)

34. Marcuse, *Die Permanenz der Kunst,* p. 53.

CHAPTER FIVE

The Rise and Fall of Historical Temporality

5.1 Historical Explanation in Ancient Greece and in the Middle Ages

The development of historical consciousness is centred around three fundamental sets of problems:

1. the determination of the historical agency;

2. the perception of change not merely as lapse of time, but as a movement that possesses an intrinsically cumulative character, hence implying some sort of advancement and development;

3. the implicit or conscious opposition between universality and particularity, with a view to achieve a synthesis of the two in order to explain historically relevant events in terms of their broader significance which, of necessity, transcends their immediate historical specificity.

Naturally, all three are essential for a genuine historical conception. This is why it is by no means sufficient to state in generic terms that "man is the agent of history" if, either, the nature of historical change itself is not adequately grasped, or the complex dialectical relationship between particularity and universality is violated with regard to the subject of historical action. Likewise, the concept of human advancement as such, taken in isolation from the other two dimensions of historical theory, is easily reconcilable with a thoroughly ahistorical explanation if the supra-human agency of "Divine Providence" is assumed as the moving force behind the postulated change.

In this sense, Aristotle's complaint against historical writing—ranking historiography known to him well below poetry and tragedy, in view of its "less philosophical"[1] character—is fully justified. Not because the original meaning of the Greek term of history—derived from "istor," i.e., "eyewitness"—indicates the danger of too great a reliance on the limited standpoint of particular individuals who themselves participate in, and hence have some vested interest also in reporting, the events in question in an unavoidably biassed way. The issue was even more intractable than that. It concerned the very nature of the historian's enterprise itself as manifest in the apparently insoluble contradiction between the particularistic point of departure and evidence as displayed in the chronicled actions, and the generic "teaching" or conclusion one was supposed to derive from them. In other words, it was the inability of the historians of Antiquity to master the dialectical complexities of particularity and universality which carried with it the necessary consequence of remaining trapped at the level of anecdotal particularism. And since it was, of course, inadmissible to leave things at that, the "non-philosophical" and anecdotal particularism of ancient historiography had to be directly turned into moralizing universality, so as to claim the reader's attention on account of its asserted general significance.

On the other hand, the historiography of the Middle Ages violated the dialectic of particularity and universality in a contrasting way, setting out from quite different premisses and determinations in relation to which the "eyewitness" of ancient history completely lost its relevance. The representative systems of the Middle Ages were characterized by the radical obliteration of the life-like vitality of actual historical particularity. Instead, they superimposed on the chronicled events and personalities alike the *abstract universality* of a religiously preconceived "philosophy of history" in which everything had to be directly subordinated to the postulated work of Divine Providence, as positive or negative instances—that is, illustrative "exemplifications"—of such Providence.

Thus, according to Saint Augustine, the author of the greatest religiously inspired philosophy of history:

> in the torrential stream of human history, two currents meet and mix: the current of evil which flows from Adam and that of good which comes from God.[2]

This is why it is argued against all those who, in Saint Augustine's view, fail to understand the real purpose of Divine intervention in human affairs—manifest even through the imposition of inhumanities which, on the face of it, are difficult to reconcile with the Divine Purpose—that:

> if they only had sense, they would see that the hardships and cruelties they suffered from the enemy came from that Divine Providence who makes use of war to reform the corrupt lives of men. They ought to see that it is the way of Providence to test by such afflictions men of virtuous and exemplary life, and to call them, once tried, to a better world, or to keep them for a while on earth for the accomplishment of other purposes.[3]

5.2 "Divine Providence" in Bourgeois Philosophies of History

The privileged role assigned to Divine Providence in explaining historical development—which renders extremely problematical, if not altogether meaningless, the very notion of a genuinely human historical agency—is, of course, not confined to the Middle Ages. It surfaces at much later stages as well, irrespective of the state of scientific knowledge and of the overwhelming evidence provided by the dynamics of the ongoing socio-historical interchanges which invite secular explanations. The reasons for this, at times, can be clearly located in conservative, indeed profoundly reactionary, social interests, as evidenced by the writings of romantic philosophy and historiography, for instance.

Thus, Friedrich Schlegel argues in the same epoch which produces the historical conception of Hegel—the age of the French as well as of the industrial revolution—that:

> The Creator has not reserved to Himself the beginning and the end alone, and left the rest follow its own course; but in the middle, and at every point also, of its progress, the Omnipotent Will can intervene at pleasure. If He pleases He can instantaneously stop this vital development, and suddenly make the course of nature stand still; or, in a moment, give life and movement to what before stood motionless and inanimate. Generally speaking, it is in the divine power to suspend the laws of nature, to interfere directly with them, and, as it were, to intercalate among them some higher and immediate operation of His power, as an exception to their development. For as in the social frame of civil life, the author and giver of the laws may occasionally set them aside, or, in their administration, allow certain cases of exception, even so is it, also, with nature's Lawgiver.[4]

The reactionary intent behind Schlegel's arbitrary assertions is fairly obvious. It becomes even clearer when he draws a direct parallel between the "Wisdom of the divine Order of Things" and of the "divine Order in the History of the World and the Relation of States"[5] in order to justify the principle according to which "power emanates from God" and therefore strictly forbids us to "*violate or forcibly subvert any established right*, whether essentially sacred or hallowed only by prescription."[6]

However, this kind of social apologetics is by no means a necessary feature of all historical theories which, for one reason or another, continue to make references to the categories of traditional theology. For, strangely enough, the historical conceptions of the bourgeoisie *never completely* succeed in freeing themselves from the determinations which make them incorporate the mysteries of "Divine Providence" into their explanatory framework. Not even when the underlying sociopolitical intent is, on the whole, quite progressive and fundamentally secular in character.

Thus Hegel, for instance, who represents the unsurpassed peak of such historical conceptions, concludes his *Philosophy of History* with the following lines:

> That the History of the World, with all the changing scenes which its annals present, is this process of development and the realization of Spirit—this is the true *Theodicaea,* the justification of God in History. Only this insight can reconcile Spirit with the History of the World—viz., that what has happened, and is happening every day, is not only not 'without God', but is essentially his work.[7]

Hegel is, of course, perfectly well versed in the dialectic of particularity and universality at the level of *philosophical abstraction.* He writes in his *Philosophy of Right*:

> The element in which the universal mind exists in art is intuition and imagery, in religion feeling and representative thinking, in philosophy pure freedom of thought. In *world history* this element is the actuality of mind in its whole compass of internality and externality alike. World history is a court of judgement because in its *absolute universality,* the *particular*—i.e. the Penates, civil society, and the national minds in their *variegated actuality*—is present as *only ideal,* and the movement of mind in this element is the exhibition of that fact.[8]

Since, however, the ideological interests inseparable from Hegel's social horizon compel him to retain the fiction of "aggregates of individuals in civil society," as we have seen in the last chapter, the actual relations must be depicted upside down, so as to be able to deduce the "variegated actuality" of bourgeois particularism from, and reconcile it with, the "absolute universality" of actually accomplished world history and its claimed ideality. Thus, we are offered an apologetic definition of world history in terms of "the necessary development, out of the concept of mind's freedom alone, of the moments of reason and so of the self-consciousness and freedom of mind." And to complete the "dialectical circle" of the Hegelian construct—which conflates the moments of ideality and actuality in the interest of its openly professed reconciliation with the present—we are told that: "This development is the *interpretation* and *actualization* of the *universal mind*."[9]

In reality, though, historical development is thoroughly unintelligible either in terms of self-oriented particularity or with reference to the ultimately mysterious unfolding of some abstract universality, be that the openly theological varieties of "Divine Providence" or the Hegelian notion of the "universal mind."

Accordingly, there can be no solution to the dilemmas of past theories without conceiving the agency of *actual* history as the practical unity of *particular and universal* determinations embodied in a *real collective subject,* in contrast to the idealistic "movement of the mind" or the circularly self-anticipating fulfilment of the a priori assumed "destiny of reason."

This is why the incompatibility of an empirically existent collective subject with the individualistic presuppositions of bourgeois thought must lead to extremely problematical results.

- On the one hand, it must lead to defining the collective dimension of historical development—in Vico, Kant, Hegel and others, though under a variety of different names—as the "Cunning of Reason," with its mysterious ways of realizing its own plan over and above the heads of the individuals.

- On the other hand, it must carry with it a desperate attempt to eliminate, by the wishful postulates of unsustainable "ought-to-be," the contradictions involved in such a solution of the relationship between the individual and collective aspects of historical development.

- Moreover, this dubious preponderance of "ought" must be in evidence even when, paradoxically, the philosopher in question (like Hegel, for instance) is—in general philosophical terms—consciously opposed to the vacuous remedies one can derive from mere "ought-to-be."

HEGEL'S CASE IS PARTICULARLY INSTRUCTIVE in this respect. For he recognizes both the radical contrast between ancient and "modern theory," and the severe dilemmas implicit in the solutions of the latter. He writes:

> Plato in his *Republic* makes everything depend upon the Government, and makes Disposition—an *ex animo* acquiescence in the laws—the principle

> of the State; on which account he lays the chief stress on Education. The modern theory is *diametrically opposed* to this, referring everything to the *individual will*. But here we have *no guarantee* that the will in question has the *right disposition* which is essential to the *stability of the State*.[10]

However, when he attempts to sustain the viability of the modern system that has to operate on the ground of "the Idea of Right" in conjunction with "men's subjective will," he can offer no real solution. He merely asserts that "In regard to the latter [subjective will], the main feature of *incompatibility* still presents itself, in the requirement that the *ideal general will should* also be the *empirically general*—i.e. that the units of the State, in their *individual* capacity, *should rule*, or *at any rate take part* in government."[11]

Thus, although Hegel is prepared to water down the requirements of an adequate relationship between the individuals and the state to the minimal criterion of "at any rate take part in government," instead of effectively "ruling" or controlling the conditions of their own life, as the "modern principle" itself would prescribe, he cannot claim that the contradiction involved in the new arrangements is solved thereby. He has to admit—appealing at the same time to the "ought" of future history as the would-be solution—that in the modern state

> The particular arrangements of the government are forthwith opposed by the advocates of Liberty as the mandates of a particular will, and branded as displays of arbitrary power. The will of the Many expels the Ministry from power, and those who had formed the Opposition fill the vacant places; but the latter having now become the Government, meet with hostility from the Many, and share the same fate. Thus *agitation and unrest* are perpetuated. This *collision*, this nodus, this problem is that with which *history is now occupied*, and whose solution *it has to work out* in the future.[12]

As we can see from Hegel's terms of reference, even when he is willing to acknowledge the presence of "agitation, unrest and collision," the overall framework of explanation remains thoroughly individualistic, recognizing only aggregates of individuals as supporters of government or opposition participating in the rather dubiously characterized conflicts. The underlying social contradictions as articulated around the focal point of irreconcilable material (and class) interests are not recognized by him, let alone would he acknowledge their objective pointers in the direction of a possible solution. Hence the gratuitous suggestion which ascribes the role of agency—as the carrier of the hoped-for solution—to an abstractly personified "future history" constitutes the logical completion of the individualistic presuppositions of this theory.

5.3 Vico's Conception of Civil Society and History

The philosophy of Giambattista Vico offers an outstanding example of both the positive accomplishments and the necessary limitations of bourgeois historical conceptions.

He addresses himself to all three fundamental dimensions of historical consciousness mentioned above. Indeed, one of Vico's greatest insights is the recognition "that the world of civil society has certainly been made by men. . . . Whoever reflects on this cannot but marvel that the philosophers should have bent all their energies to the study of the world of nature, which, since God made it, He alone knows; and that they should have neglected the study of the world of nations, or civil world, which, since men had made it, men could come to know."[13]

At the same time, Vico also understands that the historical process cannot be explained simply in terms of the acts of particular individuals who pursue their conscious subjective aims. For the outcome, bewildering as it may sound, is often diametrically opposed to the original intentions. To quote his reflections on the subject, which unmistakably anticipate the Hegelian notion of the "Cunning of Reason":

> It is true that men have themselves made this world of nations (and we took this as the first incontestable principle of our Science, since we despaired of finding it from the philosophers and philologists), but this world without doubt has issued from a mind often diverse, at times quite contrary, and always superior to the particular ends that men had proposed to themselves; which narrow ends, made means to serve wider

> ends, it has always employed to preserve the human race upon this earth. Men mean to gratify their bestial lust and abandon their offspring, and they inaugurate the chastity from which the families arise. The fathers mean to exercise without restraint their paternal power over their clients, and they subject them to the civil powers from which the cities arise. The reigning orders of nobles mean to abuse their lordly freedom over the plebeians, and they are obliged to submit to the laws which establish popular liberty. The free peoples mean to shake off the yoke of their laws, and they become subject to monarchs.[14]

However, while it is explicitly stated that "the world of civil society is made by men," Vico's historical conception, just like that of Hegel, breaks down at the crucial point. He, too, becomes entangled in the—from the standpoint of political economy insurmountable—difficulties concerning the relationship between particularity and universality as well as between temporality and transhistoricity. For within such horizons the real subject of history cannot be a trans-individual collective agency which could offer a solution to those problems. Rather, inasmuch as the historical agency is said to be working through the acts of individuals who are used by the "hidden hand" in the service of its own "hidden design," it must be *supra*-individual, in contrast to *trans*-individual. And, of course, it can only assert its *supra-individual* authority over the limited particular individuals by being also *supra-human*. A solution which is, undoubtedly, compatible with the required individualistic model of explanation, although the price that must be paid for adopting it involves the incorporation of an openly acknowledged mystery into programmatically rational and enlightened systems of thought.

VICO, LIKE ALL THOSE WHO PIONEERED THE STANDPOINT of political economy, is quite conscious of the role of labour[15] in historical development. He also shares with them a view of human nature according to which men are "under the *tyranny of self-love*, which compels them to make *private utility* their chief guide."[16] Such a view of human nature—a "nature" which must be, according to Vico, subdued and controlled by the "properly human"—is linked to an explanation of the advancement of both knowledge and liberty on the basis of an anthropological model.

Thus, the past failure to understand the nature of civil society and its institutions is explained by Vico as an "*aberration*" which is:

> a consequence of that infirmity of the human mind by which, immersed and buried in the body, it naturally inclines to take notice of bodily things, and finds the effort to attend to itself too laborious; just as the bodily eye sees all objects outside itself but needs a mirror to see itself.[17]

Likewise, the appearance of human liberty is made intelligible in counterposition to the human body by saying that:

> since this liberty does not come from the human body, whence comes concupiscence, it must come from the mind and is therefore properly human.[18]

That in addition to the "natural body" in which the allegedly "genus-individuals" partake, there is also their social articulation in intrinsically collective complexes, constituting a historically produced and changing "second nature" in relation to which the advancement of both knowledge and liberty can and must be explained, are considerations which, obviously, cannot find their place in this framework of thought.

Paradoxically, however, the ahistorical terms of counterposition which we find in Vico's anthropological model rebound against his historical conception as a whole. Thus, he is forced to look for "universal and eternal principles . . . on which all nations were founded and still preserve themselves,"[19] diverting thereby the quest for the historical dialectic of particular and universal into the metaphysical blind alley of timeless universality and eternality. This is why in the final analysis the providential and supra-temporal "Cunning of Reason" must take over as the true subject of history, displacing historical temporality by the "eternal," and particularity by the abstract universal. As Vico himself puts it in two key passages of his pathbreaking work:

> Our new Science must therefore be a demonstration, so to speak, of what *providence* has wrought in history, for it must be a history of the institutions by which, without human discernment or counsel, and often *against the designs of men,* providence has ordered this great city of the human

> race. For though this world has been created in *time* and *particular,* the institutions established therein *by providence* are *universal* and *eternal.*[20]

And again, after surveying how the conscious intentions of men turned into their opposite, even if to the claimed benefit of all, he concludes:

> That which did all this was *mind,* for men did it with intelligence; it was not *fate,* for they did it by *choice;* not *chance,* for the results of their always so acting are *perpetually the same.*[21]

Thus, historical temporality in the end must be suppressed so as to bring everything into line with the "political economist" conception of "human nature" and with the individualistic model of reason, knowledge and liberty directly or indirectly derived from the anthropological foundations of that alleged nature.

Naturally, Vico's "providence through the order of civil institutions,"[22] acting as the "mind" and the moving force behind the historical transformations which lead to or manifest "perpetually the same," is very far from being a traditional theological concept. Nevertheless, since the institutions of civil society—"by which, without human discernment or counsel, and often against the designs of men, providence has ordered this great city of the human race"—cannot be critically scrutinized and treated as intrinsically historical, hence changeable with regard to all their aspects (including the structurally most important ones), the ideological interest of "eternalizing the established social relations" dominates the overall construct and imposes the supra-historical mysteries of a claimed "*rational civil theology* of divine providence"[23] as the stipulated "bounds of human reason"[24] on Vico's originally intended secular and historical system of explanation.

5.4 Organic Models as Substitutes for Historical Explanation

The characterization of the *social* body, together with all its constituent parts and institutions, as an *organism,* is broadly diffused throughout the history of social and political thought. Nor is it possible, of course, to reject it on some a priori ground. Nevertheless, the question of its viability hinges on how its terms of reference are defined, i.e., whether it is seen dynamically, or as a self-enclosed and unchangeable system.

What makes extremely problematical the various anthropological models of bourgeois thought—even when they are formulated from a progressive standpoint, as, for instance, in the writings of Vico, Rousseau and Herder—is that the organic explanation constitutes for them only a *substitute* for a genuine historical view of the social process. For while the way in which such models are conceived makes it possible to account for the immediately observable functioning of the established mode of social intercourse, it only does so by avoiding the question of *genesis,* since a close scrutiny of the latter would transfer the possibility of social criticism to the plane of—historically feasible—radical negation and change.

And yet, it is precisely the historical dimension of genesis which makes intelligible the functioning of a determinate set of social relations as an *organic system* within the framework of some historically created *practical presuppositions*. For, as Marx forcefully argued:

> It must be kept in mind that the new forces of production and relations of production do not develop out of *nothing,* nor drop from the sky, nor from the womb of self-positing Idea; but from within and in antithesis to the existing development of production and the inherited, traditional relations of property. While in the *completed* bourgeois system every economic relation *presupposes* every other in its bourgeois economic form, and *everything posited is also a presupposition,* this is the case with every *organic system*. This organic system itself, as a *totality* has *its presuppositions,* and its *development* to its totality consists precisely in subordinating all elements of society to itself, or in creating out of it the organs which it still lacks. This is *historically* how it *becomes a totality*. The process of becoming this totality forms a moment of its process, of its *development*.[25]

The omission of this all-important dimension—which aims at grasping the given social totality in its *historical becoming,* in terms of its *objective presuppositions*—is not a personal failure of Vico, Rousseau, Herder and others, but a *necessary limit* of their standpoint. For the underlying material and ideological interests do not allow them to look beyond the structural framework of class society, thereby necessarily confining their critique to some secondary aspect of the established order, without questioning the framework itself, nor its historically created—and therefore also *historically transcendable*—presuppositions.

This is why the organic image itself which they use with such predilection can have no genuine explanatory value, since its real determinations (i.e. precisely those which define the organism as a developing totality) are necessarily overlooked. As a result, the postulate of "organic unity"—which is said to cement the diverse parts of society together, just as nature does in the case of the individual's body—can amount to nothing more than an *external* and rather superficial *analogy*. For through such analogical reduction the immanent historical dynamism of *both* the individual and the social organism (as systems intelligible only in terms of determinate historical conditions of *production* and *reproduction*) is wiped out and turned into a *timeless* "functionality," with more or less pronounced apologetic connotations.

SIGNIFICANTLY, IN THE MAINSTREAM of the philosophical tradition we are here concerned with, the critical investigation of the *presuppositions* of the given social totality is *systematically* avoided, ignoring the question of how the existing order *becomes* a totality, so as to be able to maintain the circularity through which unexplained presuppositions "explain" the meaning of other presuppositions.

Thus, setting out from the given as a self-explanatory totality, the reciprocal references of the "dialectical circle" not only "explain" (and legitimate) the specific function of the various aspects, but simultaneously also confer upon them the semblance of *permanence*. Accordingly, ignoring the *historical genesis* of the system in existence fulfils its ideological function by obliterating the historical dimension of the established order also in the direction of the *future*. This is what Marx calls the "eternalization of the bourgeois relations of production" which plays a very important role in the corresponding conceptualizations of capital's epoch, from its early phases to the present.

Only the 18th and early 19th centuries seem to constitute an exception to the general rule, in that they take a giant step in the direction of a genuine historical explanation. By the middle of the nineteenth century, however, the dominant mood is that of extreme scepticism—almost to the point of cynicism—with regard to the possibility of intelligible historical development. Indeed, such mood is tellingly encapsulated in Ranke's dictum: "all events are equidistant from God."

But even in the eighteenth and early nineteenth centuries—with Vico, Rousseau, Herder and Hegel—the proposed historical explanation is not carried coherently to its conclusion. Instead, we find either the disruption of historical temporality, through the introduction of repetitive *cycles* into the overall explanatory framework, or an apologetic *closure* of historical development at its alleged climax in the European civilization of the "Germanic World," as happens to be the case with Hegel.

Thus, in the final analysis, historical development as a dynamic process is either ignored (both in the past and in relation to the future), or is allowed to enter the stage only for a very limited duration and purpose, in order to underpin the present in its "rational actuality" and, at the same time, to completely block off the future. In this sense, the adoption of a position which grants historical existence only to the past, and even that with characteristic inconsistencies, brings with it a conception of "decapitated" temporality, with far-reaching methodological implications for all aspects of the theories which operate within its ahistorical framework.

5.5 Vicissitudes of Historical Consciousness in the Twentieth Century

As to the development of this historical consciousness in the twentieth century, Hannah Arendt provides us with a representative and intriguing example. All the more so since the ever-intensifying manifestations of the contradictions and inhumanities of the capitalist social order preclude the adoption of an unproblematical defence of that order, and Arendt frequently tries to distance herself from "bourgeois privatization," consumerism and hypocrisy. Indeed, in a university discussion dedicated to the assessment of her own work she goes as far as to confess to a "romantic sympathy with the council system."[26]

And yet, notwithstanding Arendt's critical intent, privatization reigns supreme in her work, no matter how many references are made to the idealized "public realm" of the even more idealized "citizen." Not only because she admits that "I never felt the need to commit myself."[27] More important is in this respect the irreconcilable opposition she champions between *thought* and *practice*, opting for the former with the justification that "I, by nature, am not an actor."[28] And even when she acknowledges that

> The main flaw and mistake of *The Human Condition* is the following: I still look at what is called in the traditions the *vita activa* from the viewpoint of the *vita contemplativa,* without ever saying anything real about the *vita contemplativa*,[29]

no indication is given as to how one might overcome the now admitted "fallacy" (Arendt's expression). On the contrary, the diremption of thought and practice is maintained both by insisting that "to the extent that I wish to think I have to *withdraw from the world*"[30] and by reformulating the old approach in essentially the same terms.[31] It is not enough to say that "I feel that this *Human Condition* needs a second volume and I am trying to write it."[32] For, as we know also from the example of Sartre's philosophical syntheses *Being and Nothingness* and the *Critique of Dialectical Reason,* it is one thing to acknowledge the need for a corrective "second volume," and quite another to be able to deliver it, in view of the profound, but to the authors in question not visible, theoretical incompatibilities involved.

Arendt's failure to challenge the predicament of privatization, despite the sincerely felt desire to do so, is replicated in her critique of "bureaucracy"—as "rule by nobody"—in that it is formulated in a social vacuum. Indeed, her critique is sustained only by her idealization of the American Constitution of "the Founding Fathers," spelled out in conjunction with a dubious interpretation of Montesquieu which is devised for the purpose. And when she is criticized for lack of evidence from actual history and from the idiosyncratically interpreted works, all she can offer in support of the advocated position is a circularly stipulative elevation of the Weberian practice of constructing "ideal types" to the axiomatic status of an unquestionable general rule.[33]

Understandably, therefore, the propounded critique of bureaucracy remains quite impotent. It verbally opposes bureaucracy while simultaneously also accepting it on the ground that "bigness and centralization demands these bureaucracies."[34] And, in the same way, after declaring that the work of administration "can be done only in a more or less central manner," all we are offered, in place of a solution, is a dilemma from which there can be no way out:

> On the other hand this centralization is an awful danger, because these structures are so vulnerable. How can you keep these up without centralization? And if you have it, the vulnerability is immense.[35]

It would be astonishing if it could be otherwise in Hannah Arendt's system. For the critique that undermines its own ground and the possibility of any effective intervention in transforming the structural and institutional framework of society for the better—undermines, that is, by peremptorily rejecting not only the Marxian notion of superstructure, defined in terms of its dialectical reciprocities with the material ground of social practice, but also the categories of social classes, trends and movements, with the curious justification that concepts like these belong to the "nineteenth century"[36]—must be utterly powerless in the face of such self-imposed dilemmas.

NOTWITHSTANDING HER, AT TIMES BITING, POLEMICS against "the bourgeois," Arendt shares with their tradition not only the standpoint of isolated individuality—which induces her to idealize the mysterious inward "experiences between *man and himself*,"[37] so as to be able to conclude, opposing Weber to Marx, that "*World alienation,* and not self-alienation as Marx thought, has been the hallmark of the modern age"[38]—but also the other methodological characteristics which we are concerned with.

Her conception of historical consciousness, as we shall see, is inseparable from Heisenberg's extreme relativist theorization of modern science—with its quasi-mystical "principle of indeterminacy"—on which she hopes to "ground" an insurmountably sceptical notion of history.

At the same time, dualism and dichotomies are in evidence everywhere in her system, from the aprioristic separation of thought and practice to the irreconcilable opposition between the "political" and the "social." Besides, the dichotomously articulated categories are not established on the ground of ascertainable evidence but on the merely stipulated premise of formalistic definitions, coupled with a Heideggerian/irrationalistic cult of the "incident," as well as with constant polemics against *other people's* "theories and definitions."[39]

Moreover, her conscious self-identification with the standpoint of bourgeois political economy is clearly visible in her passionate defence of *private property*, arguing that:

> the word 'private' in connection with property, even in terms of ancient political thought, immediately loses its privative character and much of its opposition to the public realm in general; property apparently possesses certain qualifications which, though lying in the private realm, were always thought to be of utmost importance to the political body. . . . both property as well as wealth are historically of greater relevance to the public realm than any other private matter or concern and have played, at least formally, more or less the same role as the chief condition for *admission to the public realm* and full-fledged *citizenship*. . . . Prior to the modern age . . . all civilizations have rested upon the *sacredness of private property*.[40]

And elsewhere:

> Property is indeed very important . . . And, believe me, this property is very much *in danger*, either *by inflation*, which is only another way of *expropriating* a people, or *by exorbitant taxes*, which is also a way of expropriation. These processes of expropriation you have everywhere. To make a decent amount of property available to every human being—not to expropriate, but to *spread property*—then you will have some *possibilities for freedom* even under the rather inhuman conditions of modern production.[41]

Thus, in sophisticated contrast to the crude apologetics of Burnham's "managerial revolution" and of its more recent variants, Hannah Arendt offers us the mythology of "people's capitalism" as an *ideal to strive for,* rather than as an already *accomplished fact.* The sad truth, though, that the overwhelming majority of humankind has been and continues to be ruthlessly deprived of even the most meager possessions by precisely those who have been using private property, now for a very long time indeed, for *anything but* to establish "the possibilities for freedom," does not seem to carry much weight, if any, in Arendt's idealist, and in the face of all historical evidence strikingly *counter-factual,* scheme of remedies.

Furthermore, what makes things worse still is that the political economy of capitalist socioeconomic practices—transsubstantiated by her into the so-called "strictly economic sphere" (whatever that might be)—is dichotomously opposed by Arendt to the sphere of thought considered appropriate to political interaction, bringing with it (quite revealingly) an end to her programmatic concern with the "recovery of the public world" in the crucially important domain of our socioeconomic life. For, according to Arendt:

> Theorizing of a scientific or technical kind belongs only where there is *no room for action or debate,* in the *strictly economic sphere,* where men engage in the activities of labour and work, when they produce and consume. Here, of necessity, the category of means and ends governs their activity and their thinking about their activity, which takes the forms of calculation, planning, and administration with the aim of prediction and control. Here *efficiency* is at a premium and economy can best be served by decisions that are reasoned out by *one or a few men, rather than debated by everybody.* For what is at issue is not the variety of experience and judgement of what is best for a common world, but simply the *correct means to an end.*[42]

Thus, Hannah Arendt's dichotomies, formulated from capital's standpoint of political economy, serve an easily identifiable ideological purpose. For the insurmountable opposition between "the political" and the "strictly economic sphere" a priori exempts the latter from even the possibility of legitimate public scrutiny, with the excuse that it belongs to the domain of "*technical*" reasoning, concerned with the purely instrumental relationship of means and ends.

In other words, her approach takes for granted and simultaneously rationalizes the rule of capital under the privileged "few men" who happen to be well entrenched already in their position of command in society, exercising on behalf of the ruling class (this "nineteenth-century abstract noun") the power of economic decision making and the "strictly rational" allocation of resources. A solution based on ideological presuppositions which are indistinguishable from the postwar illusions of "the end of ideology."[43] This has been indirectly acknowledged even by one of Arendt's most sympathetic commentators who pointed out that:

> What she hoped for was a solution to the problem of poverty 'through technical means', through a 'rational, non-ideological economic development'. What this might be, she did not say. Her assumption was that technology can be 'politically neutral' — a very problematic assumption.[44]

Indeed!

5.6 "There Is Neither Necessity nor Meaning"

CURIOUSLY, WHILE ARENDT CONSTANTLY ACCUSES Marx of "abstraction" and of using an "abstract noun" in place of the plurality of men, in reality she is the one who is guilty of such practice, whenever it suits her, as in the last quotation, or in her earlier seen identification with Tocqueville's pessimistic laments about "the *mind of man* wandering in darkness." Castigating Marx, in another passage, she claims that:

> Hegel's *world spirit* reappears in Marx as man as a species-being. In each case you have ruled out or counted out the *plurality of men*. There are not men whose acting together and against each other finally results in history. But there is *one giant noun,* and this noun is the *singular* and now you ascribe everything to this noun. This I believe, is really an *abstraction.*[45]

In truth, however, what could be more of a "giant noun" and vacuous abstraction than Arendt's own notion of "the world-alienation of man"? Furthermore, what could be more obviously the *exact opposite* of Arendt's claims with regard to Marx's alleged "abstraction" than his real position? For this is how already the very "young Marx" assesses these problems in *The Holy Family,* in his scathing attack on the "Young Hegelians" in whose work "history, like truth, becomes a *person apart, a metaphysical subject of which real human individuals are merely the bearers.*"[46] And in his critique of Feuerbach he repeatedly makes it clear that

> The social structure and the state are continually evolving out of the life-process of *definite individuals* . . . Feuerbach . . . *posits 'Man' instead of 'real historical man'*. . . . He does not see that the sensuous world around him is not a thing given direct from all eternity, remaining ever the same, but the product of industry and of the state of society; and, indeed [a product] in the sense that it is an historical product, the result of the activity of a *whole succession of generations, each standing on the shoulders of the preceding one,* developing its industry and its intercourse, and modifying its social system according to the changed needs.
>
> Thus he never manages to conceive the sensuous world as the total living sensuous activity of the *individuals* composing it; therefore when, for example, he sees instead of healthy men a crowd of scrofulous, overworked and consumptive starvelings, he is compelled to take refuge in the 'higher perception' and in the ideal '*compensation of the species*,' and thus to *relapse into idealism* at the very point where the communist materialist sees the necessity, and at the same time the condition, of a *transformation* both of industry and of the social structure. As far as Feuerbach is a materialist he does not deal with history, and as far as he considers history he is not a materialist. With him materialism and history diverge completely.
>
> This [Marx's own] conception of history . . . has not, like the idealist view of history, to look for a category in every period, but remains constantly on the real ground of history; . . . It shows that history does not end by being resolved into 'self-consciousness' as 'spirit of the spirit', but that each stage contains a material result, a sum of productive forces, a historically created relation to nature and of *individuals to one another,* which is handed down to *each generation* from its predecessor. . . . This sum of productive forces, capital funds and social forms of intercourse, which *every individual and every generation* finds in existence as something given, is the real basis of what the philosophers have conceived as '*substance*' and '*essence of man*' . . .
>
> The real, practical dissolution of these phrases, the removal of these notions from the consciousness of men, will, as we have already said, be affected by altered circumstances, not by theoretical deductions.[47]

When an author speaks as clearly as Marx does on the subject at issue, the complete misreading of his works is highly symptomatic. In Arendt's case it is closely linked to her dichotomies of "theory" versus "practice," "understanding" versus "doing," "thinking" versus "commitment," the "political" versus the "social" and the "stricly economic sphere," the "world-alienation of man" versus the manifestations of real socioeconomic alienation in all spheres of human activity, etc. If we read them in conjunction with one another, it clearly transpires that they constitute a coherent set of ideas, whatever one may think of their ideological substance. Their common denominator is what Marx pinpointed in his analysis of Young Hegelian "Absolute Criticism." Namely that the latter has learnt from Hegel's *Phenomenology of Mind,* just like Hannah Arendt from the philosophical tradition to which she belongs, despite her criticisms:

> at least the art of converting real objective chains that exist outside me into merely ideal, merely subjective chains, existing merely in me and thus of converting all external sensuously perceptible struggles into pure struggles of thought.[48]

That is why the claimed authenticity of "non-participation" and "withdrawal from the world," expressed in Arendt's opposition to commitment and in her idealization of the "*vita contemplativa*," must find their terms of reference—stamped with the seal of full approval—in the mystifying notions of the "silent dialogue between me and myself," the "plurality within us, the me and myself" and the "habit of living together explicitly with oneself," etc. For so long as critical attention remains focused on such concerns, the oppressive reality of capital's "strictly economic sphere"—with all its "real objective chains" that exist in the historically given society—can remain in effective control of the lives of the real individuals. Abrogating to itself legitimacy with the force of self-evidence on the ground of its alleged ability to regulate with pure "rationality" and "efficiency" the process whereby the required "means" are allocated to the realization of the (apparently uncontentious) "ends."

IN THE SAME VEIN, Arendt's characteristic interpretation of history sets out from a diagnosis of the impact of science and technology on the "world-alienation of man" which is said to be the hallmark of modern developments, as referred to already. It is presented in her essay on "The Concept of History" as follows:

> The fundamental fact about the modern concept of history is that it arose in the same sixteenth and seventeenth centuries which ushered in the gigantic development of the natural sciences. Foremost among the characteristics of that age, which are still alive and present in our own world, is the *world alienation of man,* which I mentioned before and which is so difficult to perceive as a basic condition of our whole life because out of it, and partly at least *out of its despair,* did arise the tremendous structure of the human artifice we inhabit today . . . The shortest and most fundamental expression this world-alienation ever found is contained in Descartes' famous *de omnibus dubitandum est.*[49]

Significantly, the position of Descartes must be as completely misrepresented in this conception of "world-alienation" as Marx's. For the Cartesian methodological principle of doubt is only the *point of departure* of a general approach which in its explicitly stated positive aspirations aims at the constitution of *secure knowledge.* By contrast, Arendt's orientation is utterly pessimistic, offering scepticism not as a methodological point of departure but as the *terminus ad quem*, i.e., the desolate ideological *conclusion* according to which

> The modern age, with its growing world-alienation, has led to a situation where man,[50] wherever he goes, encounters only himself. . . . In the situation of radical world-alienation, *neither history nor nature is at all conceivable.* This twofold loss of the world—the loss of nature and the loss of human artifice in the widest sense, which could include all history—has left behind it a society of men who, without a common world which would at once relate and separate them, either live in *desperate lonely separation* or are *pressed together into a mass.* For a *mass society* is nothing more than that kind of organized living which *automatically* establishes itself among human beings who are still related to one another but have lost the world once common to all of them.[51]

In place of the necessary evidence to substantiate such conclusions of despair, all we get is a set of arbitrary assertions. They are derived from a suggested analogy between the Heisenbergian relativist interpretation of modern science and the world of politics, claiming that "While *trouble* throughout the modern age has as a rule started with the *natural sciences* and has been the consequence of experience gained in the attempt to know the universe, this time the refutation rises simultaneously out of the *physical* and the *political* fields."[52] And the meaning of such developments—in the spirit of Heisenberg's "indeterminacy principle"—is supposed to be "quite literally that *everything is possible* not only in the realm of ideas but in the field of reality itself."[53] Consequently, according to Arendt: "*Any order, any necessity, any meaning* you wish to impose will do. This is the clearest possible demonstration that under these conditions *there is neither necessity nor meaning*."[54]

Thus, a pessimistic relativism—a cross between Ranke and Heisenberg—guides Arendt's assessment of historical interpretations, described as "purely mental constructions . . . which are equally well [and, of course, equally badly] supported by facts."[55] At the same time it is asserted with regard to the present that "The contemporary decline of interest in the humanities, and especially in the study of history, which seems *inevitable* in all *completely modernized countries,* is quite in accord with the first impulse that led to modern historical science."[56]

Furthermore, even in relation to the past it is claimed by Arendt, on the ground of a curious *counter-factual* reasoning, that:

> Vico, who is regarded by many as the father of modern history, would hardly have turned to history under modern conditions. He would have turned to *technology*; for our technology does indeed what Vico thought divine action did in the realm of nature and human action in the realm of history.[57]

The underlying intent of such reasoning is, of course, the complete relativization of everything, so that one should be able to claim that "everything is possible" and that "there is neither necessity nor meaning."

In this sense, Heisenberg's extreme relativism is a "heaven sent gift" which helps to confer the semblance of scientific respectability on a blatantly ideological position. It is directed at discrediting not simply Vico, the great 18th century forefather of bourgeois historical theory (who, in any case, is immediately "rehabilitated" by the counter-factual-conditional assertion that "under modern conditions" Vico, very sensibly, "would have turned to technology"). The stakes championed in this line of reasoning are much higher. For the true object of Arendt's relativistic attack is the Marxian conception of historical development which argues that the individuals who constitute society do in fact, and indeed in a tangible and meaningful sense, "make their own history." Accordingly, we are told by Arendt that:

> Today this quality which *distinguished history from nature* is also a *thing of the past*. We know today that though we cannot 'make' nature in the sense of creation, we are quite capable of starting new natural processes, and that *in a sense we 'make nature,'* to the extent, that is, that we *'make history.'* It is true we have reached this stage only with the *nuclear discoveries*, where natural forces are let loose, unchained, so to speak, and where the natural processes which take place would never have existed without direct interference of human action.[58]

What is particularly revealing about such ideological eagerness is not simply the complete misrepresentation of the claimed radical novelty of the man-made natural processes themselves.[59] It is the author's willingness to reduce the complex dialectical significance of human action to the incomparably less complex and largely mechanical level of the nuclear physical processes referred to in Arendt's sceptical inverted commas.

What is here rejected by Arendt's sceptical reductionism is the possibility of meaningful human action which does indeed amount to making history in the very precise sense of not being at the mercy of "Divine Providence," or of "History writ large";[60] the Marxian meaning of making history which recognizes the objective constraints and the frequently unavoidable reversals involved in the efforts of generations of individuals who pursue their material and ideal objectives across the long trajectory of cumulative transformations.

Among other things, Marx is accused of being guilty of "the confusion of politics with history"[61] and of "meaning" with "end." With regard to the latter, we are told by Arendt that "The *growing meaninglessness of the modern world* is perhaps nowhere more clearly foreshadowed than in this identification of meaning and end."[62] This is said to be fatal because "the moment such distinctions are forgotten and meanings are degraded into ends, it follows that ends themselves are no longer safe because the distinction between means and ends is no longer understood, so that finally all ends turn and are degraded into means."[63]

And this is the point where the ideological motivations at the roots of Arendt's conception of history, together with the target they are meant to demolish, come to the fore with greater clarity. For she asserts—after paying a left-handed compliment to Marx which turns out to be a crude distortion of his position—that

> What distinguishes Marx's own theory from all others in which the notion of '*making history*' has found a place is only that he alone realized that if one takes history to be the object of a process of fabrication or making, there must come a moment when this 'object' is *completed*, and that if one imagines that one can 'make history,' one cannot escape the consequences that there will be an *end to history*. . . . In this context it is important to see that here the process of history, as it shows itself in our calendar's stretching into the infinity of the past and the future, has been abandoned for the sake of an altogether different kind of process, that of making something which has a beginning as well as an end, whose laws of motion, therefore, can be determined (for instance as *dialectical movement)* and whose innermost content can be discovered (for instance as *class struggle)*., This process, however, is incapable of guaranteeing men any kind of immortality because its end cancels out and makes unimportant whatever went before: in the *classless society* the best mankind can do with history is to *forget the whole unhappy affair*, whose only *purpose* was to abolish itself.[64]

NOW WE ARE IN A BETTER POSITION to understand why it is necessary to equate the Marxian conception of open-ended historical development with Hegel's personification of "History" and the "World Spirit," as well as with the Hegelian notion of the "end of history," despite Marx's repeated, and often even sarcastic, comments directed explicitly against Hegel and his followers on the issues involved. For, as a result of such practice of "reductive equation," both the genuine achievements of the Hegelian approach and their radical extension by Marx to an irrepressibly historical account of human development—including his challenge of "historical necessity" as "eine *verschwindende Notwendigkeit*," i.e. a necessarily "*vanishing or disappearing necessity*"[65]—can be thrown overboard and replaced by the vacuous, not to say totally absurd, notion of "our calendar's stretching into the *infinity* of the past and the future."

On the cosmic time-scale of "infinity," the stretch of human history is "infinitesimal" and, presumably, negligible or meaningless. And, of course, the point of adopting this perspective is that it can be readily brought in line, by the propounders of pessimistic relativism, with their view of "growing world-alienation"; the "growing meaninglessness of the modern world"; the "inevitability" of the loss of historical interest "in all *completely modernized* countries" (at which point, it seems, "our calendar's stretching into the infinity of the future" conveniently comes to an end); the impossibility to conceive "either history or nature"; the desolate predicament of "modern man living in desperate lonely separation or pressed into a mass"; the fateful realization that "everything is possible" and therefore "there is neither necessity nor meaning"; the collapse of "overall historical interpretations"—but, of course, not of the miopic little or large fact-heaps of "modern" historiography—under the weight of the recognition that they are nothing but "purely mental constructions," devoid of even the possibility of real supporting ground that might favour any one of them somewhat more than any other; and the like.

It should be needless to say—yet it seems necessary to do so—that human history has both a beginning and an end, no matter how far the latter might lie ahead of us in the future. But, of course, the real issue at stake here is not the historically remote beginning and end of the human species; it is the far more limited time-span of specific social formations, involving the historical determination of their limits of viability.

Accordingly, any attempt to replace the dialectical categories which grasp the *historical specificities* of social formations—together with all their "disappearing necessities"—by the empty generality of "our calendar's stretching into the *infinity* of the past and the future," amounts to no more than a self-congratulatory rationalization of trying to run away from some difficult, and from the standpoint of capital insoluble, problems. Problems which concern, on the one hand, the requirement to explain the conditions of *genesis* of the social formation in question and, on the other, the necessary acknowledgement of its inescapable *limits*. For the two together firmly define, in one direction, with regard to the past, the "beginning," and, in the direction of the future, the "end" of all social structures and forms of interchange.

IN THE PRESENT CONTEXT we must remind ourselves of some issues discussed by Marx in a little known passage of *Capital*. For by focusing attention on the objective and subjective constituents of the irrepressible historical dynamics, they help to dispel any idea of "mechanical reductionism." The passage in question reads as follows:

> To the extent that the labour-process is solely a process between *man and nature,* its *simple elements* remain *common to all social forms* of development. But *each specific historical form* of this process further develops its *material foundations* and *social forms*. Whenever a certain *stage of maturity* has been reached, the *specific historical form is discarded* and makes way for a *higher* one. The moment of arrival of such a *crisis* is disclosed by the depth and breadth attained by the contradictions and antagonisms between the *distribution relations,* and thus the specific historical form of their *corresponding production relations,* on the one hand, and the *productive forces,* the production powers and the development of their *agencies,* on the other hand. A conflict then ensues between the *material development* of production and its *social form*.[66]

It is necessary to underline here two major considerations:

1. the principal factors (man and nature; production and distribution relations; productive forces and their agencies) and their interrelations which determine the irrepressible dynamism of the historical process, and

2. their validity, *mutatis mutandis,* under *all* social forms, which follows from the first.

- With regard to the *first,* it is important to bear in mind that the term "each specific historical form"—as contrasted by Marx with the "simple elements" of the labour-process that remain "common to all social forms"—indicates the inherently historical character not only of the different "social forms" but also of their corresponding "material foundations." For if the material foundations themselves are not articulated in a specific historical form, it is then impossible to make intelligible not only the historical character of the "relations of production," but also the organic connection between the latter and the fundamental socioeconomic metabolism of the given society. In other words, in that case the relationship between the "material base" and the "superstructure" must assume the form of a one-sided, mechanical determination, instead of a dialectical reciprocity. (This is indeed how it is pictured by many.) For a material complex whose constituent parts are not produced in the course of a dynamic historical process to which the parts themselves actively contribute—in contrast to the one-sidedly subordinated parts of a no matter how complicated machine—could never constitute a dialectically interrelated overall complex.

- Moreover, the *distribution relations* and the *production relations* form a—by no means unproblematical—dialectical unity. The given unity of production and distribution relations is necessarily problematical in the sense that it is the *outcome* of the (for the time being) successful resolution of the tensions (and contradictions) inherent in it, and as such it must be *constantly reproduced* in order to maintain the stability of the historically established social form. (Obviously, it would be very foolish to take for granted the automatic and permanently successful resolution of such tensions and contradictions.)

- And the final point to underline here is that the concept of "material foundations" is crudely oversimplified if it is forgotten that the "productive forces and productive powers" of society are *inseparable* from their human *agencies* and from the evolving social consciousness of such agencies. For it is precisely through the ongoing development of the agencies themselves—thanks to the constant intervention of which the narrowly or literally material elements of the socioeconomic metabolism are activated and "come to life" in a specific form—that the "material foundations" of society are objectively defined as historically articulated and dynamically changing dialectical complexes.

- As to the *second* point, the socialist conception of a future socioeconomic interchange that envisages the removal of the *antagonistic* contradictions of society, cannot do away with the irrepressible dynamism of the historical process itself. (Hence accusations of "Messianic" and "Millennial socialism" are completely out of place with regard to the Marxian conception.) For that, one would not only have to eliminate all conceivable *unevenness of global development,* together with the objective tensions and contradictions necessarily inherent in the latter, but—more importantly—also the evolving human agencies of an immensely complex and interlinked overall process would have to be replaced by some uniform and rather primitive *mechanism:* a blatant absurdity, if ever there was one.

- To imagine that a future socialist society could be run on the basis of the self-regulatory mechanism of "rational efficiency" as such, amounts to no more than the reformulation and perpetuation of the *capitalist myth* of efficiency. It forgets that "efficiency" is a *value* which must be spelled out in terms of specific *human objectives,* even if under the conditions of generalized commodity production—and the universal reification that goes with it—"rational efficiency" (dictated in fact by capital's unique mode of economic and social control) appears as the "neutral instrumentality" of "maximizing economy," and in that disguise as the self-evident regulatory principle of the one and only economically viable mode of social interchange. Now quite apart from the fact that the historical tendency of capitalist "efficiency" is the production of formerly unimaginable *waste,* rather than the "maximum of economy," the question is *always*—and that includes, of course, all conceivable socialist societies—"efficient" *in terms of and in relation to what?*

- In reality there is no such thing as Hannah Arendt's "strictly economic sphere," which could then be run on the basis of a mythical "rational efficiency" and its uncontested (for "rationally" uncontestable) "pure instrumentality." There is, instead, an always particular and necessarily "biassed" *value-determination* of "efficiency," which is inseparable from both the objective *constraints* of the historically established (but changing) *material foundations* and from the *relative inertia* of the institutionally articulated specific *social forms* as *rooted in* (but by no means of necessity always *tyrannically ruled by)* their material foundations.

- Once the *tyrannical rule* of capital's material determinations is removed from the social individuals' horizon, the need for the value-determination of society's regulative principles—as feasible in terms of the historically prevailing material and institutional constraints—does not disappear with it. This is why the reproduction of the various objective and subjective factors enumerated in the passage quoted from Marx, under all social formations (though, of course, with their changing historical qualifications, in the sense indicated by the potential removal of the now prevailing socioeconomic antagonisms), reproduces at the same time the irrepressible dynamism of the historical process as well.

IT IS THE INABILITY TO CONTEMPLATE the inescapable temporal and structural limitations and the ultimate supersession or "end" of the established socioeconomic formation that brings with it the profoundly antihistorical fantasy of "infinite stretch," presented as the scientifically grounded historical explanation of the "growing world-alienation of the modern age" and of the "world alienation of modern man."

This is why Arendt's ideological fire must be directed against the idea that the historical process might have some *laws of motion,*[67] identified as *dialectical movement* which manifests itself through the irreconcilable structural contradictions and antagonisms of social life and through the painful reality of the *class struggle*. And, above all, what makes the Marxian conception radically incompatible with Hannah Arendt's vision is that Marx envisages a *classless society* in which

> socialized man, the *associated producers,* rationally regulate their interchange with nature, bringing it *under their common control,* instead of being ruled by it as by the blind forces of nature; and achieving this with the least expenditure of energy and under conditions most favourable to, and worthy of, their human nature.[68]

This is what must be categorically rejected from the point of view of the idealized "strictly economic sphere" in which "one or a few men" take all the decisions and the overwhelming majority is not even allowed to discuss the matters that so deeply affect their life; let alone could it be contemplated that they should be allowed to take hold of the levers of control, as *associated producers,* who continue to regulate their socially articulated interchange with nature in accordance with the ends and tasks (i.e., a coherent range of planned and humanly fulfilling *activities,* in sharp contrast to the division of labour, tyrannically subordinated to *commodity-targets)* which they consciously adopt for themselves.

Sadly, at such key point in the argument Arendt presents us with a totally unrecognizable Marx. For, as is fairly well known, Marx explicitly counterposes "*real history*" to "*prehistory*," in an attempt to define the *qualitative* differences between the history of class societies (in which manifold blind determinations tend to rule the life of the individuals) and the societies of the future in which class antagonisms are overcome and the associated producers are able to make history—subject to changing, but nonetheless very real, constraints which *no historically specific social form can escape or ignore*—in accordance with their own design.

Yet, the Marxian position must be crudely misrepresented. This is done by claiming that he reduces the historical process to the process of mere "*fabrication*," and by asserting that Marx adopts such an utterly fallacious solution so that he should be able to announce the "*completion*" and the "*end of history*" in the classless societies of the future.

Equally, Marx could not be clearer in his rejection of historical conceptions—religious or otherwise—in which some a priori *purpose* is hypostatized, as it is done, for instance, in the Hegelian idea of "history as theodicy."[69] Astonishingly, however, Hannah Arendt tells us not only that Marx attributes such purpose to history, but that he defines, rather absurdly, the "only purpose of history" as the self-contradictory design "to abolish itself," while in fact she is the one who maintains that "in the situation of radical world-alienation neither history nor nature is at all conceivable," as we have seen a moment ago.

However, the most peculiar of Arendt's distortions is the claim that in Marx's "classless society the best mankind can do with history is to forget the whole unhappy affair." This assertion is rather bewildering, in the first place, because it falsely ascribes to the Marxian conception ideas and implications which are totally alien to it. And even more so, secondly, because the cosmic pessimism to which the contorted indignation of the sentence purports to object is precisely what we are offered by Arendt herself—in her essay on "The Concept of History" as well as in *The Human Condition* and elsewhere—in her gloomy diagnoses of the "growing meaninglessness of the modern world" and of the alleged disappearance of not just "meaning," but also of "order" and "necessity" from it.

5.7 "If Sense There Be, It Escapes Our Perception": from Ranke and Tocqueville to Sir Lewis Namier and Beyond

Thus, the enlightened historical conception of the bourgeois philosophical tradition—which produces some significant accomplishments in the eighteenth and early nineteenth centuries, especially when the all-engulfing historical dynamic of the revolutionary turmoil breaks through the horizon of the philosophers concerned—leaves its place to progressively more pervasive scepticism and pessimism, from the decades that follow Hegel's death to our own times. Ranke and de Tocqueville set the tone, preaching the "equidistance" of everything from God as well as the desolateness of our inescapable predicament which makes "the mind of man wonder in darkness," as quoted with approval by Arendt.

Nor is it possible to envisage an easy escape from the dilemmas and contradictions of such approaches to history. For, once they assert that the major contending historical theories are "purely mental constructions," devoid of ascertainable factual basis—and therefore strictly "incommensurable" already on that account, not to mention their mythical "equidistances"—nothing can be really done in order to remove the contradiction of wanting to be at the same time both generically *sceptical* (i.e., programmatically *groundless,* as a blanket measure of self-defence, devised to deflect a priori all possible criticism), and yet *firmly grounded* in the "sound theoretical refutation" of their chosen adversaries (more often than not Marx and his followers, of course).

The celebrated historian, Sir Lewis Namier, sums up with pessimistic scepticism—tempered with the self-assured dogmatism of those who know that their class holds the reins of power—the anti-historical "philosophy of history" which predominates in the bourgeois ideologies of the twentieth century. As he puts it, in favour of describing "intersecting *patterns,*" after rejecting—just like Arendt[70]—the viability of investigating "envenomed *struggles*" (because "such inquiry would take us into *inscrutable depths* or into an *airy void*"): "there is no more sense in human history than in the changes of the seasons or the movements of the stars; or if sense there be, it escapes our perception."[71]

With the adoption of such views, all genuine achievements of the Enlightenment tradition in the field of historical theory are completely overturned. For the outstanding figures of the Enlightenment attempted to draw a meaningful line of demarcation between nature that surrounds *homo sapiens* and the man-made world of societal interaction, in order to make intelligible the rule-governed specificities of socio-historical development which emerge from the pursuit of human objectives. Now, in complete contrast, even the rationality and legitimacy of such reflections is denied with categorical firmness. Thus, historical temporality is radically suppressed and the domain of human history is submerged into the cosmic world of—in principle "meaningless"—nature.

We are told that we can only "understand" history in terms of the immediacy of *appearance*—so that the question of taking control of the underlying *structural determinations* by grasping the *socioeconomic laws* at work cannot even arise—while resigning ourselves to the paralyzing conclusion that "if sense there be," it cannot be found any more in historically produced and historically changeable social relations, shaped by human purpose, than in cosmic nature, hence it must forever "escape our perception."

Naturally, the pessimistic scepticism of theories of this kind—which, however, do not hesitate to set themselves up as stern castigators of all "overall conceptions" (exemplified also by the "postmodern" tirades against "grand narratives")—need not oppose social practice in general in the name of the otherwise stipulated necessary "withdrawal from the world." The need for the latter arises only when major structural change—with reference to some *radical* overall conception—is implicit in the advocated action.

So long as everything can be contained within the parameters of the established order, the "unity of theory and practice" need not be condemned as one of Marx's many alleged "confusions." On the contrary, under such circumstances it can be praised as a highly positive aspect of the intellectual's enterprise. Just as we find it, in fact, in Sir Lewis Namier's observation according to which "it is remarkable how much *perception is sharpened* when the work serves a *practical purpose* of absorbing interest," with reference to his own study, "The Downfall of the Habsburg Monarchy," the fruit of work "in Intelligence Departments, first under, and next in, the Foreign Office."[72]

Thus, historical scepticism, no matter how extreme, is quite selective in its diagnoses and in the definition of its targets. For if the subject at issue involves the possibility of envisaging major structural transformations—and, therefore, the elaboration of the strategies required for "making history," in this tangible practical sense—then it preaches the "meaninglessness" of our predicament and the unavoidability of the conclusion that "if sense there be, it escapes our perception." On the other hand, however, when the question is: how to sustain with all the necessary means and measures the established order, despite its antagonisms, and how to divide the spoils of—or how to move into the vacuum created by—a dying Empire: the Habsburg Empire, such "practical purpose of absorbing interest," in the service of the Intelligence Departments of another doomed Empire, the British, will miraculously "sharpen perception" and lay to rest the troublesome nuisance of scepticism.

SADLY, THIS IS HOW THE EMANCIPATORY QUEST of the Enlightenment tradition ends in the theory and practice of modern bourgeois historiography. The great representatives of the bourgeoisie in the ascendant attempted to found historical knowledge by elucidating the power of the human historical subject to "make history," even if, for reasons which we have seen above in various contexts, they could not consistently carry through their inquiry to the originally intended conclusion. Now every single constituent of their approach must be liquidated.

The very idea of "making history" is discarded, with undisguised contempt for all those who might still entertain it, since the only history that should be contemplated is the one *already made,* which is supposed to remain with us to the end of time. Hence, while it is right and proper to chronicle the "Downfall of the Habsburg Empire," the intellectual legitimacy of investigating the objective trends and antagonisms of historical development which foreshadow the necessary dissolution of the British and French Empires—or, for that matter, also of the politically/militarily much more mediated and diffused postwar structures of overwhelmingly U.S.-dominated global imperialism—all this must be a priori ruled out of court.

In the same way, the reluctant acknowledgement of the individuals' limitations in imposing the adopted state policy decisions "of absorbing interest" on historical development—an admission of the obvious which, nevertheless, goes hand in hand with the continued diffusion of the myth of "individual consumer Sovereignty" as the claimed ideal regulator of the socioeconomic and political metabolism of "modern industrial society"—does not lead to a more realistic grasp of the dialectical reciprocities at work between individuals and their classes in the constitution of the historical subject, nor to the recognition of the inescapable *collective* parameters of historically relevant action. On the contrary, it brings the sceptical dissection and complete elimination of the historical subject, with devastating consequences for the theories which can be constructed within such horizons. For once the historical subject is thrown overboard, not only the possibility of *making* but also of *understanding* history must suffer the same fate, as the great figures of the Enlightenment had correctly recognized while trying to find solutions to the problems confronting them.

And finally, the ironical outcome of all this for the historians concerned is that their own enterprise, too, completely loses its "*raison d'être*." A predicament which they bring upon themselves in the course of attempting to undermine the ground of those who refuse to give up the closely interconnected concepts of "historical subject," "making history," and "understanding history," thereby also necessarily breaking all links with the constructive elements of the philosophical tradition to which they belong.

In the end, what is left to them as a "way out" is the arbitrary generalization and idealization of a dubious intellectual stance which must turn in its search for sceptical self-assurance not only against its social adversary but even against its own ancestry.

They try to hide the contradictions of the solutions they end up with behind the ideology of universal "meaninglessness," coupled with the apparently self-evident viability of presenting, instead, "patterns" with descriptive "completeness": a hopelessly self-defeating aspiration, if ever there was one. And they justify their programmatic evasion of comprehensive issues - from which the question of how to make intelligible the trends and necessities that emerge from the individuals' pursuit of their socially circumscribed ends cannot be eliminated—on the ground that they properly belong to the "inscrutable depths" of cosmic mysteries.

5.8 Social Antagonism and Historical Explanation

If we look for the reasons behind the depressing trajectory of this radical reversal—from the Enlightenment's preoccupation with human meaning and its progressive realization in history, to the apotheosis of cosmic pessimism and universal meaninglessness—one particular factor stands out, more than anything else, with its weighty and irreversible significance, directly affecting the philosophical tradition of our enquiry in its qualitatively altered phases of development. It concerns the objectively given conditions and possibilities of emancipation, as well as the varying social constraints involved in their conceptualizations under different historical circumstances.

In truth, already the emancipatory quest of the great historical tradition of the Enlightenment suffers from the constraints which induce its major representatives to leave the question of the historical subject nebulously and abstractly defined (or undefined). This is due partly to the individualistic presuppositions of the philosophers who belong to this tradition, and partly to the potentially antagonistic heterogeneity of the social forces to which they are linked at the given phase of historical confrontations. Thus, what we encounter here, even under circumstances most favourable to the articulation of bourgeois historical conceptions, is the—at first latent, but inexorably growing—presence of untranscendable social antagonisms which find their way to the structuring core of the respective philosophical syntheses.

Understandably, therefore, the closure of the historical period in question, in the aftermath of the French Revolution and the Napoleonic wars, brings to light a truly ambivalent achievement. On the one hand, it gives rise to the greatest bourgeois conceptualization of the historical dynamics, at the highest level of generalization, magisterially anticipating within the abstract categorial confines of its horizons the objective logic of capital's global unfolding, coupled with truly epoch-making insights into the key role of labour in historical development. On the other hand, however, it also produces the formerly unimaginable expansion of the *mystificatory arsenal* of ideology.

Significantly, the two are combined in the internally torn and even in its own terms extremely problematical synthesis of the Hegelian system; with its "identical Subject/Object" and its "cunning of Reason" in place of the real historical subject; with the reduction of the historical process to the "circle of circles" of the self-generating "progress of the Concept only," in his construction of the categorial edifice of *The Science of Logic* as well as in the claimed "true Theodicy" of *The Philosophy of History*; and with the suppression of historical temporality at the critical juncture of the present, self-contradictorily ending up with the biggest lie of all one can possibly champion in a theory that purports to be historical—namely that "Europe is *absolutely the end of history*"[73]—after defining the task of "Universal History" as the demonstration of "how Spirit comes to a *recognition and adoption of the Truth.*"[74]

- There can be nothing surprising, therefore, in the fact that the situation becomes progressively worse as the formerly latent social antagonisms unfold and capital's new exploitative order is consolidated in the postrevolutionary period, in the course of major clashes and class confrontations, under the hegemony of the bourgeoisie. As a result, it is no longer possible to leave the question of the emancipatory historical subject abstractly undefined, nor indeed to keep the issue of emancipation itself separate from the clearly identifiable grievances of domination and exploitation.

- Thus, to define historical advancement in terms of the generic "progress of *mankind*"—not to mention the Hegelian "progress of the Concept only"—completely loses its relevance once the lines of demarcation are redrawn on socioeconomically specific conflictual lines in the actuality of social practice itself. To persist with optimistic promises and expectations, wedded to vague categorial frameworks—which were understandable at the time when the "Third Estate" was still rather undifferentiated—becomes extremely difficult.

- Such attitude to history can be maintained all the less, since a variety of socially critical conceptualizations, too, appear in the period between the French Revolution and the revolutions of the 1840s, parallel to the growing social polarization, culminating in the Marxian conception of the new social order with reference to capital's structural antagonisms and to the emancipatory role of the class-conscious proletariat.

IN THIS SENSE, hand in hand with the consolidation of the postrevolutionary social order go some highly significant conceptual transformations.

At first, the sociohistorical substance, as well as the explanatory value, of "*class struggles*" is recognized by bourgeois historians, even if they try to insert this concept into an increasingly more conservative overall framework. Later, however, all such categories must be completely discarded as "nineteenth century concepts," characteristically ascribing them to Marx (although Marx himself never claimed originality in this respect) in order to be able to get rid of an intellectual heritage without embarrassment. The Enlightenment quest for emancipation suffers the same fate of being relegated to the remote past in all its major aspects, more and more being referred to—at best—as a "noble illusion."

Since the question of *emancipation* itself is inseparable from the tangible practical issue of how to overcome *exploitation,* the two—frequently conjoined—strategies open to the modern bourgeois approach are:

1. to define the terms of reference of emancipation *introspectively*, as a matter which concerns the relationship between "me and myself"; and

2. to discredit, as "confusion" and/or "delusion" all those concepts which cannot be mystificatorily "internalized" (like: "making history"); those which attempt to make intelligible the objective trends and determinations of historical development (i.e., "understanding history"); and, last but not least, all those efforts which try to identify the conditions of meaningful intervention of the "historical subject" in the unfolding historical process, with the aim of bringing the blind forces that emanate from capital's intrinsic constitution under conscious human control.

When, "from the standpoint of political economy" (which represents the vantage point of capital's established order) the question is how to *prevent* that history be made by the subordinate classes in furtherance of a new social order, the historical pessimism of "growing meaninglessness," and the radical scepticism that tries to discredit the very idea of "making history," are perfectly in tune with the dominant material and ideological interests.

At the same time, by contrast, the social forces engaged in the struggle for emancipation from the rule of capital cannot give up either the project of "making history" or the idea of instituting a new social order. Not on account of some perverse inclination toward messianic "holism," but simply because the realization of even their most limited *immediate objectives*—like food, shelter, basic health-care and education, as far as the overwhelming majority of humankind is concerned—is quite inconceivable without radically challenging the established order whose very nature consigns them, *of necessity*, to their powerless position of structural subordination in society.

Thus, the articulation of a genuine historical conception, and the defiant assertion of the validity of its "totalizing" orientation, with the practical objective of "making history," are inseparable from all real emancipatory challenge to the ruling order. By the same token, on the opposite side of the social divide, the symbiosis of historical pessimism and scepticism with the ideology of "anti-holistic social engineering" is equally understandable. For—notwithstanding some differences of emphasis in certain contexts, in accordance with their division of labour in the shared ideological enterprise in the service of the prevailing *status quo*—their common denominator is the radical suppression of historical temporality and the aprioristic declaration of the utter meaninglessness of envisaging the "overall" (or "holistic") possibility of "making history."

But historical pessimism and scepticism, in its unholy alliance with "piecemeal social engineering" (which is really only the other side of the same coin), offers a "bonus" as well to the forces bent on the preservation of the *status quo*.

The point is that the social strategies of emancipation must be asserted under the *actually given* relation of forces which, at the present conjuncture, is still heavily weighed down against them, in capital's favour, despite the *historical* anachronism of its socioeconomic order. Thus, it seems, only partial successes are feasible under the prevailing circumstances, and frequently even they have to suffer the consequences of the unfavourable relation of forces. Consequently, every failure or major setback seems to strengthen the hand of historical scepticism, spreading its influence well beyond those who are the natural beneficiaries of the continued maintenance of the *status quo*.

In this important practical sense, the suppression of historical temporality is probably the most powerful methodological device in the arsenal of the ruling ideology.

NOTES

1. As Aristotle puts it:

   "The truth is that, just as in the other imitative arts one imitation is always one thing, so in poetry the story, as an imitation of action, must represent one action, a *complete whole*, with its several incidents so closely connected that the transposal or withdrawal of any one of them will disjoin and dislocate the whole. For that which makes no perceptible difference by its presence or absence is no real part of the whole.

   "From what we have said it will be seen that the poet's function is to describe, not the thing that has *happened,* but a kind of thing that *might* happen, i.e., what is possible as being probable or *necessary*. The distinction between historian and poet is not in the one writing prose and the other verse—you might put the work of Herodotus into verse, and it would still be a species of history; it consists really in this, that the one describes the thing that has been and the other a kind of thing that might be. Hence poetry is something *more philosophic* and of graver import than history, since its statements are of the nature rather of *universals*, whereas those of history are *singulars*. . . . Of simple Plots and actions the *episodic* are the worst. I call a Plot episodic when there is neither probability nor necessity in the sequence of its episodes." Aristotle, *Poetics,* chapters 8 and 9.
2. Saint Augustine, *City of God,* Image Books, Doubleday & Co, New York, 1958, p. 523.
3. Ibid., p. 41.
4. Friedrich Schlegel, *The Philosophy of Life, and Philosophy of Language, in a Course of Lectures,* George Bell & Sons, London, p. 116.
5. Ibid., pp. 114, 140, 163, 186.
6. Ibid., pp. 328–9.
7. Hegel, *The Philosophy of History*, Dover Publications Inc., New York, 1956, p. 457.
8. Hegel, *The Philosophy of Right*, Clarendon Press, Oxford, 1942, p. 216.
9. Ibid.
10. Hegel, *The Philosophy of History*, p. 449.
11. Ibid., p. 452.
12. Ibid.
13. Giambattista Vico, *The New Science,* Cornell University Press, Ithaca,

1970, pp. 52–53.

14. Ibid., pp. 382–3.
15. See the section in which Vico insists that "the family fathers, having become great . . . through the labours of their clients, began to abuse the laws of protection and to govern their clients harshly." Ibid., p. 377.
16. Ibid., p. 58.
17. Ibid., p. 53.
18. Ibid., p. 376.
19. Ibid., p. 53.
20. Ibid., p. 60.
21. Ibid., p. 383.
22. Ibid., p. 384.
23. Ibid., p. 59.
24. Ibid., p. 65.
25. Marx, *Grundrisse,* Penguin Books, Harmondsworth, 1973, p. 278.
26. *Hannah Arendt: The Recovery of the Public World,* edited by Melvyn A. Hill, St. Martin's Press, New York, 1979, p. 327. Of course, she immediately adds: "the council system, which *never was tried out.*" The actual historical instances of the council system, from the Paris Commune to some recent attempts at asserting its practical importance for a socialist transformation of society, do not seem to count. Not even as "tried out." For the social horizon with which Arendt identifies herself cannot come to terms with the socialist project. It prefers to label and summarily dismiss it as inseparable from "totalitarianism."
27. Ibid., p. 306.
28. Ibid., pp. 333–7. And to the questioner who asks: "What are you? Are you a conservative? Are you a liberal? Where is your position within the contemporary possibilities?," she answers:

    "I don't know. I really don't know and I've never known. And I suppose I never had any such position. You know the left think that I am conservative, and the conservatives sometimes think I am left or I am a maverick or God knows what. And I must say I couldn't care less. I don't think that the real questions of this century will get any kind of illumination by this kind of thing. . . . I never was a socialist. I never was a communist. I come from a socialist background. My parents were socialists. But I myself, never. I never wanted anything of that kind. So I cannot answer the question. I never was a liberal. I never believed in liberalism. . . .

"So you ask me where I am. I am nowhere. I am really not in the mainstream of present or any other political thought. But not because I want to be so original—it so happens that I somehow don't fit. . . . I don't mean that I am misunderstood. On the contrary I am very well understood. But if you come up with such a thing and you take away their bannisters from people—their safe guiding lines (and then they talk about the breakdown of tradition but they have never realized what it means! That it means you really are out in the cold!) then, of course the reaction is—and this has been my case quite often—that you are simply ignored. . . . And, well, you know, I don't reflect much on what I am doing. I think it's a waste of time. You never know yourself anyhow. So it's quite useless. This business that the tradition is broken and the Ariadne thread is lost. Well, that is not quite as new as I made it out to be. It was, after all, Tocqueville who said that 'the past ceased to throw its light onto the future, and the mind of man wonders in darkness.' This is the situation since the middle of the last century, and, seen from the viewpoint of Tocqueville, entirely true."

29. Ibid., p. 305.
30. Ibid., p. 304.
31. See in this respect Ibid., pp. 303–6.
32. Ibid., p. 306.
33. "Well, of course, I did something like Montesquieu did with the English Constitution in that I construed out of the American Constitution a certain ideal type. . . . Actually we all do that. We all make somehow what Max Weber called the 'ideal type.' That is, we think a certain set of historical facts, and speeches, and what have you, through, until it becomes some type of consistent rule." (Ibid., p. 329.)
34. Ibid., p. 327.
35. Ibid., p. 328.
36. "Believe me, bureaucracy is a reality much more [revealing or disclosing] today than class. In other words, you use a number of abstract nouns which were once revealing, namely, in the nineteenth century." (Ibid., p.319.) Lenin, too, is "so nicely nineteenth-century, you know. All this we do not believe any longer." (Ibid., p. 324.)
37. Arendt, *The Human Condition,* Doubleday Anchor Books, New York, 1959, p. 230. Or, as she puts it elsewhere: "the habit of living together

explicitly with oneself, that is, of being engaged in that silent dialogue between me and myself." (Arendt, "Personal Responsibility under Dictatorship," *The Listener*, August 6, 1964.)

38. Arendt, *The Human Condition*, p. 231. It is, of course, a characteristic misrepresentation to claim that Marx's concern is "*self*-alienation." His interest in unravelling how the "alienation of labour" assumes a central role in the functioning of society under the rule of capital, deeply affecting all facets of life, from material production to religious images and philosophical conceptualizations, is focussed on highly objective dialectical determinations and processes whose meaning cannot be reduced to and encapsulated by subjectivist terms like "self-alienation."
39. "The only gains one might legitimately expect from this *most mysterious* of human activities [i.e., thought] are *neither definitions nor theories,* but rather the slow, plodding discovery and, perhaps, the mapping survey of the region which some incident had completely illuminated for a fleeting moment." Arendt, "Action and the Pursuit of Happiness," paper delivered at the Meeting of the American Political Science Association, September 1960. Quoted in Melvyn A. Hill's thoughtful essay, "The Fictions of Mankind and the Stories of Men," in Hill (ed.), Op.cit., p. 296.
40. Arendt, *The Human Condition,* p. 56.
41. Melvyn A. Hill (ed.), op.cit., p. 320.
42. Ibid., p. 287.
43. No wonder, therefore, that Daniel Bell greeted the publication of Hannah Arendt's works with so much enthusiasm. (Needless to say, the sympathy was fully reciprocated. For Arendt, too, recommended Daniel Bell's book, *Work and Its Discontents,* as "an excellent criticism of the vogue of 'human relations'." See *The Human Condition,* p. 346.)
44. Elisabeth Young-Bruehl, "From the Pariah's Point of View: Reflections on Hannah Arendt's Life and Work," in Hill (ed.), op.cit., p. 24.
45. Hill, ed., op.cit., pp. 323–4.
46. Karl Marx and Frederick Engels, *Collected Works*, Vol. 4, Lawrence and Wishart, London, 1975.
47. Marx and Engels, *Collected Works*, Vol. 5, pp. 35, 39, 41, 53–4, 56.
48. Marx and Engels, *Collected Works*, Vol. 4, pp. 82–3.
49. Arendt, "The Concept of History," *Between Past and Future: Six Exercizes in Political Thought,* Meridian Books, Cleveland and New York, 1963, p. 53.

50. Here we have again the "abstract singular noun" for which Arendt—quite wrongly, as we have seen—castigates Marx.
51. Arendt, "The Concept of History," pp. 89–90.
52. Ibid., p. 86.
53. Ibid., p. 87.
54. Ibid., pp. 88–9.
55. Ibid., p. 86.
56. Ibid., p. 58.
57. Ibid., pp. 57–8.
58. Ibid., p. 58.
59. Arendt's suggestion is, in fact, rather astonishing, since the nuclear processes in question—or at least their constituents which are being combined into a great variety of "man-made" processes—do indeed exist in nature, even if not necessarily in our immediate terrestrial environment. However, the mystificatory inflation of the claimed ability of modern science and technology to "make nature" is used by Arendt in order to empty the concept of "making history" of all real meaning. For to assert that we can only make history in the sense in which we can "make nature" amounts to saying that we cannot make it at all, since in "making nature"—with which the process of making history is arbitrarily equated by Arendt—the term "making" is used in a purely *figurative* sense.
60. Marx is very critical in this respect not only of the Young Hegelians, but of their philosophical forefather as well. He writes in *The Holy Family*:

> Hegel's conception of history presupposes an Abstract or Absolute Spirit which develops in such a way that mankind is a mere mass that bears the Spirit with a varying degree of consciousness or unconsciousness. Within empirical, exoteric history, therefore, Hegel makes a speculative, esoteric history, develop. The history of mankind becomes the history of the Abstract Spirit of mankind, hence a spirit far removed from the real man. . . . Already in Hegel the Absolute Spirit of history has its material in the Mass and finds its appropriate expression only in philosophy. The philosopher, however, is only the organ through which *the maker of history, the Absolute Spirit,* arrives at self-consciousness retrospectively after the move-

> ment has ended. The participation of the philosopher in history is reduced to this retrospective consciousness, for the real movement is accomplished by the Absolute Spirit unconsciously. Hence the philosopher appears on the scene *post festum*. (MECW, Vol. 4, pp. 85–6.)

Naturally, Marx makes it amply clear how diametrically opposed his own position is to such abstract personification of History. He puts this in the most emphatic way when he writes that "*History* does nothing." (Ibid., p. 93. Marx's italics.) At the same time, while conscious of the constraining conditions under which history must be made, he insists on the *real power* of individuals to transform the conditions of their existence and thereby establish the "realm of freedom" not simply *on* but also *beyond* the original foundation of the "realm of necessity." See in this regard not only our quotations from *The Holy Family* and *The German Ideology,* but also some celebrated passages from *Capital* and from the *Grundrisse* concerned with the "realm of freedom."

61. Arendt, "The Concept of History," p. 77.
62. Ibid., p. 78.
63. Ibid., p. 79.
64. Ibid., pp. 79–80.
65. For a detailed discussion of these problems, see my essay on "Kant, Hegel, Marx: Historical Necessity and the Standpoint of Political Economy" in *Philosophy, Ideology and Social Science*, Harvester/Wheatsheaf, London, 1986.
66. Marx, *Capital,* Vol. 3, Foreign Languages Publishing House, Moscow, 1959, p. 861.
67. There is a predilection among Marx's critics to present his dialectically qualified views on the laws of historical development—of which social consciousness is an integral part—as a generic and mechanical "natural law." It is a particularly crude distortion in this respect when someone claims that in Marx's view "people's thoughts and ideas are a kind of *vapour* . . . which mysteriously rises from the 'material foundations.'" (Patrick Gardiner, *The Nature of Historical Explanation,* Oxford University Press, 1961, p. 138.)

    As we have seen above, Marx in fact insists that the development of the "productive forces" and "production powers" of society is inseparable from "the development of their *agencies*," which demonstrates the complete meaninglessness of the accusation that he reduces people's thoughts and ideas to "a kind of vapour which mysteriously rises from the material foundations," since the people themselves organically belong to such foundations.

Further, it is also ignored that for Marx the concept of "material foundations" contains not only the historically changing "productive forces" and "production powers"—in their inseparability from their ***human agencies***—but also the dynamically developing "production and distribution relations" of society. The "laws of motion" of the historical process must be made intelligible in terms of the dialectical interdeterminations of all such objective and subjective conditions, as centred in the Marxian vision around the *historical agency* and its developing social consciousness. But, of course, it is much easier to maintain the semblance of a "sound critique" if the silly caricature of "vapour mysteriously rising from matter" can be substituted for the dialectical complexities of the materialist historical conception.

68. Marx, *Capital,* vol. 3, p. 800.

69. "Hegel himself confesses at the end of the *Geschichtsphilosophie* that he 'has considered the progress of the concept only' and has represented in history the '*true theodicy*'." *(The German Ideology,* Marx and Engels, *Collected Works*, Vol. 5, p. 61.) Naturally, Marx had no greater sympathy for the propounders of the "hidden purpose" and the "hidden hand"—who directly idealized the materiality of bourgeois market relations—than for Hegel's speculative mystifications.

70. To quote Arendt: "*Class struggle*—to Marx this formula seemed to unlock all the secrets of history, just as the law of gravity had appeared to unlock all the secrets of nature. Today, after we have been treated to one such history-construction after another, to one such formula after another, the question for us is not whether this or that particular formula is correct. In all such attempts what is considered to be *meaning* is in fact no more than a *pattern*—to *mistake a pattern for a meaning,* and he certainly could hardly have been expected to realize that there was almost ***no pattern into which the events of the past would not have fitted as neatly and consistently as they did into his own***." Arendt, "The Concept of History," pp. 80–81.

71. Sir Lewis Namier, *Vanished Supremacies: Essays on European History, 1812–1918,* Penguin Books, Harmondsworth, 1962, p. 203.

72. Ibid., p. 7.

73. Hegel, *The Philosophy of History*, p. 103.

74. Ibid., p. 53.

CHAPTER SIX

Dualism and Dichotomies in Philosophy and Social Theory

6.1 The Hidden Premises of Dichotomous Systems

The philosophers who share "the standpoint of political economy" (i.e., the standpoint of capital, according to Marx) tend to present us with dichotomies and dualistically articulated "solutions" to the problems at stake. In Hannah Arendt's case, for instance, "understanding" is opposed to "doing," "theory" to "practice," the "political" to the "social," "judgement" to the "technical reasoning" of the "strictly economic sphere," etc. The fact that the technical imperatives of production—both within a given factory and in the organization of the productive apparatus as a whole—are based on the fundamental, and capitalistically most vital, *social* premise of the *forcible separation of labour* from the *means* of production, *must* remain outside the framework of such reasoning.[1] It must remain so as a matter of ideological determination which has a vested interest in assuming the existing "organic system" as simply *given*, refusing to consider the dynamics of its *genesis* and potential *dissolution:* both identifiable (with relative ease from a radically different social standpoint) in the focal point of the system's *antagonistic presuppositions*.

It cannot be stressed enough, the *necessary presuppositions* of the given socioeconomic system do not reside in an obscure region of the remote *past,* so as to relegate the question of their assessment to the realm of purely academic interest. On the contrary, they constitute one of the most vital dimensions of the constantly unfolding *present,* with far-reaching theoretical and practical implications as regards the feasible social alternatives and strategies. For, no matter how antagonistic in their inner determinations, the presuppositions themselves must be—as, indeed, to our own days they are—successfully *reproduced* in the overall process of capital production and reproduction, together with all of the other constituent parts of the system in question; if, that is, the productive system of so-called "modern industrial" and "post-industrial" society is not to disintegrate under the weight of its manifold contradictions.

There is a tendency to disregard this crucial aspect of the societal reproduction process, thanks to the mystificatory power of the dominant ideology. For, as a rule, the latter has an immense positional advantage in choosing the terrain as well as in marking out the parameters within which theoretical debates must be conducted in historical periods of relative stability. And, of course, the ruling ideology fully exploits that advantage by taking for granted its own (unmentioned) ideological premisses—which happen to coincide with the established order's necessary practical presuppositions for successful self-reproduction—as the uncontestable terms of reference of all legitimate "technical reasoning" as well as "value-judgement."

Naturally, the systematic theoretical *separation* of the (eternalized) *functional characteristics* of the given system from the investigation of their *dynamic,* past as well as present, *presuppositions* (which are one-sidedly and fallaciously assigned to the "specialized" field of academic historiography, if considered at all), and thereby the *obliteration* of the ideologically most embarrassing and directly challengeable dimension of capital's reproduction process, is itself an integral part of the overall process of societal reproduction. Indeed, this is one of the most important ways in which the ruling ideology actively helps to articulate and modify, in accordance with the changing circumstances but within well marked structural limits,[2] the complex network of—individual and collective, as well as material and ideal—determinations which secure and safeguard the continued reproduction of the established social order, with all its practical presuppositions.

It is not too difficult to see that the dualistic methodology and the dichotomous articulation of the categories are very useful weapons in the service of the dominant ideological interests. For their combined effect is the imposition of extremely problematical lines of demarcation on the way in which the identified problems can be evaluated.

Such categorial and methodological lines of demarcation, in their more or less explicit stipulative functions, amount to the establishment of rigid taboos (like the claimed categorical impossibility to derive "ought" from "is," "values" from "facts," etc.). As a result, the dynamic link between the given structure of the social totality on the one hand, and its original historical constitution and ongoing transformations, on the other, is completely obfuscated.

Thus, it is by no means surprising that the tension between the *structural* (or "synchronic," "systematic," "structural/functional") and the *historical* (or "diachronic," "genetic") aspects of theory should be so endemic to this entire philosophical tradition. Nor indeed that the manifestation of this tension should culminate in the twentieth century in the most extreme conceptualizations of dualism and dichotomies through various forms of "*structuralism*" and "historicism" which confront one another in their reified separateness.

6.2 The Functional Imperative of Operational Exclusiveness

In the social totality itself the inherited and always rigidly reasserted presuppositions of the established productive system, and its more transient features, are reproduced simultaneously. They are reproduced as inextricably conjoined elements of a unified, organic process. Indeed, the organic character of society's self-reproduction asserts itself in virtue of the *practical inseparability* of its various dimensions under normal circumstances.

To put it another way, in any historically given social totality the *valuational* (or "axiological") and *functional* (in capitalist society as a rule also "technical/technological") determinations are so closely intertwined that even theoretically they cannot be clearly separated without adopting a critical vantage point vis-à-vis the established system. For, as a result of the relentless process of practical confounding, the structurally dominant and institutionalized values tend to appear in a technical/instrumental guise (precisely because they happen to be already institutionalized), assigning only their adversaries to the realm of contestable values.

Accordingly, since the established order must take itself for granted as being "beyond contest" in its fundamental structural articulation, its already institutionalized values can easily assume the cloak of pure instrumentality. At the same time, *critical* values—i.e., values that appear openly as such, without the disguise of uncontentious instrumentality—must be condemned as "*heresy*," or more recently as "*oppositional irrationality*," "*emotivism*," etc.

The perverse practical confounding manifest in these phenomena can be clearly identified in such institutions, for instance, as the "Holy Inquisition." For while in its claims to be the "defender of the faith" against all heresy the Holy Inquisition openly asserts values, the specific set of values advocated in that way is never allowed to be considered as one of a possible multiplicity of (contestable) *alternative sets*. On the contrary, it must be presented as the one and only conceivable regulator and instrumental framework of the divinely ordained social whole.

Moreover, since the crucial issue from the standpoint of the established order is always the effective control of the practically dominant instrumentality, the open admission of the latter's association with values is feasible only so long as the socially entrenched set of values can sustain its *exclusive* claims to existence, as in the case of the Holy Inquisition itself.

There can be no "tolerance" at the level of the dominant instrumentality. This is why as soon as (in the course of actual historical development) values are admitted to belong to *legitimately competing* alternative sets—not in the aftermath of the miraculously advancing "principle of rationality" and "calculation," but as a result of the unfolding class struggle in which the bourgeoisie in the ascendant still plays a positive role—the practical relationship of instrumentality to values requires a drastic realignment.

In this sense, parallel to the consolidation of capital's socioeconomic order, the contest of the rival sets of values must be transferred to a *sepa-*

rate realm, where their confrontations cannot endanger the practical functioning of the new structure. For what decides the issue in the end is the *practical intolerance* of the one and only set of operational rules with which capital's mode of social control is actually compatible, notwithstanding the broadly diffused ideology of "pluralism."

In reality the much publicized "pluralism" has for its terms of reference the *plurality of capitals* only, but *never* the possibility of instituting a meaningful valuational and functional alternative to the rule of capital itself.

The practically enforced rule of operational *exclusiveness* (on the plane of the dominant instrumentality) corresponds to an objective *functional imperative* of the given socioeconomic system, and it must prevail precisely in that form. In complete contrast, the ideology of "tolerance" with regard to alternative sets of values arises at a time in history when the bourgeoisie is still an "outsider" and therefore must negate the regulatory "intolerance" of the old order that prevents its advancement. Once, however, the bourgeois order of society is consolidated and capital can assert its *structural intolerance* as a matter of course, "tolerance" itself must be exiled to the separate sphere of abstract and impotent values.

Thus "competition" is admissible as right and proper so long as it can be contained within the limits that correspond to the plurality of capitals. Should such competition, though, assume the form of a new set of values that envisages or implies a real functional alternative to the given framework of structural intolerance, it must be disqualified and, if necessary, repressed with all means at the system's disposal. For nothing may be allowed to disturb the "rational functionality"—i.e., the specific mode of valuational and instrumental determination—of the established order.

SINCE ANY PARTICULAR SOCIAL ORDER is compatible with only one fundamental set of values at the level of its operational/instrumental structures, there must be historically specific ways in which the rival sets—which arise spontaneously out of the objective contradictions and antagonisms of the given socioeconomic order itself—are practically dealt with. The *exclusiveness* mentioned above is a *functional imperative* of all social orders, since the fundamental regulator of the social metabolism cannot be other than a *totalizing* one. Nevertheless, the specific historical forms in which this functional imperative prevails in different social formations can be radically different from one another.

The contrast becomes clearer if we remind ourselves of the fact that capital must establish its own credentials in the course of historical development against a social-economic order which claims the absolute validity of "divine commands" with regard to what happens to constitute two of the principal obstacles to the progressively unfolding power of capital.

- The first concerns the practical dogma of "non-alienability of land" whose abolition is absolutely vital to the development of capitalistic agriculture.

- And the second major obstacle that cannot be tolerated by the bourgeoisie in the ascendant is the Christian prohibition imposed on "usury" (interest), or "profit upon lending without alienation of capital," to put it in the language of the heated controversies of the age.

Thus, capital must define itself, at first, as an admittedly *historical*—but on that score by no means less legitimate and viable, nor indeed with regard to its future aspirations less permanent—*global alternative* to the established order.

This is obviously in sharp contrast to the attitude of its established social adversary. For the latter categorically rejects the very idea of a possible alternative to itself in its exclusive self-identification with the only admissible set of values for which it claims not merely historical but *divine* lineage, in order to justify its a priori superiority to all conceivable contingency. (The Holy Inquisition is of course only a particular institutional expression—under rather special historical circumstances—of this direct structural coincidence and open identification of *absolutized values* with *dominant instrumentality.*)

However, also in the case of capital, its self-definition as an alternative set of—historically constituted—values is by no means the end of the process. For the ultimately always prevailing functional imperative of exclusiveness—anticipated, in a curious way, by the bourgeois conceptualization of the world: one that forcefully *rejects* "eternalization" in its theological/intolerant form and at the same time *reconstitutes* it in a new secular form by claiming to have *Reason as such* (in its atemporal and in principle incontestable absoluteness) on its side—must reassert itself once capital is in overall control of the social metabolism.

Significantly, therefore, in the course of capital's historical development we can witness a radical shift in the meaning of the concept of "alternative." For one thing, it loses its formerly *global* sense—i.e., its properly axiological dimension—which is in principle transferred to the separate "*realm of values.*" At the same time, in the spirit of the practically prevailing new partiality, a strictly *limited* sense of "alternative" is retained on the *functional/instrumental* plane, corresponding to the innermost structural determination of capital as the *plurality of competing*—and in that narrow sense "alternative"—*capitals.*

Furthermore, both on account of the limited functional definition of the meaning of "alternative," and in virtue of the dualistic separation of the "realm of values" from the "realm of facts," capital acquires the appearance of an eminently "rational" system. And while in reality these shifts of meaning are objectively imposed upon capital itself—in that as a specific mode of overall social control capital can neither recognize the legitimacy of any real alternative to its own rule, nor can it constitute an *alternative* to its own mode of operation in any meaningful sense of the term—the prosaic functional imperative of *totalizing operational exclusiveness* is rationalized and idealized by bourgeois philosophy as the paradigm of "rational functionality."

6.3 Ruling Values Disguised as Instrumental Complexes: The Illusions of Value-Free Functionality

Naturally, the stipulated transfer of the axiological meaning of "alternative" to a separate realm is essentially a sham. It cannot be other than a sham because the values intrinsic to capital's mode of economic operation and social control must remain the *unmentioned global presuppositions* and *unquestionable practical premises* of the established order, as has been indicated already. Indeed, they must be (and unceremoniously they are) enforced as such—directly or indirectly, as the circumstances require—with incomparably greater practical efficacy than what the Holy Inquisition could ever even dream about with regard to its own claims to divinely sanctioned law-enforcement.

Thus objectively, in the actual mode of functioning of this system, the contradiction in values is in no way eliminated or transcended by the adoption of the dualistic categorial framework. It is merely hidden away by postulating the radical separation of "facts"—i.e., the operational/instrumental/functional determinations of the social complex—and "values."

However, there can be no operational/functional determination of a *social* complex (as opposed to that of a limited *mechanical* complex or machine) which is not simultaneously also a *value-determination*. As such, it involves not only some "original choices," but also *"ongoing choices"* between more or less conflicting alternatives (with far-reaching social implications for each) in necessarily changing situations, as well as the constant reassertion of the viability of the earlier choices, inasmuch as they are being reproduced, in preference to rival possibilities. Consequently, the contradiction of values reaches down to the inner core of the given system and cannot be resolved in the real world within the confines of capital's structural determinations.

This is why the dualistic "solution" is the only way out of the underlying difficulty. For the generally adopted philosophical dualism is apparently in a position to remove the contradiction in question by abstractly stipulating, on the basis of nothing more than its own decree, that *"there can be no contradiction in values"* (Kant). The contradiction here referred to consists in this that capital *is*—in its historical genesis and objective constitution—an *alternative* (to its predecessor) which, however, *is not* a genuine alternative, because it cannot tolerate any alternative to itself; hence the end of history and the concomitant "eternalization" of the already established socioeconomic relations once capital is effectively in command of the vital socioeconomic processes.

The adoption of this arbitrary postulate brings with it the convenient dissolution of the problems at stake. For taking the categorical postulate of a priori non-conflictuality in values as the point of departure, one can derive from it two further—ideologically required and "conclusive"—propositions:

1. "values must belong to a radically different realm" where they cannot be contradicted by actuality; and

2. since, in virtue of (1), values belong to a realm to which considerations of fact *("questio facti")* do not and cannot apply, the identified contradictions in value (which we can abundantly perceive in the actuality of the established order, until we decide to blind ourselves to all such evidence through the acceptance of the dualistic categorial matrix itself) are not really contradictions in value, and therefore they are devoid of any real philosophical (in contrast to merely "contingent" and "hypothetical") significance.

But there is yet another important aspect to this dualistic dissolution of the problem. For it not only transfers the questions of value to a separate realm but simultaneously also deprives them of their *social dimension*. What continue to be recognized as belonging to the social sphere proper are only the—allegedly value-free—determinations of operational instrumentality and functionality. Values as such are supposed to concern the individuals as mere individuals only (who have their own "private demons" in Weber's terminology[3]), whether the choices and "moral imperatives" associated with them are conceived in accordance with the commands of Kantian "practical reason" or degraded to the level of philosophically unjustifiable "emotionalism."

Dualism thus prevails both in the form of inventing and opposing *abstract individuality* to the reality of the *social individual,* and in divorcing the value-determinations of the social complex from their functional and instrumental manifestations. And, of course, on both counts the dualistic philosophical remedies arise in response to the untranscendable contradictions of capital's socioeconomic practices, providing for them an imaginary solution that rationalizes the world of reified appearance and individualistic fragmentation. Thanks to the "fetishism of commodity" and the mystifyingly subdivided—yet even more mysteriously unified—structure of productive machinery, the semblance of operational and functional/instrumental "neutrality" dominates in the real world of social reproduction, infecting social consciousness, too, with the illusions of "value-free rational functionality" through which the given order successfully establishes its claims to absolute legitimacy.

UNDERSTANDABLY, AGAINST SUCH HEAVY ODDS it is not only difficult but well nigh impossible to formulate a critical alternative to the dualistically compartmentalized conception of values within the framework of the dominant ideological discourse, with its pretences to "methodological neutrality."

As a matter of universally valid rule which asserts itself with particular severity in the circumstances of generalized commodity production, only under the conditions of major crises can the question of envisaging an alternative framework of (defiantly value-laden) practical premises for an operationally viable new socioeconomic system arise in the field of theory, in response to some already unfolding social practice. By the same token, historical periods of relative stability are characterized by the paralyzing impact of the *instrumentally disguised ruling values* which impose themselves with the greatest ease on the overwhelming majority of the subaltern classes as the "common sense of the age."

On another plane, such periods of sustained stability tend to produce functionalist and structuralist types of intellectual syntheses, often successfully penetrating into the ranks of the ruling ideology's potential antagonist, as the strange vicissitudes of "Marxist structuralism"[4] demonstrated not so long ago both in Europe and in Latin America, under circumstances which greatly favoured capital and compelled its adversary to adopt a *defensive* posture.

Inevitably, therefore, the appearance of a coherent, all-embracing social alternative (i.e., what may be rightfully termed a "hegemonic alternative") involves directly challenging the anti-historically articulated claims to "rational functionality" and "natural organicity" of the historically prevailing social metabolism. At the same time, it also involves a defiant critical assault on the formerly veiled sets of values from which the established modality of social metabolism is in fact structurally inseparable. This open contestation of the ruling values, together with their functional/instrumental equivalents, is necessary in order to establish the credentials of the alternative framework with regard to all dimensions of social life, from the most limited practical functions of material interchange to those which require the comprehensive restructuring of the complex network of value-production and reproduction.

6.4 Ideological Roots of Methodological Dualism

As an example, let us consider the profound interconnection between the apparently "strictly technical" laws of the established mode of production and the underlying, clearly value-laden, social determinations of the same system. To quote Marx:

> The rule, that the labour-time expended on a commodity should not exceed that which is socially necessary for its production, appears, in the production of commodities generally, to be established by the mere effect of competition; since, to express ourselves superficially, each single producer is obliged to sell his commodity at its market-price. In Manufacture, on the contrary, the turning out of a given quantum of product in a given time is a *technical law* of the process of production itself.[5]

However, to stop at this point would—and in the eyes of those who identify themselves with the "standpoint of political economy" in fact one *does*—carry with it the acceptance of "the absurd fable of Menenius Agrippa, which *makes man a mere fragment of his own body*,"[6] on account of its undeniable practical realization as the totally dehumanizing technical law of the capitalist workshop in which "Not only is the detail work distributed to the different individuals, but the individual himself is made the automatic motor of a fractional operation."[7]

In reality, of course, the technical articulation of production is only the *end-result* of a long historical process which involves the radical (and in its human aspects extremely brutal)[8] *overthrow* of formerly established productive practices, together with all their corresponding "technical laws"; the *forcible separation* of human productive activity (labour) from the conditions of its exercise (the means of production), as mentioned above; the callous exploitation and disregard of even the *natural substratum* of human existence,[9] in direct subordination to the reifying requirements of a determinate mode of production; and the imposition of a new system of values, with a *hierarchical and despotic* regulation of the production process itself, embodied in a *global* system of *domination and exploitation* which rules every single aspect of life under the system of generalized commodity production, from the directly material exchange-relations to the most mediated intellectual and artistic pursuits.

Furthermore, the smooth running and the economically viable ("rationally efficacious" and "calculable") *continuity* of capitalist production, in accordance with its "technical laws," is inconceivable without the *constant* reproduction of *all* these presuppositions—at whatever cost—under the ultimate supervisory power of the *capitalist state*. This remains true even if the unashamedly violent modalities of direct state intervention in the exercise of society's reproductive functions need not surface without the pressure of all-embracing crises. As historical experience shows, however, they come to the fore with predictable regularity whenever the vital practical presuppositions of the ruling socioeconomic order are themselves endangered. Thus, significantly, under the circumstances of fundamental crises it becomes necessary to cast aside the otherwise much more convenient regulatory devices of "liberal ideology."[10] They are replaced by "states of emergency" whose declared purpose is the reconstitution of the formerly prevailing conditions of capitalist "normality," arbitrarily equated with "law and order" as such.

THUS, THE ACCEPTANCE OF THE TECHNICAL LAWS of capitalist production at their face value, as "purely technical laws," or, analogously, the postulation of the "technical reasoning" and "instrumental rationality" of commodity production, on the arbitrary assumption of a "strictly economic sphere" (which is by definition exempted from historical qualifications and, of course, contradictions), is extremely problematical, to say the least.

Of necessity, such an approach produces systematically distorted conceptualizations, in conformity to the ideological interests which circumscribe the social horizon of the philosophers involved. For, an adequate understanding of the true nature and relative economic viability of the technical laws themselves requires situating them within the *unified* framework of the social production and reproduction process, with all its presuppositions and axiological determinations. The ability to do so, however, necessitates in its turn the adoption of a critical vantage point from which the ongoing unification of the heterogeneous and antagonistic social determinations into a viable *social* organism first becomes visible.

Naturally, the latter is inconceivable without the simultaneous identification of the structural *and historical* limits of the given mode of practical unification, as opposed to its long established ideological misrepresentation as a "natural organism." By contrast, the various dualistic approaches articulated by the philosophical tradition which we are concerned with depict these relationships in a most disconcerting way. For they superimpose on the complex unity and practical inseparability of the axiological and functional dimensions an a priori scheme of some sort.

Such schemes are meant to establish the *insurmountable* diremption of the identified dichotomies, for the purpose of transferring the question of value to an independent, self-contained "realm." And in this respect it does not really matter that some of the philosophers who engage in these practices do not actually *call* their a priori construct by its proper name, in contrast to Kant, for instance, who does. For they stipulate, nonetheless, the untranscendable separation of social value and technical functionality on the ground of aprioristic assumptions.

- Accordingly, behind the *methodological dualism* that divorces the historically given *end-result* from its necessary practical *premises,* we find the more or less conscious *ideological intent* characterized by Marx as the "eternalization of the established relations of production."

- Compartmentalizing the world of experience the way in which methodological dualism does—i.e., by divorcing the historically established and constantly reproduced presuppositions of the system from its fictitiously atemporal structural articulation, thus arbitrarily reducing everything to its present functionality—blocks out from view the system's vulnerable strategic core against which a radical challenge must be mounted by the social adversary. If, that is, the latter is to have any hope at all of asserting its own vision as a viable practical alternative, coherently spelled out in all its major aspects, from the directly axiological determinations to the corresponding "technical" dimensions.

- However, the methodological dualism of separating the given from its practical presuppositions renders another very important service as well to the ruling ideology. For, thanks to the institutionally secured ability of the latter to impose its own (unmentioned) presuppositions on theoretical debate, the substantive issues of social conflict are transformed into matters of "purely methodological" concern, since the *dualistic compartmentalization* is *ipso facto* also an ideologically motivated *reduction*.

- As a result, the advocacy of the new, contesting set of values is in principle deprived of the ground in relation to which it could be considered representative of a veritable social alternative, to be contested as such, in substantive terms. In other words, it is a priori deprived of any "operational" or "functional" significance in virtue of the dominant ideological discourse's automatic refusal to recognize (within the imposed matrix of dualistic/reductive categorizations) the legitimacy of the contestant's critical posture vis-à-vis the "strictly economic," etc. "realm."

Thanks to the successful imposition of such methodological premises, the values and corresponding social strategies in question can be debated no end with reference to a separate "value-realm" and its "practical reason," methodologically counterposing the latter to the "realm of facts," to the world of "technical/administrative/instrumental rationality," etc., but the outcome by definition cannot affect the "realm of is." And in the meantime, of course, the necessary practical presuppositions of the ruling order can be reproduced in the course of capital's enlarged self-reproduction, undisturbed even by the possibility of theoretical question marks over the fate of the established relations of production.

6.5 The Inward-Oriented Subject of Philosophical Discourse

Naturally, the methodological dualism which results from the socially determined separation of the given from its necessary presuppositions, and the concomitant postulation of dichotomies and antithetical "realms" (not to forget the fetishistic hypostatization of mutually opposed human "faculties"—like the "faculty of theoretical reason" as against that of "practical reason"—to match the self-contained character of the postulated realms), must be directly related to all the other methodological characteristics of this tradition. For they happen to constitute a closely interlocking system in which the various parts not merely are compatible with, but also reciprocally reinforce one another, even if they do so in a contradictory fashion, in keeping with the very nature of capital as "the living contradiction" (Marx).

We can better appreciate this by reminding ourselves of some closely related points. Accordingly, "the standpoint of isolated individuality" is very far from being a philosophical blessing even in the eyes of its adherents. It is most ironical that the solution adopted by both the materialist and the idealist philosophers of this tradition, in order to surmount the contradictions of their social standpoint, creates many more problems than it can resolve. For their hypostatization of a generic "human nature" in which the individuals partake as "genus-individuals," instead of constituting a viable answer to the problems which generated the need for this hypostatization in the first place, only intensifies their dilemmas.

What happens, in fact, is that predicating the direct "organic" relationship between the egotistic/isolated individual and the human species merely *displaces* the original difficulties to other areas. As a result, the thinkers who share the standpoint of isolated individuality are presented with mysteries of their own making from which they cannot extricate themselves.

These mysteries confront them wherever they look, as evidenced by the way in which they tackle all major issues of philosophy, from their inquiry into the nature of knowledge to the opposition they set up between "subject" and "object," the "particular" and the "universal," "appearance" and "essence," "fact" and "value," "theoretical" and "practical" philosophy, "for-itself" and "in-itself," and the like. The irony is that their genuine but quite hopeless attempt to bring to a common denominator isolated individuality and the human species, in accordance with capital's standpoint of political economy, only reproduces the objects of their initial perplexity with a vengeance, in the form of a forbidding range of dichotomies, dilemmas and paradoxes whose resolution remains, of necessity, beyond their reach.

The untranscendable dualism is present, right from the Cartesian beginnings, in the way in which the issues themselves are perceived and defined in relation to the philosophical "Subject." For the immanent complexities of social practice (concerned in the real world with the realization of tangible objectives) are transformed into mystifying, and at the level of isolated subjectivity absolutely insoluble, theoretical riddles. Also, the more extensively capital's power unfolds and consolidates itself, bringing under its control the social metabolism in its entirety, the more the philosophical conceptualizations of universally reifying commodity production by the representatives of this tradition tend to reduce everything to the question: "How can cognition as such get beyond its subjective immediacy and reach its object?" (Husserl).

Moreover, they impose upon themselves two hopelessly constraining conditions which in the end guarantee the failure of their epistemological quest.

First—with the exception of a handful of philosophers whose example only strengthens the rule—by conceiving the subject as the self-referential inwardness of the *ego,* even if under a number of different names.

And second, by stipulating for all (including themselves) a scholastic, and ultimately solipsistic, rule according to which the task imposed upon the subjectivity of cognitive consciousness with regard to its object must be accomplished "rigorously within the sphere of immanence."

- Thus, paradoxically, the world of capitalist reification, which is *de facto* impenetrable from the point of view of isolated individuality, produces the alienated Subject of philosophical discourse.

- This "Subject" is an abstract, speculative, and to a large extent arbitrary philosophical construct, derived by way of the systematic and *reductive obliteration* of the social characteristics of all real individual subjects.

- Considered in relation to the philosophical problematic of which this inward-orientated Subject is supposed to be the bearer, the principal function of its constitution is to reinforce the impression of impenetrability and uncontrollability, changing the ontological

> status of alienated and reified existence from *de facto* to *de jure,* as if it *could not be otherwise.*

This ideologically crucial shift from *de facto* to *de jure* is achieved by declaring the manifold *actual* dualisms of the prevailing mode of production—to which we shall return in a moment—perfectly to correspond to the postulated dualistic "ontological structure" of "authentic being." For nothing could legitimate and eternalize the given social order with greater ideological efficacy than its claimed supra-historical identity with the absolute ontological determinations of being itself.

6.6 From "Unreconciled Dualism" to Dualism of Reconciliation

The merit for the most remarkable attempt to overcome the dichotomies of this tradition within the constraints of its social horizons belongs, again, to Hegel.

Indeed, in some respects he produces lasting solutions to some of the dichotomies of his predecessors, as demonstrated by his biting critique of Kant, for instance. As Lukács recalls, "Hegel pours scorn in a number of places on Kant's 'soul-sack' in which the different 'faculties' (theoretical, practical, etc.) are lying and from which they have to be 'pulled out'."[11]

Equally, Hegel is very critical of Solger's inconsistency and ultimate failure to carry out his promised philosophical programme, in that Solger remains trapped within "unreconciled dualism" despite his explicit intention to go beyond it.[12]

Furthermore, Hegel clearly perceives that the rigid opposition of "Intelligence" to "Will," and the corresponding dualism of "is" and "ought" leads to what he calls "bewildering contradictions." For:

> While Intelligence merely proposes to take the world *as it is,* Will takes steps to make the world what it *ought to be.* Will looks upon the immediate and given present not as solid being, but as mere semblance without reality. It is here that we meet those *contradictions* which are so *bewildering* from the standpoint of *abstract morality.* This position in its 'practical' bearings is the one taken by the philosophy of Kant, and even by that

> of Fichte. The Good, say these writers, has to be realized: we have to work in order to produce it: and Will is only the Good actualizing itself. If the world then were as it ought to be, the *action of Will would be at an end.* The Will itself therefore *requires that its End should not be realized.*[13]

However, in the end the Hegelian way of resolving the identified contradictions turns out to be no solution at all. For it merely transfers the—rightly criticized—dualisms from one plane to another, reproducing even the ought-ridden character of the overall approach of his philosophical predecessors in the form of his own ideal postulates. This is how Hegel argues his case:

> it is the process of Will itself which abolishes finitude and the contradiction it involves. The *reconciliation* is achieved when Will in its result *returns to the presupposition* made by *cognition.* In other words, it consists in the *unity* of the theoretical and practical *idea.* Will knows the end to be its own, and Intelligence apprehends the world as the notion actual. This is the *right attitude* of rational cognition. Nullity and *transitoriness* constitute only the *superficial features* and not the *real essence* of the world. . . . All *unsatisfied endeavour* ceases, when we recognize that the *final purpose* of the world is accomplished no less than ever accomplishing itself. Generally speaking, this is the *man's way of looking;* while the *young imagine* that the world is utterly sunk in *wickedness,* and that the first thing needful is a *thorough transformation.*[14]

Thus, in place of *"unreconciled dualism"* we end up with a peculiar *dualism of reconciliation* which explicitly rejects the possibility of a *thorough transformation* of the world as contrary to the *"final purpose"* and *"real essence* of the world." This apologetic Hegelian dualism locates "superficial features" and "transitoriness" (Hegel's categories directed against all those who have the temerity of acknowledging the need for a thorough transformation of the existent) on one side, and the "real essence" (corresponding to the reconciliatory "right attitude of rational cognition" towards what Hegel himself is forced to admit to be "unsatisfied endeavours," which he nevertheless wants us to consider adequately and satisfactorily accomplished) on the other.

It is highly significant that this Hegelian solution bolsters up its claims to rationality by arbitrarily declaring that what it finds socially unacceptable belongs to the domain of "youthful imagination," whereas the resignatory complicity with the *actual diremptions and contradictions* of real life qualifies in its perverse terms for the maturity and dignity of "the man's way of looking" at the world in its essentiality. This is the same pseudo-solution and dissolution of the problem which we find in Hegel's *Philosophy of Mind* where he declares that "the man" (as opposed, again, to the youth):

> must recognize the world as a *self-dependent* world which in its *essential* nature is already complete, *must accept the conditions* set for him by the world and wrest from it what he wants for himself. As a rule, the man believes that this *submission* is only forced on him by necessity. But, in truth, this *unity* with the world *must* be recognized, not as a relation imposed by necessity, but as *the rational*. The rational, the divine, possesses the absolute power to actualize itself and has, *right from the beginning, fulfilled itself;* . . . The world is this actualization of divine Reason; it is only *on its surface* that the *play of contingency* prevails.[15]

The advocated "*unity* with the world" is, thus, an empty *postulate*—a speculatively transfigured "ought"—and a thoroughly conservative one at that. For such "ought" preserves and idealizes the established world, despite its more or less openly admitted contradictions, as "in its essential nature already complete." Moreover, in the spirit of the Hegelian reconciliatory dualism, it is also declared that the postulated "completeness" of the world's "essential nature" corresponds with full adequacy to "the rational," in opposition to the misconceptions of all those who fix their eyes merely on the "surface play of contingency." And the aprioristic construct of "mature man versus impatient emotional youth"—which is devised in order to suit the Hegelian conception of *rationality as resignation*—reproduces the dualism inherent in the standpoint of capital's political economy even on the plane of anthropology, attempting to escape from the newly created difficulty by postulating at the same time the earlier discussed "process of the *genus* with the *individual*."[16] No wonder, therefore, that Hegel's solutions with regard to dualism and dichotomies remain at the level of partial negations of Kant, Fichte, Solger and others, reproducing, even if in characteristically Hegelian terms, the same contradictions which he tries to leave behind.

ADMITTEDLY, THE HEGELIAN SOLUTIONS are formulated from a relatively higher vantage point than those of his predecessors. Nonetheless, his system exhibits the historical limitations of their shared social orientation and conceptual framework in an even more striking form, due to the more open manifestation of the fundamental social antagonism between capital and labour in his age than at an earlier stage of development.

We can witness the reappearance of the common methodological and ideological parameters of the standpoint of political economy in that Hegel can accomplish no more than a pseudo-transcendence of the identified, and partially criticized, dichotomies and dualistic oppositions, in the purely speculative realm of the Notion. But even more revealing is in this respect the dualistic framework of his entire philosophical system in which the logico/deductive *categories* are superimposed on the *actuality* of the historical world, liquidating in the end their historicity.

Nor should it come as a surprise that Hegel's curious "dualism *malgré lui*"—i.e., one that is all the more revealing precisely because often it asserts itself against the philosopher's explicit anti-dualistic intentions—is just as pronounced in the Hegelian theory of the state as in his *Science of Logic* and in *The Philosophy of History*. Accordingly, the dualistic opposition between "civil society" and the "State" which we are offered in the Hegelian *Philosophy of Right,* with its thoroughly ought-ridden "resolution" of the antagonisms of Civil Society through the subsumption of the latter under the idealized State, reproduces the same determinations which shape the conceptions of all major intellectual figures of the epoch. Thus, Marx's critique of the "mystical dualism" of the Hegelian solutions identifies an important methodological characteristic which is inseparable from the legitimating ideological intent common to all those who share capital's standpoint of political economy.

The Hegelian "opposition of *in-itself* and *for-itself,* of consciousness and self-consciousness, of *object* and *subject* . . . is the opposition, within thought itself, between abstract thinking and sensuous reality or real sensuousness."[17] Thanks to such conceptualization of the dichotomies, the contradictions of real life—inherent in capital's unyielding power of alienation—can be both acknowledged (for a fleeting moment) and made permanently to disappear through their "appropriating" reduction into abstract *"thought entities."* A reduction that carries with it, of course, the ideologically motivated elimination of their *social determinateness*. To quote Marx:

> the appropriation of what is estranged and objective, or the annulling of objectivity in the form of *estrangement* (which has to advance from indifferent foreignness to real, antagonistic estrangement) means equally or even primarily for Hegel that it is *objectivity* which is to be annulled, because it is not the *determinate* character of the object, but rather its *objective* character that is offensive and constitutes estrangement for self-consciousness.... A peculiar role, therefore, is played by the act of *superseding* in which denial and preservation—denial and affirmation—are bound together. Thus, for example, in Hegel's *Philosophy of Right, Private Right* superseded equals *Morality,* Morality superseded equals the *Family,* the Family superseded equals *Civil Society,* Civil Society superseded equals the *State,* the State superseded equals *World History*. In the *actual world* private right, morality, the family, civil society, the state, etc., remain in existence, only they have become . . . moments of motion.[18]

It is, thus, Hegel's ambivalent attitude to the antagonisms of the actual world—his perception of their significance from capital's vantage point, coupled with an idealist refusal to acknowledge their untranscendable negative implications for the given order in the framework of the unfolding historical development—which is responsible for producing this curious "philosophic dissolution and restoration of the existing empirical world."[19]

Witnessing the appearance of a social agency which contests the structurally enforced domination of its being by private property (capital), Hegel is too great a thinker simply to ignore the potential explosiveness of the basic social antagonisms in the historical process of which he is a most acute observer and interpreter. Nor can Hegel envisage, however, a world from which the structural dominance of private property could actually disappear. Hence his transformation of the dichotomies of real life into "thought entities" in terms of which the desired reconciliatory pseudo-transcendence can be accomplished. Accordingly, "*Private Property* as a *thought* is transcended in the *thought* of morality." An intellectual strategy which Hegel can pursue untroubled because "this superseding *leaves its object standing* in the real world."[20]

6.7 Moralizing Apriorism in the Service of the "Commercial Spirit"

Another revealing aspect of the ubiquitous dualism and dichotomies is the radical transformation of moral discourse in post-Cartesian philosophy. What we are offered bears no resemblance to the thoroughly realistic categorial framework of Aristotelian Ethics, for instance. In sharp contrast, in the post-Cartesian philosophical universe we are confronted with characteristic bourgeois conceptions of morality of which Kant's *Critique of Practical Reason* is the supreme—and within the horizons of his class quite unsurpassable—example.

The solutions of such ethics are directly derived from the assumed dualistic conception of being which in their turn the aprioristically stipulated "conclusions" circularly underpin, in the spirit of the Kantian "primacy of Practical Reason."

Within the parameters of this dualistic ontology, the hypostatized realm of "ought" represents the *impotent counter-image* to the real world in which, after all, the "moral intentions" of the idealized individual—who is said to belong to the "noumenal" or "intelligible" world as far as the ground of his moral determinations and deliberations is concerned—must find their manifestations in the form of real actions.

Moreover, the dichotomous compartmentalization of being yields very convenient ideological corollaries, in perfect harmony with the standpoint of political economy. For after stipulating, as Kant does, that "pure *a priori* legislating reason has no regard for *empirical* purposes such as are comprised under the general name of happiness,"[21] he can reconcile the most blatant contradictions and inhumanities of real life with the requirements of "pure *a priori* legislating reason" by insisting that:

> The *general equality* of men as subjects in a state coexists quite readily with the *greatest inequality* in degrees of the *possessions* men have...

> Hence the general equality of men also coexists with *great inequality of specific rights* of which there may be many.[22]

Thus the dualistic ontology and the dichotomy between *de facto* and *de jure* derived from it serve a thoroughly apologetic function. For they *legitimate,* in the name of nothing less than "pure *a priori* legislating reason," the worst iniquities of the *"de facto"* existent (i.e., the hierarchical structural determinations of domination and subordination within the antagonistic *class parameters* of the established order) by declaring their perfect consonance with the lofty imperatives of such "a priori legislating reason."

Since, in terms of the practical premises at the roots of such a vision, the contradictions of the real world cannot be done away with but, on the contrary, must be preserved *and justified,* the "corrective" role of morality must be confined to idealistic exhortations addressed to the individual, with reference to the impotent counter-image of actuality under the rule of "ought." And, significantly, in this regard it does not seem to make any difference at all whether the general philosophical framework in which the ought-ridden ethical propositions appear is a materialist or an idealist one. For the untranscendability of the basic social contradictions from the standpoint of political economy produces a *moralizing apriorism* of some kind in all cases, no matter how different the particular systems in other respects.

Adam Smith, for instance, is highly realistic in his grasp of some of the most glaring contradictions of the established order, recognizing that

> Till there be property there can be no government, the very end of which is to secure wealth and to defend the rich from the poor.[23]

Indeed, he does not even hesitate to acknowledge that as a result of the irresistibly unfolding "commercial spirit . . . the minds of men are contracted and rendered incapable of elevation. Education is despised, or at least neglected, and heroic spirit is almost utterly extinguished,"[24] adding to all this what sounds, at least by implication, as a strong indictment of the prevailing iniquitous relations, namely that "*the people who clothe the world are in rags themselves.*"[25]

However, precisely because Smith simultaneously also advocates, with boundless enthusiasm, the universal triumph of the "commercial spirit," there is nothing he can offer in opposition to the criticized phenomena, except moralistic laments about the "drunkenness, riot and debauchery" of the working classes whose sons lose in his view "the benefit of religion, which is a great advantage, not only considered in a pious sense, but as it affords them subject for thought and speculation."[26]

Smith cannot extricate himself from the contradiction of wholeheartedly approving the structural foundations of the social order whose negative manifestations he would like to condemn in limited contexts. Thus, he has to resort to aprioristically postulating a number of vague "natural" determinations — like *"disposition," "propensity," "inclination,"* etc.—in order to explain (or rather: in order to be able to run away from the need to explain) some complex, and from his standpoint totally insoluble, social contradictions. He tells us, in this spirit, that

> This *disposition* to admire, and almost to worship, the rich and the powerful, and to despise or, at least, to neglect persons of poor and mean condition, though *necessary both to establish and to maintain the distinction of ranks and the order of society,* is, at the same time, the great and most universal *cause of the corruption of our moral sentiments.*[27]

As we can see, Adam Smith's feeble lament about the "corruption of our moral sentiments" is immediately contradicted and invalidated by the philosopher himself on two counts:

1. by asserting that the object of his criticism arises from a natural "disposition" (hence it is unabatable); and

2. by concluding that the guilty disposition in question is in any event *necessary* for the establishment of social hierarchy and for the permanence of the "order of society" as such.

Further still, in case someone might begin to worry about the potential consequences of such moral corruption—which we *cannot* help, nor indeed *should* we attempt to interfere with in the "empirical world" of the "commercial spirit" and its practical necessities, even if "ideally/morally" we *ought* to—Smith reassures us in the same work that "the sentiments of *moral approbation and disapprobation* are founded on the most vigorous passions of *human nature,* and, though they may be somewhat *warped,* cannot be entirely *perverted.*"[28]

In this way, even if the *form* of moral apriorism which we find in Smith and others who write in the same idiom is different from the Kantian variety, its *substance* is exactly the same. Nor is this profound *structural affinity* of the respective philosophical systems—which appear to be diametrically opposed at first sight—really surprising at a closer look. For, in view of their shared standpoint of bourgeois political economy, the fundamental determinations of the hierarchical social framework—the "distinction of ranks and the order of society" in Smith's words, and "the greatest inequality in possessions and specific rights" in Kantian terminology—cannot be seriously questioned by either of them.

As a result, not only must the moral apriorism of all those who accommodate themselves within such horizons be simply *assumed as given* (whether on the ground of an alleged "human nature" or as a special "faculty of reason"), but also its role must be defined as a merely ideal opposition to the empirically given which it cannot significantly alter.

THUS, IN POST-CARTESIAN CONCEPTIONS of morality we are presented with a system of *"double book-keeping"*: one for the ideal world of "ought" (where, during the optimistic phase of development of the bourgeoisie in the ascendant, the "corruption of our moral sentiments" and the "power of evil" cannot be allowed simply to prevail, either in view of the claimed ultimate incorruptibility of "human nature" itself, or because "ought implies can,"[29] etc.), and the other for serving the prosaic reality of the "empirical purposes" that emanate from the exploitative determinations of the idealized "commercial spirit."

However, the inner contradictions of this approach surface even within its own terms of reference when the moral philosopher—who shares the standpoint of political economy—crosses swords with the political economist proper. They are forced to cross swords not only because they conceptualize different aspects of the same contradictory situation but above all because the solutions advocated in one context cannot be kept in a self-enclosed compartment but reveal their radical incompatibility with the other.

Moreover, ironically at times the moral philosopher and the political economist happen to be one and the same person, as the predicament of Adam Smith and Michel Chevalier, for instance, illustrates it. In such cases the ideological edifice of dualistic compartmentalization collapses before our very eyes as soon as we compare the contradictory statements made by the thinkers in question in their different capacities. In this way the standpoint of political economy comes to grief both in moral philosophy and in the field of political economy through displaying its inner contradictions. For, as Marx observes:

> It stems from the very nature of estrangement that each sphere applies to me a different and opposite yardstick—ethics one and political economy another; for each is a specific estrangement of man and focuses attention on a particular round of estranged essential activity, and each stands in an estranged relation to the other. Thus M. Michel Chevalier reproaches Ricardo with having abstracted from ethics. But Ricardo is allowing political economy to speak its own language, and if it does not speak ethically, this is not Ricardo's fault. M. Chevalier abstracts from political economy in so far as he moralizes, but he really and *necessarily* abstracts from ethics in so far as he practises political economy. The reference of political economy to ethics . . . can only be the reference of the laws of political economy to ethics. If there is no such connection, or if the contrary is rather the case, can Ricardo help it? Besides, the opposition between political economy and ethics is only a sham opposition and just as much no opposition as it is an opposition. All that happens is that *political economy expresses moral laws in its own way.*[30]

Indeed, political economy necessarily abstracts from ethics so as to be able to express the postulated moral laws in its own way, in accord with its own fundamental tenets. But, equally, ethics must abstract from the "empirical" so as to be able to legitimate the laws of political economy in *its* own way.

In the case of "double book-keeping" post-Cartesian ethics this curious correlation amounts to maintaining simultaneously both that "practical reason" (or its empiricist equivalent) is deeply concerned with fundamental moral values (in consonance with the impervertible "moral sentiments" of "human nature," or in tune with the "categorical imperatives" that emanate from the "noumenal world," etc.), and yet that its high sounding commands do not apply to the task of redressing even the "greatest inequalities" in the world of "empirical purposes."

Conveniently, therefore, in the "realistic" versions of post-Cartesian moral apriorism the "corruption of our moral sentiments" can be both virtuously noted and practically disregarded; just as in the Kantian conceptualization of "Practical Reason" from the standpoint of political economy the moral maxims demanded from the individual can be both modeled on the "form of the natural law" and relegated to a separate noumenal world, in order to avoid facing up to conflicts in value as they necessarily arise from the antagonisms of the real world.

It comes as no surprise, therefore, that Weber's "private demons"—conceived in the dualistic spirit of this long established philosophical tradition, even if in the formulation of the specific Weberian dichotomies the imagery and the conceptual apparatus are adjusted to the pessimistic Spengler-like vision of their author's conflict-torn age—can offer nothing but unashamedly subjective and arbitrary "world-views," as well as the corresponding range of irreconcilable "private values," to the self-oriented individual, in an irrationalistic and thoroughly hopeless opposition to the public world of facticity in which the struggle against the inhumanities of the "commercial spirit" must be won or lost.

6.8 The Dominance of Counter-Value in Antinomous Value-Relations

Returning to a problem indicated earlier, all these ideologically convenient dualisms and dichotomies of political economy and philosophy—not least the opposition between *de facto* and *de jure* through which the dehumanizing contingency of the existent can be elevated to the glorified status of "de jure" unalterable lawfulness—cannot be explained simply in terms of the internal conceptual determinations of the various theories concerned. For they become intelligible only if we relate them to the manifold actual dualisms and antinomies of the prevailing socioeconomic order from which they necessarily arise.

As regards the latter, at the core of commodity society's dichotomously articulated structure of domination and subordination we are confronted by the most absurd of all conceivable dualisms: the opposition between the *means* of labour and *living labour* itself.

This perverse practical dualism finds its tangible manifestation across the long trajectory of capital's historical developments in the irreconcilably antagonistic—yet not merely by political economy and philosophy "eternalized" but also materially/institutionally safeguarded and constantly reinforced—interaction and unstable structural dependency between *capital* and *labour*. The irrepressible conflictuality of this interaction and the instability resulting from it make it imperative to *reproduce* the relationship between capital and labour as a form of structural dependency, secured through a complex network of partial determinations which all display an intrinsically dichotomous character and are uneasily integrated into a dualistic overall framework. And precisely because capital's whole system of actual dualisms—burdened with vital reproductive functions—cannot possibly afford to be a neutral one, notwithstanding the great assortment of spurious theoretical claims to "value-neutrality" which we are familiar with, the historically given dual structures are not ordered in the social world "laterally," but in strict hierarchical *subordination* to one another.

This is a determination of paramount importance, bringing with it far-reaching consequences for theory. For the unsurpassable practical imperative of super- and sub-ordination—without which the capital system quite simply could not function at all, whatever the ideological wishful thinking encapsulated in the slogans of "people's capitalism" and "share-owning democracy"—means that *one* side of the relationship, of necessity, *dominates* the other, no matter how inextricably it must rely on the dominated side for its own sustenance. Inevitably, therefore, on the plane of socioeconomic life itself this kind of lopsided dualistic interrelationship can only temporarily stabilize itself through the production and reproduction of rigid hierarchies and increasingly centralized and reified institutional devices of control, thereby foreshadowing major explosions and ultimately a structural breakdown, in place of flexible mediations and dialectical transitions.

As to the theoretical consequences involved, they can be summed up with reference to how badly all attempts at dialectically overcoming the recognized dualisms and dichotomies must suffer within such parameters that happen to be circumscribed by the standpoint of political economy.

They are condemned to failure even when the philosopher in question is as great a dialectician as Hegel himself. For once the prevailing socioeconomic system of super- and sub-ordinations is taken for granted (as it must be, of course, from the standpoint of capital's political economy), the announced programme of "dialectical mediation" between reified extremes invariably turns out to be a *sham* mediation. It amounts to no more than direct or indirect social apology, and the promise of "dialectical unity" (to replace the more or less openly acknowledged dualisms and dichotomies) as well as the programme of realizing "universality" (in "transcendence" of the opposing, and again dualistically defined, partialities) prove to be nothing but vacuous, ought-ridden, and within the advocated horizons totally unrealizable *postulates*.

There can be no theoretical solution to the identified dualisms and dichotomies so long as the ongoing social processes themselves constantly reproduce the antinomies of real life which give rise to such philosophical conceptualizations. This is why in the end even the most genuine dialectical enterprise must be defeated by the resistance of capital's actuality and has to take refuge on the imaginary desert island of its own ideal postulates and fictitiously universalistic conceptual "transcendences."

IF WE NOW TAKE A CLOSER LOOK at the absurd practical dualism of opposing the *means* of labour (capital) to *living* labour, we find not only that the former dominates the latter but also that through such domination the only truly meaningful subject/object relationship is completely *overturned* in actuality, resulting in similarly overturned conceptualizations.

Paradoxically, the ground from which this thorny issue arises could not be more tangible. For the actual relationship between subject and object, in its original constitution, is inseparable from the conditions of production and reproduction of the human agency and from the assessment of the object (the means and material of production) without which no social metabolic reproduction—through the historically specific mode of human interchange with nature—is conceivable. Yet, through the refracting prism of philosophical mystification (ideologically linked to insurmountable class interests), the tangible substance of the underlying concrete material and social relationships is metamorphosed into a metaphysical riddle whose solution can only take the form of some unrealizable ideal postulate, decreeing the *identity* of subject and object. And precisely because the issue, in its fundamental structural determination, concerns the relationship between the *working subject* and the object of its productive activity—which under the rule of capital cannot help being an intrinsically exploitative relationship—the possibility of disclosing the real nature of the problems and conflicts at stake, with a view of transcending them in other than a purely fictitious form, must be practically non-existent. For inasmuch as the thinkers—be they bourgeois political economists or philosophers—identify themselves with the standpoint (and corresponding material interests) of capital, they must envisage a "solution" in a way that leaves the practically overturned relationship between the working subject and its object in reality itself absolutely intact.

As a result of the practical overturning of this vital relationship in the real world, the true subject of essential productive activity is degraded to the condition of a readily manipulable object. At the same time, the original object and formerly subordinate moment of society's productive interchange with nature is elevated to a position from which it can usurp the role of human subjectivity in charge of decision-making.

This new "subject" of institutionalized usurpation is in fact a pseudo-subject, since it is forced by its fetishistic inner determinations to operate within extremely limited parameters, substituting its own blind material dictates and imperatives—to which then really "there can be no alternative"—for the possibility of consciously adopted design in the service of human need.[31]

Characteristically, parallel to these developments we find that philosophy either simply codifies (and legitimates) the stark opposition between subject and object in its naked immediacy, or makes an attempt to "overcome" it through the ideal postulate of an *"identical subject and object."*

The latter is, of course, a thoroughly mystical proposition which takes us absolutely nowhere, since it leaves the existing dualism and inversion of the relationship concerned in the actual world exactly as it was before the appearance of such "transcending criticism." And precisely because the practical dualism and overturning of the subject/object relationship is constantly *reproduced* in actuality, we are repeatedly presented in philosophy, in one form or another, with the problematic of subject/object duality, as seen from the standpoint of capital and its political economy. For a social standpoint of that kind cannot possibly question the actuality of this *inversion,* let alone capital's exploitative domination of labour corresponding to it. Consequently the solution of the problem at issue remains permanently beyond its reach as set by the blind material imperatives of its own pseudo-subjectness.

In this sense there is indeed here before us a curious "subject/object identity," even if its unvarnished reality could not be more different from its abstract philosophical conceptualization and idealization. It consists in the totally arbitrary identification of the *object* (means of labour/capital) with the position of the *subject* (by way of deriving the "self-consciousness" or "subject-identity" of philosophical discourse from the thinkers' self-identification with the objectives that emanate from the material determinations of capital as *self-positing subject/object*), coupled with the simultaneous elimination of the *real subject* (living labour, the working subject) from the philosophical picture. No wonder, therefore, that the elusive quest for the "identical subject/object" persists to our own days as a haunting philosophical Chimera.

ANOTHER PRACTICAL DUALISM of the greatest importance in capitalist society is manifest in the relationship between *exchange* and *use.* Again, just like in the perverted subject/object relationship, exchange succeeds in one-sidedly dominating use in direct proportion to the degree to which generalized commodity production stabilizes itself and *overturns* the former dialectical primacy of use over exchange, asserting also in this respect its rigid material determinations and interests with total disregard for the consequences.

As a result of these developments, use-value corresponding to need can acquire the right to existence only if it conforms to the aprioristic imperatives of self-expanding exchange-value. It is therefore doubly ironical that one of the principal philosophies of the epoch should consider itself the champion of *"Utilitarianism"* at a time when all genuine concern for *non-profitable utility* is ruthlessly obliterated and replaced by the universal commodification of objects and human relations alike, thanks to the apparently irresistible forward march of the "commercial spirit" whose triumph the selfsame philosophy wholeheartedly approves.

To appreciate the full import of this structural subordination of use to exchange in capitalist society, we have to situate it in the context of a number of other important practical dualisms which have a direct bearing upon it—notably the interrelationship between *abstract* and *concrete, quantity* and *quality,* and *time* and *space.*

- In all three instances we should be able to speak, in principle, of a *dialectical* interconnection. However, on closer inspection we find that in their historically specific manifestations under the conditions of commodity production and exchange the objective dialectic is subverted by capital's reified determinations and *one* side of each relationship rigidly dominates the other.

- Thus the *concrete* is subordinated to the abstract, the *qualitative* to the quantitative, and the living *space* of productive human interactions—whether we think of it as "nature at hand" in its immediacy, or under its aspect of "worked-up nature," or indeed take it as the work-environment in the strictest sense of the term, or, by contrast, with reference to its most comprehensive meaning as the vital framework of human existence itself under the name of the *environment* in general—is dominated by the tyranny of capital's *time-management and time-accountancy*, with potentially catastrophic consequences.

Moreover, the way in which all four complexes are brought into a common interplay with one another under the determinations of capital greatly aggravates the situation. For, contrary to Lukács's at times Weberian reading of Marx in *History and Class Consciousness,* the problem is not that the "contemplative stance" of labour *"reduces* space and time to a common denominator and *degrades time to the dimension of space"*[32] but, on the contrary, that *"Time is everything, man is nothing."*[33] The *reduction* we find here concerns *labour* in its *qualitative specificity,* and not time and space as such. A reduction indeed through which qualitatively specific and rich "compound labour" is turned into thoroughly impoverished "simple labour," simultaneously also asserting the domination of the *abstract* over the *concrete* as well as the corresponding domination of *exchange-value* over *use-value*.

THREE QUOTATIONS FROM MARX help to clarify these connections. The first comes from *Capital* and contrasts the position of Political Economy with the writings of classical antiquity:

> Political Economy, which as an independent science, first sprang into being during the period of manufacture, views the *social division of labour* only from the standpoint of manufacture, and sees in it only the means of producing more commodities with a given quantity of labour, and, consequently, of cheapening commodities and hurrying on the *accumulation of capital*. In most striking contrast with this accentuation of *quantity* and *exchange-value,* is the attitude of the writers of classical antiquity, who hold exclusively by *quality* and *use-value*. . . . If the growth of the quantity is occasionally mentioned, this is only done with reference to the greater abundance of *use-values*. There is not a word alluding to *exchange-value* or to the cheapening of commodities.[34]

The second quotation highlights the way in which the *reduction* exercised by the political economists obliterates the *social determinateness* of individuals—depriving them thereby of their *individuality,* since there cannot be true individuality and particularity in abstraction from the rich multiplicity of social determinations—in the service of the dominant ideological interests. It reads as follows:

> Society, as it appears to the political economist, is *civil society,* in which *every individual* is a totality of needs and only exists for the other person, as the other exists for him, in so far as each becomes a *means* for the other. The political economist *reduces* everything (just as does politics in its *Rights of Man*) to *man,* i.e., to the *individual* whom he *strips of all determinateness* so as to class him as *capitalist or worker*.[35]

The concern expressed in the third quotation is in close affinity with the previous one whose implications point to the dialectic of true individuality arising from the manifold mediations of social determinateness. This is opposed by Marx to the reductive abstraction of the political economists who directly link *abstract individuality* and *abstract universality*. The passage in question brings into focus the relationship between simple and compound labour and the subordination of men to the rule of quantity and time. In Marx's words:

> Competition, according to an American economist, determines how many days of simple labour are contained in one day's compound labour. Does not this reduction of days of compound labour to days of simple labour suppose that simple labour is itself taken as a measure of value? If the mere quantity of labour functions as a measure of value regardless of quality, it presupposes that simple labour has become the pivot of industry. It presupposes that labour has been equalized by the subordination of man to the machine or by the extreme division of labour; that men are effaced by their labour; that the pendulum of the clock has become as accurate a measure of the relative activity of two workers as it is of the speed of two locomotives. Therefore we should not say that one man's hour is worth another man's hour, but rather that one man during an hour is worth just as much as another man during an hour. Time is everything, man is nothing; he is at the most time's carcase. Quality no longer matters. Quantity alone decides everything; hour for hour; day for day.[36]

Thus, within the framework of the existing socioeconomic system a multiplicity of formerly dialectical interconnections are reproduced in the form of perverse practical dualisms, dichotomies, and antinomies, *reducing human beings to a reified condition* (whereby *they* are brought to a common denominator with, and become replaceable by, "locomotives" and other machines) and to the ignominious status of *"time's carcase."* And since the possibility of practically manifesting and realizing the *inherent worth* and human specificity of all individuals through their essential productive activity is blocked off as a result of this process of *alienating reduction* (which makes "one man during an hour worth just as much as another man"), *value* as such becomes an extremely *problematical concept*. For, in the interest of capitalist profitability, not only can there be no room left for the actualization of the individuals' specific worth but, worse still, *counter-value* must unceremoniously prevail over value and assert its absolute domination as the one and only admissible practical value-relation.

Adam Ferguson candidly admits this in one of the most important sections of his magisterial *Essay on the History of Civil Society* (1767):

> Every undertaker in manufacture finds, that the more he can subdivide the tasks of his workmen, and the more hands he can employ on separate articles, the more are his expenses diminished, and his *profits increased*. . . . Nations of tradesmen come to consist of members who, beyond their own particular trade, are *ignorant of all human affairs,* and who may contribute to the preservation and enlargement of the commonwealth, without making its interest an object of their regard or attention. Every individual is distinguished by his calling, and has a place to which he is fitted. The savage, who knows no distinction but that of his merit, of his sex, or of his species, and to whom the community is the sovereign object of affection, is astonished to find, that in a scene of this nature, *his being a man does not qualify him for any station whatever;* he flies to the woods with amazement, distaste and aversion. . . . Many mechanical arts, indeed, require no capacity; they succeed best under a *total suppression of sentiment and reason;* and *ignorance* is the mother of industry as well as of superstition. Reflection and fancy are subject to err; but a *habit* of moving the hand, or the foot, is independent of either. Manufactures, acccordingly, prosper most where the *mind is least consulted,* and where the workshop may, without any great work of imagination, be considered as *an engine, the parts of which are men.*[37]

This is the context in which we can clearly identify the practical ground for the erection of the dichotomous ethical edifices which we have seen earlier. For the destruction of the relationship in which "facts" and "values," "is" and "ought" are inseparably joined together in the—not metaphysical but even to Ferguson's "savage" palpably self-evident—"inherent worth" and demonstrable "merit" of particular individuals engaged in their everyday life-activities, inevitably carries with it radical consequences for value as such. It is sundered into a *narrow utilitarian* aspect (corresponding to the needs of capital accumulation and universal commodification in the world of "is"), and into an "*ideal* aspect" that—to no avail—counterposes the elusive "moral worth" of its separate "realm of ought" to the well-entrenched actuality of the existent.

IN THE DUALISM of *distribution* and *production* we meet with the same characteristic of rigid determination, in that the one-sided distribution (class-expropriation) of the—strategically all-important—means of production predetermines the structural parameters of production for as long a historical epoch as the prevailing system of distribution can assert itself.

This is the absolute blind spot of all those who adopt capital's standpoint of political economy, even when they happen to be as great thinkers as Adam Ferguson. For on this vital issue even this outstanding (and rather neglected) figure of the Scottish Enlightenment can offer nothing but fairy-tales and circular pseudo-explanations, expecting us to believe that "The *accidents* which *distribute* the means of subsistence unequally, *inclination,* and *favourable opportunities,* assign the different occupations of men; and a sense of *utility* leads them, without end, to *subdivide* their professions."[38]

Thus, the mere assumption of "accidents," "inclination," "favourable opportunities," and "a sense of utility" are meant to explain (and legitimate) the existing structural inequalities while, significantly, the key problem concerning the one-sided expropriation of the *means of production* is *conflated* into the vague generality of "accidents distributing the *means of subsistence* unequally," removing thereby the dimension of *class conflict.* As a result, it is conveniently obfuscated that distribution in capitalist society means first of all the distribution of human beings into antagonistic social classes, from which the domination of production in a hierarchically ordered way necessarily follows, in close conjunction with all the other fundamental dualisms and practical antinomies of the given order which we have seen above.

Hegel, too, fails to get to grips with the dialectic of production and distribution, whatever his intentions and claims to the contrary. This is visible also in the context of the peculiar "universality" which he offers to us while maintaining the absolute—i.e. in his eyes philosophically grounded—legitimacy of the established social class-relations.[39] At this point it must be stressed that also Hegel *conflates* means of *production* with means of *subsistence,* as well as *work* with *socially divided labour,* so as to be able to glorify what he calls *"universal permanent capital."*[40] He derives the latter from a fictitious "ideality" that emerges from the Hegelian conceptual transformations which mirror the perverse *inversion* of the corresponding relations in actuality.

Thanks to such quasi-mystical philosophical deduction of the contingent actuality of the "commercial spirit" from the "Absolute Idea," the eternalized social order of "universal permanent capital," and the structural inequality inseparable from it, can be defended in the name of superior "dialectical Reason" against the *"folly of the Understanding* which takes as real and rational its abstract *equality* and its 'ought-to-be,'" and forgets that

> Men are made *unequal by nature,* where inequality is in its element, and in *civil society* the *right* of particularity is so far from annulling this natural inequality that it *produces it out of mind* and *raises* it to an inequality of skill *and resources,* and even to that of *moral and intellectual* attainment.[41]

What we witness here is most revealing about the importance of ideological determinations for idealist and materialist/empiricist methodologies alike. Admittedly, the latter had no difficulty in conflating their alleged *"natural* necessities"—like Adam Smith's "propensity to exchange and barter" and other so-called characteristics of "human nature," said to be in perfect harmony with the established modality of socioeconomic interaction—with the historically given state of affairs, since it had no quarrel with nature itself on philosophical grounds.

Not so, however, the idealist philosophers, like Hegel, who could not help being *hostile* even to the mention of the word "nature," since nature represents in their eyes the philosophically inferior domain of "sensuous determinations." And yet, we find that, in accordance with the ideological interests which Hegel shares with the materialist philosophers and political economists of his class, he does not hesitate for a moment to conflate *natural necessity* (the Hegelian dictum that "men are made unequal by nature," which fallaciously equates the self-evident *diversity* of nature with the socially created and by no means unproblematical *inequality* of men among themselves) with *historical contingency* in order to mould *"absolute philosophical necessity"* out of such—for an idealist thinker truly astonishing—alloy.[42] For in this way Hegel succeeds in conferring upon the historically created and *historically alterable* inequality of "civil society"—an inequality now ideally metamorphosed into "the *right of particularity*" on the purely assumptional idealist ground that "the objective *right of the particularity of mind* is contained in the *Idea*"[43]—the status of *de jure* forever existent.

6.9 The Supersession of Dichotomies: The Question of Social Agency

To sum up: the interminable succession of philosophical dualisms and dichotomies in the writings conceived from the standpoint of capital's political economy—e.g., theory/practice; thought/being; subject/object; for-itself/in-itself; world-views/factual knowledge; immanence/transcendence; noumenal/phenomenal; essence/appearance; essence/existence; form/content; value/fact; ought/is; reason/emotion; Reason/Understanding; freedom/necessity; individual/species; private/public; political/social; state/civil society; de jure/de facto; and many more—remains thoroughly unintelligible without the manifold practical dualisms and antinomies of the socioeconomic order which the dualistic methodologies of this tradition both express and help to sustain in their own way, with forceful ideological commitment and efficacy. We have also seen that the objective dichotomies and antinomies of capital's historical contingency constitute:

1. a closely *interlocking* system of determinations in which

2. *one* side of the various dualisms in question *dominates* the other,

3. on the basis of a perverse *overturning* and *inversion* of some vital objective relationships,

4. thereby establishing *rigid hierarchies* which a priori reject

5. the possibility of dialectical *mediations* and workable *transitions*

6. toward a *structural* change.

This is why philosophical dualism so easily triumphs in the post-Cartesian conceptual universe, preaching one-sided solutions (or the a priori impossibility of arriving at the required syntheses) where only a dialectical approach could begin to cope with the problems. Indeed, the success of even Hegel's conscious and rather unique attempt at dialectically overcoming the dichotomies of his predecessors is confined to the most abstract regions of the *Phenomenology* and the *Logic,* precipitating again into "unreconciled dualism"—complemented in his system by the abstract advocacy of making "reconciliatory Reason" triumph over the critical temptations of the "Understanding"—as soon as this great originator of the objective idealist dialectic turns his attention to more tangible issues and tries to subsume under his general categories the irreconcilable antagonisms of the real world.

Thus, the "diremptions," alienations and reified oppositions of actuality assert themselves in the end on all planes, defeating even the greatest theoretical efforts to squeeze coherent dialectical solutions—*ex pumice acquam* ("water from stone")—out of the hopelessly constraining objective parameters of a divided social world whose stubborn structural antagonisms the thinkers in question try to "reconcile" and defend.

The methodology of dualistic and dichotomous conceptualizations that ultimately always prevails, even when a conscious attempt is made to "sublate" it, is the necessary concomitant of such ideological predicaments. It has its inseparable corollaries:

1. in the *conflation* of vital distinctions under allegedly unalterable general determinations and thereby the convenient obliteration of their potentially explosive sociohistorical specificities;

2. in the *circularity* that results from being tossed to and fro between the two poles of the openly reasserted and accepted dichotomies, or indeed of the "unreconciled dualisms" that bewilderingly reemerge after a thinker, like Hegel, thought to have done away with them;

3. in the absence of genuine *mediations,* even when the philosopher is abstractly aware of their importance;

4. in the mere assertion of vacuous *postulates*—like the ought-ridden advocacy of "unity" and "universality," on the ground of uncritically defended *partiality*—in place of objectively underpinned theoretical syntheses and socially viable practical strategies; postulates made necessary both by the idealization of indefensible partial interests and concomitant inequalities, and by the absence of proper mediations just mentioned.

Polarization is the objective rule, *"reconciliation"* (without significantly changing the social ground of such polarization) the wishful remedy. This is how the standpoint of capital's political economy circumscribes the conceptual horizon of post-Cartesian theory.

BY IMPLICATION, if we want to envisage the possibility of dialectical syntheses in place of the dualisms and dichotomies here surveyed, it is necessary to adopt a very different theoretical vantage point, one from which the fundamental antagonisms of the given socioeconomic order can be recognized for what they really are, rather than being explained away by "reconciliatory Reason."

This involves, of course, the identification and adoption of categories adequate to grasping the dynamic historical specificity of social being. Categories through which the key regulators of the socioeconomic and cultural/ideological intercourse become visible, instead of being obliterated by means of those ideologically motivated conceptual conflations which we have repeatedly encountered even in the writings of very great thinkers. For it is impossible to come to grips with such philosophical dualisms without referring them to the vantage point of a social agency whose practical intervention in the real world indicates the possibility of *actually* overcoming the now materially sustained antinomies and dichotomies, on the basis of the consciously articulated *collective* action of the *social* individuals.

The categories in question are, of course, radically incompatible with the *individualistic* categorial framework in terms of which those who share the standpoint of political economy try to deal with the dichotomy of *subject/object,* for instance, offering at best some highly dubious "syntheses" of the dichotomy between self-oriented subjectivity and the comprehensive social world while reproducing the contradiction between fragmented/partial knowledge and "totalizing consciousness." Thus, the very least we can say in favour of the adoption of the Marxian "standpoint of the *social* individual" is that the solutions articulated within individualistic categorial frameworks cannot help being abstract-imperatival even when they are spelled out in a "descriptive" form.

As an example we may think of Adam Ferguson's "statesman" whose collective or "combined" wisdom is derived from treating others as his *tools* (see note 38); or of Hegel's "Cunning of Reason" that relates to the individuals—even to the so-called "world-historical individuals"—in much the same way, only this time dressed up in solemn idealist costume. For even if we take such solutions at their face value, the underlying contradiction between the requirements of "totalizing consciousness" and the inescapable limitations of self-oriented partiality (no matter how "aggregated") is by no means "superseded." It is only temporarily hidden from sight by the reconciliatory acceptance of, and resignation to, the existing state of affairs.

But just as the dualisms and dichotomies of the post-Cartesian philosophical tradition arise from the soil of a determinate social practice, by the same token it is impossible to think of theoretically resolving them simply through the adoption of a new categorial framework, without envisaging at the same time an alternative social order from which the *practical* antinomies of capital's historically specific system can be removed. To take one example only, the earlier mentioned tyranny of capital's *time-accountancy* (which reduces living labour to a mere "factor of production," or to a subordinate component of the category of "unit costs" in current economic parlance) and the lopsided dualism and domination of the social world implicit in it, can only be superseded in a qualitatively different framework of *social accountancy* (i.e., a truly *socialist* accountancy), oriented towards the conscious self-determination of their productive interchanges by the social individuals at all levels. This is the way Marx puts it:

> In a future society, in which *class antagonism* will have ceased, in which there will no longer be any *classes, use* will no longer be determined by the *minimum* time of production; but the *time* of production devoted to an article will be determined by the degree of its *social utility*.[44]

As we can see, here the categories of "classes," "class antagonism," and "social utility" are linked to the conception of a new social order as objectively inherent in (or arising from) the contradictions of the given historical form. This is how it becomes possible to anticipate the supersession of the dichotomies of *use* and *exchange, time* and *space, production* and *distribution,* etc., provided that we are willing to acknowledge their social embeddedness in antagonistic class relations, envisaging at the same time the radical transformation of the latter through appropriate social action. The same goes for all the other dualisms, dichotomies, and antinomies which we have encountered in the course of this survey. But, of course, to do so implies parting company with capital's standpoint of political economy and isolated individuality.

NOTES

1. Hannah Arendt waters down the problem of *expropriation* to that of "exorbitant taxes." The function of such upside-down categorization is to turn the privileged *expropriators* (who happen to pay the "exorbitant taxes") into the real victims of the system. Beyond that, only a "residual" problem is acknowledged: the undeniable persistence of poverty; Arendt, however, expects that to be be resolved by "neutral technical means."

   Such a solution is, of course, an empty "ought," conceived in the spirit of systematically avoiding the structural problem of capitalist exploitation. The whole conceptual framework is constructed in such a way that the permanent structural presupposition of expropriation and exploitation—the forcible and legally safeguarded separation of labour from the means of production—should not even appear on the horizon, let alone assume the strategic centre of the social confrontation. This is why the political sphere and its potential role in intervening at the level of economic exploitation must be conceptualized by Arendt the way in which we find it in her writings. For, once the structural foundations of the system are taken for granted, the margin of political action against the acknowledged inequalities is practically meaningless, and the recommended solution is nothing but an empty "ought." As her sympathetic commentator, Elisabeth Young-Bruehl, recalls with some bafflement:

> "[Arendt] wanted a solution to the problem of poverty that did not, does not dictate a form of government." (E. Young-Bruehl, "From the Pariah's Point of View," in Melvyn A. Hill (ed.), *H. Arendt: The Recovery of the Public World.* St. Martin's Press, New York, 1979, p. 24.)

With that proviso, both the established socioeconomic system and the "form of government which it dictates" can continue their rule, leaving the problem of "poverty" (which is itself *relative* to the general wealth of the given society, while expropriation/exploitation is a *structural absolute)* to the totally vacuous "ought-to-be" of "strictly economic technical neutrality."

2. It is also worth noting in this context that the position of the essentially negative ruling ideology, and the practical consciousness of its antagonist (whose objective is the replacement of the established system by a positively defined new social order, with qualitatively different presuppositions for the continued societal reproduction) cannot be considered *symmetrical.*
3. This is how Weber puts it: "One thing is the Devil and the other God as far as the individual is concerned, and the individual must decide which, *for him,* is God and which the Devil. And this is so throughout the orders of life. . . . let us go to our work and satisfy the 'demand of the day'—on the human as much as the professional level. That demand, however, is plain and simple if each of us finds and *obeys the demon* holding the threads of *his* life." Weber, *Gesammelte Aufsätze zur Wissenschaftslehre,* Tübingen, 1922, pp. 545 and 555. (Quoted in Lukács, *The Destruction of Reason,* Merlin Press, London, 1980, pp. 616 and 618.)
4. Structuralism in general had its hey-day in the postwar period of economic expansion and consensus politics. Thus, at the time of its confident intellectual empire-building it could happily welcome the spread of its influence even in the form of "Marxist structuralism," notwithstanding the profound incompatibility between historical materialism and anti-historical structuralism. In the same way, it is highly revealing that "Marxist structuralism"

had its greatest success in Latin America; a continent dominated in those days by various military regimes which forced the left into an understandably defensive position. And the obverse side of this relationship prevailed as well. For once the crisis of capital was signalled by the end of the "economic miracles" (both in Europe and in Latin America), coupled with the reactivation and intensification of social antagonisms—in Europe in the form of the collapse of consensus-politics and in Latin America through the demise of several military dictatorships—we could also witness the complete disintegration not only of mainstream structuralism but also of "Marxist structuralism" as an intellectual force.

5. Marx, *Capital,* Vol. 1, Foreign Languages Publishing House, Moscow, 1959, p. 345.

6. Ibid., p. 360.

Early capitalist developments create "a productive mechanism whose parts are human beings." (Ibid., p. 338.) In the manufacture period, "the handicraft continues to be the basis. . . . It is just because handicraft skill continues, in this way, to be the foundation of the process of production, that each workman becomes exclusively assigned to a partial function, and that for the rest of his life, his labour-power is turned into the *organ of this detail function.*" (Ibid., pp. 338–9.)

Yet, it would be quite wrong to ignore the natural and historical foundations on which such developments arise, seeing in them something uniquely capitalistic, as we find this in the Weberian quasi-mystical (as well as question-begging) deduction of "life-calling" from the "spirit of capitalism" (and *vice-versa).*

There is a much more tangible grounding to all such developments than the "spirit of capitalism" which Weber needs in order to provide a "refutation" of the Marxian account. (We may note here in passing that even his admirers admit that "Weber has made his academic reputation by attacking Marxist determinism's economic reductionism." Ephraim Fischoff, "The Background and Fate of Weber's *Wirtschaft und Gesellschaft,*" in Max Weber, *The Sociology of Religion,* translated by E. Fischoff, introduction by Talcott Parsons, Methuen & Co., London, 1965, p. 282.)

As Marx rightly stresses: "the conversion of *fractional* work into the *life-calling* of one man, corresponds to the tendency shown by earlier societies, to *make trades hereditary;* either to *petrify them into castes,* or whenever definite historical conditions beget in the individual a tendency to vary in a manner incompatible with the nature of castes, to *ossify them into guilds*. Castes and guilds arise from the action of the same natural law that regulates the differentiation of plants and animals into species and varieties, except that, when a certain degree of development has been reached, the heredity of castes and the exclusiveness of guilds are *ordained as a law of society*. 'The muslins of Dakka in fineness, the calicoes and other piece goods of Coromandel in brilliant and durable colours, have never been surpassed. Yet they are produced without capital, machinery, division of labour, or any of those means which give such facilities to the manufacturing interest of Europe. . . .' [*Historical and Descriptive Account of British India,* by Hugh Murray and James Wilson, &c., Edinburgh, 1832, vol. II, p. 449.] It is only the special skill accumulated from generation to generation, and transmitted from father to son, that gives to the Hindu, as it does to the spider, this proficiency." (Marx, ibid., pp. 339–40.)

What is specific about early capitalist developments is not the operation of some economic forces in accordance with the regulative principle of "life-calling,"—let alone the mysterious emergence of the latter as a self-sustaining *"ethos"* from the "protestant spirit of capitalism." As a matter of fact, the allegedly demiurgic "spirit of capitalism" was preceded, as far as "life-calling" was concerned, by thousands of years of well established, and often even legally enforced, material practices in different parts of the world, some of which at least must have been known to Weber. Rather, the innovatory contribution of these developments consists in the confinement of the worker's attention to a *fractional* operation, on very sound (even if profoundly dehumanizing) economic grounds which favour the full unfolding of the capitalistic division of labour. For, as Marx points out in continuation of our last quote:

> And yet, the work of such a Hindu weaver is very complicated, compared with that of a manufacturing labourer. An artificer who performs one after another the various fractional operations in the production of a finished article, must at one time change his place, at another his tools. The transition from one operation to another interrupts the flow of his labour, and creates, so to say, gaps in his working-day. These gaps close up so soon as he is tied to one and the same operation all day long; they

vanish in proportion as the changes in his work diminish. (Ibid., pp.340–1.)

7. Ibid., p. 360. And Marx adds here in a footnote: "Dugald Stewart calls manufacturing labourers 'living automatons . . . employed in the details of the work.' "

8. As Marx puts it:

> Primitive accumulation plays in Political Economy about the same part as original sin in theology. Adam bit the apple, and thereupon sin fell on the human race. Its origin is supposed to be explained when it is told as an anecdote about the past. In times long gone by there were two sorts of people; one, the diligent, intelligent and above all *frugal élite*; the other, lazy rascals, spending their substance, and more, in riotous living. . . . Thus it came to pass that the former sort accumulated wealth, and the latter sort finally had nothing to sell except their own skins. . . . Such insipid childishness is every day preached to us in the defence of property. . . . In actual history, it is a notorious fact that *conquest, enslavement, robbery, murder,* in short, *force,* play the greatest part. In the tender annals of political economy, the idyllic reigns from time immemorial. Right and 'labour' were from the beginning of time the sole means of enrichment, the present year of course always excepted. As a matter of fact, the methods of primitive accumulation are anything but idyllic. . . .
>
> The proletariat created by the breaking-up of the bands of feudal retainers and by the *forcible expropriation* of the people from the soil, this 'free' [*vogelfrei,* i.e. 'free as a bird'] proletariat could not possibly be absorbed by the nascent manufactures as fast as it was thrown upon the world. On the other hand, these men, suddenly dragged from their wonted mode of life, could not as suddenly adapt themselves to the discipline of their new condition. They were turned *en masse* into beggars, robbers and vagabonds, partly from inclination, in most cases from stress of circumstances. Hence at the end of the 15th and during the whole of the 16th centuries, throughout Western Europe a bloody legislation against vagabondage. The fathers of the present working-class were chastised for their *enforced transformation* into vagabonds and paupers. Legislation treated them as '*voluntary' criminals,* and assumed that it *depended on their own good will to go on working* under the old conditions which in fact *no longer existed.*

In England this legislation began under Henry VII.

Henry VIII. 1530: Beggars old and unable to work receive a beggar's licence. On the other hand, whipping and imprisonment for sturdy vagabonds. They are to be tied to the cart-tail and whipped until the blood streams from their bodies, then they are to swear on oath to go back to their birthplace or to where they have lived the last three years and to 'put themselves to labour'. *What grim irony!* In 27 Henry VIII. the former statute is repeated, but strengthened with new clauses. For the second arrest for vagabondage the whipping is to be repeated and *half the ear sliced off;* but for the third relapse the offender is to be *executed as a hardened criminal* and enemy of the common weal.

Edward VI.: A statute of the first year of his reign, 1547, ordains that if anyone refuses to work, he shall be condemned as a *slave* to the person who has denounced him as an idler. The master shall feed his slave on bread and water, weak broth and such refuse meat as he thinks fit. He has the right to force him to do any work, no matter how disgusting, with whip and chains. If the slave is absent for a fortnight, he is condemned to *slavery for life* and is to be branded on forehead or back with the letter S; if he runs away thrice, he is to be *executed as a felon*. . . .

Out of the poor fugitives, of whom Thomas More says that they were forced to thieve, '*72,000 great and petty thieves were put to death*,' in the reign of Henry VIII. [Holinshed, *Description of England,* Vol.1, p. 186.] In Elizabeth's time, 'rogues were trussed up apace, and there was not one year commonly wherein *three or four hundred* were not devoured and eaten up by the gallowes' [Strype, *Annals of the Reformation and Establishment of Religion, and Other Various Occurrences in the Church of England during Queen Elizabeth's Reign,* 2nd ed., 1725, Vol. 2]. According to this same Strype, *in Somersetshire alone in one year 40 persons were executed,* 35 robbers burnt in the hand, 37 whipped and 183 discharged as 'incorrigible vagabonds'. Nevertheless, he is of the opinion that this large number of prisoners does not comprise 'even a fifth of the actual criminals, thanks to the negligence of the justices and the foolish compassion of the people', and that the other counties of England were not better off in this respect than Somersetshire, while some were even worse off. (Marx, ibid. pp. 713–4 and 734–6.)

In the last decades of the 17th century, in accordance with capital's standpoint of political economy, the great idol of modern liberalism: John Locke—an absentee landowner in Somersetshire as well as a highly paid Government official—preaches the same "insipid childishness" described by Marx. He insists that the cause of "The growth of the poor . . . can be nothing else but the relaxation of discipline and corruption of manners; virtue and industry being as constant companions on one side as vice and idleness are on the other. The first step, therefore, towards the setting of the poor on work . . . ought to be a restraint of their debauchery by a strict execution of the laws provided against it [by Henry VIII. and Edward VI.]." (Locke, "Memorandum on the Reform of the Poor Law," in H.R. Fox Bourne, *The Life of John Locke,* King, London, 1876, Vol. 2, p. 378.)

Receiving annually the near astronomical remuneration of around £1,500 for his services to Government (as a Commissioner at the Board of Trade: one of his several offices), Locke does not hesitate to praise the prospect of the poor earning "a penny per diem" (Ibid., p. 383), i.e., a sum approximately *1,000 times lower* than his own income from one of his governmental offices, which he takes, of course, as wholly justified. Not surprisingly, therefore, "The value of his estate at death—nearly £20,000, of which £12,000 was in cash—was comparable to that of a well-to-do London merchant." (Neal Wood, *The Politics of Locke's Philosophy,* University of California Press, Berkeley, 1983, p. 26.) Quite an achievement for someone whose principal source of revenue is milking the—admittedly more than willing—state!

Moreover, being a true gentleman, with a very high stake to protect, he also wants to regulate the movements of the poor through the draconian measure of *passes,* proposing:

> That all men begging in maritime counties without passes, that are *maimed* or *above fifty years* of age, and all of *any age* so begging without passes in inland counties nowhere bordering on the sea, shall be sent to the next house of correction, there to be kept at *hard labour* for three years." (Locke, "Memorandum on the Reform of the Poor Law," op.cit., p. 380.)

And while the brutal laws of Henry VIII. just referred to wanted to slice off only *"half* the ear" of the *second* offenders, our great liberal philosopher and state official—one of the leading figures of early English Enlightenment—suggests an improvement on such laws by solemnly recommending the loss of *both* ears, to be administered already to *first* offenders. These are his words:

> That whoever shall counterfeit a pass shall *lose his ears* for the forgery the *first time* that he is found guilty thereof, and the second time that he shall be transported to the *plantations* [to become a slave there], as in case of *felony*." (Ibid.)

At the same time, in his "Memorandum on the Reform of the Poor Law" Locke also proposes the institution of workhouses for the children of the poor from a very early age, arguing that

> The children of labouring people are an ordinary burden to the parish, and are usually maintained in idleness, so that their labour also is generally lost to the public till they are *twelve or fourteen* years old.
>
> The most effectual remedy for this that we are able to conceive, and which we therefore humbly propose, is, that, in the fore-mentioned new law to be enacted, it be further provided that *working schools* be set up in every parish, to which the children of all such as demand relief of the parish, *above three and under fourteen years of age* . . . shall be *obliged* to come. (Ibid., p. 383.)

Locke's chief concern is how to combine severe work discipline and religious indoctrination with the maximum of economy. He follows Edward VI.'s guidance on how the slave-master "shall feed his slave on bread and water, weak broth and such refuse meat as he thinks fit," with one significant difference, in that he removes even "refuse meat" from his royal example's miserly list:

> If therefore care be taken that they [the children] have each of them *belly-full of bread* daily at school, they will be in no danger of famishing, but, on the contrary, they will be healthier and stronger than those who are bred otherwise. Nor will this practice cost the overseers any trouble; for a baker may be agreed with to furnish and bring into the school-

> house every day the allowance of bread necessary for all the scholars that are there. And to this may be also added, without any trouble, *in cold weather,* if it be thought needful, *a little warm water-gruel;* for the same fire that warms the room may be made use of to boil a pot of it.
>
> Another advantage also of bringing children thus to a working school is that by this means they may be *obliged to come constantly to church* every Sunday, along with their schoolmasters or dames, whereby they may be brought into some sense of religion; whereas ordinarily now, in their idle and loose way of breeding up, they are as utter strangers both to *religion and morality* as they are to *industry.* (Ibid., pp. 384–5.)

Thus, the measures that had to be applied to the "labouring poor" were radically different from those which the "men of enlightenment" considered suitable for themselves. In the end it all boiled down to naked power relations, enforced with utmost brutality and violence in the course of early capitalist development, irrespective of how they were later rationalized in the "tender annals of political economy."

Naturally, the idea that the growth of the poor and unemployed has its cause in the "relaxation of discipline and corruption of manners," and that people's inability to find work is to be attributed to the absence of "their own good will," can never be abandoned by the representatives of capital. The British Tory Minister of Employment a few years ago advised more than three million unemployed to get on their bikes (which they could not afford to buy) and look for a job (i.e., to look for "the old conditions that no longer existed"). This advice was later followed by government regulations implementing savage cuts in Social Security benefits and in State Pension funds. And Margaret Thatcher's Conservative Government introduced yet another measure of which even John Locke (though perhaps not Henry VIII.) would have been proud. The measure in question was designed to compel the unemployed young to *move on* in search of (non-existent) work-opportunities after *two weeks* of staying in one place on the "Costa del Dole." The idea that one should also "slice off the ears" of first offenders has not yet been revived, as far as I know.

9. One of the most important aspects of this problem is that generalized commodity production ruthlessly exploits even the natural propensities of human existence, in that with the development of the capitalist workshop:

> Not only have we here an increase in the productive power of the individual, by means of co-operation, but the creation of a new power, namely, the collective power of masses. Apart from the new power that arises from the fusion of many forces into one single force, mere social contact begets in most industries an *emulation and a stimulation of animal spirits* that heighten the efficiency of each individual workman. Hence it is that a dozen persons working together will, in their collective working-day of 144 hours, produce far more than twelve isolated men each working 12 hours, or than one man who works twelve days in succession. The reason of this is that man is, if not as Aristotle contends, a political, at all events a *social animal.* (Marx, ibid., p. 326.)

What we are concerned with here is not simply a specific social relationship, but one which simultaneously also manifests the individual's inherent connection with the human species. For:

> . . . the special productive power of the combined working-day is, under all circumstances, the social productive power of labour, or the productive power of social labour. This power is due to co-operation itself. When the labourer co-operates systematically with others, he strips off the *fetters of his individuality,* and develops the *capabilities of his species.* (Ibid., p. 329.)

However, since the whole process must be subordinated under capitalism to the imperatives of self-expanding exchange-value, the positive achievements of developing the productive powers of the species are inevitably contradicted by the inhuman impact of the adopted work practices on the individual producers. For "constant labour of one *uniform* kind *disturbs* the intensity and flow of *man's animal spirits,* which find *recreation and delight* in mere *change of activity.*" (Ibid., p. 341.)

Further: the intellectual faculties of the workers are equally badly affected as a result of the capitalistic division of labour, involving not simply technical "specialization," but both the systematic *divorce* of their powers of control from the labourers, and the lining up of these powers *against* them. To quote Marx:

The *knowledge*, the *judgement*, and the *will*, which, though in ever so small a degree, are practised by the independent peasant or handicraftsman, in the same way as the savage makes the whole art of war consist in the exercise of his personal cunning—these faculties are now required only for the workshop as a whole. *Intelligence* in production *expands in one direction*, because it *vanishes in many others*. What is lost by the detail labourers, is concentrated in the capital that employs them. It is a result of the division of labour in manufactures, that the labourer is brought face to face with the *intellectual potencies* of the material process of production, as the *property of another* and as a *ruling power*. This *separation* begins in simple co-operation, where the *capitalist* represents to the single workman, the *oneness and the will* of the *associated labour*. It is developed in manufacture which cuts down the labourer into a detail labourer. It is completed in modern industry, which makes *science* a productive force distinct from labour and presses it into the *service of capital*. ('The *man of knowledge* and the *productive labourer* come to be widely *divided* from each other, and *knowledge*, instead of remaining the handmaid of labour in the hand of the labourer to increase his productive powers . . . has almost everywhere arrayed itself *against labour* . . . systematically deluding and leading them [the labourers] astray in order to render their muscular powers entirely mechanical and *obedient*.' (W. Thompson, *An Inquiry into the Principles of the Distribution of Wealth*, London, 1824, p. 274.)

In manufacture, in order to make the collective labourer, and through him *capital, rich in social productive power*, each *labourer* must be made *poor in individual productive powers*. '*Ignorance* is the mother of industry as well as of superstition. *Reflection* and fancy are subject to err; but *habit* of moving the hand or the foot is independent of either. Manufactures, accordingly, prosper most where the *mind is least consulted*, and where the *workshop* may be considered as an *engine, the parts of which are men*.' (Adam Ferguson, *An Essay on the History of Civil Society*, Edinburgh, 1767, p. 280.) As a matter of fact, some few manufacturers in the middle of the 18th century preferred, for certain operations that were *trade secrets*, to employ *half-idiotic* persons. (J.D. Tuckett, *A History of the Past and Present State of the Labouring Population*, London, 1846. Marx, ibid., pp. 361–2.)

Thus, the alienating requirements of the capitalistic production process prevail even against spontaneous natural inclination, nullifying the objective possibilities of the many-sided development of the human faculties, in the interest of maintaining the stranglehold of capital's mode of control over society as a whole.

10. Tragtenberg rightly stresses the liberal/social democratic ancestry of authoritarian corporatism, all the way down to Nazism: "A teoria da empresa-instituiçâo desenvolveu-se na Alemanha, sob Weimar, com Rathenau e Neumann, sendo depois adotada pelo nazismo, che reconheçeu a importância politico-social da empresa." (Mauricio Tragtenberg, *Administraçâo, Poder e Ideologia,* Editora Moraes, Sâo Paulo, 1980, pp. 13–14.)

    We should also recall here the complete consonance of Max Weber's Bonapartist views on "democracy" and its "Leader" with those of General Ludendorff, one of Hitler's earliest champions.

    For an insightful analysis of the relationship between big business and dictatorial developments in Brazil see Octavio Ianni, *A Ditadura do Grande Capital,* Civilizaçâo Brasileira, Rio de Janeiro, 1981.

11. Lukács, *History and Class Consciousness*, Merlin Press, London, 1971, p. 140.
12. "Solger fängt mit einer *unversöhnten Dualismus* an, obwohl seine ausdrückliche Bestimmung der Philosophie ist, nicht in einem Dualismus befangen zu sein." Hegel, *Sämmtliche Werke,* Jub. Ausgabe, Vol. 20, p. 169.
13. Hegel, *Logic: Encyclopaedia of the Philosophical Sciences,* Part I., Clarendon Press, Oxford, 1975, p. 291.
14. Ibid.
15. Hegel, *Philosophy of Mind,* Clarendon Press, Oxford, 1971, p. 62.
16. Ibid., p. 64.
17. Marx, *Economic and Philosophic Manuscripts of 1844,* Lawrence & Wishart, London, 1959, p. 149. Marx's emphases.
18. Ibid., pp. 159–62. Marx's emphases.
19. Ibid., p. 150.
20. Ibid., p. 163.
21. Kant, "Theory and Practice: Concerning the Common Saying: This May Be True in Theory but Does Not Apply to Practice," in Carl J. Friedrich (ed.), *Immanuel Kant's Moral and Political Writings,* Random House, New York, 1949, p. 416.

22. Ibid., pp. 417–18.
23. Adam Smith, *Lectures on Justice, Police, Revenue, and Arms,* in Herbert W. Schneider (ed.), *Adam Smith's Moral and Political Philosophy,* Hafner Publishing Company, New York, 1948, p. 291.
24. Ibid., p. 321.
25. Ibid., p. 320.
26. Ibid., p. 319.
27. Adam Smith, *The Theory of Moral Sentiments,* in H.W. Schneider (ed.), op.cit., p.102.
28. Ibid., p. 225. This is all the more remarkable since Smith's proposition with regard to the constitution of moral values on the basis of "our sentiments of moral approbation and disapprobation" is advanced in direct contrast to "our sentiments concerning beauty of every kind." For immediately before the lines quoted above, Smith insists that: "The principles of the imagination, upon which our *sense of beauty* depends, are of a very nice and delicate nature, and *may easily be altered by habit and education.*"
29. A Kantian formula which asserts with categorical moral absoluteness that "since you ought to do it, you can," no matter how completely incapacitating the conditions which you must encounter in the empirical world.
30. Marx, *Economic and Philosophic Manuscripts of 1844*, p. 121.
31. An interesting example is Merleau-Ponty. For while he rightly castigates the dualism of Sartre's philosophy (in *Les aventures de la dialectique,* 1955), he can only oppose to it a watered-down version of the Hegelian "subject-object identity." At the same time Merleau-Ponty also remains wedded to the vacuous postulate of abstract "universalism." See in this respect his sharp exchange with Sartre as recorded in their "Intervention à un Colloque organisé par la *Société Européenne de Culture* à Venise," 25-31 March 1956, *Comprendre,* September 1956.
32. Lukács, *History and Class Consciousness,* p. 89.
33. Marx, *The Poverty of Philosophy, Collected Works*, Vol. 6, Lawrence and Wishart, London, 1975, p. 127.
34. Marx, *Capital,* Vol. 1, pp. 364–5.
35. Marx, *Economic and Philosophic Manuscripts of 1844*, p. 129.
36. Marx, *The Poverty of Philosophy,* op.cit., pp. 126–7.
37. Adam Ferguson. *An Essay on the History of Civil Society,* edited, with an introduction, by Duncan Forbes, University Press, Edinburgh, 1966, pp. 181–183.

38. Ibid., p. 180.

    Due to the blindness which he shares with the whole tradition of classical political economy and philosophy as regards the real problem of distribution, even Ferguson's sharp diagnosis of what he himself considers to be the necessary defects of the capitalist system is in the end watered down. Thus, in a reconciliatory gesture he curiously mixes up genuine insight with an uncritical embellishment of the ruling order by suggesting that "if many parts in the practice of every art, and in the detail of every department, require no abilities, or actually tend to contract and to limit the views of the mind, there are others which lead to general reflections, and to enlargement of thought. Even in manufacture, the genius of the master, perhaps, is cultivated, while that of the inferior workman lies waste. The statesman may have a wide comprehension of human affairs, while the tools he employs are ignorant of the system in which they are combined." Ibid., p. 183.

39. See in particular his *Philosophy of Right*, Clarendon Press, Oxford, 1942, pp. 122–34.
40. Ibid., p. 130.
41. Ibid.
42. Hegel resorts to a similar device in *The Philosophy of History* (p. 96) when it suits his prejudices. Describing the "African character" he asserts that "the Negroes indulge that perfect contempt for humanity, which in its bearing on Morality and Justice is the fundamental characteristic of the race," contrasting the behaviour of the "African race" with that of the bearers of "the principle of the North"—i.e., the colonizing Europeans—by a positive reference to the *instinctually* correct behaviour "among us." Since, however, such an argument is in no way consonant with the spirit of his own philosophy, he has to add to this sentence a curious afterthought: *"if we can speak of instinct at all as appertaining to man."* But if indeed within the confines of idealist philosophy we cannot speak of instinct at all as appertaining to man, what could be the point of using it the way Hegel does—just as he uses a fictitious natural law which is supposed to have made men "unequal by nature"—other than having it both ways, betraying through such eagerness and concomitant philosophical inconsistency his ideological interests?
43. Hegel, *The Philosophy of Right,* p. 130.
44. Marx, *The Poverty of Philosophy, Collected Works*, Vol. 6, p. 134.

CHAPTER SEVEN

The Postulates of "Unity" and "Universality"

7.1 The Incorrigible Circularity and Ultimate Failure of Individualistic Mediation

Since the standpoint of isolated individuality is an untranscendable methodological characteristic of the whole tradition, the philosophically inescapable attempt to go beyond its mere particularity is a recurrent preoccupation, bringing its own dilemmas.

On the one hand, facing up to the problem itself is unavoidable because the universalistic aspirations of philosophy cannot be openly abandoned while consciously remaining within its framework and subscribing to its traditional requirements. On the contrary, they must be constantly reaffirmed with all the greater insistence the more problematical is the claim to universality of the particular philosophies concerned, in view of their incorrigibly individualistic grounding. And on the other hand, precisely because the standpoint of isolated individuality circumscribes the horizon of the philosophies in question, the attempt to go beyond mere particularity within its structural constraints produces not only an inherently *dualistic* conceptual framework, as we have seen in chapter 6, but also one in which the dimension of "unity and universality" is only *assumed*, *postulated* or *hypostatized*, but never really established.

Thus, in such problematical appeals to "unity" and "universality," we are offered aprioristic "guarantees" as a way out of the dilemmas of the self-oriented ego and its (bourgeois) class-equivalent, instead of viable solutions to the difficulty of relating the isolated individual to a tenable social setting. It is enough to recall in this respect the line of development that goes from Descartes' "ontological argument" to Leibniz's "absolute monad," not to forget Spengler's totally mystifying notion of "monads without windows." Likewise, we may refer here to a variety of "universalizing" strategies in the post-Cartesian philosophical domain, from Kant's attempt to establish the validity of the "categorical imperative" of his *Individualethik* with reference to the "intelligible world" all the way down to what Husserl opaquely calls "the systematic unfolding of the all-embracing A priori innate in the essence of a transcendental subjectivity . . . the universal logos of all conceivable being."[1] All such philosophical strategies can do no more than underline the impossibility of squeezing the desired "unity" and "universality" out of the fragmented multiplicity of isolated individualities.

Hegel is, of course, thoroughly dissatisfied with the Leibnizian solution of the "absolute monad." However, when he spells out the reasons for his critical rejection of Leibniz's answer, his own corrective can only consist in directly linking the assumed "principle of intro-Reflection or individuation" and the aprioristrically stipulated "*absolute unity* of form and content" to a definition of "Reflection as *self-relating negativity*" and "*self-repulsion*" out of which the "positivity" of "positing and creating"[2] is mysteriously derived.

Husserl confesses that "the problem of all-embracing genesis" which he intends to unravel "presents *so many enigmas*."[3] And no wonder. For he merely *decrees* that "with the systematic progress of transcendental-phenomenological explication of the apodictic ego, the transcendental sense of the world must also become disclosed to us."[4] Just as in the other representative figures of this philosophical tradition, Husserl's solution, too, is derailed because of his failure to produce an adequate concept of *mediation*. He can only see mediation in terms of the "*I, the mediator*"[5] through which the social world "receives existential sense . . . as something appresented *analogically*."[6]

Understandably, therefore, the "intermonadic" unity and universality postulated by Husserl is nothing more than an ever more desocialized twentieth century version of the Hegelian "intro-reflection" which in Husserl assumes the form of absolutized inwardness. According to him:

> The path leading to a knowledge absolutely grounded in the highest sense, or (this being the same thing) a philosophical knowledge, is necessarily the path of *universal self-knowledge*—first of all *monadic*, and then *intermonadic*. We can say also that a radical and universal continuation of Cartesian meditations, or (equivalently) a *universal self-cognition*, is philosophy itself and encompasses all *self-accountable science*. The Delphic motto, 'Know thyself!' has gained a new signification. Positive science is a science *lost in the world*. I must *lose the world* by *'epoché'*, in order to regain it by a *universal self-examination*. 'Noli foras ire', says Augustine, 'in te redi, in interiore homine habitat veritas.' ('Do not wish to go out; *go back into yourself*. Truth dwells in the *inner man*.')[7]

And that is how the quest for the "systematic unfolding of the universal logos of all conceivable being" and for the "absolute grounding" of "universal concrete ontology" and "universal and concrete theory of science" on the foundations of the "*egology* of the primordially *reduced ego*"[8] ends. Just as Hegel suggested, "mediation bends back its end into its beginning,"[9] completing the methodological/ideological circle from which there can be no escape.

At the same time, this is how the quest for the "mastery of man over nature" also ends, defeated by the inherently antagonistic determinations which must prevail in capitalist society with regard to the "mastery of men over men." This way of ending the once confidently proclaimed positive "mastery of man over nature" is due to the circumstance that a non-antagonistic and constructive mastery of human beings over the conditions of their social existence is the key also to an adequate—historically sustainable rather than destructive—mastery of their social metabolic reproductive processes in relation to nature. If that vital condition is violated, due to the antagonistic inner determinations of the prevailing social order, the philosophical circle—or "circle of circles" acknowledged by Hegel—becomes ever tighter, rendering impossible any effort to overcome its narrowing horizon and the limitations associated with it.

Naturally, the problems are greatly intensifid by the absence of the concept of proper social mediation in the dominant philosophical discourse. It is no help in this respect to rely on the quasi-mythical notion of "intermonadic inter-subjectivity" in place of real mediation. For it is impossible to squeeze out of "inter-monadic subjectivity" the required—and required in the sense of being historically viable and long term sustainable—social mediation.

THE "MANY ENIGMAS" REFERRED TO by Husserl also present themselves as a great puzzle directly addressed to the self-oriented ego. For, in his words, "I, the mediator, do not understand how I shall ever attain others and myself as 'one among others', since all other men are 'parenthesized' . . . and I recognize only reluctantly that, when I 'parenthesize' myself qua man and qua human person, I myself am nevertheless to be retained qua ego."[10] Thus, the journey proposed by Husserl can only be an "inward" journey, envisaging the radical "loss of the world" as the necessary condition of its problematical success.

No doubt, the *isolated "mediator"* of the advocated "egology of the primordially reduced ego" can offer a monadic self-affirmation to those who are concerned with the possibility of a journey to the coreless "core"—like Peer Gynt's paradigmatic onion—of the socially "parenthesized inner man." The trouble is, though, that the "universality" which one can derive from the methodological imperatives of such journey can never amount to more than the *purely exhortatory* projection of unrealizable *abstract postulates*.

Peer Gynt himself must realize, toward the end of Ibsen's dramatic poem, that a journey without appropriate human concerns and relationships—in the words of the great Norwegian poet and dramatist: a journey which would be meaningful and justifiable only if its guiding principle veritably "distinguished humans from hill trolls" who are said to be satisfied with the crudely self-oriented motto: "Troll, *to thyself be enough!*"[11] —is most reprehensible. Ibsen makes it clear on the same page that by "hill troll" he means the egoist. Indeed, at an earlier stage of his journey Peer Gynt himself proudly declares that his *selfishly negative definition* of his self as living "for-and-within-one's-self-existence"[12]—for which he must be blamed in the final account as having *"utterly failed in his pur-*

pose in life"[13]—was his deliberate choice. As he boastfully puts it at that earlier stage in his life:

> What ought a man to be?
> Well, my short answer is 'Himself' . . .
> Guarding himself and his possessions,
> a thing he cannot do when burdened
> with someone else's weal and woe.[14]

However, reflecting in the final act on the sense, if any, of such an existence, Peer Gynt compares the particular phases of his own life-journey, with self-wounding irony, to the coreless layers of an onion held in his hand and feverishly peeled in an attempt to reach its hoped for solid centre, exclaiming when he fails to find it:

> What an incredible number of layers!
> Don't we get to the heart of it soon?
>
> [He pulls the whole onion to pieces.]
>
> No, I'm damned if we do. Right down to the centre
> there's nothing but layers—smaller and smaller . . . [15]

And when at the very end of Ibsen's drama Peer Gynt is fatefully confronted by the implications and the consequences of such a journey, as having been wastefully pursued by a coreless person, only Solveig's devoted love can save him from the fate of being melted down into button fragments by *The Button Moulder*, sent to call him to account by the mysterious *Master*. Peer Gynt thus cries out, desperately looking for confirmation of a meaningful human self-identity with a solid core, when facing Solveig who is the purest embodiment of humanly valid devotion and love:

> Where has Peer Gynt been since last we met?
> Where? Since he sprang from the mind of God?
> Can you tell me that? If you cannot tell,

I must go down to the shadowy land.
Where was I Myself—complete and whole?
Where? With God's seal upon my brow?

And this is Solveig's deeply moving and redeeming, although by Peer Gynt's past life quite undeserved, answer:

In my faith, in my hope, and in my love.[16]

In this way, when at the very end of this great work the foreboding words of *The Button Moulder* resound, leaving even then still unresolved the stark alternative of Peer Gynt's doom or escape, the last words of Ibsen's dramatic poem we hear are those which are sung with generous devotion by Solveig. First we hear the ominous words of the *Master*'s messenger:

THE BUTTON MOULDER'S VOICE [behind the hut]

Peer, we shall meet at the last cross-roads,
and then we shall see if . . . I'll say no more.

But they are countered by the serenely caring voice of Solveig, hinting in this way by Ibsen at the possibility of a very different fate for Peer Gynt:

SOLVEIG [singing more loudly in the sunshine]

I will cradle you, I will guard you;
sleep and dream, dearest son of mine.[17]

Thus, thanks to Solveig—whose innermost human core is deeply loving care—in the final words of Ibsen's play the prospect of escaping his somber fate appears for Peer Gynt. In this unexpected way a redeeming fate is opened up to him, in the same way as at the end of *Faust* to Goethe's hero, when divine intervention rescues him—and only divine intervention can at that point rescue him—from the clutches of Mephistopheles, after Faust loses his wager with the devil.

NATURALLY, THIS KIND OF POETIC LIBERTY and striking intervention—often even a complete reversal of what one was induced to expect at an earlier stage of the literary plot's unfolding: in Peer Gynt's final act the potential redemption of an unredeemably self-oriented "monadic" individual—is wholly appropriate to creative literature. For in that domain only the fully elaborated overall complexity of the artistically created and appropriately completed world—in its unique way of metaphorically embodying and transmuting the significant characteristics of the historically specific actual world from the soil of which the great work of art arises—can convey the writer's intended message. Accordingly, the kind of artistic procedure which we encounter in literature, fit for the purpose of enabling the writer to be the sovereign creator of an artistically coherent and in its own way representative world, is entirely in keeping with the innermost nature of meaningfully and organically transfigured—that is: aesthetic/non-discursive—discourse. But it has no legitimacy at all in philosophy where the thinker must formulate his or her forceful discursive claims and define the conditions under which the philosophical conception in question, advocated on the ground of the required and clearly ascertainable evidence, is supposed to assert its validity, matching the advanced claims in their properly sustainable terms of reference.

Husserl's "community of monads"[18] is an extremely problematic idea in this respect. It is Husserl's purely notional attempt to extricate himself from the untenable constraints of his *solipsistic overall conception*. But no fundamentally overturning "communal redemption" is feasible here. Husserl's attempt cannot succeed because by its very nature the proclaimed communality is no more than a merely assumed *generic decree* regarding the character of the monads. We are simply expected to take it for self-evident that "I cannot conceive a plurality of monads otherwise than as explicitly or implicitly in communion. . . . It is essentially necessary that the togetherness of monads, their mere co-existence, be a temporal co-existence and then also an existence temporalized in the form: 'real' temporality."[19] Significantly, the word "real," as set by Husserl in inverted commas at the end of this paragraph, betrays the remaining solipsism which cannot be overcome by the purely stipulating decree of "community of monads."

The way Husserl proceeds in his analysis intended to provide a solid methodological foundation to philosophy does not and cannot improve the situation. For he insists, again with categorical absoluteness, that "In respect of order, the intrinsically first of the philosophical disciplines would be *'solipsistically' reduced 'egology,'* the egology of the primordially reduced ego. Then only would come intersubjective phenomenology, which is founded on that discipline."[20] And thus in no time at all in Husserl's methodological reflections we are back to an attempt to give a monadological foundation even to the most tangible concerns of value and history. This is how Husserl argues his case:

> The intrinsically first being, the being that precedes and bears every worldly Objectivity, is transcendental intersubjectivity: the universe of monads, which effects its communion in various forms. But within the de facto monadic sphere and (as an ideal possibility) within every conceivable monadic sphere, occur *all the problems of accidental factualness, of death, of fate,* of the possibility of *'genuine' human life* demanded as 'meaningful' in a particular sense—among them, therefore, the problem of 'meaning' of history—, and all the further and still higher problems. We can say that they are the *ethico-religious* problems, but stated in the realm where everything that can have a possible sense for us must be stated.[21]

Ironically, however, the moment of truth arrives for Husserl when he genuinely tries to confront, and perhaps even to combat, the dreadful implications of the unfolding world-wide social and historical crisis—erupted on the international political stage from the Nazi menace and from the associated obvious barbarism and devastation—which he conceptualizes as *Philosophy and the Crisis of European Man.* The social and human challenge directly arising from such developments would call for a forceful social intervention that could match—and hopefully also to counter and through its effective mobilizing force also overcome—the destructive power of the adversary. But a philosophy based on the ultimate methodological foundations of solipsistic monadology cannot be of any help in that respect, given the way in which the vital relationship between *theory and practice* is defined in it.

In this way Husserl's discourse, despite the author's undoubted good intentions of addressing himself to the manifestations of the grave historical crisis of his time, tends to be hopelessly trapped in an abstract philosophical circle from which there seems to be no escape. Accordingly, we are told by him that "The *theoretical attitude,* even though it too is a professional attitude, is *thoroughly unpractical.* Thus it is based on a deliberate *epoché* from *all practical interests,* and consequently even those of a higher level, that serve natural needs within the framework of a life's occupation governed by such practical interests."[22]

Not surprisingly, therefore, when Husserl tries to "open the philosophical bracket," after his "deliberate *epoché* from *all practical interests,*" his discourse is even more problematical than when the bracket was deliberately closed by him. For under the circumstances when Husserl's lecture quoted here is delivered in Prague in May 1935, the coming *global conflagration* is already clearly visible on the horizon, with Hitler's aggressive revanchism in league with Mussolini's Fascism and with the Japanese extreme right's destructive design on its own half of the world. Together they foreshadow an explosion which would inevitably involve the whole of humankind, and thus they underline that there never has been before a more justifiable need to get deeply involved in the most urgent practical interest of forcefully moving against the threatening catastrophe. Sadly, however, the German philosopher's diagnosis is a million miles distant from the real situation and from the solution one should envisage to the all too evident social antagonisms and to the corresponding destructive trends of actual historical development.

Given his inward-oriented philosophical stance, Husserl remains hopelessly trapped within the most dubious conceptual framework of allegedly exemplary "European man" and of its totally anachronistic—if not much worse—valuational postulates, claimed by Husserl to apply with unchallengeable validity to the whole of mankind. And this line of self-disarming approach in an actual historical situation of inexorably growing danger, explicitly acknowledged by Husserl himself as a predicament of great crisis, is put forward by him in the name of a "free and universal" theoretical discourse. As Husserl puts it in his Prague lecture on *Philosophy and the Crisis of European Man:* "Philosophy has the role of a free and universal theoretical disposition that embraces at once all ideals and the one overall ideal – in short, the universe of all norms. Philosophy has constantly to exercise through *European man* its role of *leadership for the whole of mankind*."[23]

Thus, when the need for a combative practical intervention against the forces of barbarism, in the interest of human survival, is becoming ever more pressing, Husserl can offer only well-intentioned and in its aspirations noble but utterly resounding rhetorics. Such abstract philosophical rhetorics, instead of helping to mobilise those who are willing to defend the values of human advancement, actually obfuscates the real nature of the threat, already tangible as it manifests itself in the aggressive and destructive actions by that time not only prepared but well in the course of being pursued on a visibly growing scale by the Nazi adversary. These are Husserl's words:

> The crisis of European existence can end in only one of two ways: in the ruin of a Europe alienated from its rational sense of life, fallen into a barbarian hatred of spirit; or in the rebirth of Europe from the spirit of philosophy, through a *heroism of reason* that will definitely overcome naturalism. Europe's greatest danger is weariness. Let us as 'good Europeans' do battle with this danger of dangers with the sort of courage that does not shirk even the endless battle. If we do, then from the annihilating conflagration of disbelief, from the fiery torrent of despair regarding the West's mission to humanity, from the ashes of the great weariness, the phoenix of a new inner life of the spirit will arise as the underpinning of a great and distant human future, for the spirit alone is immortal.[24]

In reality "European man"—with its ferocious class-determined imperialist ambitions and irreconcilable antagonisms – is the *problem* and not the *solution*. In the face of the grave contradictions of capital's actually existing social order the abstract appeal to an idealized philosophy—which projects "the West's mission to humanity," in the spirit of an "intermonadic inter-subjectivity" erected on the ultimate foundations of "the egology of the primordially reduced ego" and its "absolutized inwardness"—cannot possibly offer a way of overcoming the crisis acknowledged by Husserl himself. The categories in which he is trying to characterize it are woefully inadequate to grasping the social gravity of the unfolding developments. Indeed, his characterization deliberately *abstracts* from the *historically determinate practical social dimension* of the dangers, in the hope of providing thereby an absolute philosophical foundation—conceived in the problematical spirit of "intermonadic intersubjectivity"—both to his own diagnosis and to the envisaged solution.

The social sphere is thus compressed into the confines intelligible in terms of the vision of *"I the mediator"*: a self-oriented subject quite incapable of measuring up to the dramatic historic task. Even at the very end of Husserl's reasoning we are only presented with the elusive notion of "a new inner life of the spirit," without any explanation as to why and how the presumed (but by no means philosophically demonstrated) original "inner life of the spirit" of allegedly exemplary "European man" has been lost and in what way it could be reconstituted with lasting validity and effectiveness, so as to fulfil "the West's mission to humanity."

THUS, EVERYTHING REMAINS rather mysteriously enveloped in the most abstract determinations of utterly powerless "ought-to-be," unable to go beyond the level of mere postulates. Although Husserl exemplifies this methodological characteristic in an extremely pronounced form, it is by no means confined to his philosophy. He shares it with the long philosophical tradition to which he belongs. For the socially vital question of *mediation* is—and must always remain—extremely problematical within the historical confines of capital's social order.

This is primarily due to the objective dominance of the capital system's perversely ahistorical and circularly self-serving, as well as necessarily alienating, *second order mediations*,[25] in place of the fundamental *first order mediations* of social metabolic reproduction as such. They are uncritically assumed and rationalized by the thinkers who conceptualize the world from the vantage point of capital's established economic and social order.

Accordingly, the intractable nature of the problem whereby the individuals are unceremoniously subsumed under *antagonistic class determinations* must remain beyond the conceptual horizon of the thinkers concerned. This circumstance inevitably vitiates their concept of mediation in an incurably individualistic way. For they have to avoid like plague the acknowledgement of class antagonisms which prevail in the established social order, since they conceptualize that order from capital's unremediable vantage point. Instead of recognizing their real nature, they reduce the untranscendable social antagonisms—which precisely as structurally untranscendable social antagonisms cannot be mediated—into aggregative individual vicissitudes and conflicts, so as to make them amenable to be dealt with through individualistic mediation and balancing. And in this respect it is of secondary importance whether the projected solution of mediation was supposed to be accomplished through *"I the mediator"* or through any number of its soulmates. What matters is that in this way the thinkers in question are compelled to directly transfigure their advocated method of individualistic mediation into a pseudo-universalistic postulate of some kind.

This is why even in the greatest of the bourgeois conceptions of world history—in the Hegelian philosophy—mediation must "bend back its end into its beginning,"[26] thereby not only completing "the circle of circles,"[27] but at the same time also "transcending mediation"[28] itself as such in a speculative metaphysical way, while leaving the (from the very beginning assumed) system of historically untenable capitalist second order mediations absolutely intact.

7.2 "The Process of the Genus with the Individual": The Reconciliatory Function of Anthropological Models

As we have seen in the last section, Husserl wishfully postulated the solution of actually existing capitalist society's perilously aggravating problems - exploding in his time in Nazi barbarism—through the *"heroism of reason."* This high-sounding projection of the advocated way out from the very real historical crisis in his Prague lecture was, if anything, even more illusory than Hegel's appeal to the totally unsubstantiated idea of solving the dilemmas which he indicated in his *Philosophy of History*—with reference to the otherwise by him uncritically idealized modern phase of historical development—through the agency of *"future history,"* after peremptorily asserting that we have already reached in the "rational actuality" of the present, in full adequacy to the unfolding development of the World Spirit, *"the end of history."*

These unreal solutions are no marginal inconsistencies or defects which could be rectified through critical reasoning. On the contrary, they are the irreplaceable central constituents of a philosophical horizon in which they have the function of filling in the structurally insurmountable gaps inherent in the social conception of the respective thinkers. The ideologically most telling practical presuppositions of the rationally acceptable social order assumed by the philosophers in question, in tune with their individualistic stance, induce them to avoid, bypass, or characteristically transfigure the fundamental social antagonisms of their age. This is due to the profound and structurally dominant vested interests inseparable from their own standpoint, corresponding to the uncriticizable vantage point of capital which happens to be more or less consciously internalized and ideologically rationalized by them.

In this sense the individualistic articulation of the key tenets of a historical conception is not a corrigible position. In the Hegelian philosophy it arises from the great German philosopher's perception of social conflict in terms of the unalterable givenness of apologetically usable "aggregative individualities." Inevitably, this has far-reaching consequences for the philosopher's overall view.

To be sure, the social world is constituted by separate individuals. But they are always an integral part of a determinate social setting which confers upon their behaviour some well definable orienting constraints, in accordance with the objective determinations of the given social structure itself. If the philosopher abstracts from such objective structural determinations and presents, instead, the individuals as abstractly self-defining entities, or as speculatively devised "genus-individuals" (not to mention their transformation into Husserlian monads), in that case he bars before himself the road to finding a plausible historical explanation to future developments and to the resolution of some major social dilemmas whose challenging nature he acknowledges. This is why in Husserl's case, given his hopelessly individualistic stance, as we have seen above, the pure rhetorics of "the heroism of reason" is called upon to bring about the fundamental change genuinely desired by him. His concept of the "heroism of reason" is postulated as mysteriously suitable to overcome "the crisis of European existence" and the menacing "barbarism of spirit." This is an utterly fragile philosophical projection, introduced by Husserl in place of the required historical analysis of the clearly identifiable destructive forces at work in the given historical situation of tangibly real Nazi barbarism, rather than the vague and abstract "barbarism of Spirit," and completely failing to identify the necessary social forces which could overcome them on a lasting basis. For such forces could not conceivably be derived from the solipsistic "intermonadic subjectivity."

As regards Hegel's position, the postulate of "future history" is at best the evasion of this grave problem. For it is not enough to admit that within the framework of the—by Hegel as a rule greatly idealized—modern state "agitation and unrest are perpetrated," leading to "collision,"[29] if the underlying objective determinations are misdiagnosed as due to the improper "disposition" of the *"individual will"* toward the state. For in that case the immediately added proviso—personifying history in the future tense, so that it should wishfully stipulate the untroubled way of overcoming the identified contradiction by saying that "this collision, this nodus, this problem is that with which history is now occupied, and whose solution it has to work out in the future"[30]—in actuality amounts to absolutely nothing. This is because the philosophically eternalizable representation of the nature of social and political conflict as directly emanating from the behaviour of "aggregative individualities" is itself false, fully in tune with capital's self-interested and self-idealizing vantage point. It is this tendentiously self-idealizing bourgeois conception of the "individual will," said to be corrigible with regard to its now still problematical "disposition," which inevitably carries with it the gratuitous projection of the conveniently problem-solving agency of "future history" as the totally unfounded "ought-to-be."

This approach characteristically prevails in the Hegelian conception without acknowledging in the slightest the antagonistic and ultimately explosive character of the hierarchically ordered and accordingly irreconcilable *class basis* of the historically dominant social conflicts. For the myth of the "rational actuality" of the established social order cannot be disturbed by the thought of the hierarchically ordained and structurally irreconcilable objective antagonisms. By contrast, aggregative individualities may be amenable to corrective intervention, targeting their temporarily defective disposition in relation to the unquestionable "rationality" of the modern state. This is how the circularity of the definition of the "individual will" and its *required* (as well as truly *appropriate)* disposition toward the idealized state obligingly matches the ultimate circularity of the Hegelian philosophy according to which *"what is rational is actual and what is actual is rational."*[31]

No one should have any illusions about the socially reconciliatory character of this heavily ought-burdened approach, despite Hegel's protestations against the presence of "ought-to-be" in his own philosophy. For while he insists that his "science of the state," depicting the state as "inherently rational," is intended by him to be "poles apart from an attempt to construct a state as it ought to be," his claimed science nevertheless turns out to be precisely a reconciliatorily idealized "ought" by decreeing that the state equals "the ethical universe."[32] And the consciously pursued reconciliation is rendered even explicit when Hegel adds to such assertion that "To recognize reason as the rose in the cross of the present and thereby to enjoy the present, this is *the rational insight which reconciles us to the actual.*"[33]

As we know only too well, Husserl's "heroism of Reason" did not accomplish what it was expected to do. Nor did Hegel's "future history" resolve the contradictions conceptualized by the great German philosopher as "agitation, unrest and collisions," despite the one hundred and eighty years elapsed since the formulation of his postulate. On the contrary, the irreconcilable antagonisms of our hierarchically structured social order greatly intensified in the intervening period, to the point of acutely threatening today the very survival of humanity. No wishful postulates like the "appropriately disposed individual will"—in its capital-apologetic support for the claimed "ethical universe" of the state—let alone the mysterious "Heroism of Reason" as the saviour of Husserl's "inter-monadic" universe, can extricate humankind from the very real danger of putting an end to history itself.

THE KIND OF TENDENTIOUSLY individualistic conceptualization of the objective antagonisms of the established social order which we have just seen, and the equally tendentious use of organic and anthropological models is closely connected. Their common denominator is the function which they are called upon to fulfil in the overall social and historical conception of the respective thinkers.

The notorious role assigned by Menenius Agrippa to the organic image, according to which the interconnected functions of the human body are supposed to justify the gruesome inequalities dominating the life of the plebeians in the social body, is blatantly obvious in this respect. This totally apologetic view was presented by the Roman Senator to the common people, who were staging their forceful protest on the hill of Monte Sacro, in order to make them willingly accept "their place"—declared to be the right and proper place—in society.

Later the problem of organic analogy and the use of anthropological models had become rather more complicated. This was due to the critical attitude assumed by the progressive philosophical approaches against the earlier dominant notion of *theologically defined providence* in explaining historical change and its religiously sanctified, as well as in a most authoritarian way regulated, institutional setting. Thus Vico's earlier quoted insistence that "the world of civil society has certainly been *made by men*"[34] introduced a radical emancipatory contrast between traditional theology and what he called "the *rational civil theology* of divine providence."[35] He articulated this contrasting approach as a thoroughly secular conception, even if he could not consistently carry through his intended historical design to its logical conclusion. And the characteristic limitations of his historical conception which we have seen earlier, in sections 5.3 and 5.4 above, were due precisely to the uncritical constituent of the organic postulate. The same type of limitations are recognizable in all theories which attempt to reduce the social order—a multifaceted order which is in actuality constituted as an immensely dynamic and historically always changing complex of complexes—to some aspects of the individuals' naturally regulated human body.

In the last analysis all such reduction can only yield some more or less superficial analogy, despite the unquestionable emancipatory intent. For the socioeconomically tendentious postulate of "organic unity"—said to cement the diverse parts of the *social* body together in exactly the same way as nature ties together and determines the functioning of the human *individual's* body—ignores the crucial question of the *historical becoming* of the assumed "organic totality" of society, so as to be able to disregard (and often even explicitly to rule out on the claimed ground of "organic completeness" and corresponding circular functionality) the possibility of *significant change* in the historically given social order. It is therefore by no means surprising that even the most progressive bourgeois historical conceptions, from Vico and Rousseau to Herder and Hegel, remained captive of their own uncritical presuppositions of the right and proper social structure, perceived and theorized by them from capital's unalterably self-serving vantage point.

The organic/anthropological model of the philosophers just mentioned also contains a revealing *cyclic* and repetitive element, which is contrary to a genuine historical explanation. To be sure, in Vico's philosophy the cyclic determination of the long scale historical process is inseparable from his secular enlightenment intent. Likewise in Herder's conception of history. Equally, also in Rousseau's case the enlightenment orientation remains always dominant. But Rousseau's way of applying to the historical process the organic/anthropological model also contains a revealing proviso about the danger (and ultimate inadmissibility) of revolutionary upheavals, as we shall see in a moment. Most strikingly, though, even in the Hegelian system the sequential "ages of man" lead back to a cyclic closure of the "life-process." This is done in the Hegelian philosophy in the name of a new beginning or renewed cycle of the postulated aprioristic development, with reference to the "old man" who—through a somewhat arbitrarily conceptualized but in terms of social apologetics by Hegel much needed twist—returns "to the childhood in which there is no opposition."[36]

In his *Discourse on Political Economy* Rousseau offers a most detailed analogy between the general *"body politic"*—which he considers a truly *living* body—and the body of man. As he puts it: "The sovereign power represents the head; the laws and customs are the brain, the source of the nerves and the seat of the understanding, will, and senses, of which the Judges and Magistrates are the organs: commerce, industry, and agriculture are the mouth and stomach which prepare the common subsistence; the public income is the blood, which a prudent economy, in performing the functions of the heart, causes to distribute through the whole body nutriments and life."[37] He goes on to say, in preparation to his severe warning about the right and proper functioning of the state, that "The life of *both bodies* is the *self* common to the whole, the reciprocal sensibility and internal correspondence of all the parts. Where this communication ceases, where the *formal unity* disappears, and the contiguous parts belong to one another only by juxtaposition, the *man is dead,* or the *State is dissolved.*"[38] In this way he is enabled to conclude, thanks to the authority conferred upon his comparisons by the fact that what is at stake is the *order of nature,* that "The body politic, therefore, is also a *moral being* possessed of a *will; and this general will,* which tends always to the preservation and welfare of the *whole* and of *every part,* and is the source of the laws, constitutes for all the members of the State, in their relations to one another and to it, the rule of what is *just or unjust.*"[39] Thus, by the end of Rousseau's grandiose reasoning the firm *moral postulates* are inextricably intertwined with the declared insurmountable naturalness of the whole edifice. The organic/anthropological model thus becomes the foundation of a monumental—and to our own days profoundly influential—political conception in which the advocacy of practical expediency can never be divorced from the consideration of moral rightfulness.

However, the moral postulates are expected to accomplish too much in Rousseau's system. Even when the crying contradictions of a social and historical order are amply in evidence, the good work of the moral/political imperative—prescribing the absolute observance of the law and the rejection of all scepticism which might query that "everything ordained by the law is lawful"[40]—is supposed to counter any idea of a revolutionary intervention in the historical process. Rousseau's views are spelled out with peremptory finality on this issue, relying in this case rather uncritically on the organic/anthropological model:

> There are times in the history of States when, just as some kinds of *illness* turns men's heads and makes them forget the past, periods of violence and *revolutions* do to *peoples* what these crises do to *individuals:* horror of the past takes the place of forgetfulness, and the State, set on fire by civil wars, is born again, so to speak, from its ashes, and takes on anew, fresh from the jaws of death, the *vigour of youth.* . . . But such events are rare; they are *exceptions,* the cause of which is always to be found in the *particular* constitution of the State concerned. They cannot even happen *twice* to the same people, for it can make itself free as long as it remains barbarous, but not when the civic impulse has lost its vigour. Then disturbances may destroy it, but *revolutions cannot mend it:* it

> needs a *master*, and not a *liberator*. Free peoples, be mindful of this maxim: *'Liberty may be gained, but can never be recovered.'*[41]

Thus, unhappily, the anthropological model greatly weakens Rousseau's insight into the nature of social development by confining revolutions—ironically only a short space of time from one of the greatest of them: the French Revolution of 1789 of which he becomes a most revered hero—to a non-repeatable historical phase, no matter how grave might be the causal determinations which necessitate a revolutionary social and historical transformation. The moral postulate of the right and proper "body politic" must prevail also in this respect. Clearly, the point of Rousseau's strictures against revolutionary upheavals is the assertion of the moral "ought-to-be." For he wants to shake people out of their indifference toward the right course of action, so that—by becoming "mindful of his maxim" about Liberty—they can save themselves from the fate of "disturbance and destruction." As we can see in the passage just quoted from *The Social Contract,* the vision of health in its counter-position to *"illness"* is, again, the orienting principle, said to apply with equal validity to individuals and to peoples. But by disqualifying in this way, in accordance with the organic/anthropological model, the viability of revolutionary interventions in the historical process, Rousseau rules out of court one of the most fundamental explanatory forces of humanity's development, despite the unparallelled radicalism of his diagnosis of the prevailing crude violations of not only the *substantive* but also the elementary *formal* requirements of equality.

AT THE PEAK OF THE ELABORATION of the progressive bourgeois historical conceptions Hegel offers by far the most ingenious version of the organic/anthropological model. For he is not contented simply with Rousseau's characterization of the *"body politic"* by analogy with the *living human body*. He adds a remarkable new dimension by directly relating the requirements of social development, as stipulated in his philosophy by the a priori anticipated self-realization of the world spirit, to the life process of the individual human being, from *childhood* to *old age*. Significantly, however, also his own version clearly displays the contradictions due to the uncritical orientation of such approach toward the established social and economic order. As mentioned before, even the idea of cyclic repetitiveness[42]—constraining the views of his great predecessors—finds a place in the Hegelian system, contributing thereby to the weakening of the genuine historical accomplishments of his philosophy.

As we know, Hegel adopts Ricardo's belief that the economic laws manifest in the complicated reproductive processes of the capitalist order "are not merely observed uniformities within a given economic system but universal and inexorable necessities."[43] Thus in his conceptualization of the nature and functioning of the social order around him Hegel presents us with a vision according to which the development of the individual human being—from childhood to old age (and in the last stage back to childhood)—closely matches the requirements of the right and proper substantiveness and universality of the self-realizing "world mind" and its appropriate embodiment in world history and in the ethical universe of the modern state.

As Hegel puts it, "The sequence of ages in man's life is rounded into a notionally determined totality of alterations which are produced by the *process of the genus with the individual*."[44] The apologetic/conformist nature of the stipulated development of the *genus individual* is clear enough from the beginning of Hegel's characterization of the unfolding process. For according to him "This contradiction of the immediate individuality and the substantial universality implicitly present in it, establishes the life-process of the individual soul, a process by which the immediate individuality of the soul is made *conformable to the universal*, actualizing the latter in the former and thus raising the initial, simple unity of the soul with itself to a *unity mediated by the opposition*, developing the initially abstract universality of the soul to concrete universality."[45] And he goes on to decree that "The *genus* is truly realized *in mind, in Thought,* in this element which is homogeneous with the genus."[46]

By defining his terms of reference in this way Hegel is able to equate the human *genus individuality* with *rationality* and *inner universality,* as required by the reconciliatory orientation of his philosophical system. Accordingly, the idea of entering into conflict with the "rational actuality" of the given world can only be envisaged as a strictly transient feature, admissible only in the still immature state of the *youth* who "unlike the child is no longer at peace with the world."[47] In the age of *manhood,* however, such attitude and behaviour would amount to totally reprehensible *hypochondria,* and indeed to "a *diseased frame of mind.*"[48]

The ideally conformist stage of manhood in the sequential ages of man is presented in the Hegelian philosophy, in the name of "right" and "rationality"—and even as fully appropriate to "the interest of right, ethics, and religion"[49]—in a form of discourse full of *"must-be."* Curiously, this form of reasoning is adopted by Hegel despite his protestations against the idea that the conformity prevailing in manhood arises on the basis of *necessity.*

To give a fair and accurate view of Hegel's reasoning in this respect, it is necessary to quote his words at some length. Talking about the proper way in which the *man* is supposed to behave he writes:

> he *must recognize* the world as a self-dependent world which in its essential nature is *already complete, must accept the conditions* set for him by the world and wrest from it what he wants for himself. As a rule, the man believes that this *submission* is only forced on him by *necessity.* But, in truth, this *unity with the world must be recognized,* not as a relation *imposed by necessity,* but as *the rational.* The rational, the divine, possesses the absolute power to actualize itself and has, *right from the beginning, fulfilled itself;* it is not so impotent that it would have to wait for the beginning of its actualization. The world is this actualization of divine Reason; it is only on its surface that the play of contingency prevails. It can claim, therefore, with at least as much right, indeed with even greater right, than the adolescent to be esteemed as complete and self-dependent; and therefore the man behaves quite rationally in abandoning his plan for completely transforming the world and in striving to realize his personal aims, passions, and interests *only within the framework of the world,* of which he is a part. Even so, this leaves him *scope for an honourable, far-reaching and creative activity.* For although the world *must be recognized as already complete* in its essential nature, yet it is not a dead, absolutely inert world but, like the life-process, a world which perpetually creates itself anew, which *while merely preserving itself,* at the same time progresses. It is in this *conservation and advancement* of the world that the man's work consists. Therefore, on the one hand we can say that the man *only creates what is already there;* yet on the other hand, his activ-

> ity *must* also bring about an advance. . . . Therefore, men can find satisfaction and honour *in all spheres* of their practical activity if they accomplish throughout *what is rightly required of them* in the particular sphere to which they belong either by *chance*, outer *necessity*, or *free choice*.[50]

Thus the conveniently uncritical notion of the "genus-individual," with his pseudo-anthropological determinations fully matching the postulated "rationality of the world" and its "self-fulfilling completeness right from the beginning," enables Hegel to legitimate and ideologically rationalize the necessary *conformity* to the established order. By transferring the question of development to the plane where the *individuals*—who are said to embody the determinations of their *genus*—exhibit through their behaviour the generic characteristics of the eternalized sequential "ages of man" (to which they can rightfully only resign themselves if they do not want to be disqualified under the label of having a "diseased frame of mind"), the contradictions of the real world disappear from view. In place of the actually existing world of irreconcilable structural antagonisms, gruesome social inequality, and enforced class hierarchy which dominate the "life-process" of the overwhelming majority, we are presented with a picture in which every individual can find fulfilment "in all spheres of their practical activity if they accomplish what is rightly required of them." For, miraculously, they are all supposed to have at their disposal "scope for an honourable, far-reaching and creative activity," even the elsewhere idealized "pauper"[51] and the labouring masses of the people condemned to the "life-activity" of the most alienating and dehumanizing monotonous routine, according to the "rational" prescriptions of the socially undefined ages of man. One could hardly imagine a more apologetic depiction of the established social and economic order.

The arbitrarily propounded "genus individuality" is required—and by no means only in the Hegelian philosophy—because from the analogy of a strictly *individual* human being it would be impossible to derive the (aprioristically postulated) generalizations about the *social body*. At the same time, given the way in which the established social order is structured, the alternative way of depicting the individual on a societal scale, as a genuine *social individual* endowed with positive co-operative characteristics in relation to the objectively given potentialities of an alternative social order, is historically premature. After all, the age of Hegel was contemporary only to the emergence of the idealistic and in practical terms utterly unviable *utopian socialist* counter-images to the existent.

Nevertheless, at a certain point of actual historical development the generalizations based on the hypostatized "genus-individuals" were both emancipatory, in contrast to past religious conceptions and corresponding authoritarian constraints, and at the same time uncritical/conservative/apologetic in relation to the established, hierarchically structured and incurably exploitative, socioeconomic order, perceived from capital's then *relatively* progressive vantage point. But, understandably, the apologetic dimension had to become more prominent with the inexorable consolidation of the capitalist order. This is why it turned out to be more problematical in Hegel's philosophy than in the writings of his predecessors. For Hegel was situated in time at the historically most significant juncture when the potentially viable hegemonic alternative of labour appeared on the horizon and *began* to assert itself as a combative force in the first skirmishes of the socialist movement. This important correlation is underlined by the fact that the philosophical genius of Hegel—inspired in the first place by the social and political earthquakes erupting in the dramatic aftermath of the French Revolution and the Napoleonic wars, of which he was a most acute and sympathetic observer—succeeded in elaborating the most monumental and systematic attempt to come to terms both with the positive potentialities and the inherent contradictions of the bourgeois horizon, even if in a speculative form.

Yet, the sequential "ages of man" could not help being a thoroughly apologetic conception, just like the *"unity"* and *"universality"* proclaimed to be inherent in the tendentiously characterized life-process. The life-process conceived in that way by Hegel is extremely problematical in that it operates with the help of an aprioristic logico-metaphysical concept of simply declared "mediation," instead of a historically intelligible and identifiable category of *social mediation*. This is because the apologetic *conclusion*—and the underlying *raison d'être*—of the whole enterprise is itself assumed from the very beginning.

This revealing circularity is accomplished by Hegel in much the same way as we see it decreed in Kant's theory of the insuperable "asociability" of individual human beings in "civil society," due to the presumed ground that the propensity of individuals to behave antagonistically toward each other is, as a genus-determination, *"innate in men."*[52] Naturally, the underlying motivation in the Kantian and Hegelian philosophy is also much the same: the assertion of the absolute consonance of the bourgeois social and political order with the postulated, but never demonstrated, determinations of *"human nature"* which, if true, would automatically confer the appropriate determinations of *necessity* and *universality*—notwithstanding the *historical contingency* and the painfully obvious *discriminatory particularism* of actually existing society—on the established order. In Kant's own eyes the justification for the gloomy assertion of insuperable "asociability" is that "one cannot fashion something absolutely straight from *wood which is as crooked as that of which man is made.*"[53] And the "proof" of the peremptorily assertive "conclusion" of the Kantian philosophy is nothing but the arbitrary assumption of the nature-determined crookedness of "innate human nature" itself: a veritable, socially inspired, philosophical *vicious circle.* In the Hegelian philosophy the self-serving assumption of a logico-metaphysical concept of mediation produces a no less problematical result.

Since the socially apologetic consonance of "manhood" with the absolute requirements of the self-realizing world spirit is the real orienting principle (i.e., the often veiled *terminus ad quem)* of Hegel's reasoning, whereby the mature man is called upon to *"recognize the objective necessity and reasonableness of the world as he finds it,"*[54] the particular steps leading to this tendentiously "concluding assumption" are strictly subordinate to the postulate of the overall design. For Hegel insists, in the form of a most curious justification of the historically unfolding "life-process" of the individual human beings, as we have seen above, that "The rational, the divine, possesses the absolute power to actualize itself and has, *right from the beginning, fulfilled itself:* it is not so impotent that it would have to wait for the beginning of its actualization."[55]

Thus we are invited to start with the logico-metaphysical construction according to which "The *soul,* which at first is *completely universal,* having in the way we have indicated *particularized* itself and finally *determined itself to the stage of individuality,* now enters into *opposition* to its inner universality, to its substance." From this initial definition of opposition Hegel is able to derive both his somewhat mysterious concept of "mediation" and the philosophically required "concrete universality." This is how his argument runs immediately after the last quoted sentence: "This contradiction of the immediate individuality and the substantial universality implicitly present in it, establishes the life-process of the individual soul, a process by which the immediate individuality of the soul is made *conformable to the universal,* actualizing the latter in the former and thus raising the initial, *simple unity* of the soul with itself to a *unity mediated by the opposition,* developing the initially *abstract universality* of the soul to *concrete universality*."[56] Thus everything takes place in the domain of the Hegelian conceptual deductions, based on the aprioristically stipulated logico-metaphysical "conclusive assumptions" which make it possible for him to assert with categorical finality that the self-actualizing rational has "right from the beginning fulfilled itself." And, naturally, from this kind of determination of Hegel's terms of reference—regarding abstract logico-metaphysical "contradiction," "unity mediated by the opposition," and the "concrete universality" of the properly particularized soul—it follows with equally categorical absoluteness that in the age of "manhood" (the apologetic *terminus ad quem* of his reflections on genus-individuality), *any* departure in the actually existing world from the ideally postulated *conformity to the universal* (that is, any attempt to practically challenge the imperatives of the established order of "civil society" and its "ethical state") must be disqualified as the manifestations of "a diseased frame of mind."

Finally, it is necessary to say something about the thoroughly apologetic and ahistorical character of the peculiar cyclic/repetitive constituent in Hegel's sequential ages of man. Again, the terms of reference in Hegel's theorization of old age are defined in such a way, in sharp contrast to the definitional characteristics of appropriately integrated and rationally conforming manhood, that they should lead back to the notional ideality of his *terminus ad quem* from two directions: from the far receding memory of the unruly youth, on the one hand, and the dull predicament of the old man, on the other. Thus we are invited to accept that "The old man lives without any definite interest, for he has abandoned the hope of realizing the ideals which he cherished when he was young and the future seems to hold no promise of anything new at all; on the contrary, he believes that he already knows what is universal and substantial in anything he may yet encounter. The mind of the old man is thus turned only towards this universal and to the *past* to which he owes the knowledge of this universal."[57] Even the knowledge and wisdom acquired by the old man in the course of his life turns out to be utterly pointless. For his accumulated wisdom, "this lifeless, complete coincidence of the subject's activity with its world, leads back to the *childhood* in which there is *no opposition.*"[58]

Thus everything can start all over again with the circular "movement" from childhood to old age leading absolutely nowhere from the conformist "rational actuality" of the present, as embodied with full adequacy in the pretended genus-individuality of the unquestioningly submissive man. In order to envisage a real historical movement and a significantly different solution beyond the resigned sterility of the old age, as described by Hegel, it would be necessary to appeal to the idea of *renewal,* with reference to actually existing social forces capable of bringing about such renewal, instead of the apologetic circularity of the postulated *repeat* of childhood. But the precondition of that solution would be the radically critical assessment of capital's vantage point. And that is obviously quite inconceivable for Hegel.

What Hegel must, instead, opt for—given the overall determinations of his philosophical conception, wedded to capital's vantage point, and the tangible constraints of his social and historical predicament—is a peculiar version of the cyclic/repetitive model. The way in which he theorizes old age, in order to provide yet another justification for the total submissiveness of manhood in the sequence of ages, takes him to a literally *dead end.* At that point there is no more *movement,* and there cannot be any: a condition fatal to a purported historical conception which is supposed to match the unfolding rationality of the self-realizing world spirit. It is no consolation to say in that respect, as Hegel does in his *Philosophy of Right,* that "Philosophy in any case always comes on the scene too late . . . As the thought of the world, it appears only when actuality is already there cut and dried after its process of formation has been completed. The teaching of the concept, which is also history's inescapable lesson, is that it is only when actuality is mature that the ideal first appears over against the real and that the ideal apprehends this same real world in its substance and builds it up for itself into the shape of an intellectual realm. When philosophy paints its grey in grey, then has a shape of life grown old. By philosophy's grey in grey it cannot be *rejuvenated* but only understood. The owl of Minerva spreads its wings only with the falling of the dusk."[59]

And yet, in his *Philosophy of Mind* Hegel is compelled to do precisely what he says in the lines just quoted that it cannot be done. For having reached the *dead end* due to the perverse requirements of his social apologetics—embodied in the conformist "manhood" and its justificatory counter-image in the old man on his way to actual death—Hegel has to invent a *pseudo-movement* where no real historical movement is feasible. And the only way he can do that is by arbitrarily *"rejuvenating the world"* through the imposition of the fictitious "new beginning" of *childhood* in the eternalized sequence of ages, in accordance with the cyclic/repetitive model of his genus-individuality. Only the doubly apologetic and thoroughly ahistorical nature of the adopted cyclic/repetitive approach can thus enable Hegel to project the continuation of the "life-process" beyond the notionally completed dead end. Accordingly, thanks to the *semblance* of a movement amounting to mere *repetition,* and never to meaningful *renewal,* capital's idealized "rational actuality" can go on forever, without any feasible challenge to its alienating rule.

The sterile *memory of the past* dominates the vision of the old man, emptying thereby both "universality" and "substantiveness" of their real significance. At the same time, the old man's lifeless coincidence as a subject with his world is rejected by Hegel on the ground that it is devoid of *opposition.* However, we should have no illusions about these terms of reference. For both the memory of the past—the Hegelian *Erinnerung*—and the logico-metaphysical concept of *opposition* (which plays such an important part in Hegel's concept of *mediation)* are rather problematical. In the Hegelian conceptual universe the opposite of "Erinnerung" is *"Entäusserung."* And the latter means for Hegel: *objectifying alienation* which is unthinkable without some kind of activity and movement. In that sense this pair of opposites undoubtedly goes beyond the lifeless predicament of the old man. But in what way? Certainly not by envisaging a historically viable transformation of the existent. For the Hegelian philosophy as a whole asserts the *absolute insurmountability of alienation* as the innermost ontological determination of the "rational actuality" of the existent. And in that way, too, the circularity of the genus-individual's life-process, from childhood to an old age hopelessly dominated by past memory, and back to the age of childhood (not in reality but as a tendentious generic postulate), highlights the reconciliatory character of the organic/-anthropological model in Hegel's philosophy. For the opposition between "Erinnerung" and "Entäusserung" can only underline the *triumph of alienation,* in many places rendered also explicit in the Hegelian system.

7.3 Fragmentation and "Longing for Unity"

Husserl, in his own way of approaching the important question of *fragmentation*—by him most problematically always confined to the domain of idealistic philosophical discourse—talks about *"the longing for a fully alive philosophy."*[60] And he diagnoses the apparently intractable problems in this way:

> The *splintering* of present-day philosophy, with its perplexed activity, sets us thinking. When we attempt to view western philosophy as a *unitary science,* its decline since the middle of the nineteenth century is unmistakable. The comparative unity that it had in previous ages, in its aims, its problems and methods, has been lost. . . . Instead of a *unitary living philosophy,* we have a philosophical literature growing beyond all bounds and almost without coherence. . . . The philosophies lack the *unity of a mental space* in which they might exist for and act on one another. . . . Cannot the *disconnectedness* of our philosophical position be traced back ultimately to the fact that the driving forces emanating from the *Meditations* of Descartes have lost their original vitality—lost because the *spirit* that characterizes radicalness of *philosophical self-responsibility* has been lost? Must not the demand for a philosophy aiming at the ultimate conceivable freedom from prejudice, shaping itself with actual autonomy according to ultimate evidences it has itself produced, and therefore *absolutely self-responsible*—must not this demand, instead of being excessive, be part of the fundamental sense of genuine philosophy?[61]

As we can see, Husserl can find nothing wrong with maintaining the illusion of the "absolute self-responsibility" of philosophy. He is looking for a "mental space" in which the "splintering" varieties of philosophies could somehow find their commendable unity. Thus, again, the reasons why the, by Husserl deplored, fragmented philosophical discourses have lost their claimed unity, which they were supposed to have prior to the middle of the nineteenth century, is not raised at all. It is simply asserted by him that the trouble is due to the circumstance that the driving forces of the *Meditations* developed by Descartes have lost their original vitality. And why have they lost it? Apparently "because the *spirit* that characterizes radicalness of *philosophical self-responsibility* has been lost." In this way everything remains tied to a circular assumption—well in tune with the author's aprioristic conclusion and illusorily corrective recommendation—which invariably refuses to address the established social and historical framework and the dramatically changing horizon of the developments of which modern philosophy itself is an integral part, but only a part. It should come as no surprise at all that this is the same kind of circularly self-referential reasoning which we have witnessed above—concerning the total unreality of *"the heroism of Reason"* postulated in the Prague lecture by Husserl—as the recommended remedy to the catastrophe-threatening Nazi barbarism of his time.

In truth, the "original vitality" of Descartes's position is also presented by Husserl as hopelessly inadequate to his own projection of "absolutely self-responsible philosophy." He speaks of "prejudices" leading to nothing less sinful than *"absurdity"* which in his eyes was supposed to dominate the intellectual climate when Descartes conceived his *Meditations*. As he puts it: "Unfortunately these prejudices were at work when Descartes introduced the apparently insignificant but actually *fateful* change whereby the ego becomes a *substantia cogitans,* a separate human 'mens sive animus', and the point of departure for inferences according to the principle of *causality*—in short, the change by virtue of which Descartes became the father of *transcendental realism, an absurd position* . . . Descartes erred in this respect. Consequently he stands on the threshold of the greatest of all discoveries—in a certain manner, has already made it—yet *he does not grasp its proper sense,* the sense namely of *transcendental subjectivity,* and so he does not pass through the gateway that leads into *genuine transcendental philosophy*."[62]

Thus, if the Cartesian "original vitality" is already irretrievably captive, under the circumstances of its own time, as "an absurd position," which must be categorically rejected from the standpoint of Husserl's self-enclosed and accordingly commended "genuine transcendental philosophy," in that case the mysterious "loss" is only a purely rhetorical device in support of the advocated "transcendental subjectivity." This is so because the loss of *"an absurd position"* in philosophy is, if anything, an intellectual advancement and not a *fateful derailment*, as the author claims. In fact the Husserlian rejection of Descartes's unforgivable position—his all too obvious concern with *causality* and *realism*, and thus with the relevance of the unfolding scientific development of his time to the actually exising world, in the envisaged positive service of the "mastery of man over nature"—is required by Husserl precisely because *it has not been lost,* but because *he himself wants to lose it*. Indeed, he must lose it in order to provide a solipsistic foundation to the absolutized inwardness of his "*egology* of the primordially *reduced ego*," in the spirit of his "monadology," and at the same time to the "systematic unfolding of the all-embracing A priori innate in the essence of a transcendental subjectivity," as we have seen above.

If we want to do something about the historically produced and socially most damaging problems of fragmentation, together with the related negative trends of intellectual development, like the "splintering of philosophy" in Husserl's words, we must assess them in their appropriate—and by their very nature all-embracing—socioeconomic, political and cultural setting. One cannot make the deplored impact of such developments even minimally intelligible in and through the self-referentiality of philosophy; not to mention the necessary failure to positively affect their underlying causal determinations on a lasting basis in their overall complexity. And in this respect it makes no difference whatsoever how heightened might be the rhetorical claims attached to the postulated remedial intervention if everything remains confined to the self-oriented domain of philosophy itself. Not even if we are willing to entertain Husserl's notion of the postulated "*absolutely self-responsible*" role of "transcendental subjectivity."

The painful limitation of this approach—inseparable from Husserl's methodological horizon—is that the solipsistic correction to Descartes's "absurd position" leads the author into a blind alley. He abstracts as completely from the social and historical framework in which the Cartesian conception was born as from the actual circumstances of his own time when the ever more severe problems of social fragmentation, compartmentalization and the socially defenceless "splintering" of the intellectual enterprise continue to assert their negative impact with growing intensity. He is trying to elaborate an aprioristic, *timeless* method of categorical projections in response to an eminently *historical* predicament. He wants to overcome what he calls "the splintering of present-day philosophy, with its *perplexed* activity"[63] by his own method of apodictic certainty and supra-historical universal validity, proclaimed on the postulated absolute foundations of the *"radicalness of philosophical self-responsibility"* which in his eyes needs no tangible social and historical references, apart from the dubious generic assertion that something has been lost. In this way we are presented with the closure of the methodological circle centred on the "absolute inwardness" of self-referential philosophy through which Husserl can *"lose the world* by *'epoché.'"* [64] But the price that must be paid for such closure of the methodological circle—not simply by Husserl but in general by humanity, thanks to the more or less conscious advocacy of the clearly identifiable unfolding trend of the destruction of nature in our time—is that it becomes philosophically easier to abandon all concern with the Cartesian original programme of the "mastery of man over nature" and its necessary connection to a historically sustainable non-adversarial relationship among human beings. And no one can deny the disastrous consequences of that historical failure today.

SARTRE, DESPITE ADOPTING as a young man the phenomenological method, emphatically rejects Husserl's solipsism already in his early synthesizing work, *Being and Nothingness.* At the same time he calls the Husserlian transcendental subjectivity not only *useless* but even a *disaster.* This is how Sartre argues his case:

> Formerly I believed that I could escape solipsism by refuting Husserl's concept of the existence of Transcendental 'Ego'. At that time I thought that since I had emptied my consciousness of its subject, nothing remained there which was privileged as compared to the Other. But actu-

> ally although I am still persuaded that the hypothesis of a transcendental subject is useless and disastrous, abandoning it does not help one bit to solve the question of the existence of Others. . . . Because Husserl has reduced being to a series of meanings, the only connection which he has been able to establish between my being and that of the Other is a connection of knowledge. Therefore Husserl can not escape solipsism any more than Kant could.[65]

In his much later work, *The Problem of Method,* Sartre attempts to provide a historically concretized analysis of the nature and motivating ground of the Cartesian enterprise. As he puts it: "The analytical, critical rationalism of the great Cartesians has survived them; born from conflict, it looked back to clarify the conflict. At the time when the bourgeoisie sought to undermine the institutions of the Ancien Régime, it attacked the outworn significations which tried to justify them. Later it gave service to liberalism, and provided a doctrine for procedures that attempted to realize the 'atomization' of the Proletariat." And in the same context Sartre also clearly underlines the way in which the historical vantage point of capital was reflected, however tenuously, in the varieties of the Cartesian approach, by saying that "In the case of Cartesianism, the action of 'philosophy' remains *negative;* it clears the ground, it destroys, and it enables men, across the infinite complexities and particularisms of the feudal system, to *catch a glimpse of the abstract universality of bourgeois property*."[66] Accordingly, there can be no legitimacy at all for treating in a timeless fashion either the historically more distant Cartesian tenets or the reconsideration of the question of the Cartesian legacy under the circumstances of the twentieth century.

In the same way, Sartre is rightly critical of Husserl's general approach when he writes: "Husserl could speak of *apodictic certainty* without much difficulty, but this was because he remained on the level of *pure, formal consciousness* apprehending itself in its *formality;* but, for us, it is necessary to find our apodictic experience in the *concrete world of History*."[67] This is an important point not only in relation to Husserl but in terms of its general philosophical validity. Nevertheless it is rather ironical that even the "Marxisant" Sartre, despite his awareness of the need to elucidate "the concrete world of history," in order to make the historical process truly intelligible, remains in his *Critique of Dialectical Reason* confined to *"the formal structures of history,"* as mentioned before.

The difficulties become as a rule most pronounced in Sartre's philosophy when he has to address the ideologically most intertwined question of the historical subject. In contrast to Kant, who in his "Idea for a Universal History with Cosmopolitan Intent" and elsewhere was still trying to organically relate the particular individuals to the most comprehensive category to which they belonged, namely humanity, the passing of time in bourgeois conceptions of history shows a significant *involution* in this respect. Thus in the Heideggerianized conception of atheistic existentialism, exemplified by Sartre's *Being and Nothingness,* we are presented with the following reasoning:

> But if God is characterized as radical absence, the effort to realize humanity as ours is forever renewed and *forever results in failure.* Thus the humanistic 'Us'—*the Us-object*—is proposed to each individual consciousness as an ideal *impossible to attain* although everyone keeps the *illusion* of being able to succeed in it by progressively enlarging the circle of communities to which he does belong. This humanistic 'Us' remains an *empty concept,* a pure indication of a possible extension of the ordinary usage of the 'Us'. Each time that we use the 'Us' in this sense (to designate suffering humanity, sinful humanity, to determine an *objective historical meaning* by considering man as an *object* which is *developing its potentialities)* we limit ourselves to indicating a certain concrete experience to be undergone in the presence of the absolute Third; that is, of God. Thus the limiting concept of humanity (as the totality of the *Us-object)* and the limiting concept of God imply one another and are correlative.[68]

Yet, despite this kind of slanted characterization, "humanity as ours" does indeed exist, even if under the present historical circumstances still in a gravely alienated form. For under the now prevailing conditions humanity asserts itself as the antagonistically articulated *world history,* embodied in the inescapable realities of the *world market* and the apparently uncontrollable, self-imposing, *division of labour on a world scale.* Nor indeed does the concept of mankind developing its objective potentialities imply the formulation of an impossible ideal, viewed from the standpoint of the 'absolute Third', God. That kind of false conception can arise only from fallaciously characterizing humanity as an 'Us-*object*," and man as an *"object which is developing its potentialities,"* as Sartre does in the quoted passage. For, contrary to all varieties of mystificatory atheistic existentialism, only as the *genuine subject* of historical transformation can humanity be made intelligible in the present context.

All that is required to make sense of "humanity as ours" is to grasp the disconcerting reality of the material and ideal/ideological structures of domination in the dynamic process of their objective unfolding and potential dissolution; not from the standpoint of the mystifying "absolute Third" but from the vantage point of the inter- and trans-individual *historical subject.* If, however, the philosopher—wedded to an individualistic conception of the social process—assumes the nature of *conflict* as inherent in the "ontological solitude of the For-itself," as Sartre does in his *Being and Nothingness,* in contrast to his much later *Critique of Dialectical Reason,* in that case the historical process as such (in the absence of a plausible historical subject) becomes extremely problematical to him, if not altogether devoid of intelligibility.

Similar considerations apply to the realistic assessment of the important question of the feasible interaction of the major forces in actually existing society and the possibility of producing a historically viable outcome. If that is not done, we end up with predicating the aprioristic stalemate of atomistically conceived individuals depicted within the framework of arbitrarily proclaimed pseudo-ontological postulates. To quote Sartre again:

> The oppressed class can, in fact, affirm itself as a *We-subject* only in relation to the oppressing class.... But the experience of the 'We' remains on the ground of *individual psychology* and remains a simple symbol of the *longed-for unity of transcendences.* . . . The subjectivities remain out of reach and *radically separated.* . . . We should hope in vain for a human 'we' in which the intersubjective totality would obtain consciousness of itself as a unified subjectivity. Such an ideal could be only a *dream* produced by a passage to the limit and to the absolute on the basis of *fragmentary, strictly psychological experiences.* ... It is therefore useless for humanity to seek to get out of this dilemma; one must either transcend the Other

> or allow oneself to be transcended by him. The essence of the relation between consciousnesses is not the *Mitsein* [being with]; it is *conflict*.[69]

As we can see, Sartre's gloomy picture—decreeing the absolute insurmountability of the presumed "ontological" predeterminations which constitute the categorial framework of *Being and Nothingness*—starts with the totally gratuitous assertion that the concept of the "We-subject" is utterly meaningless without its opposition to the *oppressing class* as its elementary condition of intelligibility. Moreover, such opposition itself to the oppressing class, in its unavoidable collectivist aspiration, is utterly misconceived and is condemned to failure. The whole question of even raising the possibility of the "We-subject" (as a proper "we") *acting* in such a way that it should bring about a qualitatively different social order is dismissed by Sartre on an arbitrary definitional ground which is totally devoid of any socially identifiable foundation. It is circularly dismissed by him on the "conclusive" *assumption* according to which anything the "We-subject" might attempt to do necessarily disqualifies its professed aim of asserting in practice its feasible strategic objectives—as a genuine collective enterprise—on account of hopelessly *deluding* itself. For, in Sartre's view, its misconceived action must be condemned under the category of *"fragmentary, strictly psychological experiences."* Thus even the most remote possibility of a viable *historical alternative* to capital's rule—which is of course inconceivable without the not only negating/combative, but also in the longest term positively sustainable, intervention by an appropriate *historical subject* in the process of meaningful social transformation—is categorically (and categorially) ruled out. It must be ruled out because the historical process, with its objectively existing and identifiable social actors, is reduced by Sartre to the more or less haphazard vicissitudes of *individual psychology*. As a matter of aprioristically proclaimed ontological determinations the "We-subject" is supposed to be constituted by an illusory—and worse than that, self-deluding—coalescence of individualistic psychological experiences leading absolutely nowhere. No meaningful transformatory historical enterprise can be squeezed out of that.

In this way the methodological circle—peremptorily assuming as established what should be in fact philosophically demonstrated—is closed again, despite the undoubted presence of historical references in Sartre's *Being and Nothingness* and also in his critique of Husserl. But, of course, in the vision of the early Jean-Paul Sartre history is tendentiously depicted from capital's vantage point, dense with Heideggerian type eternalization of the prevailing order.[70] To be sure, *alienating fragmentation,* in a variety of its forms, is recognized in *Being and Nothingness*, even if primarily in the form of psychological experiences, decreeing at the same time that the subjectivities involved necessarily "remain out of reach and *radically separated.*" Accordingly, we are told that it is utterly vain to hope that the intersubjective totality of individuals, aiming to constitute themselves as a "We-subject" against the oppressing class, might obtain consciousness of themselves "as a unified subjectivity." In this characteristically qualified way Sartre does not deny the fact of *"longing for a unified subjectivity"* as an important preoccupation—and not only intellectual preoccupation—in the twentieth century. But he emphatically rules out the possibility of its realization. For the tendentious reduction of social and historical antagonisms to individual psychological experiences carries with it the paralyzing implication that the "We-subject" can be nothing more substantive than "a simple *symbol* of the *longed-for unity of transcendences.*" And even that is by no means the bleakest part of closing Sartre's ontological and methodological circle in *Being and Nothingness*. Rather, it is the desolate and declarative conclusion-assumption according to which "it is *useless for humanity* to seek to get out of this dilemma; one must either transcend the Other or allow oneself to be transcended by him. The essence of the relation between consciousnesses is not the *Mitsein*; it is *conflict.*" Besides, the conflict in question is not a potentially progressive social confrontation but the ubiquitously diffused psychological conflict of separate individuals, splintering all sides of the social divide into an infinity of monadological fragments. Thus alienating fragmentation is destined to remain forever the "human predicament," in the spirit of the proclaimed existential ontology of *Being and Nothingness.* At the same time all longing for a socially effective transformatory unity of the forces capable of instituting a historically feasible alternative hegemonic order, beyond the destructiveness of capital's structural determinations, is condemned to the futility of a hopeless irrational enterprise.

FOR A NUMBER OF REASONS the most representative figure who passionately addressed the basic problems discussed in this section was the Hungarian philosopher, György Lukács.

First, because he was engaged in productive theoretical writing over an exceptionally long period of almost seventy years. He started his publishing career in some of the important Hungarian cultural organs in 1902, and he carried on writing one of his most important synthesizing work, *The Ontology of Social Being,* until he died in 1971. Inevitably, his orientation as a creative thinker had gone through significant, and in the present context highly relevant changes in those long decades, as we shall see below.

Second, because—due to his social background, as the son of the Austro-Hungarian monarchy's most influential banker with far-reaching international connections, a very rich and politically consequential actor, even on Count István Tisza, the Prime Minister—the young Lukács experienced the dilemmas of capitalist fragmentation and alienation at the *inner core* of the capitalist exploitative order. In that sense for the young Lukács a spontaneous adhesion to his "natural" We-subject, in the Sartrean scheme of things confined to "the ground of *individual psychology,*" could only have meant siding with the *oppressing class,* and not with its historical adversary: an utterly insensitive and retrograde choice which he could not make. In fact Lukács, despite his extremely privileged background, rebelled against that prospect from a very early age, siding instead more or less consciously with the socially well grounded revolutionary orientation of the greatest Hungarian poet of the age, Endre Ady. This choice anticipated to a significant extent his more radical turn toward the end of the First World War. Indeed, also after he moved to Germany in 1909, closely collaborating for years with some leading intellectuals of that country, like Georg Simmel and Max Weber, and returning temporarily to Hungary only in the aftermath of the erupting war, he always retained his ethically rebellious stance. It is not surprising, therefore, that he sharply dissented from the chauvinistic enthusiasm for the war-adventure of German imperialism even by people like Thomas Mann (greatly admired by the literary critic Lukács for a long time before the war) and his own friend Max Weber. Thus the young Lukács's position of a *critical outsider*—not only in relation to German culture and history but also vis-à-vis the mainstream of the contemporary Hungarian theoretical conceptions exemplified by the journal *Nyugat* (Occident)—continued to shape his creative orientation in all of his major writings, until he had to make an irretrievably radical choice in the middle of the revolutionary turmoil of 1917–1918.

And third, because in the course of his intellectual and political development Lukács reached a stage when he became convinced that it was necessary to distance himself from the categorial framework of all of his major early works, including *Die Seele und die Formen* (Soul and Form, in Hungarian 1910, in German 1911), *Aesthetic Culture* (in Hungarian 1913), and *Die Theorie des Romans* (Theory of the Novel, 1916). This came about because he embraced Marxism both as a philosopher and as a politically engaged militant.

Two points are particularly relevant in this respect. First, that Lukács's way of critically confronting the categorial arsenal of his own youthful writings was an *organic* development and not the kind of "conversion" all too well known in the twentieth century, which can be just as easily undone by the people involved as it can surface in their life in the first place. Thus his critical stance in relation to the cultural developments of his time, dominated by his own class, was not defined from a remote distance, let alone from the aprioristic position characteristic of many sectarian writings. It was articulated from the vantage point of someone who himself acutely experienced from the *inside* the dilemmas that deeply affected the creation of valid intellectual achievement. In this way he was capable of assuming not only a critical but also a *self-critical* attitude to the determinations and dilemmas in question. The second point that must be made in this respect concerns the way in which Lukács, thanks to his organic philosophical development which always firmly rejected the idea of starting with a self-servingly convenient but really untenable *tabula rasa,* was able to put also the self-critically examined categories of his own early work into *historical perspective*. In other words, he never sacrificed the relevant *continuities* for the sake of some hastily and one-sidedly assumed *discontinuities,* in the name of a more or less arbitrarily proclaimed *"radically new"* in the cultural and political domain.

This is how one of the outstanding intellectual achievements of the twentieth century could be grounded on secure *dialectical* foundations, respectful of the historical evidence reaching into the core of the present from the past. A burdensome past that could not be simply left behind but had to be overcome—in the sense of the profoundly insightful Hegelian category of being "aufgehoben"; that is, superseded/preserved/raised to a higher level—by turning to positive use the potentially emancipatory elements of its contradictory legacy. Lukács's encounter with Marxism provided for him the vantage point from which the evaluation of capital's historical epoch could be attempted, with all its bewilderingly complex and intertwined aspects.

This radical turn had opened for Lukács the door to the possibility of undertaking in due course the kind of overall *synthesis* for which he could only be *longing,* utterly in vain, as a young thinker, in his eloquent advocacy of the need to engage in, as well as in several of his failed attempts to actually write, a wide-ranging philosophical *system.*[71] Naturally, the self-critical evaluation of his own—even today much acclaimed—early works was accomplished on that basis. But it was by no means a one-way street. The fact that he was able to situate the critically and self-critically examined concepts and dilemmas in a comprehensive Marxian historical perspective, giving them the weight and significance they deserved, contributed in a positive and lasting sense to his own future development, notwithstanding the most problematical character of the categories which the young Lukács shared for almost two decades with some of his contemporaries.

ALREADY IN 1909 LUKÁCS RESPONDED in highly positive terms to the work of Thomas Mann. Feeling great affinity for the way in which Mann treated objectivity, highlighting its dilemmas and apparent insecurity, Lukács wrote in one of his review articles:

> objectivity can perhaps never exist without a certain irony. The most serious regard for things is always somewhat ironic, for somewhere or other the great gulf between cause and effect, between the conjuring of fate and the fate conjured, must become obvious. And the more natural the peaceful flow of things appears, the truer and deeper this irony will be. Admittedly it is only in *Buddenbrooks* that this emerges so clearly, as it were, from a single source. In the later writings this irony of Mann takes

> on diferent forms, yet its deepest root remains this feeling of dislocation from, and *longing for, the great vegetative community.*[72]

Like Thomas Mann, the young Hungarian philosopher felt the same dislocation from, and the same longing for, an objective synthesis and unity in a world in which the gulf between "cause and effect," "intention and result," "value and reality," appeared to be ever increasing. But, of course, for him irony could not bring the longed for solution.

The somewhat rhetorical abstractness of the young Lukács's general level of inquiry—the categories of "soul and forms" (*die Seele und die Formen*), "value and reality" (*Wert und Wirklichkeit*), "the height of being" (*Gipfel des Seins*), "pure constraint on the pure will" (*der reine Zwang auf den reinen Willen*), "the pinnacle of being" (*der Hohepunkt des Daseins*), and the like—prevented him from identifying those concrete mediations which could transcend the rejected immediacy by moving toward a concrete totality, and not toward some hypostatized "metaphysical essenses," as happened to be the case in his early works.

If one started—as the young Lukács did—from the premise that the philosophical system could offer "the icy, final perfection,"[73] the margin of the critic's activity had to be a rather illusory one. For the most abstractly defined entities of the "system" were assigned the metaphysical value-quotient of the always elusive "finality of perfection." The problem of necessary and in its appropriate context valid mediation, despite the recognition of the "bad immediacy" of naturalism, symbolism, etc., remained totally unresolved. That was the main reason why the young Lukács was defeated in the end, forced to look for a solution where it could not be found: in a "Kierkegaardized" and mystically inclined opposition to "the system." Even when a few years later Lukács tried to incorporate into his own vision some important themes and methods of Hegel, he could not escape the temptations of pursuing the discourse of Kierkegaardian paradox. Thus, at an astronomical distance from the Hegelian definition of truth as *the whole,* he asserted that "Truth is only subjective—perhaps; but *subjectivity* is quite certainly *truth.*"[74] No wonder, therefore, that the mature Lukács spoke with misgivings about a "Kierkegaardized Hegel" with reference to this phase in his own intellectual development.

The young Lukács could only project "*longing for the system,*"[75] admitting at the same time, even if with a question mark attached to it, "*the ultimate hopelessness of all longing.*"[76] His reflections on this complex of problems were spelled out with the profound originality of his essay on "The Metaphysics of Tragedy." This is how his line of argument ran:

> Tragedy is the becoming real of the concrete, *essential nature of man.* Tragedy gives a firm and sure answer to the most delicate question of platonism: the question whether *individual* things can have idea or *essence.* Tragedy's answer puts the question the other way round: only that which is individual, only something whose individuality is carried to the uttermost limit, is adequate to its idea—i.e. is really existent. That which is *general,* that which encompasses all things yet has no colour or form of its own, is *too weak in its universality,* too *empty in its unity,* ever to become real. . . . The *deepest longing of human existence* is the metaphysical root of tragedy: the *longing of man for selfhood,* the longing to transform the narrow peak of his existence into a wide plain with the path of his life winding across it, and his meaning into a daily reality.[77]

This line of reasoning, with its forcefully expressed concern for *universality* and *unity* centred on the necessity to be engaged in an authentic quest for selfhood, inevitably led Lukács to questioning the nature and apparently fateful self-imposing power of history. His paradoxically heightened views were summed up in this way: "History appears as a profound symbol of fate—of the regular accidentality of fate, its arbitrariness and tyranny which, in the last analysis, is always just. Tragedy's fight for history is a great war of conquest against life, an attempt to find the *meaning of history* (which is immeasurably far from life) in life, to extract the meaning of history from life as the true, *concealed sense of life.* A sense of history is always the most living necessity; the *irresistible force;* the form in which it occurs is the *force of gravity* of mere happening, the irresistible force within the flow of things. It is the necessity of everything being connected with everything else, the *value-denying necessity;* there is no difference between small and great, meaningful and meaningless, primary and secondary. What is, had to be. Each moment follows the one before, unaffected by aim and purpose."[78]

In this way—due to the characterization of the meaning of history as the "concealed sense of life," asserting itself as "the irresistible force of gravity within the flow of things" and as "value-denying necessity"—the fundamental orienting principles of the individual's life had to be relativized to the extreme, wiping out the lines of demarcation between "small and great," "meaningful and meaningless," as well as "primary and secondary," and thereby leaving in the end no margin at all for the exercise of *aim and purpose.* A bleak picture indeed which could only be made even bleaker by stressing, again in the form of a relentless paradox, that historical necessity is both the nearest to life and the furthest from it. The impact of operating with such a categorial framework had to be all-pervasive irrationality, rendering most problematic even the idea of personal longing. For the fate of not being able to escape the desolate predicament of "*blind tools of a dumb and alien taskmaster*" was supposed to loom large at the end of the road. This is how the young Lukács had put it:

> History, through its *irrational reality,* forces *pure universality* upon men; it does not allow a man to express *his own idea,* which at other levels is *just as irrational:* the contact between them produces something alien to both—to wit, *universality. Historical necessity* is, after all, the nearest to life of all necessity. But also the furthest from life. The realization of the idea which is possible here is only a roundabout way of achieving its essential realization. . . . But the whole life of the whole man is also a roundabout way of reaching other, higher goals; his deepest *personal longing* and his struggle to attain what he longs for are merely the *blind tools of a dumb and alien taskmaster.*[79]

The qustions hopelessly unanswerable by Lukács at the time of writing "The Metaphysics of Tragedy," in 1910, were: could one find meaning in history in a radically different way which did not appear as a mysterious "force of gravity"? Was it necessary for history to assert itself through the postulated meaningless turmoil of particular "happenings" and to reveal an intelligible order to the individual only when everything was irretrievably buried in the past already? How could the apparently irreconcilable opposition between value and historical actuality be overcome? Was it the unavoidable predicament of humanity that those who are said to reach the height of self-fulfilment and realize "the longing of man for selfhood" should be "shattered against the All"?[80] How could one rescue the individuals engaged in their struggle for the wholeness of life—which they are said to be equally longing for—from being dominated by an irrational universality? Could one envisage mastering history not in abstractly hypothesized universalistic terms but in such a way that the personality of the individuals involved in the enterprise of authentic self-fulfilment should find genuine outlets for its proper and in the real world sustainable actualization?

In order to answer in a credible way these questions, it was necessary to enter a different universe of discourse. However, the categorial and methodological framework of the young Lukács's general approach, despite the much admired formal accomplishment of many of his essays, made that impossible.

THE QUESTION OF FRAGMENTATION appeared in the writings of the young Lukács time and again, under many of its aspects. Thus, in relation to the requirements of sustainable knowledge he ruefully complained that "Human knowledge is a psychological nihilism. We see a thousand relations, yet never grasp a genuine connection. The landscapes of our soul exist nowhere; yet in them, every tree and every flower is concrete."[81] This view was linked in *Soul and Form* to an untenable conception of ethics, exemplified by the following lines:

> *Form* is the highest judge of life . . . an *ethic*; . . . The validity and strength of an ethic does not depend on whether or not the ethic is applied. Therefore only *a form which has been purified until it has become ethical* can, without becoming blind and poverty-stricken as a result of it, *forget the existence of everything problematic and banish it forever from its realm.*[82]

Naturally, for as long as Lukács maintained such a position he barred his own road to finding a way out of his self-imposed maze of contradictions. For an ethic that could "*forget the existence of everything problematic and banish it forever from its realm,*" for the sake of becoming "purified form," inevitably condemned itself not only to being blind and poverty-stricken but also to total irrelevance.

In order to elaborate a creatively sustainable approach it was necessary for Lukács to undertake a radical reexamination of his conception of both ethics and form. The first major step in that direction was made by him in *The Theory of the Novel.* In that work Lukács's earlier rather vague ethical rebellion started to acquire a more tangible and in its intent more radical frame of reference, even if for the time being only a "purely utopian" one, according to the retrospective judgement of the mature Lukács. As he had put it in 1962, in the Preface to a new edition of *The Theory of the Novel*, it was utopian because "nothing, even at the level of abstract intellection, helped to *mediate* between subjective attitude and objective reality."[83] And he added:

> *The Theory of the Novel* is not conservative but subversive in nature, even if based on a highly naive and totally unfounded utopianism—the hope that a natural life worthy of man can spring from the disintegration of capitalism and the destruction, seen as identical with the disintegration, of the lifeless and life-denying social and economic categories.[84]

The unworkable in *The Theory of the Novel,* according to the mature Lukács, was that he tried to formulate in his youthful work "a conception of the world which aimed at a fusion of '*left*' ethics and '*right*' epistemology, ontology, etc. . . . a left ethic oriented towards radical revolution coupled with a traditional-conventional exegesis of reality."[85]

Another important consideration that must be taken into account in this respect was Lukács's—no longer "Kierkegaardized"—assessment of Hegel in the 1920s. The new approach to Hegel was in general most positive, but at the same time also firmly critical precisely because of the great German philosopher's treatment of the categories in relation to which Lukács himself had to radically modify his position. It was spelled out by Lukács in his important article on "Moses Hess und die Probleme der idealistischen Dialektik." These were the main points of Lukács's penetrating analysis:

> Hegel's tremendous intellectual contribution consisted in the fact that he made theory and history dialectically relative to each other, grasped them

> in a dialectical reciprocal penetration. Ultimately, however, his attempt was a failure. He could never get as far as the *genuine unity of theory and practice;* all that he could do was either fill the logical sequence of the categories with rich historical material, or rationalize history, in the shape of the succession of *forms, structural changes, epochs,* etc., which he raised to the level of *categories* by sublimating and abstracting them. Marx was the first who was able to see through this false dilemma. He did not derive the succession of categories either from the logical sequence, or from their historical succession, but recognized 'their succession as determined through the relation which they have to each other in bourgeois society'. In this way, he did not merely give dialectic the real basis which Hegel sought in vain, he did not merely put it on its feet. But he also raised the critique of political economy (which he had made the basis of dialectics) out of the fetishistic rigidity and abstractive narrowness to which economics was subject, even in the case of its greatest bourgeois representatives. The critique of political economy is no longer one science along with others, is not merely set over the others as a 'basic science'; rather, it embraces the whole world of history of the *'forms of existence'* (the categories) of human society.[86]

In this context we can see that the ground on which Lukács now praised Hegel was that "he made theory and history dialectically relative to each other, grasped them in a dialectical reciprocal penetration." In other words, Hegel offered a dialectical conception of *totality*, in absolute contrast to Lukács's earlier seen *subjectivist* conception of truth. At the same time, on the critical side of the now proposed evaluation of these problems, the question of "*unity,*" in contrast to the young Lukács's reflections on the subject, was no longer subsumed under the idea of *"longing,"* whether feasible or hopeless, but acquired a most tangible frame of reference within the requirements of a genuine *unity of theory and practice*. Moreover, the *categories* through which the world of experience—including all genuine quest for selfhood—could be made intelligible, had to be extricated from their idealistically rationalizing, sublimating and abstracting integument.

The most important of all for Lukács's development in this respect was the radical reexamination of the category of *form*. In the past, as we have seen above, the broadly used category of "*Form*" was idealized by Lukács, to the point of even wanting to equate it, in its bewilderingly "purified" variety, with a thoroughly unreal kind of *ethic.* Thus, whereas in the past the "forms" were conceived by the young Lukács as a set of abstract speculative—even if poetically embellished[87]—categories, now they have been understood, in their Marxian sense, as the crucial ***Daseinsformen*** of contemporary capitalist society. Accordingly, they could not be theorized by themselves, nor indeed as emerging ready made from a hypostatized philosophical and aesthetic domain, but only as the fundamental *"forms of existence"* of human society itself. That was the only way to confer upon them their far-reaching explanatory relevance, including the elucidation of the way in which they are shaping—in their capacity of *"übergreifendes Moment"* (that is, as a factor of ultimately overriding importance), asserted in the sense of the *dialectical reciprocity* on the basis of which the categorial *Daseinsformen* of society are themselves articulated and historically transformed—also the philosophical and aesthetic domain.

To be sure, at this point in his development, when Lukács wrote "Moses Hess und die Probleme der idealistischen Dialektik," he was already formulating his ideas within a socialist framework of discourse. Much earlier in his life, in 1910, he contemplated for a fleeting moment the relevance of socialism. But the young Lukács dismissed it without any serious examination of its potential role, in the name of its alleged failure to live up to the demands of the quasi-mystically conceived category of "soul" in his early writings. All he could say at the time of writing "Aesthetic Culture," in his speculative mood, was that although "the only hope could be in the proletariat, in socialism . . . it seems that socialism does not possess the *religious power* which is capable of filling the *entire soul:* a power that characterized primitive Christianity."[88]

Significantly, his radical reassessment of the categories of his youthful writing carried with it for Lukács also an essential change in relation to his approach both to the world of artistic creation and to ethics, with an enduring validity for the rest of his life. Two brief quotations can clearly illustrate this change. The first put it into relief—in an obvious contrast to Hegel's conception of world history as "the true *Theodicaea,* the justification of God in History"[89]—that "every real work of art is an *anti-Theo-*

dicaea in the strictest sense of the term."[90] And the second made the for Lukács seminally important emancipatory point that "*Ethics* is the crucial field of the fundamental, all-deciding struggle between *this-worldliness* and *other-worldliness,* of the real superseding/preserving transformation of human particularity."[91] This is how the categories discussed in this section, which originated within the conceptual framework of thinkers who in their time had expressed in one way or another their dilemmas and misgivings about their own class's oppressive rule, have been put in a proper historical perspective and transferred with moving authenticity by Lukács—who experienced from the inside the same dilemmas and misgivings in his youth—into a very different universe of discourse.

7.4 "The Ideal General Will Should Also Be the Empirically General Will"

The title of this section is taken from the concluding pages of Hegel's *Philosophy of History*. It refers to the—in Hegel's view hopelessly contradictory—embodiment of the principles of Liberalism in the modern state. This way of ordering in the modern world the life of the particular individuals and the complicated legislative processes of the state represents an insoluble dilemma for Hegel, as we have seen it admitted in his wishfully postulated projection of how the "perpetrated agitation, unrest and collision," according to the Hegelian scheme of things characteristic of the liberal state, would have to be worked out by the—to our own days very far from obliging— "future history."

Understandably, this was a matter of fundamental importance to Hegel. For, true to his idealization of the "Protestant principle in its secular aspect," as it was supposed to have been incorporated in the state by Frederick the Great of Prussia, Hegel asserted that the Prussian king "did not side with one party or the other, he had the *consciousness of Universality*, which is the profoundest depth to which Spirit can attain, and is Thought conscious of its own inherent power."[92]

The reasoning behind this boundless idealizing conclusion concerned nothing less than the postulated nature of "*the German world*" which represented the combined philosophical and world historic climax of the Hegelian system as a whole. As Hegel made it clear, "The German world appears at the fourth phase of World History. This would answer in the comparison with the periods of human life to its *Old Age.* The Old Age of Nature is weakness; but that of *Spirit* is its perfect maturity and *strength,* in which it returns to *unity* with itself, but in its fully developed character as *Spirit.*"[93] We have seen earlier that Hegel solved the philosophical problems arising from the Old Age in the periods of human life through the circularity of the return to childhood, as quoted above. Here he solved it through his *definitional decree* whereby in the case of *Spirit* Old Age was equivalent to "*perfect maturity and strength.*" And he *had to* find this kind of solution. For it was a necessary requirement of Hegel's overall philosophical conception that a forever lasting *reconciliation* should take place in the course of World History between the "Secular principle" and the "Spiritual principle." On the one had, according to Hegel, such reconciliation was inconceivable prior to the German world. And on the other hand, the *all-important defining determination* and absolute legitimation of the fourth and concluding phase of the Hegelian conception of world history was precisely the postulated *permanent reconciliation* of those two principles which had to constitúte an *absolutely unshakable unity*. This had to be the case because "The Secular *ought to be* in harmony with the Spiritual principle."[94] It is that harmony which is supposed to be fully accomplished in the German phase of world history. For at that irreversible phase Spirit

> produces its work in an intellectual shape and becomes capable of realizing the Ideal of Reason from the Secular principle alone. Thus it happens, that in virtue of elements of *Universality,* which have the principle of Spirit as their basis, the empire of Thought is established actually and concretely. The antithesis of Church and State vanishes. The Spiritual becomes reconnected with the Secular, and develops this latter as an independently organic existence. The State no longer occupies a position of real inferiority to the Church, and is no longer subordinate to it. The latter asserts no prerogative, and the Spiritual is no longer an element foreign to the State. *Freedom has found the means of realizing its Ideal*—its true existence. This is the *ultimate result* which the process of History *is intended to accomplish.*[95]

Moreover, this ideal state of affairs is supposed to remain with us forever; just like the rule of capital is expected to prevail in world history for the rest of time. For "length of Time is something entirely relative, and the element of Spirit is *Eternity*. Duration, properly speaking, cannot be said to belong to it."[96]

GIVEN ITS SHARP CONTRAST to this vision, it is not at all difficult to imagine that Hegel had to find the already existing and potentially even more dominant state formation of Liberalism utterly bewildering. He could neither minimize its historical relevance, nor could he contemplate any admissible solution to the total *"incompatibility"* which he identified in Liberalism between "men's subjective will"[97] and the absolute requirement of the "consciousness of Universality" that he praised—as fully appropriate to the harmony which he also asserted between the Protestant principle and the Secular principle—in the attitude to the State by Frederick the Great.[98]

Naturally, the obvious contradiction between the Liberal state formation and his own conception of the ideally accomplished Germanic State was not a minor historical complication in the Hegelian scheme of things. On the contrary, it represented a massive intrusion which happened to be most revealing about the categorial and methodological framework, as well as the postulated completion of both philosophy and world history, as articulated in the Hegelian system. For it was categorically asserted by Hegel that

> Truth is the *Unity of the universal and subjective Will;* and the *Universal* is to be found in the *State,* in its laws, its universal and rational arrangements. The State is the Divine Idea as it exists on Earth. . . . Law is the objectivity of Spirit; volition in its true form. . . . *when the subjective will of man submits to laws—the contradiction between Liberty and Necessity vanishes.*[99]

Now Hegel had to admit that instead of submitting to the requirements of the idealized "ethical" state's "universal and rational arrangements," *men's subjective will* apparently carried on asserting its demand that "the ideal general will should also be the empirically general—i.e.

that the units of the State, in their individual capacity, should rule, or at any rate take part in government."[100] Hegel could not consider legitimating any other form of rationality than what would aprioristically correspond to *"the essential destiny of Reason"* which was *"destined to be realized"*[101] in the "eternal present" of Spirit and in its "perfect embodiment—the State."[102] Since he viewed the world from the vantage point of capital, Hegel could not possess the concept of structurally rooted *class antagonisms.* For such a concept would vitiate the postulated framework of unquestionable "rational actuality" of the social system whose standpoint he shared with the greatest representatives of bourgeois political economy, including Adam Smith. Even less could he entertain for a moment the idea that a fundamentally different—and historically sustainable—rationality might actually arise from the potentially positive unfolding of the *social* (and not tendentiously misrepresented *atomistic/individualistic)* antagonisms. Understandably, therefore, Hegel could argue only in this way:

> Not satisfied with the establishment of rational rights, with freedom of person and property, with the existence of a political organization in which are to be found various circles of civil life each having its own functions to perform, and with that influence over the people which is exercised by the intelligent members of the community, and the confidence that is felt in them, *'Liberalism'* sets up in opposition to all this the *atomistic principle*, that which insists upon the *sway of individual wills;* maintaining that all government should emanate from their express power, and have their express sanction.[103]

Thus Hegel's negative attitude was determined by the circumstance that the state form of "Liberalism" did not conform to his own idealized state conception in which the *"subjective will"* and the *"rational will"* find themselves in complete *"unity,"* under the "Universality of Reason," imaginarily resolving thereby the *"contradiction between Liberty and Necessity."* Ultimately sharing the same social standpoint as his presumed adversary, Hegel could not submit to criticism the fundamental vacuity of the liberal position. Namely, that as the exploitative beneficiary of capital's structurally (and therefore by its very nature irreconcilably) antagonistic order it could have nothing whatsoever to do with the *substantive* ("empirical") requirements of making the *general will* effectively prevail in all domains of social life. For what the liberal state formation perpetrated was the rule of the *plurality of capitals*—switching intermittently from *some* of its strictly mandated personifications to *others*—against the *structurally subordinate class of labour*. Thus it did not simply "perpetrate the subjective will of the Many"—sometimes in Government and sometimes in Opposition—against which Hegel complained. But to notice that a radically different kind of vacuity was quite impossible from capital's vantage point which Hegel fully shared also with liberalism.

FROM THE UNCHALLENGEABLE STANDPOINT of his own approach Hegel did not hesitate to decree in his *Philosophy of History*, in the form of a categorically asserted postulate, that

> The only Thought which Philosophy brings with it to the contemplation of History, is the simple conception of *Reason;* that Reason is the Sovereign of the World; that the history of the world, therefore, presents us with a rational process. . . . On the one hand, Reason is the *substance* of the Universe; viz., that by which and in which all reality has its being and subsistence. On the other hand, it is the *Infinite Energy* of the Universe; since Reason is not so powerless as to be incapable of producing anything but a mere ideal, a mere intention . . . It is the *infinite complex of things,* their entire Essence and Truth.[104]

On the way towards defining his own position, one of Hegel's great German ancestors, Leibnitz, enters the picture. Hegel makes an important reference to Leibnitz's method in relation to their common concern, called by Hegel "a justification of the ways of God." At the same time Hegel also underlines a major difference between them in this respect. This is how he characterizes the problem:

> It was for awhile the fashion to profess admiration for the wisdom of God, as displayed in animals, plants, and isolated occurrences. But if it be allowed that Providence manifests itself in such objects and forms of existence, why not also in Universal History? This is deemed too great a mat-

> ter to be thus regarded. But *Divine Wisdom, i.e., Reason,* is one and the same in the great as in the little; and we must not imagine God to be too weak to exercise his wisdom on the great scale. Our intellectual striving aims at realizing the conviction that what was *intended* by eternal wisdom, is actually *accomplished* in the domain of existent, active Spirit, as well as in that of mere Nature. Our mode of treating the subject is, in this aspect, a Theodicaea—a justification of the ways of God—which Leibnitz attempted metaphysically, in his method, i.e., in indefinite abstract categories—so that the ill that is found in the World may be comprehended, and the thinking Spirit reconciled with the fact of the existence of evil.[105]

The big difference was, in contrast to Leibnitz, that Hegel's Theodicaea had to be *positive* through and through. Its inalterable positive orientation was a crucial characteristic of the Hegelian philosophy in its entirety. This was the case even when some of the far from marginal assertions of the Hegelian system—like "what is rational is actual and what is actual is rational," for instance—were spelled out with a tone of unconcealed resignation, without altering thereby in the slightest the overall philosophical claim of positivity and finality. Not surprisingly, therefore, many instances of such claimed positivity had to be judged *false positivity* by all those, including Marx, who refused to bring their own position into conformity to the eternalized vantage point of the capital system.

Given the *aprioristic positivity* of the Hegelian system, *reconciliation* (or "*harmonization*") speculatively always had to prevail in it. In Hegel's view "nowhere is such a *harmonizing view* more pressingly demanded than in Universal History; and it can be attained only by recognizing the *positive* existence, in which the negative element is a *subordinate, and vanquished nullity*. On the one hand, the ultimate design of the world must be perceived; and, on the other hand, the fact that this design has been *actually realized* in it, and that evil has not been able permanently to assert a competing position."[106]

Assuming this kind of positive postulate as absolutely prevailing in the Universe under the Sovereignty of Reason, it was inconceivable for Hegel to entertain a different idea about the necessary embodiment of Reason in the State than what he actually stipulated. Accordingly, this is how Hegel treated the doubts that might arise at all on this score and had to be firmly laid to rest:

> There *may be* various opinions and views respecting laws, constitution and government, but there *must be* a disposition on the part of the citizens to regard all these opinions as subordinate to the *substantial interest of the State,* and to insist upon them no further than that interest will allow; moreover nothing must be considered *higher and more sacred than good will towards the state.*[107]

This is why Hegel could not contemplate any other intelligible explanation for the failure to conform to his own conception of the ideal "ethical State" than the particular individuals' irrational refusal to bring their "subjective will" under the absolute authority of the "rational will."

His conclusions were, therefore, unalterable by any actually existing alternative state formation, like the liberal, for instance, which he could only consign to the work of "future history." And that strange notion of "future history" was itself rather arbitrarily hypostatized. For the only sense in which such a thing could make any sense at all in Hegel's scheme of things in relation to the State would be if it created *total conformity* to the model of the "ethical State" with which he fully identified himself. In other words, if that "future history" was *not future at all,* since it existed already in the "eternal present" of actually accomplished world history, in its final—Germanic—phase of development, together with its ideal state formation.

What had to be unquestioningly respected, according to Hegel, was that "the History of the World is nothing but the development of the Idea of Freedom. But Objective Freedom—the laws of *real* Freedom—demand the *subjugation of the mere contingent Will*—for this is in its nature formal. If the Objective is in itself Rational, human insight and conviction *must* correspond with the Reason which it embodies, and *then we have* the other essential element—*Subjective Freedom*—also *realized.*"[108]

THUS THE WHOLE EDIFICE of the Hegelian philosophy—which equated *Reason* embodied in it with nothing less than the *Divine Wisdom*[109]—was supposed to be, precisely on account of its divinely ordained rationality, absolutely unassailable for all time to come. Every *"principle"* worthy of philosophical interest according to Hegel had its place allocated in it, moving from the "abstract" to the "concrete," and all of them were brought together within the unfolding framework of World History itself, which was said to display "the justification of the ways of God," with the idealized Hegelian State at its unchallengeable apex.

Yet on closer inspection it transpires that the whole edifice is erected on the foundations of categorically asserted *postulates,* and by no means only with regard to the assertion of "unity" and "universality," as predicated by the entire philosophical tradition under review.

For a start, we are confronted by the postulate that "the rational, the divine, possesses the absolute power to *actualize itself* and has, right from the beginning, *fulfilled itself,*" as we have seen above. Moreover, if doubts might be entertained about such categorical assertions, Hegel offers us, repeatedly, a side-tracking assurance, regarding the unquestionable *power* of the divine, by saying that "it is not so *impotent* that it would have to wait for the beginning of its *actualization.*" Or: "Reason is not so *powerless* as to be incapable of producing anything but a mere idea." And again: "we must not imagine God to be *too weak* to exercise his wisdom on the great scale." Once we enter this framework of discourse, consenting on the ground of *definitional self-evidence* that no one could or should wish to suggest that the divine and its assumed identity with Reason might be "impotent," "powerless," and "too weak," the original postulate implicit in Hegel's categorical assertion about the "self-fulfilling actualization" of the divine order—or the "World Spirit"—in the positive unfolding of World History, as reflected in Hegelian philosophy, acquires its legitimacy and timeless validity.

The closure of *actual human history,* in the name of the arbitrarily postulated "eternal present" corresponding to the time frame of the Spirit, is not less problematical. We are told by Hegel that "we have, in traversing the past . . . only to do what is *present*; for philosophy, as occupying itself with the True, has to do with the *eternally present.* Nothing in the past is lost for it, for the Idea is ever present; Spirit is immortal; with it there is *no past, no future,* but an *essentially now. . . .* The life of the ever present Spirit is a *circle* of progressive embodiments . . . The grades which Spirit seems to have left behind it, it still possesses in the depths of its *present*."[110] This view is inseparable from the assertion of the World Spirit's "*final aim*" and its fully adequate actualization in the *present*. To say that Spirit preserves the past in the depths of its present is one thing. But to say that "there is no past, *no future*" is quite another. For what he really asserts in that way is that there can be no meaningfully different *future* for human beings and for their historically created institutions: a profoundly *apologetic* position. And he maintains that position so that he should be able to hail the idealized State as the final embodiment of the Divine Idea "as it exists on earth." And that kind of actualization of the World Spirit was always so intended, in accordance with its postulated "final aim." For in the State "Freedom has found the means of realizing its Ideal—its true existence. This is the *ultimate result* which the process of History *is intended to accomplish*," as we have seen it decreed by Hegel on page 110 of his *Philosophy of History*.

Hegel's conception of "*unity and universality*" was subsumed under his definition of Truth in its relationship to the State. For he insisted that "Truth is the *Unity* of the *universal* and *subjective Will*; and the Universal is to be found in the State, in its laws, its universal and rational arrangements." He recognized that this was a difficult matter. But he could see only one way of solving the problem inherent in the relationship between the individuals' subjective will and the State, while always insisting on the vital necessity of its solution. And, of course, the solution advocated by Hegel had to be the unquestioning *submission* of the subjective will to the Divine Idea embodied in the laws of the State. At the same time, when asserting the rightful imperative of submission, he also optimistically postulated that "when the subjective will of man *submits* to laws—the contradiction between Liberty and Necessity vanishes." And he went even further than that, by talking about the necessary *subjugation* of the subjective or contingent will. And again he did not hesitate to equate the *subjugation* of the particular individuals' "contingent will" with the realization of Freedom. Indeed, in this case with the realization of *Subjective Freedom*. His earlier quoted reasoning started with the "*if*" clause but culminated with the Hegelian conclusion conveniently derived from a *must*. These were his words: "*If* the Objective is in itself Rational, human insight and conviction *must* correspond with the Reason which it embodies, and *then we have* the other essential element—*Subjective Freedom*—also realized."

But *what if* we have to question the fundamental Hegelian reconciliatory postulate that "what is rational is actual and what is actual is rational"? Could that create a margin of legitimate action for the individuals? Not for the sake of displaying in a capricious and irrational way their "mere contingent will" but in order to creatively intervene in the ongoing historical process, for the realization of their consciously chosen and on a lasting basis sustainable objectives? Or must we resign ourselves to the "submission" and "subjugation" of the "subjective and contingent will" by the actually existing individuals? And to do so in the interest of the *speculative* realization of "*unity and universality*" aprioristically prejudged by the requirements of the idealized State, contenting ourselves with the kind of purely notional *"subjective Freedom"* that one can squeeze out of the relationship defined in such terms? Naturally, to enter properly into answering these questions it would be necessary to pursue a very different line of ideological and methodological enquiry.

It is most ironical that Hegel's strictures about the unrealizability of the "ideal General Will" as "empirically general" do not really apply to Liberalism. For Liberalism never intended, and moreover never in the future could intend, the practical embodiment of the ideal principles of the General Will into its state legislative framework. Its appeal to the "Many" deplored by Hegel served very limited electoral purposes, never altering in any way the structural framework of the established socioeconomic order. Also in its original formulation the theory of the General Will did not envisage its translation into readily available state practices. It was attempting to set the *morally commendable* regulative principles of legislation and administration, so far in vain in history. Nevertheless, the actualization of some aspects of the "empirically general will" remain feasible under suitably changed societal conditions. But to institute the regulative principles applicable with validity under such conditions would require the radical redefinition of the historical subject, in actual social practice, as a genuine communal subject, in contrast to both the "aggregative individualities" of mainstream bourgeois philosophy and the Hegelian speculative personification of World History.

7.5 Unification through the Material Reproduction Process

To the extent to which it is practicable under the circumstances of class society, "unification" is carried on as a matter of course by the complex material reproduction process itself, which cannot be divorced from the powerful tools and institutional arsenal of the ruling ideology. Only in periods of acute crisis is this relationship significantly upset. We should remember in this respect that revolutionary upheavals, overturning for shorter or longer periods of time this kind of normality, arose from such acute crises, in the aftermath of major military disasters, from the Paris Commune of 1871 to the 1917 Russian Revolution, not to forget the social earthquakes in Eastern Europe which followed the defeat suffered in the Second World War alongside Nazi Germany.

Naturally, the fact that the ruling ideology enjoys overwhelming support by the overall complex of the material reproduction process itself does not mean that in the conceptualizations of their concern for "unity" and "universality" by the thinkers who adopt the vantage point of capital the actual power relations of structural hierarchy and domination might be acknowledged, with some corrective intent. Not even when they assert—and tendentiously idealize—their commitment to *reform.* On the contrary, the real meaning of their discourse on *"social unity"* and *"equitable universality"* is meant to be used as the obvious and unobjectionable *evidence* for the projected *rational improvement* which is supposed to be taking place in society, thanks to the explicitly stated enlightened commitment of the thinkers concerned.

However, the postulated improvements are always confined to the *vicious circle* of consumable *distribution,* in its absolute dependency on the unmentionable, let alone changeable, property relations of *production.* It is relevant in this regard that even a philosophical genius, like Hegel, can commit the elementary fallacy[111] of *conflating* the means of *production* with the means of *subsistence,* in the interest of eternalizing the world of capital, as mentioned before. This is a most revealing fallacy which would call for much more than the usual "correction" confined to the philosophical domain. For the nature of the underlying problem is that once the means and the material of production are most iniquitously distributed in the historically created world among a tiny minority of people, namely among capital's structurally privileged and happily obliging personifications, such predetermination of the societal reproduction process imposes on even the best intentioned distribution of the capitalistically produced commodities allocated for individual consumption its strictly *prejudged* limit. That way of controlling production itself invariably calls for, and simultaneously also *justifies,* the "rational/consensual tightening of the belt" by the working classes—in contrast to all fictitious reform—whenever the unquestionable imperatives of production (and concomitant capital-expansion) so demand. At the same time, since the presumed reforming institutions of social reproductive interchange—from the hierarchically ordained particular workshops to the all-embracing market, and from the cultural and educational institutions of the established order to the dominant political decision making bodies of society—are necessarily prejudged by the same determinations, there can be no question of significant change. This is how abstracting in self-enclosed theoretical discourse—about the claimed reforming "unity and universality"—from the overpowering role of the material reproduction process can only obfuscate and mystify matters, irrespective of how consciously this line of approach is pursued by the particular thinkers.

Accordingly, in this framework of discourse all talk about "unity" and rationally adopted "unification" —postulated on the imaginary ground of the full "reciprocity" and "mutuality" of all individuals in society, projecting thereby the self-evident realization of the "universal interest"—must remain extremely problematical. For what is tendentiously omitted from the adopted picture is the brutally enforced original distribution of the people into antagonistically opposed social classes, allocating the overwhelming majority of them at the time of the "primitive accumulation of capital" to the structurally and hierarchically subordinate class, controlled for a long time in history even with the most oppressive forms of punishment, including the mass extermination of the so-called "vagabonds." And when the workers' inescapable *economic compulsion* makes superfluous the earlier forms of brutal political control, since capital-expansion can be secured primarily through the modality of the ubiquitously prevailing economic compulsion, backed up by the legislative framework of the capitalist state, the fiction of full reciprocity becomes a commonplace. At the same time the most important dimension of the *structurally enforced hierarchical social division of labour*—carrying with it the unalterable allocation of the overwhelming majority of the people to the economically exploited subordinate class—disappears from view. It is transubstantiated into a purely *technical division of labour,* which should not be questioned by any sane person, of course.

THIS IDYLLIC VIEW OF THE SOCIAL UNIVERSE is characteristic of all major thinkers of bourgeois political economy who adopt, as axiomatically valid, the vantage point of capital. Hegel follows in their footsteps, transferring their idyll to the most abstract level of philosophical generalization. He insists that

> The universal and objective element in work lies in the abstracting process which effects the subdivision of needs and means and thereby *eo ipso* subdivides production and brings about the division of labour. . . . At the same time, this abstraction of one man's skill and means of production from another's completes and makes necessary everywhere the dependence of men on one another and their *reciprocal relation* in the satisfaction of their other needs. . . . When men are thus dependent on one another and reciprocally related to one another in their work and the satisfaction of their needs, subjective self-seeking turns into a contribution to the satisfaction of the needs of *everyone else.* That is to say, by a *dialectical advance,* subjective self-seeking turns into the *mediation* of the particular through the universal, with the result that each man in earning, producing, and enjoying on his own account is *eo ipso* producing and earning for the enjoyment of everyone else.[112]

To be sure, Hegel cannot deny that compulsion is somehow involved in this process. But he ideally transubstantiates also the compulsion into an organic constitutive moment of the best of all conceivable worlds. This is how his reasoning continues immediately after the last quoted words: "The compulsion which brings this about is rooted in the complex *interdependence of each on all,* and it now presents itself *to each* as the *universal permanent capital* which *gives each the opportunity,* by the exercise of his education and skill, to *draw a share from it* and so be assured of his livelihood, while what he thus earns by means of his *work* maintains and increases the general capital."[113] But what about those who do not work yet have much more than their "livelihood" secured to them through their a priori established privileges, embodied in their—by Hegel idealized and by the "ethical state" forcefully protected—private property? That kind of embarrassing question, which would undermine the projected idyllic finality of the World Spirit's determinations, cannot find its place in any discourse conceived from the vantage point of capital. For the fiction of full "reciprocity" and "mutuality" must be maintained at all cost, despite all evidence to the contrary.

Naturally, we cannot abstract from the objective reality of *mediation* asserting itself in these relations. Nothing could work in the social world without it. But only in speculative philosophy can actual mediation be defined as we have seen it done by Hegel, even if some of its constituents are borrowed from the classics of political economy.

If it were true, as Hegel asserts, that we must put our faith in the interchange of the fundamental "principles" of particularity and universality, in that case the best we could expect in the "rational actuality" of the existent through the good work of such principles would be the kind of "reciprocity" and "mutuality" which would seem to overcome the problem of the predicated selfishness (or subjective self-seeking) of each individual—by turning their "complex interdependence" into universally shared enjoyment—without changing in the real world anything at all. For this miraculous transformation is said to come about thanks to the way in which "subjective self-seeking turns into the *mediation* of the particular through the universal," producing thereby a permanently sustainable and harmonized relationship of each and every one of the particular individuals among themselves. And they do not even have to consciously change their former egotistic self-assertion because *mediation itself*—in Hegel's words the "*mediation* of the particular through the universal"—is destined to do it automatically for them: by redefining the character of universal "*subjective self-seeking itself*" as *universal enjoyment*. In this way what is inherently problematical—due to the assumed fixity of selfish "human nature"—becomes insuperably praiseworthy, just like in the Chronicles of bourgeois political economy.

However, the question of mediation cannot be treated as a speculative interchange of abstract philosophical principles. The real problem is not *individualistic mediation* happily completed and positively absolved from all possible blame by the principle of universality, as depicted by Hegel. Rather, it is the *conflictual/adversarial mediation* involved in the way in which the potentially most destructive *power relations* are managed in actually existing society through the complex interchange of its antagonistically opposed classes.

If a thinker speculatively abstracts from the insuperably conflictual class relationship characteristic of capital's social order, ignoring the fact that the two fundamental classes of society constitute the hegemonic alternative to each other (as all those who conceptualize the world from capital's vantage point abstract from it, avoiding like plague the subject of structurally rooted class antagonism), in that case the conflicts that are nevertheless identified, since they cannot be hidden from sight even in the most reconciliatory approaches, are bound to be arbitrarily reduced to individualistic vicissitudes, so as to be transfigured in due course into spurious virtues, as we have seen above. This is done despite the fact that one cannot make intelligible the functioning of the established social order simply in terms of the interactions of arbitrarily conceptualized *"genus individuals,"* no matter how many, instead of adequately depicting the most complicated and multi-dimensionally conflictual *actual mediations* through which the *social individuals* are related both to their own class and to the class of their historical adversary. The tendentious failure to grasp *antagonistic social mediation* in this way, since it cannot be brought into agreement with the standpoint of capital, denies not only the intelligibility of the actual historical process as a whole.[114] It removes at the same time also the *margin of meaningful intervention of the social individuals*—irrespective of which side of the social divide they find themselves—in the contradictorily unfolding historical process, notwithstanding the professed ideology of "Freedom." For it is impossible to make intelligible the historical process even minimally without giving its due weight to the most active involvement of the *social*—as opposed to the arbitrarily conceptualized *isolated self-seeking*—individuals. Assuming for the fictitious "genus individuals" the fixity of "self-seeking human nature" offers no solution whatsoever in this respect.

In Hegel's case we find that—*reversing the actual causal order*—he mystifyingly depicts the vital determination of being *self-seeking / egotistic* as if it was directly emanating from the individuals themselves, although in reality it is immanent to capital's insurmountable ontological ground. Such a historically constituted ontological ground was in reality *imposed on the individuals* who could not opt out from operating within the framework of the given social metabolic order. Consequently, the individuals had to *internalize* the system's *objective self-expansionary imperative*—without which that system as such could not possibly survive—as if it sprang out of the inner core of their own *nature-determined* personal aims and purposes. In this way Hegel was able not only to produce a philosophically absolutized dualism of capital's social order (its "civil society" and its "ethical political state") but also to glorify the historical development corresponding to the claimed "realization of freedom," fully in tune with the ultimate design of the World Spirit.

THE NEARER WE GET TO OUR OWN TIME the more intractable these problems become. Against the undeniable historical background of two devastating world wars in the twentieth century, as well as countless social upheavals experienced on a massive scale—which should not have happened at all if there was any substance in the fairy tales of the universally benevolent "hidden hand" and in the equally fanciful Hegelian projection of full reciprocity and "universal enjoyment" produced by the *"mediation* of the self-seeking particular through the universal"—the postulates of "unity and universality" continue to be constantly renewed in the mainstream of bourgeois theory, even if with an increasing dose of cynicism and hypocrisy. Now the idyllic saga talks about "people's capitalism" and "individual consumer sovereignty" (to be exercised by the capitalistically devoted housewives who "shop around" in the more or less identical supermarkets), not to mention the endlessly repeated words of "Liberty" and "Democracy" in political discourse. And to crown all this blessing, we are also constantly promised the ultimate unity and universality of fully accomplished *globalization,* whereafter with absolute certainty every single individual shall live in great happiness.

The trouble is, though, that our social and historical reality could not be more disturbingly different. For we have reached a stage in the capital system's development when—due to the reckless husbandry and wastefulness of the established system's productive practices, visibly undermining the conditions of life on this planet, coupled with genocidal military adventures undertaken by the most powerful "democracies" in the name of "Liberty," with no indication as to how far they might still escalate—the *destruction of humanity* is on the horizon unless a radical structural change can prevail in the foreseeable future.

When the far from equitably disposed "invisible hand" had found its organized adversary in the working class movement, the unfolding socioeconomic conflicts had to be acknowledged by capital's personifications in some form. But only in order to be countered by various means, in the proclaimed interest of creating "unity" among the contending parties. One of the advocated approaches, both theorized and instituted by Frederic Winslow Taylor, claimed for itself the status of "scientific management." Its basic tenet was spelled out by Taylor in this way: "The great revolution that takes place in the mental attitude of the two parties under scientific management is that both sides take their eyes off the division of the surplus as the all-important matter, and together they turn their attention toward increasing the size of the surplus until this surplus becomes so large that it is *unnecessary to quarrel over how it shall be divided*."[115] Taylor was also propagandizing in his entrepreneurial utopia "the substitution of hearty brotherly cooperation for contention and strife."[116] But this is how he characterized (and also treated) the "brother" employed in his factory: "Now one of the very first requirements for a man who is fit to handle pig iron as a regular occupation is that he shall be so stupid and so phlegmatic that he more nearly resembles in his mental make-up the ox than any other type. . . . He is so stupid that the word 'percentage' has no meaning for him."[117]

In truth the really "stupid"—or, rather, capitalistically blind—party in this relationship was Taylor and his kind. For the personifications of capital could never even begin to understand that the real problem was not *how large is the surplus to be divided*—that could only matter temporarily, for even the most spectacularly enlarged societal production can be dissipated by irresponsible husbandry and militarist destruction, as we know in our society only too well—but *who allocates the total social product and to what ends.*

In the idyllic fairy tales of the past in which everything was supposed to be managed in the best possible way by the various conceptualizations of the "invisible hand," producing not only ever-expanding wealth but also "unity" and "universality," not to forget "universal enjoyment" for all individuals, the question of *"who"* and *"to what end"* could not possibly arise. For everything was said to be ideally settled forever by the aprioristic assumption of the rather mysterious directing authority itself, whether under the name of the "invisible hand" or the "cunning of Reason." But even after the evaporation of the hope associated with the original transubstantiation of the actual social reproduction process, when class antagonisms sharply erupted into the open, nothing more could be offered by capital's entrepreneurial personifications and their ideological apologists than the new fairy tale of remedying everything through the self-illuminating realization by the contending parties that "when they substitute friendly cooperation and mutual helpfulness for antagonism and strife, they are together able to make the surplus so enormously greater than it was in the past that there is ample room for a large increase in wages for the workman and an equally great increase in profits for the manufacturer."[118] Nothing has been changed in this respect ever since. Even the *"Welfare State"* was theorized—and instituted in a tiny fraction of the world—on the same basis, without any guarantee for the future. For even in those few countries the Welfare State was instituted only conjuncturally, taking back the relative improvements in the standard of living of the working classes to an alarming degree under the impact of capital's structural crisis.

ONE OF CAPITAL'S PRINCIPAL IDEOLOGISTS in the post-Second World War period, Raymond Aron, did not hesitate to postulate the realization of *"Western universalism,"* contemptuously dismissing at the same time all those who continued to express their critical concern about the gruesome inequality dominating the overwhelming majority of humankind as "megalomania, anti-Americanism, the political 'progressiveness' typical of Latin intellectuals whether they are on the banks of the Seine, in Havana, or in Rio de Janeiro."[119] He also peremptorily decreed that "in the age of industrial society there is no contradiction between the interest of underdeveloped countries and those of advanced countries."[120] No wonder, therefore, that he could see nothing wrong with the way in which postwar imperialism rearticulated its mode of domination. He idealized it by saying that "a *universal society* is coming into being... The West is dying as a separate 'culture', but it has a future as *the center of a universal society.*"[121]

No rational argument could alter this kind of—unreservedly apologetic and self-complacent—attitude towards the established order. Raymond Aron crusadingly championed the "Atlanticist" perspective, to be imposed under American military domination,[122] equating it with the final form of "universalism." His conception of "unification" was equally cogent. Viewing it from the "center of a universal society," from capital's vantage point, he could not see any difficulty about it, since in his view there could be no contradiction between the interest of underdeveloped countries and those of advanced countries. Accordingly, the people who had the temerity to voice their dissent had to be categorically condemned as "megalomaniac anti-American intellectuals." This is how some of the once genuine tenets of *liberalism* have been turned several decades ago into the self-righteous articles of faith of aggressive *neo-liberalism.* And ever since that time there has been no shortage in attempts to bring them up-to-date in the same spirit.

Naturally, the grave problems of our actually existing world do not disappear through the ever more vacuous postulates of "unity" and "universality." Their lack of theoretical substance does not mean that it is impossible to turn them into the practical orienting principles of dangerous neo-liberal adventurism. Especially when the immense vested interests of the military industrial complex—glorified by Raymond Aron (as we have seen in a note attached to the last paragraph) —back them up in every way, thanks to their unrivalled leverage also in the cultural domain. It is happening today far beyond the boundaries of the original—in explicit defensive terms defined—"Atlantic alliance" which had to be, and has been, redefined for the purpose of aggressive military intervention all over the world. At the same time the chronic insolubility of the problems that should be positively confronted, instead of destructively tampered with, carries the danger of humanity running out of control of its conditions of survival.

THUS, THE NEED FOR FINDING historically viable solutions to the problems of our antagonistic social order has never been more pressing. As we know, under the normally prevailing circumstances of capital's social order "unification" is achieved, even if only to a limited degree, by the material reproduction process itself. The potentially destructive power relations are successfully contained and managed in it—more or less under the force of inertia, since the stakes themselves as a rule do not involve the question of radical change—through the conflictual/adversarial mediation of their affairs by the contending classes.

This is what creates the illusion that the customary form of adversariality can be *permanently* maintained as the dominant modality of the societal reproduction process. The concept of *conflictual mediation* is in that way subsumed under the idea of *balancing,* and it is wishfully projected into the future. It is woefully ignored that even when the semblance of balancing prevails, it really works under the *causal impact* of the given material and political *power relations* favouring the ruling order, and not by itself. This is so no matter how elaborate might be the institutionalized balancing machinery. What is always omitted from the more or less cynical reasoning in praise of successful "balancing" is precisely the *nature of the conflict*—whether conjunctural or structural—and the *magnitude of the stakes* involved.

In our time, in view of the *structural crisis* of the capital system in its entirety, the conflict in question is *structural* and not conjunctural. At the same time, the magnitude of the stakes involved could not be greater. For, notwithstanding all effort to hide the contradictions under the proverbial carpet, waste and destruction is visible everywhere in our time. Thus only the historically viable institution and consolidation of the *hegemonic alternative* to capital's ever more destructive social reproductive order can offer a way out from our deepening structural crisis. Abstract postulates of unity and universality take us absolutely nowhere. Not even when they are formulated at the highest level of philosophical generalization, as we have seen in the work of Hegel.

The challenge remains the elaboration of socially viable—and no longer on the subordinate classes ruthlessly imposed adversarial—material and cultural mediations. That is, solving our problems requires the institution of qualitatively different forms of mediation through which both the now dominant practice of irresponsible husbandry, with its fatefully negative impact on nature, and the trend of escalating militarist destruction, can be permanently consigned to the past. But, of course, all that is synonymous with the radical restructuring of our established social order, in accordance with consciously chosen and forcefully pursued human design, to be achieved in the not too distant future, in the course of our inescapable historical period of transition.

No historically sustainable alternative is feasible without the radical reexamination of the *practical premises* of capital's social order. The fundamental characteristic of the long prevailing form of material and ideological mediation in our societal reproduction process is the *strictly hierarchical* and *structurally enforced domination* of the overwhelming majority of the people, corresponding to the one and only conceivable operational premise of the established order in which the *directing* functions *must be* assigned in the most authoritarian way, despite all rhetorics about "democracy" and "liberty," to the personifications of capital. For the capital system could not sustain itself even for a short time in any other way.

The necessary hegemonic alternative to the ruling order, by contrast, could not realize its objectives without the successful elaboration and institution of a *meaningfully democratic* and *fully cooperative* mode of material and cultural mediation. That kind of—qualitatively different—form of non-adversarial mediation can only be oriented by the *communally* organized productive and distributive interchanges of the social individuals among themselves. In other words, a system of *"directly social"* and not *"post festum social"* mode of societal reproduction (Marx[123]) in which *instead of* the now dominant *hierarchical social division* of labour the rational organization and *coordination* of the productive activities prevails, as consciously managed by the freely associated producers on the basis of their *substantive equality*.

The important methodological aspects of pursuing such a design are to be explored in the final chapter.

NOTES

1. Husserl, *Cartesian Meditations*, Martinus Nijhoff, The Hague, 1969, p. 155.
2. Hegel, *Science of Logic*, vol. 2, Allen & Unwin, London, 1929, p. 171.
3. Husserl, *Cartesian Meditations*, p. 35.

4. Ibid., p. 136.
5. Ibid., p.150.
6. Ibid.
7. Ibid., pp. 156–7.
8. Ibid., p. 155.
9. Hegel, *Science of Logic*, vol. 2, p. 484.
10. Husserl, *Cartesian Meditations,* p. 150.
11. Henrik Ibsen, *Peer Gynt,* translated by Peter Watts, Penguin Books edition, 1966, p. 206.
12. Ibid., p. 106.
13. Ibid., p. 201.
14. Ibid., p. 106.
15. Ibid., p. 191.
16. Ibid., p. 222.
17. Ibid., p. 223.
18. Husserl, *Cartesian Meditations,* p. 139.
19. Ibid.
20. Ibid., p. 155.
21. Ibid., p. 156. Husserl's emphases.
22. *Philosophy and the Crisis of European Man,* in Husserl, *Phenomenology and the Crisis of Philosophy,* Harper & Row, New York, 1965, p. 168.
23. Ibid., p. 178.
24. Ibid., p. 192.
25. They are briefly discussed in Sections 3.1, 3.2 and 4.4 above. For a more detailed analysis of this problem, together with the closely related issue of first order mediations, see chapter 4 of my book *Beyond Capital.*
26. Hegel, *Science of Logic*, vol. 2, p. 484.
27. Ibid.
28. Ibid., p. 485.
29. Hegel, *The Philosophy of History,* Dover Publications Inc., New York, 1956, p. 452.
30. Ibid.
31. Hegel, *The Philosophy of Right,* Clarendon Press, Oxford, 1942, p. 10.
32. All quotations in this paragraph: ibid., p. 11.
33. Ibid., p. 12.
34. Vico, op. cit. p. 52.

35. Ibid., p. 65.
36. Hegel's *Philosophy of Mind,* Clarendon Press, Oxford, 1971, p. 64.
37. Rousseau, "A Discourse on Political Economy," in Rousseau, *The Social Contract* and *Discourses,* Dent & Sons, London, 1958, p. 236.
38. Ibid.
39. Ibid., pp. 236–237.
40. Ibid., p. 237.
41. Rousseau, *The Social Contract,* in *The Social Contract* and *Discourses,* Dent & Sons, London, 1958, p. 36.
42. In Hegel's discussion of "the ages of man."
43. Note by T. M. Knox to Hegel's *Philosophy of Right,* p. 376.
44. Hegel's *Philosophy of Mind,* p. 64.
45. Ibid., p. 55.
46. Ibid., p. 56.
47. Ibid., p. 62.
48. Ibid.
49. Ibid., p. 63.
50. Ibid., pp. 62–63.
51. In the context of postulating the "second alienation" (i.e., the fictitious "supersession") of his alienated existence as a pauper in the religious experience undergone in the cathedral, where his actual conditions of alienation are supposed to disappear as a speck of cloud on the distant horizon whereby "he is equal of princes" in the eyes of God. See Hegel's *Jenenser Realphilosphie,* Leipzig, 1931, vol. 2, p. 267.
52. Kant, "Idea for a Universal History with Cosmopolitan Intent," in Carl J. Friedrich (ed.), *Immanuel Kant's Moral and Political Writings,* Random House, New York, 1949, p. 120.
53. Ibid., p. 123.
54. Hegel's *Philosophy of Mind,* p. 55.
55. Ibid., p. 62.
56. Ibid., p. 55.
57. Ibid., p. 64.
58. Ibid.
59. Hegel's *Philosophy of Right,* pp. 12–13.
60. Husserl, *Cartesian Meditations,* p. 6.
61. Ibid., pp. 4–6.

62. Ibid., pp. 24–5.
63. Ibid., p. 4.
64. Ibid., p. 157.
65. Sartre, *Being and Nothingness,* Methuen & Co., London, 1969, p. 235.
66. Sartre, *The Problem of Method,* Methuen & Co., London, 1963, p.5.
67. Sartre, *Critique of Dialectical Reason,* NLB, London, 1976, p. 35.
68. Sartre, *Being and Nothingness,* p. 429.
69. Ibid., pp. 422–9.
70. In which way Sartre attempts to go beyond the historical vision of *Being and Nothingness,* and to what extent he succeeds in dong so in his *Critique of Dialectical Reason,* is discussed at some length in my forthcoming book and companion volume to the present one, entitled *The Dialectic of Structure and History.*
71. See Lukács's posthumously published volumes, *Heidelberger Philosophie der Kunst (1912–1914)* and *Heidelberger Aesthetik (1916–1918),* edited by György Márkus and Frank Benseler, Luchterhand Verlag, Darmstadt & Neuwied, 1974.
72. Lukács, "Royal Highness," *Essays on Thomas Mann,* Merlin Press, London, 1964, pp. 135–7.
73. Lukács, *Soul and Form,* Merlin Press, London, 1974, p. 1.
74. Lukács, "The Foundering of Form Against Life," in *Soul and Form,* p. 32.
75. Lukács, *Soul and Form,* p. 17.
76. Ibid., p. 93.
77. Ibid., p. 162.
78. Ibid., pp. 167–8.
79. Ibid., p. 171.
80. Ibid., p. 160.
81. Ibid., p. 190.
82. Ibid., pp. 173–4.
83. Lukács, *The Theory of the Novel,* Merlin Press, London, 1971, p. 12.
84. Ibid., p. 20.
85. Ibid., p. 21.
86. "Moses Hess und die Probleme der idealistischen Dialektik," in *Georg Lukács: Schriften zur Ideologie und Politik,* Hermann Luchterhand Verlag, Neuwied & Berlin, 1967, p. 268.
87. The young Lukács called his own essays "intellectual poems," approving-

ly quoting in that sense the older Schlegel who first used such characterization about the work of Tiberius Hemsterhuys. See *Soul and Form,* p. 18.

88. Lukács, "Esztétikai kultúra" (Aesthetic Culture), in *Renaissance,* 1910.
89. Hegel, *The Philosophy of History,* p. 457.
90. Lukács, *Die Eigenart des Aesthetischen,* vol. 2, Luchterhand, Neuwied and Berlin, 1963, p. 837.
91. Ibid., vol. 2, p. 831.
92. Hegel, *Philosophy of History,* p. 438.
93. Ibid., pp. 108–109.
94. Ibid., p. 109.
95. Ibid., pp. 109–110.
96. Ibid., p. 110.
97. Ibid., p. 452.
98. On page 456 of his *Philosophy of History* Hegel describes what he considers the monarch's proper involvement in the affairs of the State, corresponding on the whole to Frederick's practice. This is how he puts it: "The government rests with the official world, and the personal decision of the monarch constitutes its apex; for a final decision is, as was remarked above, absolutely necessary. Yet with firmly established laws, and a settled organization of the State, what is left to the sole arbitration of the monarch is, in point of substance, no great matter. It is certainly a very fortunate circumstance for a nation, when a sovereign of noble character falls to its lot; yet in a great state even this is of small moment, since its strength lies in the Reason incorporated in it."
99. Ibid., p. 39.
100. Ibid., p. 452.
101. Ibid., p. 16.
102. Ibid., p. 17.
103. Ibid., p. 452.
104. Ibid., p. 9.
105. Ibid., p. 15.
106. Ibid., pp. 15–16.
107. Ibid., p. 449.
108. Ibid., p. 456.
109. As we have seen it in the quotation taken from page 15 of Hegel's *Philosophy of History.*

110. Ibid., p. 79.

111. See Hegel's *Philosophy of Right,* pp. 126–130. Characteristically, the exclusion of the "needy man" from the privileges conferred on their owners by private property is justified on the ground that "property is the embodiment of the free will of others." Ibid., p.128.

112. Ibid., pp. 129–130.

113. Ibid., p. 130.

114. Naturally, there is no more need to make intelligible the historical process as *open towards the future* once the world can be depicted as the *"eternal present"* of capital's social order.

115. F. W. Taylor, *Scientific Management,* Harper and Row, 1947, p. 29.

116. Ibid., p. 30.

117. Ibid., p. 60.

118. Ibid., p. 29.

119. Raymond Aron, *The Industrial Society: Three Essays on Ideology and Development,* New York, 1967, p. 40.

120. Ibid., p. 24.

121. Ibid., p. 74.

122. This is how he tried to justify his "universalism": "The *American defence budget* represents three-quarters of the total military expenditure of the *Atlantic alliance* . . . In our century, a *second class nation state* is not an adequate framework for full human expression." R. Aron, "The end of the ideology age?," in Chaim I. Waxman (ed.), *The End of Ideology Debate,* Simon and Schuster, New York, 1968, p. 29.

123. See Marx, *Grundrisse,* Penguin Books, Harmondsworth, 1973, pp. 170–172.

CHAPTER EIGHT

Method in a Historical Epoch of Transition

8.1 The Marxian Reorientation of Method

Marx's well known "Preface" to his 1859 *Contribution to the Critique of Political Economy* is most relevant in our present context. It asserts two equally important propositions. First, that capital's long established social metabolic order is the last antagonistic form of societal reproduction in human history, and, second, that the *material conditions* for overcoming the structural antagonism of the now ruling socioeconomic order are themselves created within the framework of the given bourgeois society. These are his words:

> The bourgeois mode of production is the *last antagonistic form* of the social process of production—antagonistic not in the sense of individual antagonism but of an antagonism that emanates from the individuals' social conditions of existence—but the productive forces developing within bourgeois society create also the material conditions for a solution of this antagonism. [1]

The first proposition is important because the capital/labour antagonism is a fundamental *class antagonism,* subjugating the overwhelming majority of society to the hierarchical structural domination of capital. It is a relationship of unreformable domination and subordination which could not be sustainably reproduced in a future society by reversing the roles between the dominated vast majority and the ruling small minority. For the latter would be quite incapable of reproducing on its own the primary conditions of existence even for itself, let alone for the whole of society.

As regards the vital relevance of the second proposition, it is necessary to remember that without an advanced level of productive activity, one fully adequate for satisfying the genuine needs of the totality of the social individuals—in contrast to the highly discriminatory distribution of the social product in favour of a tiny minority in the past—the conflicts and antagonisms would start all over again.[2] This is why Marx insists on the same page of the "Preface" quoted from his *Contribution to the Critique of Political Economy* that "No social order is ever destroyed before *all* the productive forces for which it is sufficient have been developed, and new superior relations of production never replace older ones before the material conditions for their existence have matured within the framework of the old society. Mankind thus inevitably sets itself only such tasks as it is able to solve, since closer examination will always show that the problem itself arises only when the *material conditions for its solution* are already present or at least in the course of formation."[3]

Two comments are required at this point, not only in order to avoid misunderstandings but also to counter some facile hostility. The first is that Marx talks only about the creation of the necessary *material conditions* within the framework of the old society, repeating the same expression several times in a short passage. He is well aware of the need for properly developing the political and cultural/theoretical—as well as the ongoing educational—conditions which present a great challenge for the future. This is why Marx stresses, in sharp contrast to utopian socialism, like the position of Robert Owen—which "divides society into two parts [the educators and the educated], one of which is superior to society"—that "the educator must himself be educated."[4] And he also refers to the unavoidable historic task of "the production *on a mass scale* of communist consciousness," which means "the consciousness of the necessity of a fundamental revolution."[5] In other words, successful completion of the historic task requires the fulfilment of a revolutionary political, theoretical, and educational undertaking to which Marx himself dedicated his whole life, precisely because these dimensions of the historical challenge in question could not be expected to be solved by the spontaneous material processes of the old society.

The second comment that must be added here concerns the gravity and urgency of the problems we have to face under the present historical conditions of capital's antagonistic order. For in that respect the post–Second World War decades of developments have rendered the situation incomparably graver than it was during the life-time of Marx. To be sure, Marx had underlined already in 1845 that, due to the alienating antagonisms of capital's mode of social reproductive control, "in the development of productive forces there comes a stage when productive forces and means of intercourse are brought into being which, under the existing relations, only cause mischief, and are *no longer productive but destructive forces*."[6] And, anticipating the meaning of Rosa Luxemburg's famous warning about "socialism or barbarism," Marx also insisted in the same work that "things have now come to such a pass that the individuals must appropriate the existing totality of productive forces not only to achieve *self-activity*, but, also, *merely to safeguard their very existence*."[7]

However, what was in the 1840s only a somewhat remote possibility even in military technological terms, is today an undeniable frightful reality. For since the time when the lines quoted above were written by Marx humanity has had to confront not only the inhumanities of two devastating world wars, together with a multiplicity of less global but most destructive military conflagrations—including the Vietnam war and the current genocidal intervention by the overwhelmingly dominant imperialist power in the Middle East—but also the prospect of a potential annihilation of the whole of humanity, and at the same time even the destruction of all life on earth, by means of the nuclear, chemical and biological weapons of mass destruction ready to be activated with the greatest ease. And as if all that were not enough by itself, the ubiquitously imposed productive practices of capital's *destructive production* are actively engaged already today in inflicting irreversible damage on *nature itself*, undermining thereby the elementary conditions of existence of humankind. Thus, while on the one side the *productive potential* that could be put, in principle, to positive use had never been even approximated in the past, on the other side the *destructive reality* of ongoing developments—both on the military and on the societal reproductive plane—not only matches but far exceeds the productive forces of humankind to the point of potentially total destruction, under the control of capital's more than willing personifications. For destruction is much easier than construction. This is what inevitably qualifies today Marx's earlier quoted sentence according to which "mankind sets itself only such tasks as it is able to solve."

AS MENTIONED IN THE LAST PARAGRAPHS of section 7.5, under the present conditions of the capital system's deepening structural crisis the elaboration of a qualitatively different, *non-antagonistic* way of mediating the social metabolism is the vital condition of success for the future. Accordingly, the necessary concern with the questions of method appropriate to mastering the severe problems and difficulties of our historical epoch of transition are closely related to this issue. The importance of this qualitatively new mediatory requirement cannot be overstated. For if it proves impossible to elaborate in the foreseeable future a non-antagonistic mode of mediating the relationship between humanity and nature as well as among the individuals themselves, that would make the feasibility of instituting a genuine socialist reproductive order itself rather bleak.

The necessary point of departure in this respect, for the reorientation of method inherited from the past, is to subject to a radical critique the established modality of social reproductive mediation under the rule of capital. This issue can be summed up with reference to the fundamental difference between *first order* and *second order mediations.* The latter, as we know them, are unredeemably *antagonistic mediations,* constituting a system of social metabolic control which must be superseded in its entirety, as a perversely *"organic system,"* and replaced by its *hegemonic alternative,* constituted and consolidated, again, as a historically viable and fully co-operative *organic system*. Marx's theory of *alienation*,[8] as the explanatory framework of capital's antagonistic second order mediations, is deeply concerned with these problems. Both his first diagnoses and solutions are articulated in his system *in statu nascendi,* written by him in Paris and published posthumously under the title of *Economic and Philosophical Manuscripts of 1844*.

The contrast between the primary and the antagonistic second order mediations is absolutely striking. The essential, for all feasible forms of societal reproduction structurally required primary mediations are:

- the necessary, more or less spontaneous, regulation of biological reproductive activity and of the size of the sustainable population, in conjunction with the available resources;

- the regulation of the labour process through which the given community's necessary interchange with nature can produce the goods needed for human gratification, as well as the appropriate working tools, productive enterprises, and knowledge by means of which the reproductive process itself can be maintained and improved;

- the establishment of suitable exchange relations under which the historically changing needs of human beings can be linked together for the purpose of optimizing the available natural and productive—including the culturally productive – resources;

- the organization, co-ordination and control of the multiplicity of activities through which the material and cultural requirements of the successful social metabolic reproduction process of progressively more complex human communities can be secured and safeguarded;

- the rational allocation of the available material and human resources, fighting against the tyranny of scarcity through the economic (in the sense of economizing) utilization of the given society's ways and means of reproduction, as far as feasible on the basis of the attained level of productivity and within the confines of the established socioeconomic structures; and

- the enactment and administration of the rules and regulations of the given society as a whole, in conjunction with the other primary mediatory functions and determinations.

As we can see, *none* of these primary mediatory imperatives in and by itself calls for the establishment of *structural hierarchies* of domination and subordination as the necessary framework of social metabolic reproduction. In sharp contrast, the second order mediations of the capital system could not be more different in character. They may be summed up as follows:

- the *nuclear family,* articulated as the "microcosm" of society which, in addition to its role in reproducing the species, partakes in all reproductive relations of the social "macrocosm," including the necessary mediation of the laws of the state to all individuals, thus directly necessary also to the reproduction of the state;

- alienated means of production and their "personifications" through which capital acquires "iron will" and tough consciousness, strictly mandated for imposing on everyone conformity to the dehumanizing objective requirements of the given social metabolic order;

- money assuming a multiplicity of mystifying and ever more dominant forms in the course of historical development all the way to the global stranglehold of the present-day international monetary system;

- fetishistic production objectives, submitting in one form or another the satisfaction of human needs (and the corresponding provision of use-values) to the blind imperatives of capital-expansion and accumulation;

- labour structurally divorced from the possibility of control both in capitalist societies, where it must function as wage-labour coerced and exploited by economic compulsion, and under the post-capitalist rule of capital over the politically dominated labour force;

- varieties of capital's state formation in their global setting, where they confront one another (at times even with the most violent means, dragging humankind to the brink of self-destruction) as self-oriented national states; and

- the uncontrolled *world market* within the framework of which the participants, protected by their respective national states to the degree feasible by the prevailing power relations, must accommodate themselves to the precarious conditions of economic co-existence while endeavouring to procure the highest practicable advantage to themselves by outwitting their competing counterparts, inevitably sowing thereby the seeds of ever more destructive conflicts.

In relation to the way in which all these constituents of the established mode of social metabolic control are linked together we can only talk about a *vicious circle*. For the particular second order mediations reciprocally sustain one another, making impossible to counter the alienating and paralyzing force of any one of them taken in isolation while leaving intact the immense self-regenerative and self-imposing power of the system as a whole. On the basis of painful historical evidence the disconcerting truth of the matter is that the capital system succeeds in imposing itself—through the structural interconnections of its constituent parts—on partial emancipatory efforts aimed at limited specific targets. Accordingly, what must be confronted and ovecome by the adversaries of the established, incorrigibly discriminatory, order of social metabolic reproduction is not only capital's positively self-sustaining force of surplus-labour extraction but also the devastating negative power—the apparently forbidding inertia—of its circular linkages.[9]

THE CONCEPTION ENVISAGING the supersession of capital's antagonistic second order mediations is inseparable from reassessing in a radical way the methodologically seminal contrast between the *standpoint of philosophy* inherited from the typical bourgeois characterization of the social order and the qualitatively different standpoint offered by Marx himself. As he had formulated the latter in number 10 of his "Theses on Feuerbach," Marx insisted that "The standpoint of the old materialism is *civil society;* the standpoint of the new is *human society,* or *social human-*

ity." At the same time, stressing the relevance of this necessary departure from the standpoint of civil society in Marx's reorientation of method, should not be confined to the old type of materialism, contrasted in this particular Thesis on Feuerbach with the Marxian advocacy of materialism. For, characteristically, the speculative idealist philosophies, including the philosophy of Hegel—with their postulate of "aggregative individualities," said to be asserting as self-seeking individuals the strictly individualistic conflicting interests of each particular individual against all of the others—are characterized by the same limitations of standpoint. Marx made that very clear in his 1859 "Preface" to his *Contribution to the Critique of Political Economy* by underlining that

> My inquiry led me to the conclusion that neither legal relations nor political forms could be comprehended whether by themselves or on the basis of a so-called general development of the human mind, but that on the contrary they originate in the material conditions of life, the totality of which Hegel, following the example of English and French thinkers of the eighteenth century embraces within the term '*civil society*'; that the anatomy of this civil society, however, has to be sought in political economy.[10]

The reason why the adoption of the "standpoint of civil society" as the general orienting principle of philosophy had to be subjected to a radical critique was because by conveniently reducing the *antagonistic social contradictions* of the established social order to the strictly personal vicissitudes of self-seeking individuals, and thereby hypostatizing such contradictions as ontologically insurmountable, the actually existent hierarchical social order remained in principle *beyond criticism.* It could carry on exactly as before with its reproductive activities within the framework of its—destructive and ultimately even self-destructive—antagonistic second order mediations. For if the real problems of social antagonism are individualistically transfigured and arbitrarily abstracted from the only setting in which they could be properly addressed, namely in so-called "civil society" itself, where the "material conditions of life" produce and constantly reproduce them, in that case the adopted methodological stance can successfully fulfil its ideological function of fully *rationalizing the existent* in a reconciliatory way. This is why Marx was pressing in our earlier quote that bourgeois society was "antagonistic not in the sense of individual antagonism but of an antagonism that emanates from the individuals' social conditions of existence," adding at the same time the crucial critical proviso that "the productive forces developing within bourgeois society create also the material conditions for a solution of this antagonism."[11] This was precisely both the kind of diagnosis of the really existing antagonisms, as well as of their potential resolution, which had to be avoided by all those who embraced in their conceptualizations of the world the eternalizing "standpoint of civil society."

Moreover, this kind of treatment of "civil society," adopted already by the great intellectual representatives of the bourgeoisie in the ascendant, had the added benefit for them that by separating the comprehensive *political* dimension of the problems from their material ground—through the imaginary abstraction of the *state* from the material reality of "civil society"—helped to create the speculative conditions for the idealization of the capitalist state itself. This characteristic approach of structural separation was doubly convenient. For what could at least in principle bring results in the real world: the necessary confrontation of the material, and closely associated political, antagonisms as they unfolded in the reproductive domain of "civil society," was categorically ruled out of consideration in view of the false conceptualization of civil society as the terrain of strictly self-seeking aggregative individuality. And, by the same token, in the idealized separate realm of the state, where the material antagonisms of society could not even be properly identified, let alone adequately overcome, the required solution of the one and only "natural order" and its unquestionable "rationality" was arbitrarily postulated, excluding all possibility of changing in the slightest the structurally entrenched hierarchical domination of labour by the unanalysable (and absolutely unalterable) practical premises and imperatives of the capital system.

Thus, to expect any remedy from such an artificially separated construct of the two "realms," so-called civil society and the idealized "ethical State," was inconceivable. The structurally enforced exploitative and oppressive material foundation of society—in which living labour was categorically separated from the means of production and thereby radically divorced from the exercise of all societal directive functions—was characteristically transfigured into the pretended mutually beneficial *equality* of freely contracting individuals (irrespective of their self-seeking but allegedly with societal harmony thoroughly compatible with personal conflicts); and the whole construct was wrapped into the reified layers of mystification appropriate to the material functioning of the unimprovable "civil society," in order to make it ideologically acceptable. At the same time, the *formal/legal* procedures of the capitalistically idealized state—which in actuality was *totally dominated* by the *necessarily presupposed material power of capital,* imposing even the most violent repressive functions (internally against its own labour force, and externally in the form of wars against other states), whenever the defence of the established social order so required—could never even begin to contemplate any significant structural change on their own. For the state's vital functions have been historically articulated as the legal, political and military (as well as in the internal class relations of capitalist society by the great variety of the police forces secured) *preservation* of the existing structures of domination and subordination. This is how it became possible for the great figure of the Scottish Enlightenment movement, Adam Smith, to idealize the rule of capital as "*the natural system of perfect liberty and justice.*"[12] And Hegel, too, had no difficulty in finding an equally reconciliatory and idealizing characterization of, and justification for, the established order by postulating that "*the true reconciliation which discloses the State as the image and actuality of reason has become objective.*"[13]

Once the actual operating conditions of capital's social metabolic order have been defined in this way, through the convenient separation of "civil society" and the State, no historically sustainable positive solution could be envisaged as the hegemonic alternative to the established mode of reproduction without exposing the total untenability of its antagonistic structural determinations. The Marxian reorientation of method was dedicated precisely to that purpose.

MARX TREATED WITH SARCASM all those who wanted to offer some limited and patronizing concessions about the form of *distribution* to consumers prevailing in capital's socioeconomic order while retaining its antagonistic mode of *production* fetishistically intact. Thus he wrote that

> it is highly *absurd* when John Stuart Mill says: 'The laws and conditions of the production of wealth partake of the character of *physical truths*. . . . It is not so with the *distribution* of wealth. That is a matter of human institutions solely.'[14]
>
> The 'laws and conditions' of the production of wealth and the laws of the 'distribution of wealth' are the same laws under different forms, and both change, undergo the same historic process; are as such only moments of a historical process.
>
> It requires no great penetration to grasp that, where e.g. free labour or wage labour arising out of the dissolution of bondage is the point of departure, there machines can only *arise* in antithesis to living labour, as property alien to it, and as power hostile to it; i.e. that they must confront it as capital. But it is just as easy to perceive that machines will not cease to be agencies of social production when they become e.g. property of the associated workers. In the first case, however, their distribution, i.e. that they *do not belong to the worker,* is just as much a condition of the mode of production founded on wage labour. In the second case the changed distribution would start from a *changed foundation of production,* a new foundation first created by the process of history.[15]

Naturally, Mill's "highly absurd" separation and contra-position of production and distribution was conceived in the interest of *eternalizing* the established reproductive order as a whole, by declaring its constituent of production as partaking of the character of *physical truths.* Accordingly, Mill could not offer other than vacuous pseudo-concessions also on distribution itself. For in his scheme of things distribution had to remain *locked into* the alleged *physically unalterable* determinations of production as such. The complete failure of all subsequent attempts in the twentieth century, from timid liberal reforms to the loudly proclaimed but in the end humiliatingly abandoned social democratic programme of transforming society—according to the recipe of "evolutionary socialism," which was supposed to be established through the method of *"progressive taxation"* instituted within the framework of the *"Welfare State"* —amply confirmed the validity of Marx's sarcasm.

At the same time, when offering pious hope for a significantly reformed mode of distribution, the most important dimension of the liberal/social democratic way of approaching the problems—through the crudely *undialectical* separation of what cannot possibly be separated in reality itself—meant that the *antagonistic mediation* of social metabolic interchange could not be conceivably altered as the necessary practical premise of social life. Changes could be projected only on the narrowest margins and fringes. And that amounted to ruling out with categorical absoluteness any idea of instituting *socialism* as the historically sustainable *hegemonic alternative to capital's social order.*

Marx's radical reorientation of method was, on the contrary, conceived in the service of making that vital advance toward the *"new historic form"* feasible. That is the reason why he underlined most emphatically in the last of his "Theses on Feuerbach" that "The philosophers have only *interpreted* the world in various ways; the point is to *change* it."[16] The qualitative change envisaged by Marx—toward which the methodologically vital *critique of political economy* as the *anatomy of the structural antagonisms of civil society* had to be directed—was summed up by him as the necessary establishment of the *communal system of production and distribution.* For only through that kind of social metabolic interchange between humanity and nature and among the individuals themselves could the vicious circle of *antagonistic mediation* be broken and replaced by a new mode of, non-antagonistic, *communal mediation.*

In this respect the central issue concerns the specific form of mediation through which the *hierarchical structural division of labour,* under the rule of capital, could give way to the *directly social* mode of reproduction of the "new historic form." In other words, it is concerned with setting the *parameters* of, and the *direction* in which—in Marx's words—"*instead of* a division of labour"[17] (whose material imperatives are unceremoniously imposed on the particular working subjects) the consciously self-controlled life-activity of the social individuals could be integrated into a both productively viable and humanly fulfilling whole.

According to Marx, under the division of labour that prevails in commodity society, the individuals are mediated among themselves and inescapably combined into an *antagonistically structured* social whole only through the capitalist system of commodity production and exchange. And the latter is ruled by the imperative of ever-expanding exchange-value to which everything else—from the most basic as well as the most intimate needs of the individuals, to the various material and cultural productive activities in which they engage in capitalist society—must be strictly subordinated.

The communal system envisaged by Marx stands in complete contrast to this antagonistically structured societal mediation which cannot help ruthlessly superimposing itself on the individuals through the value relation. The main characteristics of the communal mode of exchange are enumerated in a seminally important passage of the *Grundrisse.*[18] They are spelled out by Marx in this way:

- the determination of the working subjects' life-activity as a necessary and individually meaningful link in *directly general production,* and their corresponding *direct participation* in the available world of products;

- the determination of the social product itself as an inherently communal, general product from the outset, in relation to *communal needs and purposes,* on the basis of the special share which the particular individuals acquire in the ongoing communal production;

- the full participation of the members of society also in *communal consumption proper:* a circumstance that happens to be extremely important, in view of the dialectical interrelationship between production and consumption, on the basis of which the latter is rightfully characterized under the communal system as positively "*productive* consumption";[19]

- the planned *organization* of labour (instead of its alienating *division,* determined by the self-assertive imperatives of exchange value in commodity society) in such a way that the productive activity of the particular working subjects is mediated not in a reified-objectified form, through the exchange of commodities, but through the *intrinsically social conditions of the given mode of production itself* within which the individuals are active.

These characteristics make it quite clear that the key issue is the establishment of a historically *new mode of mediating* the metabolic exchange of humanity with nature and of the progressively more *self-determined productive activity* of the social individuals among themselves.

THE TASK OF DEMYSTIFICATION had to be firmly pursued in this regard. First, in relation to the tendentious, and with one-sided arbitrariness treated, concept of *exchange*, characteristic of the political economists and philosophers who adopt the standpoint of civil society. To quote Marx:

> The individual and isolated hunter and fisherman, with whom Smith and Ricardo begin, belongs among the unimaginative conceits of the eighteenth-century Robinsonades, which in no way express merely a reaction against over-sophistication and a return to a misunderstood natural life, as cultural historians imagine. As little as Rousseau's *contrat social*, which brings naturally independent, autonomous subjects into relation and connection by contract, rests on such naturalism. This is the semblance, the merely aesthetic semblance, of the Robinsonades, great and small. It is, rather, the anticipation of 'civil society,' in preparation since the sixteenth century and making giant strides towards maturity in the eighteenth. In this society of free competition, the individual appears detached from the natural bonds etc., which in earlier historical periods make him the accessory of a definite and limited human conglomerate. Smith and Ricardo still stand with both feet on the shoulders of the eighteenth century prophets, in whose imaginations this eighteenth century individual—the product on one side of the dissolution of the feudal forms of society, on the other side of the new forces of production developed since the sixteenth century—appears as an ideal, *whose existence they project into the past.* Not as a historical result but as history's point of departure. As the *Natural Individual* appropriate to their notion of *human nature*, not arising historically, but *posited by nature.* This *illusion* has been common to each new epoch to this day. . . . Only in the eighteenth century, in '*civil society*,' do the various forms of social connectedness confront the individual as a mere means towards his private purposes, as external necessity. But the epoch which produces this standpoint, that of the *isolated individual,* is also precisely that of the hitherto most developed social (from this stand-

> point, general) relations. The human being is in the most literal sense a *zoon politikon,* not merely a gregarious animal, but an animal which can individuate itself only in the midst of society.[20]

In the century and a half transpired since the time when these lines were written by Marx nothing had changed substantively in methodological and ideological terms in the conceptualizations formulated from the standpoint of "civil society" and political economy, corresponding to the vantage point of capital. That is, nothing apart from losing their original naïve credulity in favour of assuming an openly apologetic, and at times even cynically crusading, character, as in the case of Hayek and his ilk. Today there are no genuine *illusions* seriously entertained in such writings. But the ahistorical projection of the *capitalist exchange relations* way back even into the most remote past, and the arbitrary assumption of the idealized *naturalness of the whole system* for ideological purposes, together with the fictitious *human nature* of isolated individuality, are more strongly in evidence today than ever before.

Moreover, the fact is that in the various conceptions of "civil society" the cult of the isolated individual is grossly misrepresented. For under the rule of capital we find "the hitherto most developed" social form of societal reproductive relations in which the really existing individual "can individuate itself only in the midst of society." In other words, one cannot even begin to think about the elementary defining characteristics of capitalist individuality without its inextricable *organic links* to the most complex framework of ongoing social determinations ever known in history. This uncomfortable fact remains a fundamental contradiction of the established order, and it is totally insuperable within the structural confines of such an order.

That is precisely why *distribution* must be separated from—and imaginarily opposed to—*production,* in order to create the *deceptive plausibility* of a "natural" order oriented by (and toward) the optimal gratification of the needs of *isolated individuality,* hiding in truth the actuality of the practical presuppositions and objective material imperatives imposed by the willing agency of *capital's personifications.*

In relation to the terrain of *production* as such not even the remote *semblance* of a coherent system—one capable of arising from the *chaos of strictly individualistic interchanges* and miraculously adding up in its constitution to a totally unproblematical "globalized" socioeconomic system—could be made plausible for a moment. Only the "highly absurd" methodology of abstracting distribution from its necessary ground of (incurably prejudicial) production can create the mythology of an *equitable society* while preserving absolutely intact its *structurally enforced* discriminatory determinations. Besides, the most significant dimension of *distribution itself,* when considered in its dialectical integrality—the absolute taboo regarding the primary distribution of the means and material of production as the exclusive property of capital's personifications—is removed from (one might properly say: smuggled out of) the "highly absurd" patronizing concern with truncated "distribution" of the consumer products, as part and parcel of the mystifications conveniently derived from the "standpoint of civil society."

However, notwithstanding all methodological and ideological mystification, the fundamental underlying contradiction cannot be removed from the system. On the contrary, it is getting deeper and more intensified, so that sooner or later it must be attended to in actuality itself. For we are not talking about a peripheral or marginal feature, but about a central contradiction of the capital system in its entirety: that between the *tendency toward the increasing socialization and global integration of production* and the untouchable *private appropriation* of the total societal product, including, of course, the potentially ever more powerful means of production invented through the science of the whole of society and one-sidedly expropriated in subordination to the self-expansionary needs and determinations of capital.

No one could (or perhaps even wish to) deny today that *"globalization"*—no matter how fashionably treated as a rule—belongs to "the hitherto most developed *social* (from this standpoint, *general*) relations," in Marx's words, although capital's ideologists are no doubt likely to deny its contradictory character. Nonetheless the severe problem is that the really existing trend of globalization cannot be brought to a historically sustainable completion because of the fundamental contradiction between the significantly increasing socialization of production and the ever more exclusivistic—in its ultimate tendency *monopolistically/imperialistically* destructive—appropriation/expropriation of all of its dimensions, including its productive base.

Nor should we be credulous enough to accept the self-serving propaganda assertion according to which "globalization" is a radically new type of development as a result of which all over the world we shall live happily ever after. In reality it is inseparable from a vital category of the system's overall development, and in that way it is as old as industrial capital itself. Namely, the inexorable tendency toward the *concentration and centralization of capital.*[21] In fact the unfolding of *monopolistic developments* in general is not intelligible at all without that category. Moreover, even the monopolistic type of development is not nearly as new as people often assume. For Marx had put into relief in his *Grundrisse* already in 1857 that "As a further example of the divergent positions which the same category can occupy in different social stages: one of the latest forms of bourgeois society, *joint stock companies.* These also appear, however, at its beginning, in the great, privileged *monopoly* companies."[22]

Thus, for instance, the monopolistically privileged and militarily backed East India Company of the fairly remote past was an obvious precursor and even pathbreaker of colonial imperialism. The two world wars of the twentieth century represent an undeniable reminder of the claimed "all-round beneficial" nature of such developments. Nor should indeed anybody indulge in fantasies about the ongoing trend of "globalization" while abstracting from its profound interconnections with the most ruthless forms of imperialistic domination in its design, including the determination of its overwhelmingly dominant powers to precipitate, if and whenever it serves them, even *genocidal wars,* on the model of the imperialist past.

The Marxian reorientation of method is vitally important in all these respects. For the grave and globally intensifying contradictions of our social order cannot be permanently left under the carpet of methodological and ideological mystification. The irreconcilable contradiction between the socialization and appropriation of production—pinpointed by sharply underlining that "the epoch which produces the standpoint of the *isolated individual* is also precisely that of the hitherto most developed social (from this standpoint, general) relations in which the individual can individuate itself only in the midst of society"—must be resolved in a historically sustainable way. That is: by bringing the social metabolism in its entirety, including the satisfaction of the genuine needs of the individuals, fully in line with the necessary socialization of production, and done in such a way which can be properly controlled by the freely associated social individuals themselves.

The only conceivable way of successfully accomplishing that historic task is through the institution and consolidation of the truly *communal system* of both production and consumption, in their dialectical inseparability from one another, as always advocated by Marx. There can be no *"half-way house"* on this score, as clearly evidenced by the total failure of all reformist attempts in the past which were conceived from the methodological standpoint, and in the spirit of, a historically untenable "civil society."

ONE OF THE MOST IMPORTANT methodological issues in this respect concerns the tendentious misrepresentation and the mystifying projection of the capitalistic exchange relations way back into the remote past.

To be sure, no social life at any level of complexity is conceivable without *some form* of exchange relation. In fact the term "social" is in a sense synonymous with that. The "only" question is: what must be understood by *exchange* as genuinely inseparable from social life itself. That is what ultimately decides the matter when we are talking about the necessary *historical sustainability* of the *hegemonic alternative* to capital's social metabolic order.

However, the grave problem is that the exchange relations under the rule of capital are subjected to the tyranny of the law of value. The alienating and rigidly constraining consequences for human beings—like the domination of even the elementary needs of countless millions, dependent on use-values for satisfying their needs, and the capitalistically imposed necessity of legitimating those needs as use-values in callous subordination to the production of profitable exchange-values—is the unavoidable consequence of that.

In actuality the core meaning of the term 'exchange' refers to humanity's unavoidable *metabolic interchange with nature,* on the one hand, and the exchange relations of the *particular individuals among themselves,* on the other. This is the case irrespective of what might be the historically specific forms required for realizing the envisaged objectives of humanity's societal reproduction.

In this fundamental sense, the meaning of the category of exchange is inseparable from that of historically necessary *mediation,* clearly indicating the *processual* character of what is really at stake. In sharp contrast, under the tyranny of the law of value we are confronted by the fetishistic/reifying determinations of *commodity exchange.* For within the framework of the capital system the only way in which it is feasible to legitimate use-values corresponding to human need is to produce commodities in the service of securing *profit,* under the imperative of the ever-expanding accumulation of capital.

This is extremely problematical because in reality the satisfaction of human needs is linked to the provision of goods or *products,* whether as *objects* or as *services,* and not of *commodities.* However, under the rule of capital the meaning of "products" is grossly distorted. For they can be legitimated within the capital system's domain of production and distribution only as *commodified products,* be they objects or services. And worst of all, even the exercise of *labour power,* and therewith the survival of *living labour* itself under the rule of capital, can only acquire its legitimacy for its reproduction (i.e. for its continued survival) on condition that it is *converted into a commodity.*

Viewing the conditions of societal reproduction in its fundamental sense, as humanity's metabolic interchange with nature and the exchange relations of the particular individuals among themselves, the role assigned to *products* requires critical reflection, not to mention the *commodification of products* which must be rejected as a dehumanizing outrage. For even in relation to *products* the question cannot be avoided: how justifiable are the purposes for which they are produced when considered from the standpoint of the genuine human gratification of the freely associated individuals, and not in tune with the alienating determinations of capitalist exchange relations which necessarily commodify them, inventing and imposing on society even the most artificial "needs" (in truth artificial appetites) when the conditions of profitability so require.

In this sense, the role assigned to products can constitute only a subordinate moment in this complex of problems. The primacy belongs to the active/productive side, even if this fact is gravely distorted by the capitalist modality of *objectification* which necessarily assumes the form of *alienation* and *fetishistic reification.* Yet the plain truth of the matter is also that the capitalist commodity must be first *produced,* through the interchange and exchange of a great multiplicity of *activities,* before it can enter the market in direct pursuit of profit.

This is where we can see the great importance of Marx's advocacy of the *communal system of production and consumption* as the only feasible solution to capital's antagonistic mediations and as the viable hegemonic alternative to the established order. For, in striking contrast to commodity production and its reified exchange relations, the historically novel character of the *communal system* defines itself through its practical orientation towards the *exchange of activities,* and not simply of *products.*[23] Naturally, the allocation of products arises from the communally organized productive activity itself, and it is expected to match the directly social character of productive activity. But the point is that in the communal system the primacy necessarily goes to the *self-determination* and corresponding *organization of the activities themselves* in which the freely associated individuals engage in accordance with their need as active and creative human beings. In other words, under the communal system production would consciously take place in response to need, and above all in accordance with the individuals' basic need for *humanly fulfilling life-activity.* And since the latter is an *inherently qualitative* concern, only the *individuals themselves* can be the judges over it, as against the idealized *"Invisible hand,"* which is only a more respectable name for the tyranny of capital's law of value.

The radical shift from the established exchange relations oriented toward the production and distribution of *commodified products*—or even not fully commodified products, as in the Soviet type system—to a qualitatively different kind, based on the *exchange of activities,* is the only feasible way of replacing the ultimately destructive antagonistic modality of mediation of humanity's metabolic interchange with nature and among the individuals themselves by a socially harmonious and historically sustainable alternative. For if the activities are predetermined by prior production targets, whether they are set by the imperatives of commodity production or by a separate political authority, instead of the targets themselves being set on the basis of the conscious determinations of the individuals who engage in the various productive activities, in that case there can be no guarantee at all against antagonisms arising either over the distribution of the products, or over the way in which the activities are assigned to the producing individuals in subordination to the pre-established productive targets. This is why there can be no "half-way house" between the antagonistic modality of societal reproduction and the communal system.

Another vital reason for the establishment of the communal system advocated by Marx is the incurable *wastefulness* of all possible systems of production and distribution which are not oriented toward the consciously chosen life-activity of the associated individuals. That is, the social individuals who freely interchange their activities among themselves on the basis not of the *hierarchical division* but the *substantively equitable organization of labour,* in accordance with a *comprehensive plan* set by the individuals to themselves.

It is generally accepted that through the development of society's productive powers, including the great advancement of science, the possibility of overcoming scarcity is opened up to humanity. But the long predicted production of abundance is bound to remain an *abstract potentiality* without an adequate mode of production and distribution feasible only under the communal system. To turn the abstract potentiality of the society of abundance into its *creative actuality* requires the reorientation of the social reproduction process as a whole in such a way that the communally produced goods and services can be *fully shared*, and not *individualistically wasted,* by all those who participate in directly social production and consumption, because they choose and positively control their own activity. Short of this kind of conscious self-regulation, the resources of even the richest possible society must remain trapped within the *vicious circle of self-renewing and self-imposing scarcity* even in terms of the unrestrained appetites of relatively limited groups of people, let alone in relation to the totality of individuals.

Two final comments are in order at this point. First, that in the field of political economy and philosophy the social determination of method in capital's epoch runs *totally counter* to all this, by *eternalizing* the historically established, and in epochal terms necessarily transitory, exchange relations of the capital system and by the bewildering cult of the isolated individual in tune with it. Thus, constant engagement in the work of critical demystification remains a challenging task for us.

And the second comment to be added is that the Marxian reorientation of method puts into relief the *inseparability* of the *methodological* aspects of the encountered problems from their *substantive* dimension. For contrary to the frequent speculative and formalistic separation of method from the complex issues and contradictions of social life—in theory customarily justified on the ground that the clarification of complicated methodological points involves the investigation of the most mediated facets of philosophical discourse—does not and cannot mean that the problems of method are less concerned with the vital *substantive* issues of social life. On the contrary, often the opposite is the case, in the sense that major methodological difficulties and complications arise precisely from the extreme socioeconomic complexity and contradictoriness of the matters at stake, requiring a radically critical assessment of the substantive issues themselves in order to be able to get to grips with their methodological dimension. The Marxian reorientation of method seen in this section is a graphic example of how to bring fully to life even the most complex and in traditional philosophical discourse prohibitively abstract methodological problems by elucidating them on the basis of the vital interdependency of their fundamental dimensions.

8.2 From Hegel's "Science of Logic" to the Marxian View of Science

The radical departure of Marx from Hegel, despite his full appreciation of the great achievements of Hegelian *dialectic,* is clearly expressed already in the *Economic and Philosophical Manuscripts of 1844,* the first comprehensive articulation of Marx's fundamentally new approach to capital's alienating social metabolic order. While acknowledging that Hegel offers a monumental synthesis of philosophical development, including a unique account of *objectification* and *alienation,* Marx portrays the Hegelian way of conceptualizing the succession of categories as mere *thought entities,* in contrast to their claimed embodiment of the world of *actuality.* A key passage of Marx's *Economic and Philosophical Manuscripts of 1844,* characterizing the Hegelian system as a whole, reads as follows:

> A peculiar role is played by the act of superseding in which denial and preservation—denial and affirmation—are bound together.
>
> Thus, for example, in Hegel's *Philosophy of Right, Private Right* superseded equals *Morality,* Morality superseded equals the *Family,* the Family superseded equals *Civil Society,* Civil society superseded equals the *State,* the State superseded equals *World History.* In the *actual world* private right, morality, the family, civil society, the state, etc., remain in existence, only they have become *moments of motion.* . . .
>
> On the one hand, this act of superseding is a transcending of the *thought entity;* thus, Private Property *as a thought* is transcended in the *thought* of morality. And because thought imagines itself to be directly the other of itself, to be *sensuous reality*—and therefore takes its own action for *sensuous, real action*—this superseding in thought, which leaves its object standing in the real world, believes that it has really overcome it.[24]

At the same time Marx also puts into relief that the abstract speculative approach by Hegel to these problems arises from a determinate, reconciliatory, social standpoint. This is how he puts it:

> Hegel's standpoint is that of *modern political economy.* He grasps *labour* as the *essence* of man—as man's essence in the act of proving itself: he sees only the positive, not the negative side of labour. Labour is man's *coming to be for himself* within *alienation,* or as *alienated* man. The only labour which Hegel knows and recognizes is *abstractly mental labour.* Therefore, that which constitutes the essence of philosophy —the *alienation of man in his knowing of himself,* or *alienated* science *thinking itself* —Hegel grasps as its essence . . .
>
> The self, however, is only the *abstractly* conceived man—man begotten by abstraction. Man is egotistic. His eye, his ear, etc., are *egotistic.* In him every one of his essential powers has the quality of *selfhood.* But it is quite false to say on that account '*Self-consciousness* has eyes, ears, essential powers.' Self-consciousness is rather a quality of human nature, of the human eye, etc.; it is not human nature that is a quality of *self-consciousness.*[25]

In this way Marx's early critique of Hegel centers around two major points: both of them of quite fundamental importance. First, the Hegelian conflation of the categories of objectification and alienation, tendentiously obfuscating the nature of the latter, and the second, Hegel's speculative and reconciliatory abstraction from the vital practical problems and contradictions of the really existing world. Both of them are well in tune with the self-interested standpoint of political economy, corresponding to the structurally secured vantage point of capital at the given phase of historical development.

With regard to the first point Marx puts forcefully into relief that as far as Hegel is concerned "It is not the fact that the human being *objectifies himself inhumanly*, in opposition to himself, but the fact that he *objectifies himself* in *distinction* from and in *opposition* to abstract thinking, that is the posited essence of the estrangement and the thing to be superseded. . . . Consequently, . . . there is already latent in the [Hegelian] *Phenomenology* as a germ, a potentiality, a secret, the uncritical positivism and the equally uncritical idealism of Hegel's later works—that philosophic dissolution and restoration of the existing world."[26]

Once the two seminal categories of *objectification* and *alienation* are conflated in the way in which we find them inextricably conflated in the Hegelian philosophy from the very beginning, and not only in its final—more openly conservative—stages, nothing can be done in actuality about capital's power of alienation, no matter how dehumanizing its impact on those subjected to and suffering from it: a fact on some occasions recognized by Hegel himself. The "philosophic dissolution and restoration of the existing world" eminently succeeds in accomplishing its reconciliatory—and indeed apologetic—work in that way, leaving capital fully in control of the established social order.

Marx's second point of criticism is no less important. It concerns the much debated question of *"objective truth,"* defined by Marx in one of his "Theses on Feuerbach" in this way: "The question whether objective truth can be attributed to human thinking is not a question of theory but is a *practical* question. Man must prove the truth, i.e., the reality and power, the this-worldliness of his thinking in practice. The dispute over the reality or non-reality of thinking which is isolated from practice is a purely *scholastic* question."[27]

Thus, according to Marx, the solution not only to the speculative mysteries of idealist philosophy but at the same time also to all of the apparently intractable problems and contradictions of the actually existing social order, including those conceptualized in a characteristic way by even the greatest representatives of classical political economy, must be sought through a radical reorientation of critical thought itself, in sharp contrast to the philosophical conceptions of the past. That is, in Marx's view a qualitatively different form of approach must be sought by embracing the *"this-worldliness of thinking,"* which means that all theoretical enquiry must be firmly focused on transformatory *practice* relevant to its concerns. In this way the idea of *unifying theory with practice* acquires a fundamental importance in the Marxian conception of the world at a very early stage of its development, remaining one of its vital orienting principles all the time.

True to his very different line of approach to these problems Hegel praises in his *Science of Logic* the German language as having "many advantages over other modern languages . . . so that we must recognize here *a speculative spirit* in the language."[28] In a letter sent to Engels, one year after publishing the first volume of *Capital,* Marx comments with a touch of irony on the speculative virtues of the logical categories arising from the German and other languages. He writes: "what would old Hegel say in the next world if he heard that the general *[Allgemeine]* in German and in Norse means nothing but common land *[Gemeinland],* and the particular, *Sundre, Besondere,* nothing but the separate property divided off from the common land? Here are the *logical categories* coming damn well out of *'our intercourse'* after all."[29]

Obviously, notwithstanding the magisterial scope of the Hegelian philosophy, the gap was far too great to be bridged both on the reconciliatory identification of dehumanizing *alienation* with the theoretically as well as practically insurmountable nature of the categories of *objectification* and *externalization* in general, and on the definition of the philosopher's task in thoroughly *speculative* rather than for societal transformation crucial *practical* terms. Indeed, by the time Marx started to formulate his major ideas, i.e., in the age when the bourgeois order reached the end of its dynamic historical ascendancy, it became necessary to conceive the problems of philosophy and science in a way radically different not only from the Hegelian "Science of Logic" but also from all those approaches which continued to maintain their allegiance, directly or indirectly, to capital's standpoint of political economy. For it was unthinkable to envisage and advocate the necessary socioeconomic and human emancipation of labour and the institution of its historically viable hegemonic alternative mode of social metabolic control to the incurably antagonistic and wasteful capital system in any other way.

ACCORDING TO HEGEL "the *highest and final aim* of philosophic science is to bring about . . . a *reconciliation* of self-conscious reason with the reason which *is* in the world—in other words, *with actuality*."[30]

In this reconciliatory spirit Hegel frequently treats with open sarcasm those who offer major criticism to what he himself considers the "rational actuality." He does that in the name of the Divine order and the Idea, referring them to a philosophical domain to which considerations of historical time in his view cannot apply. As we have seen in the last chapter, he never misses the opportunity to assert that the Divine order or the Idea are "not so impotent" that they could not have fully actualized themselves already, and forever, and that, moreover, to have done so in the "eternal present." Indeed he never fails to insist that "The rational, the divine, is not so impotent that it would have to wait for the beginning of its actualization."

Hegel reiterates the same thought in his *Logic* in another context by saying that: "The actuality of the rational stands opposed by the popular fancy . . . even on the field of *politics*. As if the world had waited on it to learn how it ought to be, and was not! . . . The object of philosophy is the Idea: and *the Idea is not so impotent as to merely have a right or an obligation to exist without actually existing*. The object of philosophy is an *actuality* of which those objects, social regulations and conditions, are only the superficial outside."[31] Thus the Hegelian critique of "ought-to-be" is characteristically concerned with the total rejection of all advocacy aimed at introducing significant changes into the established social and political order.

Hegel also maintains that "unless it is a *system*, philosophy is not a *scientific* production."[32] At the same time, what he also frequently emphasizes in a forceful way is the need for, and his claim to offer to the public through the completion of his own system—while remaining sharply dismissive of "popular fancy," as we have seen above—the philosophically required and adequate *"advanced science."*

Naturally, the ground on which he rejects "popular fancy" is not epistemological elitism. Hegel is, on the contrary, a most enlightened democrat regarding the ability of the people in general to comprehend even the highest level of philosophical generalization. His ground for peremptorily dismissing "popular fancy" in all its manifestations is primarily social and political conservatism, well in tune with the general orientation of his speculative system's "advanced philosophical science." This is why he asserts in the clearest possible way that "the question as to what constitutes the State is one of *advanced science,* and not of *popular decision.*"[33] And that is, of course, not an issue of abstract conceptual disputes concerning the theory of the State but a *practical* matter of actual decision making, with serious potential impact on the *actuality* of the State, as seen and idealized by Hegel himself.

That is the reason why Hegel cannot tolerate the dangerous intrusion of the advocacy of "popular decision"—by "popular fancy" or anything else—into the State's domain of political decision making, which represents the exalted but extremely problematical "this-worldliness" of the Hegelian system. There can be absolutely no compromises on that score. Indeed, in the interest of preserving the integrality of his own conservative state theory Hegel has no hesitation whatsoever even to violate his explicitly stated rule about the rejection of "ought-to-be," when doing so suits him.

An obvious example in this respect is when—in relation to the requirements of the rightful Constitution, as formulated by Hegel himself—he categorically asserts (as indeed in tune with the general character of his state theory he *must*) that "the distinction between *commanding* and *obeying* is absolutely necessary, because affairs could not go on without it."[34] However, when it comes to *justifying* the position adopted by Hegel as "absolutely necessary," notwithstanding its contradiction to some of his own principles, he can offer nothing but an utterly vacuous—unfulfillable and never in actuality fulfilled—"ought-to-be." This is how Hegel tries to extricate himself from the conceptual maze and trap he had created for himself, regarding the advocated "distinction between those who command and those who obey":

> Yet, obedience seems *inconsistent with liberty,* and those who command *appear* to do the very opposite of that which the fundamental idea of the State, viz. that of *Freedom, requires.* It is, however, *urged* that . . . the constitution *should be* at least so framed, that *the citizens may obey as little as possible,* and the smallest modicum of free volition be left to the *commands of the superiors;*—that the substance of that for which subordination is necessary, even in its most important bearings, *should be decided and resolved only by the People*—by the will of the many or of all the citizens; though it is supposed to be thereby provided that *the State should be* possessed of *vigor and strength* as a reality—an individual unity.[35]

As we can see, the *ought-to-be* "urged" by Hegel—utterly in vain—on the Constitution, regarding the decision making power of the People, is in truth nothing but the collision between two orders of *"should be":* one wishfully advocated in favour of *"the People,"* and the other actually granted to *the State,* on account of its overwhelmingly important defining characteristics according to which the Hegelian State must have *"vigor and strength,"* in order to be able to fulfil its stipulated functions. And between these two orders of "should be" (or "ought-to-be") the absolute requirements of the State must win unreservedly in the Hegelian conception all the time. Besides, on the same page from which the last quotation is taken Hegel also tries to attenuate, and even to minimize, the contradiction between "commanding/obeying" and Freedom which he cannot help acknowledging. He does so when he says not only that those who command only *"appear"* to contradict the principle of Freedom so fundamental to his own idea of the State, but also when he adds that the enforcement of the absolute requirement of commanding and obeying by the State itself "seems only a compulsory limitation, *external to* and contravening freedom *in the abstract"* only.

Thus Hegel is perfectly consistent in both instances. That is, both when he voices his strongest possible reservation about using the imperatival form of "ought-to-be" in philosophical arguments, and when he violates the same rule and unhesitatingly asserts himself the formerly dismissed imperative of "ought-to-be" any time he needs it. Naturally, the consistency is *substantive* and not *formal.* It is not formal because his own philosophical practice clearly shows, on the contrary, the *formal violation* of his own rule. But, of course, not without a very important *substantive reason* as regards the Hegelian philosophy itself. For a careful reading of the passages we have seen above reveals that his rejection of the "popular fancy," which has the temerity to intrude into the world of "political actuality"—and Hegel's scorn for it on the ground that it dares to imagine that "the world had waited on it to learn how it ought to be, and was not!"—and the contrary example of dubiously reconciling the "absolute necessity" of commanding and obeying with the hallowed idea of Freedom, in the name of a rather vacuous but philosophically/ideologically most convenient "ought-to-be," they both fully correspond to the *substantive conservatism* (and at the same time the paradoxical consistency) of the Hegelian conception of the idealized State.

AS WE CAN SEE, Hegel in fact wholly lives up to his own definition of "the *highest and final aim of philosophic science*" as a very distinctive way "to bring about the *reconciliation* of self-conscious reason with the reason which *is* in the world—in other words, *with actuality*."

However, what is most problematical is the Hegelian definition itself. For the way in which Hegel characterizes the "highest and final aim" of his philosophical science calls for the totally apologetic submission of "self-conscious reason" to the "reason in the world" in its destructively irrational—that is, in its *alienated* and not simply objectified-externalized—form, as fully befits the social metabolic order of capital's by Hegel idealized *"actuality."* In other words, Hegel defines in the name of "self-conscious reason" itself the task of philosophy by calling for the *willing submission* of all—the submission of all, that is, apart from those who are readily disqualified by him as guilty of self-delusory "popular fancy"—to the dehumanizing practical premises and imperatives of the very far from "rational actuality" of the existent. And Hegel is doing that in an age when the great historic task—under the impact of the exploding social antagonisms of which he is an acutely observing witness—is becoming ever more pressingly the *radical change* of the world.

The fundamental methodological orienting principle of the Hegelian philosophy, centered on the Absolute Idea, is inseparable from its deeply reconciliatory ideological orientation. This is why historical temporality open towards the future must be banned from it in the name of the *"eter-*

nal present," which alone is said to be appropriate to the Absolute's methodologically encapsulated "circle of circles." In Hegel's words "The definition, which declares the Absolute to be the Idea, is itself absolute. All former definitions come back to this. The Idea is the Truth: for truth is the correspondence of objectivity with the notion."[36] And he also adds that "The Idea may be described in many ways. It may be called reason (and this is the proper philosophical significance of reason); subject-object; the unity of the ideal and the real, of the finite and the infinite, of soul and body; the possibility which has its actuality in its own self; that of which the nature can be thought only as existent, etc. All these descriptions apply, because the Idea contains all the relations of understanding, but contains them in their infinite self-return and self-identity."[37] Thus the reconciliation advocated by Hegel cannot admit to any limit in time or extent. It must be *absolute,* because the idea of the self-realizing Absolute Idea is not compatible with anything else. It is not compatible with any temporal qualification, related to potentially changing sociohistorical determinations, because the Absolute Idea as such cannot tolerate even the shadow of any departure or dissent in the future from its *"fully accomplished actuality."* And that is so precisely because the Absolute Idea must be thought of as always *fully accomplished* already: a categorical postulate constantly reiterated by Hegel himself.

We have seen at the beginning of this chapter that in Marx's view "Mankind inevitably sets itself only such tasks as it is able to solve, since closer examination will always show that the problem itself arises only when the material conditions for its solution are already present or at least in the course of formation."[38] These thoughts are reminiscent of a few lines written by Hegel which read as follows: "We may rest assured that it is the nature of *truth* to force its way to recognition *when its time has come,* and hence *never appears too soon,* and never finds a public that is not ripe to receive it."[39]

These thoughts are very similar in some respects; and yet they are worlds apart. For what is at stake in Marx's case is the tangible reality of capital's *socially antagonistic* and *hierarchically entrenched* reproductive order itself. Such antagonism is contrasted by Marx with its tendentiously distorted political economist characterization as purely "individual antagonism" corresponding to "human nature," and therefore *absolutely insur-*

mountable in the practical world of "civil society" as well as legitimately *eternalizable* in economic and political theory. Accordingly, what Marx calls for is the articulation of a historically unfolding, and in the midst of the exploding social antagonisms also veritably overdue, *actual societal change,* defined in terms of its own *objective practical premises*—as labour's qualitatively different *hegemonic alternative* order—set against capital's increasingly more destructive mode of control. This is the very precise meaning of the "this-worldliness of philosophy" passionately advocated by Marx not only in his "Theses on Feuerbach" but in all of his writings.

Hegel's appeal to the idea that truth can "force its way to recognition *when its time has come,* and hence *never appears too soon*" is also the assertion of a kind of "this-worldliness," notwithstanding the speculative attire in which it is presented to us. But it is a very different kind of "this-worldliness" precisely with regard to its crucial terms of reference. Not only because it postulates "Truth" speculatively wedded to the Absolute Idea and thereby definitionally enclosed in the circle of "infinite self-return and self-identity." The greatest problem is that almost anything—and certainly *everything* ideologically convenient in the sense of unreservedly corresponding to the standpoint of political economy, in the apologetic spirit of capital's self-serving vantage point—can be derived from such a definition of Absolute Truth. And when it yields the proposition that "Europe is *absolutely the end of History,*"[40]—as we are told by Hegel in what he explicitly calls the *"Theodicaea: the justification of God in History"*[41]—then we find ourselves confronted by the baffling experience that in the work of one of the greatest philosophers of all history *absolute falsehood* can be inextricably tied to the arbitrary speculative assertion of what he claims to be the *"Absolute Truth."* This is why the Hegelian definition of "the *highest and final aim of philosophic science,*" in its speculatively secured inseparability from *"reconciliation* of self-conscious reason with *actuality"*—which had meant justifying itself in the name of the Absolute, prohibiting through the self-same modality of ideological rationalization any *historical change* in the real world—had to be radically superseded in the Marxian system by a very different conception of science.

UNDER THE NAME OF THE "CUNNING OF REASON" and "Divine Providence," corresponding to his own version of Adam Smith's

"Invisible hand" for describing capital's reproductive modality, Hegel compares such process to a syllogism and explains that

> The Middle Term is this inward power of the notion in the shape of an *agency,* with which the object as Means is 'immediately' united and *in obedience to which it stands*. . . . Thus the Subjective End, which is the power ruling these processes, in which the subjective things wear themselves out on one another, contrives to keep itself free from them, and to preserve itself in them. Doing so, it appears as the *Cunning of Reason.*
>
> Reason is as cunning as it is powerful. Cunning may be said to lie in the intermediate action which, while it permits the objects to follow their own bent and act upon one another till they waste away, and does not itself directly interfere in the process, is nevertheless only working out its own aims. With this explanation, *Divine Providence* may be said to stand to the world and its process in the capacity of absolute cunning. God lets men do as they please with their particular passions and interests; but the result is the accomplishment of—not their plans, but his, and these differ decidedly from the ends primarily sought by those whom he employs. . . .
>
> The End achieved consequently is only an object, which again becomes a Means or material for other Ends, and so on *for ever.*[42]

The question is, in relation to capital's necessary reproductive modality allegedly safeguarded by the "Cunning of Reason" and "Divine Providence": is it so really *for ever?* Or is there a historically sustainable way of overcoming capital's reproductive "circle of circles"?

Certainly, if the actual social processes are not extricated from their reconciliatory speculative integument, so as to follow instead their consciously designed course of action, in that case the "Invisible hand"—in any one of its political economist varieties—can remain in charge of the circular reproductive modality of "civil society." It is therefore necessary not only to theoretically explain but also to *practically overcome* the forces which dominate societal interchange and derive additional strength from the mystifying character of their mode of existence.

This is where the critique of alienation and reification—which requires the demystifying definition of the category of *alienation* in its proper terms of reference, disentangled from its Hegelian submergence into *objectification/externalization*—asserts its importance. For this way of clarifying the real meaning of alienation helps to change a speculative mystery into something perfectly comprehensible. To quote a relevant passage from *The German Ideology,* the question is "how does it happen that trade, which after all is nothing more than the exchange of products of various individuals and countries, rules the whole world through the relation of supply and demand—a relation which, as an English economist says, hovers over the earth like the fate of the ancients, and with *invisible hand* allots fortune and misfortune to men, sets up empires and wrecks empires, causes nations to rise and to disappear—whereas with the abolition of the basis, private property, with the communistic regulation of production (and, implicit in this, the abolition of the *alien attitude [Fremdheit] of men to their own product),* the power of the relation of supply and demand is dissolved into nothing, and men once more *gain control* of exchange, production and the way they behave to one another?"[43] Thus, what is really needed in this regard is not a reconciliatory accommodation of the people to the alienating power of the claimed "rational actuality" but its practically effective and historically viable supersession by an alternative order. For, as an apparently mysterious imposition of the perverse rationality in question over the actual socioeconomic and historical processes, "man's own deed becomes an *alien power* opposed to him, which enslaves him instead of being controlled by him. . . . This consolidation of what we ourselves produce into *a material power above us,* growing *out of our control,* thwarting our expectations, bringing to naught our calculations, is one of the chief factors in historical development up till now."[44]

Thus the fundamental orienting principle of the Marxian conception of science becomes how to *gain control* over all aspects of the societal reproduction process, from those directly involved in the basic material conditions of existence of humankind to the most mediated theoretical and creative artistic activities in the life of the social individuals. Naturally, given the dynamic character of the problems at stake, both in relation to human development as it unfolded in the past and with regard to its consciously planned trajectory in the future, the whole approach had to be irrepressibly *historical.* In contrast to the philosophical conceptions of the past there could be no question of an ideologically convenient historical closure. For the necessary emancipatory challenges of the social being involved could not be made intelligible at all without constantly keeping in mind their historical dimension.

Accordingly, the question of "Why history?" was answered by Marx with these words: "Men have history because they must *produce* their life, and because they must produce it moreover in a *certain way*."[45] In this sense there could be nothing mysterious or speculative/metaphysical about the real historical process. On the contrary, its frame of reference was described by Marx in the most tangible terms by putting into relief the important substantive point that "*the creation of new needs is the first historical act*."[46] And he summed up the fundamental methodological orientation of the new approach in the same spirit: "We know only one science, *the science of history*."[47]

Marx firmly rejected the idea that the various domains of human intellectual activity should constitute self-contained theoretical fields of their own, with artificially opposed criteria of historical enquiry. This is how he had put it: "There is no history of politics, law, science, etc., of art, religion."[48] All these fields had to be investigated as integral parts of a coherent whole. In the same way he rejected the opposition between natural and human science, insisting that in the future "natural science will lose its abstractly material—or rather, its idealistic—tendency, and will become the basis of ***human*** science, as it has already become the basis of actual human life, albeit in an *estranged* form. *One* basis for life and another basis for *science* is ***a priori*** a lie. . . . Natural science will in time subsume under itself the science of man, just as the science of man will subsume under itself natural science: there will be *one* science."[49]

The fact that in the course of modern history natural science could become the basis of actual human life only in an *estranged form,* through capitalistic industrial and commercial developments, due to their deep-seated and hierarchically articulated *structural determinations* which by their very nature had to subjugate the creative potentiality of human labour to the imperatives of capital-expansion, was, of course, a great impediment for the future. Thus the dehumanizing actuality of such developments had to be redressed the only way feasible under the existing circumstances; that is, through the uncompromising transformation of the established social order in its entirety. And that carried with it the definition of Marxian science in its inseparability from the most radical *practical intervention* in the social transformatory process. Theoretical explanation on its own could not offer the required solutions in this respect; not even the programmatically anti-speculative kind. Nor was it sufficient to engage only in the *negation* of the given order. The capital system's negation had to be combined with demonstrating the historical viability of the necessary positive *hegemonic alternative* order, as embodied in a globally unfolding emancipatory social movement. The "Theses on Feuerbach"—advocating the *unity of theory and practice*—made it absolutely clear that *revolutionizing practice,* in the most obvious sense of its terms of reference, had to assume the central role in the Marxian conception of science. This is why for the first time in history a scientific theory of structural change was articulated and directly linked by its originator to the necessary fulfilment of the historic task of creating a *conscious revolutionary movement* capable of instituting the advocated strategy of *global transformation.*

Since the target of the Marxian critique had to be the fetishistic and alienating capital system in its entirety, with all its *structural determinations,* the category of *social structure* acquired a seminal importance in the new theory. For it was inconceivable to gain control over the life-process of societal reproduction without clearly understanding, through the act of demystification, the levers and crucial determining forces of the established social structure itself. As Marx had put it: *empirical observation* must bring out, "without any *mystification and speculation*, the connection of the social and political structure with production. The *social structure* and the *state* are continually evolving out of the *life-process of definite individuals.*"[50] Consequently, by brushing aside the speculative mystification surrounding these relations, due to the overturning power of the "fetishism of commodity" (which changes social relations into things and vice versa, things into baffling social relations), and by highlighting the connection of the formerly enigmatic treatment of the social structure and the state with the tangible life-process of definite individuals, it becomes possible to perceive "the necessity, and at the same time the condition, of a *transformation both of industry and the social structure.*"[51] That is the only way in which one can envisage liberating the definite social individuals from their enslavement in capital's reproductive "circle of circles," overcoming thereby the power of the self-asserting "Cunning of Reason" even when it is sanctified by the Hegelian "Divine Providence."

THE OVERTURNING POWER of the "fetishism of commodity" is clearly manifest in the social relationship mystifyingly depicted in philosophy under the postulate of the *identical subject-object.*

Paradoxically, this postulate played an important role in one of the most influential philosophical works of the twentieth century, Lukács's *History and Class Consciousness.* He famously asserted in it that "Hegel represents the absolute consummation of rationalism, but this means that he can be superseded only by an interrelation of thought and existence that has ceased to be contemplative, by the concrete demonstration of the *identical subject-object.*"[52] Lukács himself later strongly criticized some of the major philosophical positions adopted by him in this work of transition toward Marxism (first published in 1923), including his version of subject-object identity, characterizing them as a most problematical attempt to "out-Hegel Hegel."[53] But precisely that was the reason why Merleau-Ponty, after abandoning his former position as a radical intellectual and Jean-Paul Sartre's comrade in arms, tendentiously praised *History and Class Consciousness* in his *Adventures of the Dialectic*[54] as the classic embodiment of a somewhat mythical "Western Marxism."

Naturally, Lukács's idea of subject-object identity was very different from Hegel's. He was not talking about the "Absolute Idea" and the "World Spirit" but about the *proletariat* as the *"identical subject-object of the historical process."*[55] However, by making that switch he could not turn his "Hegel-out-Hegeling" notion into something any less speculative and idealist than the much revered Hegelian postulate. For two reasons. First, because—in contrast to the *actuality* of proletarian existence under the conditions of capital's rule over society—he could only project an *abstract potentiality* for the future, and even that only in the form of the dubious concept of the Weberian "ascribed consciousness."[56] And second, because the real issue concerning the complex relationship between subject and object is the historical *unity* of the two, both in relation to the past and with regard to the future, and not their speculatively postulated *identity.*

The problem in this respect is the perverse overturning effect of the historically unfolding social division of labour which culminates in the fetishistic capital system. An important passage from Marx's *Grundrisse* helps to throw light on the nature of the material processes, centered around the working subject and the objective conditions of this activity, which in the end are transfigured—and utterly misrepresented—in the idealist postulate of subject-object identity. The passage in question reads as follows:

> just as the working subject is a natural individual, a natural being, so the first objective condition of his labour appears as nature, earth, as an inorganic body. He himself is not only the inorganic body, but also inorganic nature as a *subject.* This condition is not something he has produced, but something he finds to hand; something existing in nature and which he presupposes. . . . the fact that the worker finds the objective conditions of his labour as something *separate* from him, as *capital,* and the fact that the capitalist finds the workers *propertyless,* as *abstract labourers*—the exchange as it takes place between *value and living labour*—assumes a historic process, however much capital and wage-labour themselves *reproduce* this relationship and elaborate it in objective scope, as well as in depth. And the *historical process is the evolutionary history of both capital and wage-labour*. In other words, the *extra-economic origin of property merely means the historic origin of the bourgeois economy,* of the forms of production to which the categories of political economy give theoretical or ideal expression. . . .
>
> What requires explanation is not the *unity* of living and active human beings with the natural, inorganic conditions of their metabolism with nature, and therefore their appropriation of nature; nor is this the result of a historic process. What we must explain is the *separation* of these inorganic conditions of human existence from this active existence, *a separation which is only fully completed in the relationship between wage-labour and capital.* In the relationship of slavery and serfdom there is no such separation; what happens is that one part of society is treated by another as the mere inorganic and natural condition of its own production. The slave stands in no sort of relation to the objective conditions of his labour. It is rather labour itself, both in the form of the slave as of the serf, which is placed among the other living things *(Naturwesen)* as inorganic conditions of production, alongside the cattle or as an appendage of the soil. In other words: the original conditions of production appear

> as *natural prerequisites,* natural conditions of existence of the producer, just as his living body, however reproduced and developed by him, is not originally established by himself, but appears as his prerequisite.[57]

As we can see, the possibility of disclosing the actual character of the relationship between the working subject and his object, together with the emancipatory potential inherent in such disclosure, arises only under the conditions of capitalism, as a result of a long process of historical and productive development. For in complete contrast to the slave who "stands in no sort of relation to the objective conditions of his labour," the working subject of "wage slavery" does indeed enter the objective framework of capitalist enterprise as a working *subject.* This is so despite the fact that his subject-character is immediately obliterated at the point of entry into the "despotic workshop," which must be run under the absolute authority of the *usurping pseudo-subject, capital,* transforming the real subject, the worker, into a mere cog in the capital system's productive machinery. And since the working subject under the capital system is condemned to the existence of an *"abstract labourer,"* because he is *propertyless*—quite unlike the slave and the serf who are by no means "propertyless" but an *integral part* of property, and therefore very far from being "abstract"—the "wage slave" is completely at the mercy of capital's ability and willingness to employ him upon which his very survival depends. This, again, could not be more contrasting with the original (primitive) relationship between the working subject and the objective (necessary) conditions of his productive activity. For that relationship is characterized by "the *unity* of living and active human beings with the natural, inorganic conditions of their metabolism with nature."

Thus the real issue of the subject-object relationship is how to *reconstitute*—at a level fully consonant with the historically achieved productive development of society—the *necessary unity of the working subjects* with the attainable objective conditions of their meaningful life-activity. The *identity* of the subject and object never existed; nor could it ever exist. But, compared to the past, the *qualitatively different reconstitution of the unity between living labour as the active subject, and the objective conditions required for the exercise of creative human energies,* in accordance with the achieved level of productive advancement, is both feasible and necessary. The opposition—and indeed under the rule of capital the *antagonistic contradiction*—between living labour and the necessary conditions of its exercise is an obvious absurdity: the dirtiest trick of the Hegelian "Cunning of Reason." The philosophical mystification manifest in the postulate of subject-object identity is the necessary corollary of this objective, nonetheless absurd, relationship as perceived from capital's vantage point. For the contradiction in question can only be acknowledged in terms that remain fully compatible with the *structural imperatives* of capital as the eternalized mode of control of the social metabolism. This is why the actually feasible social remedy of reconstituting at a qualitatively higher level the *unity of the working subject with the objective conditions of his activity* must be metamorphosed into the mystical postulate of the *identical* subject-object.

As we have seen in chapter 6, there is indeed here before us a most peculiar "subject-object identity," even if in its unvarnished reality very different from its philosophical idealization. Reflecting the *fetishistic practical overturning* of the relationship between the real *working subject* and its *object,* both as its *means* of work and its *product* as stored up labour in the form of *accumulating capital*—which thereby by usurpation assumes for itself the role of the *commanding subject*—the mystifying philosophical idealization consists in deriving the *speculative "self-consciousness"* or *"subject-identity" of philosophical discourse* from the thinkers' self-identification with the exploitative objectives that emanate from the *unalterable practical premises* of capital as *self-positing subject-object,* coupled with the simultaneous elimination of the *real subject (living* and not *stored-up* labour, the *genuine working subject)* from the philosophical picture. This is why the elusive quest for the "identical subject-object"—as a *fictitious* reconciliatory resolution of the problem, which leaves the exploitative relationship itself in the world of the pretended "rational actuality" standing—persists to our own days as a haunting philosophical Chimera.

Hegel forcefully asserts that real knowledge cannot satisfy itself with appearance but, as he puts it, must "reach a position where appearance becomes identified with essence."[58] This is how he depicts the whole process, admitting that it is not without "ambiguity" but overcoming the acknowledged ambiguity in his own way:

> This dialectic process which consciousness executes *on itself* . . . is precisely what is termed Experience. . . . Consciousness knows something; this something is the *essence* or what is *per se.* This object, however, is also the *per se,* the inherent reality, *for consciousness.* Hence comes *ambiguity* of this truth. . . . since what at first appeared as object is reduced, when it passes into consciousness, to what knowledge takes it to be, and the implicit nature, the real in itself, becomes what this entity per se is *for consciousness;* . . . It is this circumstance which carries forward the whole succession of the modes and attitudes of consciousness in their own necessity. It is only this *necessity*, this origination of the new object—which offers itself to consciousness without consciousness knowing how it comes by it—that to us, who watch the process, is to be seen going on, so to say, *behind its back.* . . . In virtue of that necessity this pathway to science is itself *eo ipso* science, and is, moreover, as regards its content, Science of the Experience of Consciousness. . . . In pressing forward to its true form of existence, consciousness will come to a point at which it lays aside its semblance of being hampered with what is foreign to it, with what is only for it and exists as an other; it will reach a position where *appearance becomes identified with essence,* where, in consequence, its exposition *coincides* with just this very point, this very stage of the science proper of mind. And, finally, when it grasps this *its own essence,* it will connote the nature of *absolute knowledge* itself.[59]

To be sure, speculatively produced "absolute knowledge," under all its names generously described on page 276 of Hegel's *Logic* quoted above, is most obliging in every way and in every context. For in its self-constitution it all comes down to grasping "*its own essence*" through the "dialectic process which consciousness executes *on itself,*" as befits the procedures of idealist philosophy.

However, when the issue is the practical necessity to overcome the enslaving dominance of *alienating* objectification, constantly reinforced by the overturning power of *commodity fetishism,* a very different way must be found to sweep away *false appearance* in order to effectively gain control over the structurally entrenched *substantive relations* of the established social order. For under the rule of capital's alienating/fetishistic mode of control—which turns the working subjects into mere objects totally dominated by capital's usurpatory subject—"a definite social relation between men assumes in their eyes the *fantastic form of a relation between things*,"[60] or in other words, it assumes the mystifying form of "*material* relations between *persons* and *social* relations between *things*."[61] As a result, "their own social action takes the form of the action of objects which rule the producers instead of being ruled by them."[62]

No speculative consciousness "grasping its own essence" could be of any help in changing this state of affairs. For the painfully pressing historical truth is and remains that "The life-process of society, which is based on the process of material production, does not strip off its *mystical veil* until it is treated as production by *freely associated men,* and is *consciously* regulated by them in accordance with a *settled plan*."[63] This is why science had to be extricated from its speculative integument. It had to be radically reorientated—in accordance with its envisaged, practically vital and effective emancipatory objectives—in its Marxian sense.

8.3 The Critique of Political Economy

All of Marx's principal works carry the title or the subtitle "A Critique of Political Economy," starting with the posthumously published 1857–58 manuscripts of the *Grundrisse zu einer Kritik der Politischen Economie* (that is: *Outlines of a Critique of Political Economy)*, followed by the book he himself published in 1859 under the title *A Contribution to the Critique of Political Economy*, and crowned by his magisterial, even if unfinished, *Capital,* which has as its subtitle *A Critique of Political Economy*. Moreover, the extensive volumes of his *Theories of Surplus-Value* also belong to the same complex of investigations. Thus, obviously, the critical settling of accounts with political economy occupied a central place in Marx's lifework.

There had to be a very good reason why Marx dedicated so many years of his life to the critical assessment of political economy. As he made it explicit in his 1859 Preface to *A Contribution to the Critique of Political Economy*, that was because he became convinced that "the anatomy of 'civil society' has to be sought in political economy."[64]

Understandably, he contrasted in the most outspoken terms "classical political economy" with "vulgar economy," saying that "by classical political economy, I understand that economy which, since the time of W. Petty, has investigated the *real relations of production* in bourgeois society, in contradistinction to vulgar economy, which deals with appearanes only, ruminates without ceasing on the materials long since provided by scientific economy, and there seeks plausible explanations of the most obtrusive phenomena, for bourgeois daily use, but for the rest, confines itself to systematizing in *a pedantic way,* and proclaiming for everlasting truths, the trite ideas held by the self-complacent bourgeoisie with regard to their own world, to them the *best of all possible worlds*."[65]

However, the sharp treatment and rejection of "vulgar economy" is of a thoroughly secondary importance in this enterprise. The real target of the Marxian critique is *classical political economy*, precisely because in its time it has investigated—admittedly from capital's vantage point—the *real relations of production* in bourgeois society. The great practical sociohistorical task is the radical supersession of the bourgeois order itself which involves, of course, the critical overcoming of those theories that embody genuine scientific discoveries revealing the nature of that social reproductive order, in contrast to their pedantic and shallow apologetic vulgarizations. That is the only way to learn from the historically known "anatomy of civil society" incorporated in the work of classical political economy. This means a learning process undertaken in order to be able to go beyond the "civil society" depicted in classical political economy, no matter how idealized the image presented by the great representatives of economic theory. For the idea of a *critical supersession* cannot be simplistically equated with the notion of a straightforward *negation and rejection.* A valid critique must incorporate also the *strong points*—i.e., the real achievements—of the scientific adversary in the dialectical sense of a *"preserving supersession"* and *"superseding preservation."*

The defining characteristics of the "new historic form" advocated by Marx—labour's hegemonic alternative to the established mode of social metabolic reproduction—must be formulated in their own terms of reference. But such a process cannot take place in a historical vacuum. The important point of theoretical contact between the existing social order and the envisaged alternative society can only be classical political economy inasmuch as the latter genuinely contains the "anatomy of civil society." For to our own days classical political economy continues to play a major role—both directly and through its apologetic vulgarizations[66]—in the regulating processes of the capitalist order. The points of criticism spelled out by Marx, or by anybody else, in order to permanently supersede the representative theoretical generalizations formulated by the classical figures of political economy from capital's standpoint, acquire their validity only if the *raisons d'être*—that is the objective structural determinations at the roots of the theories concerned—are highlighted in the sense of an "immanent critique." That is to say, a critique which acknowledges also the special circumstances and historical motivations of the thinkers in question, and not only their class limitations as viewed from the qualitatively different standpoint and necessary distance of the envisaged "new historic form."

This is why it should not come as a surprise when we read Marx's generous comments on the classics of political economy, indicating at the same time also the reasons why they *had to* adopt a limited and problematical position. To quote him:

> Political economy has indeed analysed, however incompletely, value and its magnitude, and has discovered what lies beneath these forms. But it has never once asked the question why labour is represented by the value of its product and labour time by the magnitude of that value. These formulae, which bear it stamped upon them in unmistakeable letters that they belong to a state of society, in which the process of production has the mastery over man, instead of being controlled by him, such formulae appear to the bourgeois intellect to be as much a *self-evident necessity imposed by Nature* as productive labour itself. . . .
>
> The insufficiency of Ricardo's analysis of the magnitude of value, and his analysis is by far the best, will appear from the 3rd and 4th books of this work. As regards value in general, it is the weak point of the classical school of political economy that it nowhere, expressly and with full consciousness, distinguishes between labour, as it appears in the value of a product and the same labour, as it appears in the use-value of that product. . . .
>
> It is one of the chief failings of classical economy that it has never succeeded, by means of its analysis of commodities, and, in particular, of

> their value, in discovering that form under which value becomes exchange-value. Even Adam Smith and Ricardo, the best representatives of the school, treat the form of value as a thing of no importance, as having no connection with the inherent nature of the commodities. The reason for this is not solely because their attention is entirely absorbed in the analysis of the magnitude of value. It lies deeper. The value-form of the product of labour is not only the most abstract, but is also the most universal form, taken by the product in bourgeois production, and stamps that production as a particular species of social production, and thereby gives it its *special historical character.* If then we treat this mode of production as one *eternally fixed by Nature for every state of society,* we necessarily overlook that which is the *differentia specifica of the value-form*, and consequently of the commodity form, and of its further developments, money-form, capital-form, &c. We consequently find that economists, who are thoroughly agreed as to labour-time being the measure of the magnitude of value, have the most strange and contradictory ideas of *money*, the perfected form of the general equivalent.[67]

THIS TAKES US TO AN ISSUE of the greatest methodological importance. For through the critical examination of the way in which classical political economy deals with the money-form, Marx focuses attention on a methodologically frequent—and at the same time socially most revealing —*reversal* of the actual historical relationships involved. Such reversal inevitably transubstantiates in a reconciliatory way the real nature of the ongoing processes.

Attempting to elucidate an apparently most complicated problem Marx insists that "The difficulty lies, not in comprehending that money is a commodity, but in discovering how, why, and by what means a commodity becomes money."[68] To do so, it is not enough to point out the failures and insufficiencies of the explanations offered by classical political economy. It is also necessary to underline the objective sociohistorical determinations underlying such failures. Accordingly, Marx makes it clear that "What appears to happen is, not that gold becomes money, in consequence of all other commodities expressing their values in it, but, on the contrary, that all other commodities universally express their values in gold, because it is money. The *intermediary steps* of the process vanish in the result and leave no trace behind. . . . Hence the *magic of money*. In the form of society now under consideration, the behaviour of men in the social process of production is purely *atomic*. Hence their relations to each other in production assume a material character *independent of their control and conscious individual action*. These facts manifest themselves at first by products as a general rule taking the form of commodities. We have seen how the progressive development of a society of commodity producers stamps one privileged commodity with the character of money. Hence the *riddle* presented by money is but the riddle presented by *commodities;* only it now strikes us in its most *glaring form*."[69]

What needs to be explained is thus the "magic of money" which assumes the form of the "riddle of money" inseparable from the "riddle of commodities" in generalized commodity production. But the solution of such riddles requires the adoption of the right method. The key issue here is the *"differentia specifica of the value-form"* mentioned earlier. Since—in accordance with the important methodological principle that "the key to the anatomy of the ape is the anatomy of human beings,"[70] and not vice versa, i.e., that the highest form of development opens up the possibility of explaining the lower forms—within the historically most advanced and correspondingly many-sided socioeconomic framework of development it becomes possible to find answers to the indicated "riddles." But they cannot be elucidated without a *fully comprehensive* historical analysis of human development which investigates the metabolic relationship between humankind and nature as well as among the individuals themselves, on their objective ground of determination. That is, in a way which is simultaneously *social ontological* and *comprehensively historical*. Which means an analysis of the *"differentia specifica"* that constantly bears in mind the totality of sociohistorical development leading to the most advanced phase through the demonstration of its *overall genesis*, while subsuming or incorporating in its explanatory results also the relevant defining characteristics of the earlier phases.

In this sense Marx explains that "Money is a crystal formed of necessity in the course of the exchanges, whereby different products of labour are practically equated to one another and thus by practice converted into commodities."[71] The ground on which this conversion can take place is both social ontological and historical in a comprehensive sense, going well beyond the capitalistic phase of development both in relation to the past and with regard to the future. To quote Marx:

> Objects in themselves are external to man, and consequently *alienable* by him. In order that this *alienation* may be reciprocal, it is only necessary for men, by a tacit understanding, to treat each other as private owners of those alienable objects, and by implication as independent individuals. But such a state of reciprocal independence has no existence in a primitive society based on property in common, whether such a society takes the form of a patriarchal family, an ancient Indian community, or a Peruvian Inca State. The exchange of commodities, therefore, first begins on the boundaries of such communities, at their points of contact with other similar communities, or with members of the latter. So soon, however, as products once become commodities in the external relations of a community, they also, by reaction, become so in its internal intercourse. . . . In the course of time, therefore, some portion at least of the products of labour must be produced with a special view to exchange. From that moment the distinction becomes firmly established between the utility of an object for the purposes of consumption, and its utility for the purposes of exchange. Its use-value becomes distinguished from its exchange-value. . . .
>
> The necessity for a value-form grows with the increasing number and variety of the commodities exchanged. The problem and the means of solution arise simultaneously. . . . *Nomad* races are the first to develop the *money-form,* because all their worldly goods consist of moveable objects and are therefore *directly alienable* and because their mode of life, by bringing them into contact with foreign communities, solicits the exchange of products.[72]

Thus it is necessary to understand the *historical depth* of these developments not only in order to grasp the proper nature and strength, together with the limitations, of the present form of ubiquitous generalized commodity production, but also the challenges for the future. For it is far too simplistic to envisage the institution of labour's hegemonic alternative to capital's social reproductive order by means of the political overthrow of the capitalist state. The latter is *reversible,* as painful historical evidence shows, and can only be a *part* of the transformatory task. For the historic challenge consists in going *beyond capital* in the full sense of the term, embracing all dimensions of the complex emancipatory process, including its social ontological dimensions reaching a long way back into the past, as indicated above. Thus both the proper understanding of the multi-dimensional characteristics of the established order (which through their actual historical unfolding turn that order into a genuine *organic system*) and the corresponding elaboration of the strategies required for its radical transformation (which must also envisage the alternative social metabolic order as an objectively sustainable *organic system*) can only be defined in a thoroughly historical sense.

However, what we are presented with in the tendentious conceptualizations of these processes conceived from capital's vantage point by even the greatest representatives of political economy, is an arbitrary abstraction from the "differentia specifica," i.e., the necessary and very specific objective determinations of the most developed form of *generalized commodity production* of the present. This is done for two—paradoxically complementary—reasons. First, in order to be able to project the generalized form of commodity production into the most remote past. And second, in order to draw a direct line of connection between the archaic precapitalist forms and the present. In both ways the political economist conceptualizations succeed in *obliterating the historical character* of the complex developments which had actually led from the *sporadic and local* exchange of commodities to the historically given and, due to its ultimately explosive antagonistic contradictions necessarily transient, even if in a determinate period universally prevailing, capitalist form.

Thus the characteristic political economist's theoretical images are formulated from capital's standpoint in the interest of *eternalizing* the bourgeois mode of production "as one *eternally fixed by Nature for every state of society*." What disappears in this revealing way from the picture is the *all-important dimension of historical genesis* of the end result. Its obliteration opens the gates to the complete reversal of the actually unfolding antagonistic, but structurally entrenched, relationships. As a result so many things can be totally misrepresented in a self-servingly "timeless" reconciliatory fashion.

We have seen earlier that the actual historical origin of the property relations of the bourgeois economy—whereby the means of production are privately expropriated by the personifications of capital and kept permanently under their control—is grossly misrepresented in the categories of political economy as neutrally *"extra-economic,"* hence by definition exempted from all possible critique of capitalist economic exploitation. In reality, however, we are talking about an inherently historic process—i.e., the "evolutionary history of both capital and labour"—of which the most brutal forms of capital's so-called *"primitive accumulation,"* including the extermination of more than one hundred thousand "vagrants" and "vagabonds" in England alone, is an *integral part.* Besides, the *raison d'être* of the "extra-economic" origin of the exploitative process—that is, the permanent *subjugation of labour* to a *separate commanding authority* —is fully reproduced and perpetuated under capitalism, even if in a different form. At the same time, the key issue of the violent *change* from the original *unity* of the working subject with the objective conditions of his labour to the capitalist modality in which he is *structurally separated* from those objective conditions—"a separation which is only fully completed in the relationship between wage-labour and capital"—is totally obliterated, enabling thereby both in political economy and in philosophy the conveniently false theorization of the *subject-object relationship* through which capital's usurpatory pseudo-subject can self-legitimatingly maintain its rule over labour, and of course over society as a whole, forever.

Thus, focusing attention on what really needs an explanation—i.e., in the just mentioned case the historical process of the *separation* of the means of production from living labour, and with regard to the earlier discussed mysterious "money-form" and "value-relation" the question of why the "riddle of money" is inseparable from the "riddle of commodities" in generalized commodity production—is very far from being an academic question. It goes to the heart of substantive social relations by putting into relief the vital methodological importance of their *historical dimension* and their constant violation by even the outstanding figures of political economy in the service of the *eternalization* of capital's social order.

THE FACT THAT A PRODUCTIVE ORDER constitutes an *organic system*, as capital's mode of social metabolic reproduction undoubtedly does, cannot mean at all that it is exempted from the objective conditions and determinations of its own *historical genesis,* even if such genesis is not obvious at first sight, due to the mystifying overturning power of the actual socioeconomic processes themselves, as well as to their tendentious ideological rationalizations in political economy and philosophy.

We can see this clearly explained in a methodologically most important passage from Marx's *Grundrisse.* Setting out from investigating the historical relationship between capital and landed property, this is how he defines the matter:

> if the first form of industry, large-scale manufacture, already presupposes dissolution of landed property, then the latter is in turn conditioned by the subordinate development of capital in its primitive (medieval) forms which has taken place in the cities, and at the same time by the effect of the flowering of manufacture and trade in other countries (thus the influence of Holland on England in the sixteenth and the first half of the seventeenth century). These countries themselves had already undergone the process, agriculture had been sacrificed to cattle-raising, and grain was obtained from countries which were left behind, such as Poland, etc., by import (Holland again).[73]

After summarily sketching the historical background in this way, in order to clarify these matters in relation to England (which Marx considers "in this respect the model country for the other continental countries"[74]), he spells out his general methodological points as follows:

> It must be kept in mind that the new forces of production and relations of production do not develop out of *nothing,* nor drop from the sky, nor from the womb of the self-positing Idea; but from within and in antithesis to the existing development of production and the inherited, traditional relations of property. While in the *completed* bourgeois system every economic relation *presupposes every other in its bourgeois economic form,* and everything *posited* is thus also a *presupposition,* this is the case with *every organic system.* This organic system itself, *as a totality,* has its *presuppositions,* and its development to its totality consists precisely in *subordinating all elements of society to itself,* or in creating out of it the

> organs which it still lacks. *This is historically how it becomes a totality.* The process of becoming this totality forms a moment of its process, of its development.[75]

At the same time, in direct continuation of the lines just quoted, Marx brings into focus the socioeconomically vital substantive relationship between capital and wage labour for understanding the overall historical process and the deliberate economic as well as political adjustments that must be made when the conditions of the newly unfolding developments so require in the interest of the expanding capital system. This is how he illustrates the problem with a particular historical example:

> On the other hand, if within one society the modern relations of production, i.e. capital, are developed to its totality, and this society then seizes hold of a new territory, as e.g. the colonies, then it finds, or rather its representative, the capitalist, finds, that his capital ceases to be capital without wage labour, and that one of the presuppositions of the latter is not landed property in general, but modern landed property; landed property which, as capitalist rent, is expensive, and which, as such, excludes the direct use of the soil by the individuals. Hence Wakefield's theory of colonies, followed in practice by the English government in Australia. Landed property is here artificially made more expensive in order to transform the workers into wage workers, to make capital act as capital, and thus to make the new colony *productive;* to develop wealth in it, instead of using it, as in America, for the momentary deliverance of the wage labourers. Wakefield's theory is infinitely important for a correct understanding of modern landed property.[76]

As we can see, capital's fully developed *organic system* cannot successfully maintain its necessary mode of self-expansionary reproduction without a suitably profitable domination of wage labour under all circumstances, including the rather unusual setting of a unique form of colonial expansion in Australia. For the economic domination of labour always remains the vital *presupposition* of the system, including the conditions of generalized commodity production. Naturally, landed property must be turned into *capitalist agriculture* in order to fit in a proper way into capital's organic system, otherwise precisely the organic character of that system would be disrupted. The outcome is then, obviously, a question of the relation of forces under the prevailing cicumstances. Given the historical dominance of generalized commodity production in England by the time when the need for instituting the conditions of capitalist agriculture arises in colonially occupied Australia, there can be no doubt as to the establishment of the necessary presupposition of profitable wage-labour, to be achieved through the subordination of all elements of society by capital to itself and thereby "creating the organs which it still lacks."

How exactly the presuppositions are created depends, of course, on the nature of the prevailing circumstances; obviously very different in the case of nineteenth century Australia from the *historical genesis* of the capital system in its entirety. In the present context it does not matter at all whether the establishment of the required presuppositions assumes the "gentle" form of political-economic adjustments recommended by Wakefield in nineteenth century Australia, under the fully developed conditions of generalized commodity production in the colonial "mother country," or the extreme brutality and violence of capital's *primitive accumulation* powerfully analysed in Marx's *Capital.* But it is very important to bear in mind that the development of the *capital system* as a whole has a *historical depth* and a range of *social ontological metabolic determinations*—as clearly indicated by Marx himself in some of the passages quoted from *Capital* above—incomparably greater than the few centuries of its specific *capitalist phase.* Without understanding the nature of such determinations, some of which reach back thousands of years into the past, we cannot have a proper measure of capital's *organic system,* and especially not of the challenges that must be faced and overcome through the qualitatively different *organic system* of labour's necessary *hegemonic alternative* to the established mode of social metabolic reproduction. We shall have to return to this issue in the next section, concerned with the question of "Self-Critique as a Methodological Principle." For the tragic failures and reversals of the past had much to do with the underlying problems.

The *eternalizing* orientation of political economy contradicted in every sense the important methodological principles enumerated by Marx in the *Grundrisse* quoted above. It treated its idealized socioeconomic and political order as if it "dropped from the sky or from the womb of the self-positing Idea." It was not interested in the slightest in what went on *before* its arrival on the historical stage, let alone in what might come *after it.* The questions of "before" and "after" could not constitute any part of its explanatory framework, except in the form of arbitrary projections backwards and forwards, postulated on the basis of the proclaimed unchangeable *"natural"* character of the existent.

The circumstance that "in the *completed* bourgeois system every economic relation *presupposes every other in its bourgeois economic form,* and everything *posited* is thus also a *presupposition"* was considered even by the outstanding figures of political economy the amply sufficient ground for assuming the *eternal validity* of the historically established and now dominant operating principles of their reproductive order, ignoring the fact that the kind of circular relationship between what happens to be *posited* and what is already a *presupposition* in their order is characteristic of *all organic systems,* irrespective of the duration of their *life-span;* i.e., that the relationship of that kind cannot provide any guarantee whatsoever for the future. In this way the proud *eternalization* of the given order characteristic of their approach constituted at the same time an incorrigible *vicious circle.* In other words, it was equivalent to the *circular apologetics* of the structurally entrenched mode of social metabolic reproduction, oriented towards making disappear in the theoretical images conceived from capital's vantage point both the *historical genesis* of their system and the feasibility of its *historical supersession.*

To be sure, the circularity inseparable from the theoretical eternalization offered in political economy was by no means a pure invention of the thinkers concerned. It had its roots in the *perverse circularity* of the capital system itself in its objective constitution. That is to say, it corresponded to the fact that *commodity* is both the *presupposition* and the *product* of capital's development as a globally unfolding system of societal reproduction. In this sense, without understanding the precise nature of the capital system's objective circularity—through which living labour as *objectified and alienated labour* becomes capital and, as *personified capital* confronts as well as dominates labour—there can be no escape from the vicious circle of capital's expanded self-reproduction. For the power dominating labour is the circularly transformed power of social labour itself, assuming a "stunted/travestied form" and asserting itself in the mind-boggling "*fetishistic* situation when the *product is the proprietor of the producer*."[77] In other words, "the 'social character', etc., of the worker's labour confronts him, both 'notionally' and 'in fact', as not only alien, but hostile and antagonistic, and as *objectified* and *personified* in capital."[78]

Thus, in order to be able to break out of the vicious circle of capital as the established mode of social metabolic reproduction, it is necessary to confront the fetishism of the system in its fully developed form of generalized commodity production, as reflected in and systematically conceptualized by the major figures of political economy in their "anatomy of civil society."

In this sense, while it is understandable that the eternalizing circularity of political economy *reflected,* and in a reconciliatory way *conceptualized,* the perverse but objective circularity of the capital system itself, that is by no means the whole picture. If it was, in that case the "immanent critique" generously exercised by Marx—in full recognition of the objective ground of determinations and the remarkable scientific achievements of classical political economy—should not have been transformed, as indeed it *had to be,* into a *radical critique* of the theoretical images conceived from capital's vantage point.

The weighty reason why even the classics of political economy had to be subjected to a radical critique was that their conformity to the standpoint of capital necessarily carried with it not simply "overlooking" but, worse than that, ideologically rationalizing and justifying with devotion the innermost *antagonistic structural characteristics* of the established mode of social metabolic control. Thus when the best representatives of the classical school recognized and explicitly acknowledged some blatant contradiction—as, for instance, when Adam Smith condemned the fact that "the people who clothe the world are in rags themselves," as we have seen above—such criticism, despite its to us obvious severity, remained an *isolated insight,* never putting into doubt the overall idealization of the capital system. Even Adam Smith could not see any contradiction whatsoever between the miserable conditions of life of the overwhelming majority of the people, in rags, while themselves clothing the world, and his own wholesome praise for capital's social reproductive order in its entirety as "*the natural system of perfect liberty and justice*."[79]

The major representatives of classical political economy had no motivation for a critical assessment of their established *"organic system."* It was enough for them that it was *organic* and that it functioned as a successfully *expanding* mode of controlling societal reproduction. The fact that the dynamic self-expansionary historical tendency of the capital system, based on the necessary structural subjugation of labour, was dense with ultimately explosive *antagonistic contradictions,* could not carry any weight for them. For their interpretation of the given *organic system*—which they equated with the perfect *natural* order—was incompatible with an adequate *historical* conception. This is why even a great philosophical genius, Hegel, who identified himself with capital's standpoint of political economy, had to terminate history in the *present:* by postulating colonially dominant Europe as "absolutely the end of history" in his own version of the perfect *"organic system,"* corresponding to the historically objectified, and fully realized, *eternal present* of the Absolute Idea.

The only way to formulate a genuine historical theory in Marx's age, under the motivating impact of mid-nineteenth century socioeconomic turmoil as well as major political upheavals, was by radically questioning the objective circularity of capital's *antagonistic organic system,* together with its reconciliatory conceptualizations. To be able to do that in methodologically viable terms the *standpoint of analysis* had to be shifted from the *anti-historical* vantage point of capital's organic system—a system absolutely inconceivable without the permanent subjugation and exploitative structural domination of labour—to that of labour's hegemonic alternative as a *historically open-ended organic system.*

Only those could engage in the radical critique of both the established order itself and of its reconciliatory conceptualizations who had a real insight into the nature of the dramatically unfolding socioeconomic and political developments—punctuated by revolutionary explosions due to the intensifying crises at a much more advanced stage of historical confrontations than the age of Adam Smith—and who with that insight also had a major legitimate interest not in advocating the traditional accommodatory adjustments, in tune with the standpoint of political economy, but in envisaging an *alternative* social order *beyond the incurable adversariality* of the capital system's exploitative class relations.

The fact that Marx (and his comrade in arms Engels) shared with the classics of political economy the bourgeoisie as their social background could not constitute any hindrance in this respect. On the contrary. It could only underline the new historical ground and the urgency of the change required in the strategic standpoint of orientation. For the increasing destructiveness of capital's mode of social metabolic control threatened with devastation the whole of society, including those who for the time being enjoyed its privileges. The perverse destructive logic of an all-embracing social organic system, bent on ultimately destroying nature itself as the necessary ground of human existence, implicates not only *some* of its parts but *all* of them, and thereby the system itself as a whole. Marx was acutely aware of that.

Naturally, also the envisaged alternative, in order to be historically sustainable, had to be an organic system. For a firmly established organic system of societal reproduction, developed and globally extended in all of its social ontological and historical dimensions over many centuries, could only be superseded by another organic system. At the same time, the unavoidable implication of demonstrating the genesis of capital's mode of societal control through the Marxian critique, accomplished by forcefully putting into relief the necessary historical determinations of *any* organic system of *social reproduction,* was that the same considerations had to apply to the envisaged alternative order of the "new historic form," and indeed with a major enhancement in historical consistency extending over all of its dimensions. That is to say, the alternative social metabolic order had to be conceived and instituted through enduring social practice as a *substantively equitable organic system* capable of critically examining and altering not only its more limited everyday reproductive processes, but also its most fundamental *presuppositions,* whenever the course of actual historical development would call for it.

The radical critique of political economy, in conjunction with the elaboration of the vital orienting principles of a *self-critique* free from the vitiating prejudgement of vested interests, was a necessary part of such an undertaking.

8.4 Self-Critique as a Methodological Principle

The *conscious adoption* and successful maintenance of the orienting principle of *self-critique* is an absolutely fundamental requirement of the historically sustainable hegemonic alternative to capital's social metabolic order as an organic system.

Since it cannot be allowed to conflict in any way with the necessarily *open-ended* historical determinations of labour's alternative reproductive order—on the contrary, it must be a vital guarantee against all temptations to relapse into a self-complacent closure, and thereby into the reproduction of vitiating vested interests, corresponding to the traditional pattern of the past—the envisaged and knowingly pursued faithfulness to the theoretical as well as practical operative methodological principle of self-critique needs to be embraced as a *permanent* feature of the new, positively enduring, social formation. For precisely through the genuine and continuing exercise of that orienting principle it becomes possible to correct in good time the tendencies that might otherwise not only appear but, worse than that, also consolidate themselves in favour of the ossification of a given stage of the present, undermining thereby the prospects of a sustainable future.

This is so because the flexible *coordination and consensual integration* of the necessarily varied but at first only *locally/partially adopted* measures and, as a result, potentially conflicting decisions, into a *coherent whole* is inconceivable without real self-critique. The kind of potential conflict we are here concerned with, due to the circumstance that some important measures and decisions are taken at first only locally/partially before they can be assessed on a comprehensive basis, must be in fact more unavoidable in the socialist modality of the societal reproduction process than ever before, in view of its *substantively democratic* character based on the supersession of the vertical/hierarchical division of labour. For that reason a proper way of guarding—through consciously embraced self-critique by the people concerned—against the dangers that might result from such would-be conflicts is a matter of great importance.

As mentioned in the last section, the qualitatively different *organic system* of labour's necessary *hegemonic alternative* to the established mode of social metabolic reproduction is unthinkable without the conscious espousal of *self-critique* as its vital orienting principle. At the same time, it is impossible to envisage the conscious adoption and operation of self-critique as an enduring orienting principle without a *certain type* of societal reproduction which must successfully maintain itself as a veritable organic system without the danger of being derailed from its consistently open-ended historical course of development. For we are talking about a *dialectical correlation* between the *qualitatively* different type of organic system needed in the future and the necessary orienting principle of self-critique in conjunction with which that new type becomes feasible at all.

Neither the qualitatively different new type of organic system, nor the orienting and operative principle of genuine self-critique can fully unfold and positively function without the other. However, this dialectical reciprocity cannot be allowed to constitute a convenient circle, let alone a ready-made excuse for justifying the absence of *both,* by apologetically asserting on each side that without the full-scale availability of the *other* no progress can be made in the realization of the *one* in question, or *vice versa*. For, as we know, that is how an assumed convenient circle becomes an utterly *vicious circle.* In truth the dialectical correlation between the new organic system and the organ of self-critique defines itself precisely as the *mutuality of helping each other* even at a very *early stage* of their historical development, once the need for instituting labour's hegemonic alternative arises from the profound structural crisis of capital's increasingly destructive societal reproductive order.

In view of the fact that the necessary alternative to capital's in our time ubiquitously destructive organic system must be a qualitatively different but nonetheless organic system, only the *communal* mode of societal reproduction can truly qualify in this respect. In other words, only the *communally organized system* is capable of providing the overall framework for the continuing development of the multifaceted and substantively equitable constitutive parts of the socialist mode of integration of all creative individual and collective forces into a *coherent whole* as a historically viable *organic system of social metabolic reproduction.* And the success of this enterprise is feasible only if the envisaged integration into the new type of organic system is accomplished in such a way that the parts reciprocally support and enhance each other on a *positively open-ended* basis, in the spirit of *conscious self-determination,* providing thereby to the freely associated producers the scope needed for their self-realization as "rich social individuals" (in Marx's words) through their fully sustainable form of social metabolic interaction among themselves and with nature.

This is a seminal requirement of "the new historic form" as labour's necessary hegemonic alternative to capital's social metabolic order. Evidently, the principle of self-critique is integral to the necessary spirit of conscious self-determination of the freely associated producers. But just as evidently, the self-determination of the social individuals deserves its name only if their application of the vital orienting principle of self-critique is the result of a consciously chosen voluntary act. Any arbitrary attempt at imposing the ritual of self-critique on the people from above, as we know it from the Stalinist past, can amount to no more than the painful mockery of it, with far-reaching counter-productive consequences and reversals in actual historical development.

SINCE THE COMMUNAL SYSTEM—in total contrast to capital's unalterable, even if destructively blind, self-expansionary logic—cannot count on economic determinations which *"work behind the back of the individuals,"* its only feasible way of ordering its affairs, in accordance with the voluntary determinations of the freely associated individuals, is by fully activating the orienting and operative principle of self-critique *at all levels*. This means positively activating it in accordance with the particular individual concerns all the way to the highest and most complex decision making processes of comprehensive societal interaction, with its unavoidable impact on nature. And the inevitability of that impact deeply implicates not simply the obvious time-determinations of the present but also the longest term historical dimension of the qualitatively new communal organic system's consciously designed mode of overall social metabolic control.

We have to return later in this section to the discussion of some of the contrasting determinations of the radically different communal system as the only sustainable historical alternative to capital's increasingly destructive organic system. But first it is necessary to consider the possibilities and limitations of self-critique in general terms, and not in relation to its considerably modified potentialities for contributing to the operation of the communal system.

It goes without saying that self-critique is (or at least ought-to-be) an integral part of the particular intellectuals' activity. When we think of some great intellectual achievements, irrespective of the social setting with which they are associated—like the Hegelian philosophical synthesis, for instance—the creative contribution of self-critique is clear enough, at times even explicitly stated.

However, the limitations are also clearly in evidence when we consider the negative impact of problematical *social determinations* even in the case of such monumental philosophical undertakings as the Hegelian synthesis. But this should be by no means surprising. For there are some historical situations and associated social constraints when even a great thinker finds it impossible "to jump over Rhodes," in Hegel's own words. The French Revolution and the ascending phase of the capital system's historical development offered a positive scope for the Hegelian achievement. However, due to the insuperable exploitative dimension of the capital system's innermost determinations—which assumed an increasingly more dominant form as time went by, carrying with them grave implications for the future in the bourgeois order's descending phase of development—the *uncritical acceptance* of the system's contradictions and the defence of its ultimately explosive structural antagonisms became extremely problematical, bringing with them in the Hegelian philosophy speculatively articulated conservative reconciliation.

Accordingly, as we have seen above, Marx rightly characterized the social limitation intervening against the self-critical—and in its own way also *critical*—intent of this great philosopher by underlining that "Hegel's standpoint is that of *modern political economy*."[80] The acceptance of such a standpoint carries with it, of course, far-reaching consequences. For in its spirit the unavoidable reconciliatory presuppositions and complicated practical imperatives of capital's political economy enter the picture, even if they are transubstantiated by Hegel with great consistency, deeply affecting in a speculative way the general character of an earlier quite inconceivable synthesis of philosophy. We have seen in the course of this study many instances of this reconciliatory approach, presented by Hegel in the name of the "World Spirit" from the vantage point of capital's political economy. But we have also seen that when the limitations corresponding to capital's vantage point enter the picture and undermine the critical intent—not only in the Hegelian system but also in the work of the other major thinkers who conceptualize the world from the standpoint of capital's political economy, including Adam Smith—they themselves more or less consciously *internalize* the system's most problematical practical presuppositions and objective imperatives, articulating in that way the position which embodies the fundamental socioeconomic interests, as well as the central values, of a societal reproductive order with which they identify themselves. This is what sets the ultimate limits even to their best intentioned self-critique.

Evidently, there can be no question of some kind of fatality of class-determinations in the case of the thinkers concerned. There are many intellectual and political figures, including some outstanding ones, who have successfully broken their ties with their class and have produced their radical strategic systems, with powerful revolutionary practical implications and corresponding social movements, in irreconcilable contradiction to the fundamental interests of the class into which they have been born and in relation to which they had to define their position in the course of their upbringing. It is enough to recall the names of Marx and Engels in this respect.

Of course it is true that in periods of major social turmoil and great upheavals the personal motivation of many individuals for reexamining in a radical way their own class belonging, together with the role which their privileged class happens to play under the given historical circumstances, and doing that to the point of committing themselves to a struggle for the rest of their life against the repressive functions of the class in which they have been brought up, is considerably greater than under normal circumstances. The opposite is also true, in the sense that periods of conservative political and economic success in society at large—with a small "c," sustaining even the so-called *neoliberal* phase of deeply reactionary developments in the last three decades of twentieth century history, for instance—tend to coincide with wholesale intellectual reversals and with the acceptance of rather absurd pseudo-theoretical fashions. And the latter follow at humiliatingly short intervals one another in a vain search of the people concerned for ephemerally self-serving irrational evasion.

The truth of the matter is, though, that such conjunctural events and correlations cannot settle the fundamental historical issues. Not even when we have in mind some of the outstanding representatives of political economy and philosophy who in their time identified themselves with capital's vantage point, like Adam Smith and Hegel. For the limits of a thinker's ability to assume a real *critical* stance, on the basis of his or her readiness to exercise the required *self-critique* in the process, is ultimately decided by the overall historical configuration of the interacting social forces. They necessarily involve all dimensions of development, including the elementary conditions of humanity's survival on this planet in the midst of the established order's deepening structural crisis and the concomitant destruction of nature.

With regard to this correlation it was by no means accidental that capital's ascending phase of development—to some extent favouring the adoption of a critical stance, even if a limited and selective one—resulted in the great achievements of *classical political economy*. By contrast the same capital system's descending phase had brought with it the painful theoretical impoverishment and the crass social apologetics of *vulgar economy*, which confined itself "to systematizing in *a pedantic way*, and proclaiming for everlasting truths, the trite ideas held by the self-complacent bourgeoisie with regard to their own world, to them the *best of all possible worlds*,"[81] as sharply criticized by Marx. Thus, disconcerting and potentially tragic as it happens to be, in the course of the capital system's historical unfolding even the limited scope for self-critique had to leave it space for the ideology of the system's "eternalization" and for the authoritarian practical imposition of the most retrograde policies over all actively dissenting forces, no matter how dangerous the consequences for humankind.

THE ORIGINAL SCOPE FOR SELF-CRITIQUE at the ascending phase of the capital system's historical unfolding was quite important, despite its obvious class limitations. The relevance of this connection is far from negligible because in terms of the requirements of scientific advancement in general—without which the achievements of classical political economy would be unthinkable—an element of *self-critique* is a necessary condition for a *critical understanding* of the overall subject of enquiry.

This is why Marx puts into relief the analogy between the critical element in the historical development of Christianity and a somewhat better understanding by the bourgeoisie of its reproductive order when it assumed a less mythologizing attitude towards its own mode of production. We can see this connection stressed in an important passage of Marx's *Grundrisse* in which he links the general theoretical point—concerning the principal economic categories of a more advanced historical stage of societal reproduction—and the necessary but usually neglected qualifications of that general theoretical point for the proper conceptualization of capital's socioeconomic order itself, as the most advanced form. This is how he puts it:

> The bourgeois economy supplies the key to the ancient, etc. But not at all in the manner of those economists who smudge over all historical differences and see bourgeois relations in all forms of society. One can understand tribute, tithe, etc., if one is acquainted with ground rent. But one must not identify them. Further, since bourgeois society is itself only a contradictory form of development, relations derived from earlier forms will often be found within it only in an entirely stunted form, or even travestied. For example, *communal property*. Although it is true, therefore, that the categories of bourgeois economics possess a truth for all other forms of society, this is to be taken only with a grain of salt. They can contain them in a developed, or stunted, or caricatured form, etc., but always with an essential difference. The so-called historical presentation of development is founded, as a rule, on the fact that the latest form regards the previous ones as steps leading up to itself, and, since it is only rarely and only under quite specific conditions able to *criticize itself*—leaving aside, of course, the historical periods which appear to themselves as times of decadence—it always conceives them one-sidedly. The Christian religion was able to be of assistance in reaching an objective understanding of earlier mythologies only when its own *self-criticism* had been accomplished to a certain degree, so to speak *dynamei*. Likewise, bourgeois economics arrived at an understanding of feudal, ancient, oriental economics only after the *self-criticism* of bourgeois society had begun. In so far as the bourgeois economy did not *mythologically* identify itself altogether with the past, its *critique* of the previous economies, notably of feudalism, with which it was still engaged in direct struggle, resembled the critique which Christianity levelled against paganism, or also that of Protestantism against Catholicism.[82]

The "anatomy of civil society" was produced by classical political economy on this basis, once the earlier mythologizing vision of the emerging bourgeois order became pointless in the aftermath of the victory over feudalism. This was a historical phase of boundless optimism in the new conceptions, incorporating the hopeful anticipations as well as the illusions of the Enlightenment movement in Europe. As one of Adam Smith's Scottish Enlightenment comrades, Henry Home wrote with great optimism and enthusiasm: "Reason, resuming her sovereign authority, will banish [persecution] altogether. . . . Within the next century it will be thought strange, that persecution should have prevailed among social beings. It will perhaps even be doubted, whether it ever was seriously put into practice."[83] And he was equally enthusiastic about the potentialities of the new work ethos, in contrast to the idleness of the former ruling personnel, insisting that "Activity is essential to a social being: to a selfish being it is of no use, after procuring the means of living. A selfish man, who by his opulence has all the luxuries of life at command, and dependents without number, has no occasion for activity."[84]

The self-confidence of the new approach, which produced real scientific achievements in understanding the production of wealth,[85] fully corresponded to capital's from that historic phase onwards irresistible vantage point. There seemed to be no need for self-critique in other than secondary or marginal detail. The power of capital successfully asserted itself in all domains. Not even the once troublesome political dimension could exercise any significant resistance to its advancement. On the contrary, the state itself had progressively become an integral part of the capital system's overall determinations, under the primacy of the material reproduction process. In this way everything had been subsumed and consolidated under the rule of capital as the most powerful *self-expansionary organic system,* notwithstanding its inherent but unacknowledged antagonisms. And given its unchallenged systemic dominance in actuality, it seemed obvious to all those who conceptualized the world from capital's vantage point that their organic system constituted the one and only *natural system.* This is why Adam Smith could sum it all up by saying that capital embodied *"the natural system of perfect liberty and justice,"* as we have seen above.

THE COMMUNAL ORGANIC SYSTEM, as the only historically feasible hegemonic alternative to capital's social metabolic order, cannot afford the luxury of the once boundless self-confidence and self-complacency of its predecessor. For it cannot even begin to assert and sustain itself, from the moment of its attempted self-constitution, without the conscious adoption of self-critique appropriate to the ongoing (and necessarily changing) conditions of development.

As mentioned a few pages back, the self-constituting communal system cannot count on economic determinations which "*work behind the back of the individuals*": the obvious mode of operation of capital's social metabolic order throughout its history. This kind of economic determination is well in tune with the *unconscious* character of the specific parts of capital's reproduction process—inherent in the *plurality of relatively autonomous and self-assertively expansionary capitals*—and fulfils a paradoxical *corrective* function in the system. For the individual capitalists can pursue *up to a point* their own design, in expectation of successfully achieving their particular interests, but they cannot do that *against* the fundamental systemic determinations of their shared mode of production. The fundamental systemic determinations and objective practical imperatives—which must work behind the back of the individual capitalists—forcefully impose themselves *over against* the particular excessively self-seeking decisions. For beyond a certain point the latter would tend to undermine the overall viability of the system itself as the historically dominant organic system, in view of the insuperably *centrifugal* tendency of *unconscious* (unalterably self-oriented) individual capitalist *consciousness*.

Moreover, the *unconscious consciousness* in question is simultaneously also the manifestation of incurably *adversarial/conflictual* interests and corresponding strategies. The pursuit of such interests necessarily intensifies the unconscious character of the whole process. For they render to the particular capitalists the possibility of anticipating the adversary's design and his or her responses to one's own moves—by reciprocally attempting to outwit each other as competitors through firmly established (and even legally sanctified) *concealment*—that much more *opaque.* This is one of the significant reasons why the adversariality itself is *structurally insuperable,* even if—thanks to the earlier mentioned paradoxical corrective function of the fundamental systemic imperatives which assert themselves behind the back of the individuals—the centrifugal tendency of particularistic pursuits is not allowed to get completely out of hand, since that would endanger the survival of the system as a whole.

Naturally, the insuperable adversariality inherent in the capital system is not confined to the confrontation and potential collision of particular capitalist interests. If it was only for that, some significant improvements would be feasible, as they are indeed often postulated in the form of ideological rationalizations of imaginary remedies: from the constantly propagandized fiction of "people's capitalism" to the projection of "all-embracing capitalist planning" and to John Kenneth Galbraith's universally reconciliatory "techno-structure."

However, underneath the adversariality of particular capitalist interests—indeed directly affecting also the potential form of unfolding of even the individual capitalist confrontations against one another—we find the *structurally ineliminable fundamental antagonism between capital and labour* as the rival bearers of the hegemonic alternative modes of controlling the overall social metabolic process. Capital can carry on actually doing that only on condition—and only so long as—it is capable of *preserving and enforcing the deep-seated structural antagonism* which constitutes the necessary material and ideological presupposition of its social reproductive order. And labour, on the contrary, only if it succeeds in instituting a qualitatively different mode of societal reproduction—the *communal organic system*—through historically overcoming *antagonistic adversariality altogether,* and thereby consigning on a permanent basis to the past the *structurally secured hierarchical domination* of the overwhelming majority of human beings by a tiny minority, as inherited from the capital system.

The institution and successful operation of such hegemonic alternatives is, of course, inconceivable without the *conscious* control of their life-activity by the freely associated social individuals. In this regard the *individual* and the *social* dimensions of our problem are inextricably intertwined.

It is self-evident that there can be no question of a conscious societal control of the necessary decision making processes unless the particular individuals themselves—who are expected to introduce, and in a responsible way to carry out, the decisions involved—fully identify themselves with the pursued objectives. But that circumstance does not make the issue itself a purely, or even a predominantly, personal matter. The individual and the social constituents of genuine socialist consciousness would be altogether failing in their much needed role unless they could *positively enhance* one another. For the real personal involvement of the particular individuals in the realization of the chosen objectives and strategies is conceivable only if the general social conditions themselves *actively favour* the process, instead of tending in the opposite direction, which would allow some form of *adversariality* to creep in and undermine the articulation of *comprehensively cohesive* social consciousness.

This is why only a *certain type* of social metabolic order—emphatically the communal organic system—could qualify as truly compatible with the production and the continuing positive enhancement of the required individual and social consciousness. For the institution and self-determined consolidation of that type of reproductive system is the only feasible way to overcome adversariality altogether, providing thereby full scope for the *co-operative realization* of their freely adopted conscious decisions by the individuals.

The meaning of "*co-operative*," in the full sense of the term—which is absolutely essential for sustainable socialist action—implies the ability as well as the determination of the social individuals not only to *dedicate* themselves to the implementation of determinate tasks but also to autonomously *modify* their actions in the light of the jointly evaluated consequences. This mode of *self-corrective* action could not be more different from the known varieties of being overruled by a separate authority, imposed upon them from above, or by the blindly prevailing impact of the unwanted consequences of their "*unconscious consciousness*" mentioned earlier. Such consequences inevitably arise in the social metabolic order in which economic laws and determinations work behind the backs of the individuals, in the interest of the capital system's survival, even if they directly imperil the survival of humanity.

Thus *consciousness* and *self-critique* are inseparable from one another as the orienting and operative principles of decision making and action in the communal organic system. This is well understood. For the proper self-consciousness of the individuals must incorporate their *positively disposed* awareness of the real and potential impact of their decisions and actions on their fellow human beings, which is inconceivable without freely undertaken self-critique. At the same time, the conscious guard in the communal type of societal interaction process as a whole *against* the establishment and consolidation of self-perpetuating vested interests, which would inevitably reproduce adversariality of one kind or another, and the *positive way* of preventing the formation of such vested interests through the co-operative promotion and maintenance of *substantive equality,* constitute the necessary condition for the conscious and positively inclined self-critical awareness of the social individuals in their interactions among themselves.

Moreover, there is also a dimension of this problem which *transcends* the direct experience of the particular individuals both in time and in space. For, obviously, they have a limited life-span, compared to humanity's historically unfolding overall development. And while the individuals are, of course, constitutive parts of the actually given stage of humanity's advancement, they are at the same time active members of a particular community, with its own specific history and diverse problems from which significantly different tasks may arise for them to fulfil. Especially at a relatively early stage in the development of the communal system in question, when the need for overcoming the major inequalities inherited from the past represents a much more difficult problem. Also with regard to the general time scale of development, there are some consequences of earlier determined forms of action which can be—and have to be—modified on a longer time-scale, well beyond the life-span of the generation which was responsible for consciously adopting under the once prevailing circumstances the original decisions.

However, these considerations do not undermine the vital importance of the orienting and operative principles of conscious decision making—and the appropriate self-critique closely associated with it—by the individuals in their social metabolic interchange with nature and among themselves. They only underline the need for real *solidarity* extending over the most diverse communities and across the succeeding generations. Besides, learning from the lessons of the past cannot cease to be relevant because of the adoption of the principles of conscious self-critical action. On the contrary, it can really come into its own only under circumstances when the perversely derailing adversariality of vested interests is no longer dominating societal interchange itself. It is notorious how often tragic historical events and circumstances reappear and cause further devastation, due to the refusal of the interested parties to face up to the challenge of critically reassessing them, including their own role in allowing such developments to prevail in the first place. The implosion of the Soviet type system was one of the most tragic historical experiences of the twentieth century for the socialist movement. It would be even more tragic if we could not draw the appropriate lessons from it.

THE CONSTITUTION OF THE COMMUNAL SYSTEM, through the conscious adoption and continued enhancement of self-critique, is undoubtedly a most difficult learning process. Marx anticipated the importance of such self-critique in his pamphlet on *The Eighteenth Brumaire of Louis Bonaparte* by saying that proletarian revolutions

> criticize themselves constantly, interrupt themselves continually in their own course, come back to the apparently accomplished in order to begin it afresh, deride with unmerciful thoroughness the inadequacies, weaknesses and paltrinesses of their first attempts, seem to throw down their adversary only in order that he may draw new strength from the earth and rise again, more gigantic, before them, and they recoil again and again from the indefinite prodigiousness of their own aims, until a situation has been created which makes all turning back impossible, and the conditions themselves cry out:
>
> Hic Rhodus, hic salta!
> Here is Rhodes, leap here![86]

In this sense, learning from historical experience is an important part of the process of self-critique. Especially when we are concerned with actual historical developments associated with socialist claims, as made by the Soviet system. Understandably, Marx was no contemporary to them and therefore could in no way take into account the historical specificities under which the bewildering postrevolutionary developments unfolded under Stalin in the name of "socialism in one country," and in the end have brought about the implosion of the Soviet type postcapitalist capital system. Nevertheless the way in which Marx characterized capital's fully developed order as an *organic system*, because its constituents reciprocally sustain one another—and thus calling for change far exceeding its *juridical relations* while maintaining in many respects more or less intact the capital relation, including its new form of self-assertive personifications—helps to throw light on what went wrong and offers important indications of necessary self-critique for the future. Likewise Gorbachev's grotesquely uncritical conception of "market socialism" could offer only a fantasy remedy to the system and was right from the beginning doomed to failure, paving the road to capitalist restoration.

The issue resembling the uncritical projection of "market socialism" surfaced much earlier and, understandably, it is visible again in China.[87] In the past the fantasy of market socialism appeared already in Marx's lifetime, even if then it was not called by that name. Marx made it absolutely clear what he thought of it when he stressed in the *Grundrisse* that "the idea held by some socialists that *we need capital but not the capitalists* is altogether wrong. It is posited within the concept of capital that the objective conditions of labour—and these are its own product—take on a personality toward it."[88] And he added in another passage of the same work that "capital in its being-for-itself is the capitalist. Of course, socialists sometimes say, we need capital, but not the capitalist. Then capital appears as a pure thing, not as a relation of production which, reflected in itself, is precisely *the capitalist*. I may well separate capital from a given individual capitalist, and it can be transferred to another. But, in losing capital, he loses the quality of being a capitalist. Thus capital is indeed separable from an individual capitalist, but not from *the capitalist* who, as such, controls *the worker*."[89]

It is a similarly mystifying and self-disarming conception when the relationship of capital and labour is described, in the most superficial way, as one between *buyers and sellers,* hypostatizing thereby a fictitious *equality* in place of the actually existing *structurally secured and safeguarded domination and subordination.* The total absence of critical—and *self-critical*—assessment of this relationship had a great deal to do with adopting by Gorbachev and others the absurd strategy of market socialism, bringing with it necessary failure. For in reality the relationship we are talking about is not at all a genuine *market relation*, like that between particular capitalist enterprises exchanging their products, but only its *deceptive semblance.* For the innermost *substantive* determination of the fundamental interchange between capital and labour is an *actual relationship of power under the supremacy of capital.* The real substance—as the firmly established actual *presupposition* of the relationship in question in the sphere of *production*—is deeply hidden beneath the deceptive semblance of the pseudo-equivalence of transactions in the sphere of *circulation*. As Marx had made it amply clear: "It is not a mere buyer and a mere seller who face each other, it is a *capitalist* and a *worker;* it is a capitalist and a worker, who face each other in the sphere of circulation, on the market, as *buyer* and *seller.* The relation as *capitalist* and *worker* is the presupposition for their relation as buyer and seller."[90]

Thus, from the strategically derailing and self-disarming conceptions of this kind the overall framework of sustainable social transformation—the socialist vision of a necessary historical alternative to capital's organic system—is totally missing. Its place is taken by an eclectic mixture of voluntaristic *tactical* political projections (misconceived as proper *strategic* measures) and some elements of capital's established material order. Like the wishful adoption of the so-called *"market mechanism,"* which is no simple mechanism at all but an integral constituent of capital's *organic system,* hence by its very nature quite incompatible with the envisaged change. And since the necessary strategic orienting framework of the communal organic system is nowhere even hinted at in such conceptions, there can be no room at all in them for *conscious self-critique:* the elementary condition of success of the socialist enterprise. No one should be surprised, therefore, by the restoration of capitalism.

ONE OF THE OVERWHELMINGLY IMPORTANT REASONS why only the communal organic system can meet the challenge of adopting as its normal and indefinitely sustainable mode of operation the orienting principle of conscious self-critique concerns the insuperable *post festum* character of capital's organic system of social metabolic control.

This is so even if only *some* of the defining characteristics of the old system are retained among the guiding principles of postrevolutionary developments, for whatever reason. It is, of course, well understood that some tempting constraints and responses are bound to arise on the basis of capitalist enmity, due to the well known *encirclement* of a country which attempts to break its former links with the global capital system. However, they cannot provide an *excuse,* as it was done in Stalin's Russia, for incorporating disruptive and alienating characteristics of the once prevailing mode of management—like the control of the productive enterprises strictly *from above,* as inherited from the capitalist "authoritarianism of the workshop"—into the new system. For in capital's organic system that characteristic itself is an *integral part* of some overall systemic determinations, and therefore cannot be—and indeed they are not—sustained in isolation. In the case of its capitalist version, the *authoritarianism of the workshop* is inseparable from, and is also greatly strengthened and enforced by, the *tyranny of the market.*

If, therefore, the management of the "socialist enterprise from above" (a veritable contradiction in terms) fails to produce the voluntaristically projected positive results, as it is bound to do, in that case ever repeated calls for legitimating its twin brother is also bound to surface. That is, calls for the establishment of the "socialist market economy" (another incorrigible contradiction in terms), with its own kind of uncontrollable tyranny on top of those now happily embraced through the postrevolutionary society's renewed links with the global capitalist market. As indeed they actually did.

It is a rather uncomfortable truth in this respect that the tendency to capitalist restoration in the Soviet Union did not start with Gorbachev. He only consummated it in its final variety. And it did not even start with Khruschev, several decades earlier. Khruschev only gave it a more pronounced form of practice, with its corresponding ideological legitimation. In fact the long drawn out tendency for capitalist restoration started by none other than *Stalin* himself, as I have discussed and documented it in considerable detail in *Beyond Capital.*[91] That fateful road, with its ultimately uncontrollable implications, was embarked upon more than half a century ago, when the earlier state of emergency, linked to the Second World War and to the most urgent tasks of postwar reconstruction, outlived its usefulness and had to be abandoned.

With regard to the issue of the necessary conscious self-critique for sustainable socialist development, as discussed above in relation to the individuals and their social strategies, the fact is that even partially retaining the inherited determinations of the past carries with it great difficulties for the future. This can be highlighted with the problem that the incorrigibly *post festum* character of such determinations represent a fundamental challenge for socialist transformation. A challenge which cannot be avoided, sidestepped, or postponed, but must be direcly confronted right from the beginning.

Under capital's fully developed organic system the *post festum* character of societal interchange is clearly in evidence. It has four principal aspects.

First, the *post festum* social character of productive activity itself which cannot even be imagined without the destination of its products for capital's historically established exchange relations asserted within the framework of generalized commodity production, strictly *subordinating* the selective/discriminatory legitimacy of *use-value* to the absolute requirement of *profitable exchange-value*. Only through such, highly problematical, and ultimately quite unsustainable, mediation can the production process of the capital system qualify as the most developed form of social production in history.

Second, the inalterably *post festum* character of the potential *corrective function* feasible in such a *post festum* social productive system, with regard to the incurably *adversarial/irrationalistic* interchanges of capital's productive enterprises through the *market*. Although the latter is idealized as the universally benevolent "invisible hand," even this idealization misses a vital dimension of the problem. For in its *post festum* determinations the market itself, as a set of attempted corrective socioeconomic and political power relations (characteristically misrepresented as a straightforward "mechanism"), can only *partially* cover the relevant terrain in need of remedy, even when it is hypostatized as the rationally operative "global market." It could never turn the *post festum sociality* of the productive practices themselves into controllably (rationally) social.

The third principal aspect is the necessarily *post festum* character of *planning* even in the most gigantic quasi-monopolistic enterprises. This is partly due to the overall market framework of generalized commodity production, underlined in the previous point. But not only that. An even more important factor is the fundamental structural antagonism between capital and labour, which is ineliminable from the capital system no matter how many and how varied might be the attempted remedies. They range from technical and technological as well as organizational devices, including the practices of "Toyotism"[92] and the strategy of securing "lean supply lines" in the transnational industrial enterprises, all the way to the most authoritarian forms of anti-labour legislation even in the so-called "democratic" countries.

And fourth, the *post festum* nature of the feasible adjustments when some major conflicts and complications erupt in the sociopolitical arena, whether in a given national setting or across international boundaries. Activating the openly repressive functions of the capitalist state was always the normal way of dealing with this kind of problem. In the most acute international cases this involved embarking even on major wars, including the catastrophically destructive two world wars in the twentieth century. For it always belonged to the normality of capital to operate on the basis of "war if the other ways of subduing the adversary fail." While obviously this devastating general principle has not been abandoned, as witnessed by the countless postwar military adventures in which the dominant imperialist power, the United States of America, often with its allies, has been engaged in the last few decades, including the Vietnam War and the ongoing Middle East genocide, the prospects foreshadowed by a potential third world war for the annihilation of humankind represent here a rationally insuperable constraint, underlining also in that way the total untenability of this kind of *post festum* remedy in the capital system.

To be sure, Soviet type postrevolutionary formations did not retain all four of these *post festum* characteristics in their mode of controlling the societal reproduction process. Tragically, however, some of them remained operative throughout their seven decades long history, including the failure to make the production process itself directly social. In the same way, the authoritarian retroactive character of their highly bureaucratized mode of planning and its arbitrary modification and reimposition after their regular failure, also put into relief the contradictory character of their *post festum* mode of operation. Moreover, as we all know, the eventual acceptance of the tyranny of the market—mind-bogglingly even proclaimed by Gorbachev's officially named "ideology chief" nothing less than *"the guarantee of the renewal of socialism"*[93]—sealed their fate on the road to unreserved capitalist restoration.

The grave problem in this context is that the *post festum* determination of the social metabolic processes makes it impossible to adopt the orienting and operative principle of conscious self-critique. And sooner or later the absence of that vital principle from the societies that make the first steps through their anti-capitalist political revolution in the direction of a socialist transformation is bound to derail them.

It is relatively easy to be *critical* vis-à-vis the justifiably *negated* aspects of the *past,* or even of a determinate phase of the unfolding *present.* However, the real test for the viability of the attempted socialist course of action is to be able to put into critical historical perspective also the presently *affirmed* and accepted circumstances of social development. Not gratuitously, for the sake of fulfilling some formal requirement peremptorily prescribed to the individuals, as often happened in the past, but in order to co-operatively overcome the real challenges as they are bound to arise from the given conditions of societal interchange. And, of course, that kind of *critique* is conceivable only through the consistent exercise of genuine *self-criticism,* on the basis of soberly assessing the specific time-bound determinations and the corresponding relatively *limited* validity of the already accomplished *part* in the—necessarily changing—*dynamic whole*, with its real and potential contradictions as well as with its all too frequent temptations to follow "the line of least resistance."

WE MAY LIMIT OURSELVES here to the consideration of only one, but one absolutely crucial issue: the genuine *planning process*. For among its inherent characteristics we can clearly perceive the inseparability of the *critical* and the equally important *self-critical* mode of evaluating the tasks and the associated difficulties, together with the feasible forms of remedial action whenever there may be a need for it.

It goes without saying, the socialist type of sustainable decision making and the corresponding practical management of social metabolic interchanges are inconceivable without *all-embracing planning.* A type of planning which can consensually bring together, and in a lasting way *integrate* in a coherent whole, the particular concerns and the consciously taken decisions of the freely associated individuals.

Inevitably this means that the *"crutch"* of the inherited hierarchical social division of labour—which admittedly "simplifies" for the commanding personnel many things—carries with it a heavy price for the rest. It simplifies matters for the controllers of the decision making process through the system's preestablished economic determinism which, however, deprives at the same time the working individuals of their power of decision making in the related field. Naturally, that crutch must be discarded and replaced by the exercise of the faculty of voluntarily/consciously assumed self-critical action by the social individuals, involving at the same time the acceptance of *full responsibility* for their action. This way of redefining the decision making process must be the case because the "helpful crutch" is not simply a convenient crutch but also inseparable from a heavy chain that firmly shackles the arms of the individuals to itself.

Accordingly, labour's necessary hegemonic alternative implies a radical shift from the social/hierarchical *division of labour,* with its preestablished practical imperatives, to an appropriate *combination and organization of labour,* to be accomplished within the framework of a qualitatively different communal organic system. In such a system, thanks to its ability to overcome the vitiating *post festum* determinations of reproductive interchange, in Marx's words:

> the product does not first have to be transposed into a particular form in order to attain a general character for the individual. *Instead of a division of labour*, such as is necessarily created with the exchange of exchange values, there would take place an *organization of labour* whose consequences would be the participation of the individual in *communal consumption.* In the first case the social character of production is posited only *post festum* with the elevation of products to exchange values and the exchange of these exchange values. In the second case the social character of production is *presupposed,* and participation in the world of products, in consumption, is not mediated by the exchange of mutually independent labours or products of labour. It is mediated, rather, by the *social conditions of production* within which the individual is active.[94]

Thus we are concerned here with a matter of fundamental importance. For in the only historically sustainable hegemonic alternative to capital's social metabolic order it is necessary to secure the conditions for the irreversible supersession of adversariality, which would otherwise be bound to resurface—and assert its power in the direction of capitalist restoration—from the more or less blind *post festum* determinations of societal reproduction. And that vital condition of superseding adversariality, on which so much else depends, can be secured only through the proper maintenance of the *conscious and self-critical*—that is, on a continuing basis rationally readjusted, rather than in a voluntaristic way on the recalcitrant individuals from above superimposed—all-embracing planning process.

In this sense *consciousness, self-critique,* the *supersession of adversariality,* and the *genuine planning* of societal reproduction in harmony with the autonomous determination of their *meaningful life-activity* by the social individuals themselves, are inextricably combined in making possible—beyond the anachronistic *post festum* mode of operating humanity's social metabolic interchange with nature and among the individuals—the positive institution of the *communal organic system* as the necessary historical alternative to capital's increasingly destructive organic system.

None of the conditions mentioned here can be disregarded or even partially neglected. Without the permanently maintained conscious self-critique of their forms of interchange by the freely associated individuals the communal system is inconceivable. At the same time, without the positively sustained reality of the communal system itself, which cannot be allowed to be in any way burdened with structurally sustained adversariality, the orienting principle of conscious self-critique can amount to nothing more than an empty postulate. For the qualitatively different new organic system cannot function at all without the freely adopted *conscious planning* of its vital reproductive practices—on the basis of the evaluation of the legitimately enduring elements of the past and the present, free from the dead weight of vested interests—by the social individuals. And, of course, such planning is feasible only through the positively determined *self-critique* of *all* individuals who in that way can fully identify themselves with the overall objectives of their social development. That is the necessary precondition for real *foresight* towards an open-ended future, in sharp contrast to the closure forced upon the working individuals by the incorrigible *retroactive post festum determinations* of their former societal reproduction.

Understandably, the move from the existing forms of society to the communal mode of social metabolic control is the most difficult one to make, with great obstacles and resistances on the way. Transition, by its very nature, is always difficult, since deeply embedded ways of societal interaction and individual behaviour must be significantly modified or altogether abandoned in its course of realization. In the case of a radically different way of ordering the life of the people by themselves, appropriate to the communal system, the difference is incommensurable with anything accomplished in the past.

But all that can provide no excuse for abandoning the perspective, or to water down the objective and subjective requirements of a transition to the communal system. Its full development is, no doubt, bound to take a long time. However, even at the earliest stage of its realization it is necessary to adopt the overall vision of the system, with its clearly definable criteria and characteristics some of which have been indicated above, as the *real target* of social transformation and the necessary *compass* of the journey. The orienting principles of critique and self-critique are directly relevant also in this respect.

8.5 Categorial Reflections of Social Antagonism and the Central Categories of Socialist Theory

We must constantly bear in mind that capital is not a "mere thing" but a dynamic mode of social metabolic control, with its historically developed specific command structure not only on the terrain of the material reproduction process but also in politics. It is equally important to remember in our present context that, due to the general character and inherent antagonisms of this unique mode of societal control, there is an increasingly more problematical contrast between the—customarily idealized—*actuality* of the capital system and the *categorial reflections* of its fundamental structural determinations.

Accordingly, a close attention paid to the categorial reflections themselves reveals much more about the nature of the historically changing capital system in its descending phase of development than the customary class conscious evaluation and conceptualization of the ongoing socioeconomic and political transformations by the thinkers who formulate their ideologically ever more questionable considerations from the vantage point of capital's structurally entrenched vested interests. This is so because the discussion of the categorial reflections by its very nature is bound to bring into play much more mediated concerns, often with direct references to the abstract domains of methodology, and thereby renders the open championing of the most conservative societal interests rather more difficult than what frequently happens in the combative assertion of bourgeois values in opposition to labour's substantively articulated hegemonic alternative. Indeed, the positively assumed abstract requirements of methodology for the sake of methodology are deliberately cultivated in the capital system's descending phase, in the name of "rigorous objectivity." Paradoxically, however, the unwanted consequence of assuming that stance is the opposite to what it is meant to accomplish. For instead of strengthening the position of those who uncritically identify themselves with capital's in our time extremely problematical vantage point, it tends to render the roots of ideological rationalization that much more transparent precisely by helping to focus attention on the underlying structural determinations of the system itself.

When we reach capital's present conditions of rule over society—which are predominantly retrograde and with unashamed apologetics asserted by the representatives of the ruling ideology in every field—Marx's illuminating characterization of the categories of the bourgeois order must be qualified. For Marx's assessment, in his critique of political economy, applies on the whole to the *ascending* phase of the capital system's historical development.

Talking about bourgeois society in general, Marx underlines that "it is the most complex historic organization of production. The categories which express its relations, the comprehension of its structure, thereby also allow insights into the structure and the relations of production of all the vanished social formations out of whose ruins and elements it built itself up, whose partly still unconquered remnants are carried along within it, whose mere nuances have developed explicit significance within it, etc."[95] However, the increasingly contradictory conditions that prevail in the *descending* phase of the system's development, reaching in our time the point where capital can perpetuate its rule only by directly endangering human survival as such—on the one hand through the engagement of the dominant imperialist countries (and above all the United States) in potentially catastrophic military adventures and, on the other, through the ongoing destruction of nature, acting thereby against the elementary condition of sustaining human life itself—carry with them constantly worsening determinations for the societal reproduction process, And, understandably, these changes involve not only the *emptying of their content* some of the once meaningful self-characterizations and orienting principles of the *ascending phase,* as reflected in the writings conceived from capital's vantage point by the classics of political economy and their great contemporaries in philosophy, like Rousseau, Kant and Hegel, but also the complete *falsification* of the actually existing state of affairs.

In this sense it is necessary to distinguish between the *categorial reflections of actuality*—even if transfigured and idealized, as often happened to be the case in the conceptualizations of the ascending phase of capital's development by the greatest representatives of the bourgeois order, as we have seen above—and the *cynical falsification* of the now experienced transformations and the corresponding (ultimately suicidal) aggressive strategic aspirations. In the latter respect we should recall the crudely propagandistic description of the Soviet adversary under the Reagan Presidency as *"the evil Empire,"* and the mindless regurgitation of the same propaganda slogan by President G. W. Bush against five countries denounced as *"the axis of evil,"* attempting not simply to hide but even to glorify—as the one and only feasible defence of *"democracy and liberty"*—the most brutal military aggression exercised on an escalating scale by the overwhelmingly dominant power of global hegemonic imperialism.

If we remind ourselves of what actually happened to the once sincerely advocated orienting principles of the French Revolution—*Liberty, Fraternity, Equality*—it transpires that the process of progressively emptying them of their content had started a very long time ago, already in the ascending phase. "Fraternity" quickly disappeared, of course, without a trace, never to reappear again. Also, "Liberty" had been adapted to the narrow ideological requirements of *Utilitarianism,* eliminating its positive dimension altogether.[96]

But perhaps the most drastic revision was suffered by the vital principle of "Equality"[97] while still retaining its term, and to some extent even its meaning. Tellingly, one of the truly great philosophers of all time, Immanuel Kant, was actively involved in the tendentious redefinition of equality already a few years after the French Revolution, in 1793. For he had no hesitation whatsoever in asserting that

> The *general equality* of men as subjects in a state coexists quite readily with the *greatest inequality* in degrees of the possessions men have . . . Hence the general equality of men also coexists with *great inequality of specific rights* of which there may be many.[98]

In this way "equality" was treated by Kant as a purely *formal* matter, confined to the sphere of legal relations, and even that was done with the just quoted restrictive qualification. Nor should we forget the fact that even such a revealingly restricted sense of equality was constantly violated in the most discriminatory actual practice of the law itself, in the obvious interest of the ruling order, as Rousseau made it abundantly clear at an earlier stage of societal development.

But much worse was still to come, difficult as it may be to imagine. For in twentieth century bourgeois conceptualizations the concept of equality was first confined to the domain of so-called "equality of *opportunity*," in explicit opposition to the characteristically rejected "equality of *outcome*"—which made it utterly meaningless in reality—and then *any* mention of it was completely abandoned, as a most embarrassing reminder of the past.

The concept of "Democracy" suffered the same fate. Once upon a time it was acknowledged that the social form corresponding to it carried not only formal/legal/electoral but also *substantive* connotations, implying some meaningful improvements in the material conditions of existence of the great masses of the people. Early utilitarian thinkers and some representatives of Liberalism actually advocated such improvements, even if they did it in a paternalistic way and by imagining, rather naïvely, that the envisaged improvements could be successfully secured by means of a benevolent reform of the sphere of *distribution* alone, without any need for changing the relations of *production* at all. Later the social democratic reformist tradition adopted the same approach, although for some decades it continued to pay lip service to the idea of introducing also some changes in the sphere of production, through the (never seriously attempted) institution of the bewilderingly self-contradictory idea of "evolutionary socialism." The postwar reform of the "Welfare State" in Britain, under the Labour Government, but through the inspiration of the old Liberal thinker and politician, Lord Beveridge,[99] and in collaboration with another Liberal theoretician, the economist John Maynard Keynes, was still an echo of that fairly distant past, and—given the conjuncturally favourable conditions of postwar reconstruction all over the world—it produced considerable improvement for some time in the standard of living of many people, without changing in the slightest the structural framework of capitalist society.

The great reversal had to assert itself later, when the *conjuncturally favourable* postwar expansionary phase had come to a halt, towards the end of the 1960s. That signalled also the onset of the capital system's *structural crisis*. As a result, the once sincerely advocated liberal and social democratic reformist ideas were replaced by the most ruthless imposition of *neo-liberalism,* with its repressively anti-labour legislation even in countries which traditionally considered themselves paradigms of democracy, including the United Kingdom of Great Britain. Thus the old principles of liberalism in practicable politics have been permanently consigned to the past, and at the same time the reform-oriented socialdemocratic tenets of substantively democratic transformations have been *explicitly* abandoned all over Europe through the kind of retrograde metamorphoses which we have witnessed in the conversion of the British Labour Party into "New Labour." And when we consider, as we must, also the use to which the idea of "Democracy" is now put in international affairs, in a most aggressive form through the wars of the United States, the gravity of the situation should raise alarm everywhere. For in this way the descending phase of the capital system's development not only totally *reverses* a sociopolitical trend which in the ascending phase was capable of producing some positive results, but also cynically *perverts* the important concepts through which the adopted dangerous measures could be critically evaluated and opposed, adding thereby to the monopoly of mass destructive weapons also the institutionally manipulated and enforced monopoly of thought in the name of safeguarding "Liberty."

ONE OF THE CONCEPTS MOST OFTEN PRAISED today by the personifications of capital is *globalization.* We can see also in this case the grave distortion of reality in the interest of justifying the structural antagonisms of the descending phase.

The concept of "globalization" is very far from being a real *Daseinsform* (a categorial form of being) in its Marxian sense. There can be no question of producing a synthesis of the characteristics of actual socioeconomic developments in this notion—with validity even vaguely comparable to the insights of the classics of political economy—which would reveal something structurally significant about the present trends and indicate their roots in the historical past. What we are offered, instead, under the endlessly repeated slogan of universally beneficial *"globalization,"* is the cynical embellishment of the actually unfolding—and also through direct state intervention enforced—strategies of capitalist rule, corresponding to the present phase of *imperialist domination.*

The actual, but highly contradictory, historical tendency towards the global integration of the capitalist economy goes back well over two centuries in the past. Surveying in the *Communist Manifesto,* already by that time one hundred years of dynamic international economic development, Marx and Engels put into relief that "The need of a constantly expanding market of its products chases the bourgeoisie over the whole surface of the globe. It must nestle everywhere, settle everywhere, establish connexions everywhere." They underlined in that *Manifesto* the inexorability of the objective determinations at the roots of such developments, and they talked about "industries that no longer work up indigenous raw material, but raw material drawn from the remotest zones; industries whose products are consumed not only at home, but in every quarter of the globe."[100] They did that in a *Manifesto* published not in recent years, when it has become fashionable to chatter about "globalization," in the interest of social apologetics, but way back in 1848!

However, they highlighted at the same time also the other side of the coin of international capitalist expansion. Namely that "Modern bourgeois society with its relations of production, of exchange and of property, a society that has conjured up such gigantic means of production and of exchange, is like the sorcerer, who is no longer able to control the powers of the nether world he has called up by his spells."[101] It is this side of the gravely contradictory process of the capital system's inexorable tendency towards its global economic integration which is completely missing from the cynically embellished transfiguration of the—capitalistically in the end untenable and explosive—actuality of increased exploitation all over the world into the universally beneficial fairy tale of "globalization."

The ideologists of the ruling order present the issue not only as a fictitious, categorially significant, novelty of development but also by declaring at the same time that "every sane person should happily embrace globalization," instead of daring to voice doubts about its nature and prospects of success. What they are studiously silent about is the incorrigible actuality of the *power relations* which overwhelmingly favour the dominant imperialist countries and perpetuate the long prevailing inequalities, if need be with the force of arms. They are also unrealistic enough to imagine that such deeply iniquitous and structurally enforced power relations can be eternally maintained by the principal beneficiaries of capital's social metabolic order. Thus the unashamed "eternalization" of the capital system—which started to become prominent already in the writings of "vulgar economics," at the beginning of the descending phase of development—assumes through the idealization of imperialist globalization a most acute form.

Naturally, we cannot consider this development a straightforward repetition of the past going back well over two centuries. While it is perfectly correct to stress that the inner logic of capital's self-expansionary development is inseparable from the necessity of imposing itself all over the world, there are also some *differentia specifica* that must be underlined in relation to the current trends.

First, that, contrary to the present, capital's earliest form of encroachment on the remotest parts of the world did not arise from the great inner pressures of *monopolistic* and *quasi-monopolistic* transformations of the economy in the dominant imperialist countries on a major scale.

Second, that even in comparison to the beginning of the twentieth century, *imperialism* of our time is significantly different from its form which caused the massive explosion of the First World War in 1914. Not only because the political/military occupation of former colonial territories after the First World War proved to be totally unstable, as well as highly contested both internally and internationally, and had to be followed by post-Second World War decolonization and a somewhat different variety of "neo-imperialist" domination. Even more significant in this respect was that the United States became the dominant power of the new variety of imperialism, and in our time acts—even in the form of waging major wars, from Vietnam to the Middle East—as the enforcer of *global hegemonic imperialism.* In this way the United States is unwilling to tolerate rivals in its imperialist adventures—no matter how problematical this kind of monopoly is bound to turn out to be in the not too distant future—in contrast even to Hitler's design to share global domination with Japan in the past.

And the *third* major point to stress is that the political-economic forces primarily benefitting from the "globalizing" domination of the world are the giant *transnational*—often self-servingly misnamed as "*multi*-national"—corporations, acting with the full support of their national states. Again, the companies of the United States are in the forefront of these new imperialist developments. It is also relevant in this context that the economic determination of the ongoing "globalization" on the monetary plane is characterized by the highly speculative and parasitic, as well as even on a relatively short term basis dangerously unstable, forces of finance capital, and by no means without the complicity of the capitalist state.

These are the considerations that must be added to the idyllic picture of capitalist globalization in our time.

ANOTHER PROBLEM OF GREAT IMPORTANCE in this context, underlining the need for qualifying the assessment of the seminal systemic determinations which go through a major change from the ascending to the descending phase of capital's development, is the total perversion of the category of *consumption.* The importance of this matter for the societal reproduction process as a whole cannot be stressed enough. Its most extreme form emerges under the direct impact of a most pernicious, and potentially all-destructive, modality of production in the second half of the twentieth century.

The issue is of a literally vital importance because in actuality the interconnection between production and consumption, in order to be sustainable at all on a lasting basis, must qualify as a close *dialectical* relationship of genuine *reciprocity.* Without this objective determination of the societal reproduction process the whole system becomes dangerously unsustainable. However, the capitalistically insurmountable problem here is that it is impossible to confine attention to the—manipulable—conditions of only two of the constituents of this relationship. For the necessary dialectical reciprocity between the two—that is, production and consumption considered by themselves—is inconceivable without the seminal role played in the actual constitution of their relationship by human *need*. It is the fulfilment of the role required by human need in the constitution of the dialectical reciprocity between production and consumption that becomes extremely problematical under the present conditions of historical development.

This is how Marx describes the principal characteristics of this dynamic interrelationship:

> Production not only supplies the material for the *need*, but it also supplies a *need* for the material. As soon as consumption emerges from its initial state of natural crudity—and, if it remained at that stage, it would be because production itself had been arrested there—it becomes itself *mediated as a drive* by the object. . . . Production thus not only creates an *object* for the subject, but also a *subject* for the object. Thus production produces consumption (1) by creating the material for it; (2) by determining the manner of consumption; and (3) by creating the products, initially posited by it as objects, in the form of a *need felt by the consumer*. It thus produces the object of consumption, the manner of consumption and the motive of consumption. Consumption likewise produces the producer's inclination by beckoning to him as an *aim-determining need*. . . . Production is consumption, consumption is production. *Consumptive* production. *Productive* consumption. . . . The individual produces an object and, by consuming it, returns to himself, but returns as a productive and self-reproducing individual. Consumption thus appears as a moment of production.[102]

Under the conditions of monopolistic developments in the twentieth century we witness a major distortion in these relations. For the giant corporations of the dominant countries assert their power—not simply a productively obtained economic power but one greatly inflated thanks to the political advantage enjoyed through their quasi-monopolistic position in the overall capitalist setting—also in the form of *manipulating need* and *imposing* on it whatever suits their interest in securing and maintaining profitable capital-expansion. Thus the problematical practice of stimulating "artificial appetities," because they yield easier profits than the justifiable alternatives in response to real need—a practice never completely absent from capitalist production—acquired an incomparably more diffused and structurally more significant role with the onset of the monopolistic phase of capital's history.

In the second half of the twentieth century we experience a *qualitative* change in this relationship, even when set against its already significantly worsened modality under the impact of monopolistic transformations, in comparison to the ascending phase of the capital system. The economic and political agency which imposes on society this qualitatively aggravating change, with potentially catastrophic consequences, is the *military-industrial complex,* to use President Eisenhower's apt description of it. It is an agency which is, and can only be, inseparably economic and political at the highest level. The very nature of its *"productive"* enterprise is *destruction,* ultimately concerned not with just "thinking the unthinkable," as it tends to be described with frivolous complicity, but with the possibility of humanity's complete annihilation. That is, it strives by making by far the most profitable business out of the highest possible risk-taking—not *economic* risk-taking, of which, contrary to capitalist self-mythology, it has *none,* but playing with the fire of unlimited and unlimitable destruction—whose authorization can be provided only by the state as such.

Moreover, this unique business could not possibly cover even a minimal amount of the grave economic costs involved, through customary economic processes. They must be *politically imposed* on society by the state, in its capacity as tax-enforcer backed by its monopoly of violence against all feasible recalcitrance in the matter. Accordingly, what we are confronted by in this potentially lethal development of the capital system in the second half of the twentieth century is the *total perversion of consumption* in any meaningful sense of the term.

In this kind of "consumption"—which could not be more distant from, and indeed more sharply opposed to, the category of *productive consumption* quoted above—there is neither a real *subject,* nor a human *need* which could be positively fulfilled through the consumption of the produced objects. And since in actuality, in contrast to its wishfully and irresponsibly manipulated untenable modality, consumption constitutes a dialectically combined unity with production, given their ineliminable reciprocity, there can be no question of *consumptive production* either. Their place is taken by the humiliating submission of society as a whole to the acceptance of destructive wastefulness in production as much as in consumption.

The great innovation of the military-industrial complex for capitalist developments is to obliterate in a practically effective way the vital distinction between *consumption* and *destruction.* Marx once noted that in imperial Rome alienated and independent value as consumption-oriented wealth "appears as *limitless waste* which logically attempts to raise consumption to an imaginary boundlessness by *gulping down salads of pearls* etc."[103] By comparison, the truly limitless waste of gulping down resources equivalent to billions of such salads over the years, while countless millions have to endure starvation as their inescapable "fate," succeeds in legitimating itself through the destructive practices of the military-industrial complex as totally unquestionable patriotic duty. For that complex is protected by the power of institutionalized irresponsibility, no matter how fraudulent may be its practices, amounting to astronomical magnitudes, as revealed by countless scandals.

Once upon a time the production of *use-value* was closely intertwined with the multiplication of profitable *exchange-value,* even if in subordination to the latter, and carrying with it the capital system's productive tendency for the ultimately unsustainable *decreasing rate of utilization.* Ironically, however, in our present phase of historical development, when it becomes absolutely essential to achieve a humanly meaningful *increase* in the rates of utilization, as the *only viable economy* for the future, we see the diametrical opposite, with the totally irresponsible productive tendency of the military-industrial complex toward the *zero rate.* Indeed, the military-industrial complex succeeds in "raising consumption to an imaginary boundlessness" by inventing the instant perishability of even the most durable material substances and irreplaceable "strategic raw materials" by working them up in the form of the instruments of war and destruction, which happen to be wasteful/destructive of human resources in the extreme, even if they are *never used at all.* And it can impose on society such absurd *destructive* "productive" practices with the greatest ease.

In every major capitalist country the military-industrial complex enjoys the arbitrary legitimation of the most extreme forms of waste by the state's ideologically well buttressed institutional network in which the activities of the *embezzler, paymaster, auditor, law-maker and judge are all rolled into one.* And given the prominent position of the military-industrial complex in the overall reproduction process, together with its perversely secured eminence in shaping society's scale of values, the destructive dissipation of potentially most valuable resources in society as a whole becomes acceptable and even respectable, as a valid contribution to the customarily pursued capitalist aims of growth and expansion. Thus the well known exaltation of capital's impact on societal development by some liberal economists, according to which their system is characterized by *creative* or *productive* destruction, is being turned on a frightening scale into its diametrical opposite: *destructive* production. This is how the descending phase of the capital system's development in our own time tends to completely reverse and subvert the once significant achievements of its ascending phase.

THE HISTORICALLY SPECIFIC and structurally enforced hierarchical command structure of capital's generalized commodity production emerged through a long combative confrontation with the feudal system. It was constituted on the basis of radically different principles, firmly establishing in its mature form the overwhelming primacy of the *economic extraction of surplus labour,* in the most flexible and dynamic form of the expropriation and accumulation of *surplus-value.*

This represented a sharp contrast to the essentially *political* enforcement of surplus-labour extraction and the corresponding regulation of the societal reproduction process, which proved to be increasingly anachronistic and untenable in the case of feudalism as time went by. Nevertheless, in order to succeed against its adversary, and more importantly, to consolidate itself in a sustainable way for a long historical period to come, the capital system had to establish its rule over society on the basis of a strictly ordered command structure, embracing all spheres and all levels of human life. In this sense, contrary to its self-mythology of being the ideal embodiment of *liberty, democracy* and *individual autonomy* (of which *"individual consumer sovereignty"* is a relatively recent variant), capital is nothing if not the most effectively working and structurally enforced hierarchical command structure in all history. Its superiority to all previous forms of societal command structure consists precisely in its ability to combine, as a genuine and most dynamic *organic system,* the vital requirements of humanity's elementary metabolic interchange with nature and the regulation of even the most complex and sophisticated aspects of the material, political and cultural reproduction process. Indeed, one of the most important aspects of the new command structure was that capital could successfully impose its vital reproductive determinations on society on an *ever expanding scale* over a very long historical period, even if increasingly less so in our time, due to the irreversible activation of capital's absolute systemic limits.[104]

However, the radical shift from the *politically enforced* to the primarily *economic extraction* of surplus-labour was by no means a *spontaneous*—let alone a *natural*—process, as the ideological rationalizations of the capital system like to depict it, so as to postulate the established system's eternal validity. The required historical change could not be at its origin a *spontaneous* economic transition to a more flexible new modality of societal reproduction; nor is it conceivable at all that the overwhelmingly economic extraction and accumulation of surplus-labour as surplus-value could *ever* maintain itself in power without a heavy contribution—and in fact the *ultimate guarantee* of its self-expansionary development—by the appropriate, periodically changing, and in our time considerably worsening, *political dimension.* For in the depth of this socioeconomic system we can always identify the *fundamental structural antagonism* between capital and labour, even if in different periods of history that antagonism can remain more or less *latent* and actively hidden from sight by the absurd but most effective *fetishistic* determinations of the ongoing reproduction process itself whereby *"the product is the proprietor of the producer,"* as quoted already.

In this important sense, it was quite inconceivable to establish the overwhelming domination of capital's normal, economic-extraction-oriented, production and distribution process in the first place, without the massive direct involvement not simply of politics but of the *most bru-*

tal form of politics at the time of the so-called *"primitive accumulation,"* not least under the reign of Henry VIII. In the historical period, that is, when the future labour force had to be totally deprived of any, still on the common land available, alternative means of bare survival, as well as of all possible means of production in the future, in order to be completely *subjugated* by the requirements of capital's new modality of production, and in countless thousands even executed/exterminated as "vagrants" and "vagabonds," on account of being *surplus to capital's then existing productive needs and potentialities.*[105]

Moreover, the irrepressible antagonism between capital and labour—which is and must always remain the structural foundation (paradoxically both the driving force and the ultimate weakness) of this reproductive order—makes it necessary to maintain in power a strictly hierarchical command structure, not only in the particular productive units (as exercised through the undeniable "authoritarianism of the workshop") but also in society at large, imposing on the working subjects the necessarily *top-down decision making* processes of the system as a whole. This must be the case no matter how *latent* might be the objective contradictions at a particular time. As we know from the history of postwar developments, the top-down decision making processes must prevail even when the latency of the fundamental antagonism favours the broadest acceptance of the spurious "democratic" claims—including the British Labour Government's naïve propaganda slogan about "conquering the commanding heights of the economy" (in the words of Prime Minister Harold Wilson) through the reversible, and at the first opportune moment duly reversed, measure of "nationalization," which amounted in reality to nothing more than the transfer of capitalist bankruptcy to state-imposed general taxation in a few key sectors of the economy. This kind of deceptive "positive development" tends to take place under historical circumstances when the basic structural antagonism, which remains always at the roots of the capital system, appears for the time being virtually non-existent, generating all kinds of self-disarming illusions in labour's own ranks, thanks to the ongoing process of unhindered *productive expansion,* like the post-Second World War phase of reconstruction and the conjunctural practices of the Welfare State in a handful of Western countries. Ironically, however, the Welfare State practices were just as easily reversible even in those few countries as the once loudly trumpeted nationalizations of the pretended "commanding heights of the economy," and of course under the impact of sharpening social contradictions—managed under the new political climate of "neo-liberalism," to which "New Labour" became no less willingly acclimatized than its Conservative political adversary—they have been in fact largely reversed.

PERHAPS THE MOST REVEALING ASPECT of the relationship between the economic and the political dimensions in the capital system's development is the *overall trend* itself which shows the relative dominance of one or the other in the ascending and in the descending phase.

The anti-historical projection of capital's spontaneous emergence and natural permanence, set against the actuality of the most brutal political involvement needed for the system's earliest stage of stabilization, is, of course, nothing more than laughable self-mythology. Nevertheless, it is easier to find a more rational, and in a complicated historical sense also more justifiable explanation for what actually happened—amounting to the direct political imposition of the requirements through which the historically well recorded political brutality succeeded in opening the gates towards an economically productive advancement simply incommensurable with the past—than the problematical transformations we are compelled to face in the present phase of the established order's destructive development. For in the *descending* phase of capital's mode of social metabolic control, and in the most extreme form in the course of the twentieth century, extending also into the twenty-first, we witnessed the increasing dominance of the most retrograde political forces on a frightening scale, even if frequently misrepresented by the devoted personifications of capital with the false ideology of "pushing back the boundaries of the state," propagandized with utmost cynicism. In that way humankind had to experience the most problematical *reversal* of well over two hundred years of the *overall trend,* characterized by a significantly *diminishing* role of direct political decision making in the general management of the capital system up to the middle of the nineteenth century, parallel to its *ascending* phase of development.

The theoretical visions of these changes fairly accurately reflected the changing nature of the underlying process itself. Thus Thomas Hobbes, at a relatively early stage of the transition towards a much more predominantly economic extraction and accumulation of surplus-labour as surplus-value, spoke not only about the "nature-determined" *bellum omnium contra omnes,* but at the same time, with great intellectual consistency, also advocated *Leviathan* as the corresponding—extremely powerful and absolutely necessary—political state.

Well over a century later Adam Smith, at a considerably more advanced stage of capital's ascending phase of development, was forcefully arguing in favour of a *minimal* political state, so as to give full scope to the benevolent economic guiding force of the "Invisible Hand" in his ideal scheme of things. And later still, Hegel, while acknowledging the appearance of contradictions more than his intellectual precursors who also viewed the world from capital's vantage point, had no inclination at all to turn back in the direction of legitimating arbitrary state political power. Instead, he was arguing in favour of a strictly mandated "ethical state," ruled by Reason, thus clearly restricting the power of the monarch to next to nothing.[106] Besides, even a few decades after Hegel, towards the end of capital's ascending phase, the major representatives of Liberalism and Utilitarianism wanted the state to be confined to a secondary role, so as to allow the spontaneous economic processes to fulfil their postulated positive functions.

The second half of the nineteenth century, and in a particularly pronounced way the manifestations of modern imperialist colonialism unfolding in the last three decades of it, linked to ever stronger monopolistic developments internally in the dominant countries,[107] signalled the great intensification of the capitalist state's direct political involvement in the societal reproduction process. Not surprisingly, this trend became worse in the twentieth century, bringing with it two world wars, as well as formerly unimaginable devastations, including the Nazi Holocaust and the first use of the nuclear weapons of mass destruction against civil populations in Hiroshima and Nagasaki by none other than the United States of America.

Notwithstanding all mythology in praise of capital's *natural order,* and of its spontaneously prevailing *"extended economic order,"* the truth with far-reaching systemic implications is that capital's mode of social metabolic control of the reproduction process could no longer manage its affairs without the heaviest political intervention by the state. And that problematical characteristic applied not only to the most brutal Nazi and extreme right-wing Japanese adventurism successfully prevailing for decades over a major part of our planet but also to the proposed antidotes set in motion against openly authoritarian answers to the grave crisis symptoms of the system, from Roosevelt's "New Deal" to the heavily state-sponsored practices of the "Welfare State," indicated even by its name, with dubious lasting results.

And when we add to these considerations the earlier discussed *military-industrial complex*—which could not sustain itself for a moment without the massive support it continues to enjoy by the state—as well as the neo-liberal and "neo-con" advocacy and escalating practice of destructive wars, hypocritically justified by "democratic" parliaments under obvious false pretences,[108] no one can deny the gravity of capital's structural crisis. For now the circle stretching from the brutal early facilitating role played by politics for capital's emergence and consolidation as an organic system in the age of Henry VIII, followed by its diminishing trend during the ascending phase, and back to the ever increasing role of politics, with a vengeance, in the descending phase of development, that circle has now been irretrievably closed. And nothing can constitute a more vicious circle in practical terms than this one, which can follow unimpeded its rotation around its own, really existing, *evil axis.* A rotation clearly visible in the form of ever more authoritarian state intervention in the reproduction process which can be pursued on a growing scale only by directly endangering the very survival of humanity.

THE CATEGORIAL REFLECTION of the deep-seated and ineradicable structural antagonism between capital and labour is (more or less consciously) misrepresented by all those who conceptualize the world from capital's standpoint. Even during the ascending phase of capital's development "*Society,* as it appears to the political economist, is *civil society,* in which every individual is a totality of needs and only exists for the other person, as the other exists for him, in so far as each becomes a means for the other. The political economist reduces everything (just as does politics in its *Rights of Man)* to man, i.e., to the individual whom he strips of all determinateness so as to class him as capitalist and worker."[109] And, of course, when the political economists—and the philosophers who view the world in the same way—talk about the existence of capitalists and workers, they describe them as members of a society of strictly aggregative individualities and nature-determined parts of an ideal order, as we have seen above. They do not offer the slightest acknowledgement of the fact that the relationship between capitalists and workers is constituted in actuality on the ground of the *structurally enforced antagonism* between capital and labour whose successful imposition on the subjected class must remain also in the future the condition *sine qua non* of their "natural system of perfect liberty and justice."

In this sense already the Hobbesian *bellum omnium contra omnes* is a revealing misrepresentation of the actual state of affairs, even if it remains praiseworthy on account of highlighting the permanence of conflict under the rule of capital. It is a misrepresentation not in the sense that the conflicts among individuals do not exist, which they most certainly do, but because they are not intelligible without the fundamental *class antagonism* of which they are an integral part, in that it is the basic class antagonism that sets the *stakes* for the overall confrontation between the two *hegemonic alternative classes* capable of controlling in their very different ways the sociohistorical order. The manifold individual conflicts, both among the capitalists and among the workers, are subordinate determinations of that fundamental hegemonic alternative, as much with regard to their particular practical manifestations as to their major value-orientations.

As we have seen in the previous chapter, Hegel too, mystifyingly depicted the characteristic of self-seeking/egotism as if it was directly emanating from the individuals themselves, without acknowledging that in reality they had to *internalize*[110] the established order's *objective self-expansionary imperative* which gave rise to it in fact. This is how Hegel was able to produce an idealized vision of historical development, which in his view represented the "realization of freedom," in his political economist rationalization of actuality.

The ideological justification of the exploitative practices of the productively developing capital system assumed a clearly pronounced form way back in the philosophy of John Locke. He admitted at first that "*labour*, in the beginning, gave a *right of property*."[111] But his real concern was how to justify the practical elimination of that condition, in the interest of the established, most iniquitous, order. This he did by postulating the absolutely *natural* foundation of money,[112] which is said to justify "heaping up" and "hoarding up" wealth, so that "a man may rightfully, and without injury, possess more than he himself can make use of by receiving gold and silver, which may continue long in a man's possession without decaying for the overplus."[113] Locke also thought to be able to do away with the ground of the fundamental social antagonism by stretching the concepts of *property* and *possessions* to the point where, in his view, it ceased to matter "whether his possession be of land to him and his heirs for ever, or a lodging only for a week; or whether it be barely travelling freely on the highway; and, in effect, it reaches as far as the very *being* of any one within the territories of that government."[114]

This kind of apologetics served a dual purpose. In addition to ruling out any concern with inequality, it was also devised to justify the total political submission of the dispossessed to the established political authority, in accordance with Locke's mystifying, but of course highly celebrated, idea of *"tacit consent."* For by arguing in this way he could assert and "legitimate" the unlimited obligations of the subjected people in the name of an utterly fictitious "consent," ascribed to them on the ground that they did not leave the country, and thus tacitly consented to the boundless authority of the capitalist state over them, although in actuality they did not consent to anything at all, but simply had no way of altering their precarious predicament.

But even this transparent apologetics cannot be compared to what we are forced to accept under the conditions of capital's present-day actuality. For one of Locke's principal arguments for justifying the extreme inequalities of the capital system in his age was that, thanks to the nature-determined *durable nature* of money, it has become possible to *eliminate waste* which would be otherwise inseparable from the practice of "heaping up" and "hoarding up" wealth, as befits the nature of capital's expanded reproduction. By contrast, the capital system in our own time cannot function without imposing on society—in Locke's age totally unimaginable—amounts and forms of waste, and justifying it in many different ways, including the most absurd productive and self-legitimating practices of the military-industrial complex, as we have seen above. Thus, also in this respect we see the full completion of capital's vicious circle.

And in our time, inevitably, the whole of humanity must suffer the destructive consequences of its completion.

A century after Locke, by the time Adam Smith writes his *Wealth of Nations,* capital is firmly in control of the societal reproduction process in Britain and is making undeniable progress also in other parts of the world. Understandably, therefore, the illusions concerning the natural determinations of its system, and the all-round beneficial consequences of organizing production on the basis of such a "natural" system, are greater than ever before. Thus the accent is confidently and strongly on the positive side of the perceived development, on the assertion of the irresistibly unfolding *wealth* of the nations, and the negative results of the system's productive advancement are depicted on the whole as marginal problems. In this way we see the actual social antagonisms minimized beyond recognition, due to Smith's tendency to characterize the alienating aspects of the capitalist division of labour (some of which clearly acknowledged by him) primarily as *technical*—and technically/organizationally/educationally corrigible—problems, but never as deep-seated social contradictions. As regards the assessment of the *overall* cohesion and viability of the capital system, optimism reigns supreme in Adam Smith's intellectual universe. Not surprisingly, by far his most influential concept—which generates important echoes also in other countries, including Hegel's more complicated but equally influential idea of the "Cunning of Reason" *(List der Vernunft)*—offers a vision of how capital's mysterious guiding force works for the benefit of the *whole* as well as for the well-being of each and every individual. This is how the actuality of the complicated and *deeply antagonistic mediations* of the most dynamic system of social metabolic reproduction in history could be transformed in theory—in the promising period of the industrial revolution—into the universally commendable postulate of ideal human interchange. The sobering impact of the exploding contradictions took far less than a century to assert itself.

THE CATEGORIES OF SOCIALIST THEORY, as appropriate "forms of being" in the Marxian sense, must be conceptualized on a very different basis: through the most faithful reflection of the real problems and contradictions arising from the social metabolic relations of humankind with nature and among the individuals themselves, in their actually given societal setting, in a very difficult historical period of transition towards a viable new social reproductive order.

Inevitably, a firm critical response to the long dominant theoretical images and ideological rationalizations of the capital system is an integral part of this enterprise. For we are not concerned here simply with abstract theoretical issues but with vital *practical* determinations, even when they are transfigured in a complicated speculative form in some philosophical syntheses conceived from capital's standpoint, as we could see in the course of this study. Any solution pointing in the direction of labour's historically sustainable hegemonic alternative, envisaged via the unavoidable period of transition, must set out from the *actually given* conditions of the ruling social metabolic order, with its frequently hidden but fetishistically imposed practical premises and imperatives.

A methodologically valid approach to the required theory of transition in this sense is feasible only if it satisfies two necessary conditions: (1) the clear definition of its starting point in relation to the *objective* determinations of the *actually given* structural framework of society, with its really existing contradictions and ineradicable antagonisms (which implies, of course, the critique of their tendentious conceptualizations, and, especially in the descending phase of the system's development, the increasingly more apologetic misrepresentation of the historically given state of affairs from capital's self-serving vantage point), and (2) the indication of the broad outlines of *labour's long term sustainable hegemonic alternative* to the established order.

The first issue in need of clarification in this respect is the concept of *wealth.* For even the classics of political economy could never have other than a *fetishistic* conception of wealth and poverty, due to capital's necessarily—and exclusively—*quantifying* approach to these problems. This had to be the case even at the most promising ascending phase of the system's development, including Adam Smith's *Wealth of Nations.* It is vitally important to mark here a firm line of demarcation not only in the interest of our pressing conditions of development today, with its already quite unsustainable productive practices, but even more in relation to the future. For it is inconceivable to institute labour's hegemonic alternative order—the communal organic system—on the basis of even the best-intentioned *quantification.*

The *only viable economy*, no matter how advanced a stage humankind might reach in productive powers in the future, in contrast to the necessary *wastefulness* of capital's quantifying/fetishistic inner determinations, is a mode of societal reproduction that must be oriented by *qualitative* considerations, in response to genuine *human need*. This contrast to the general approach of political economy as a whole to the absolutely crucial problem of the real economy of the future was unmistakably spelled out by Marx already in his earliest assessment of the subject. He firmly stressed that "in place of the *wealth* and the *poverty* of political economy come the *rich human being* and rich *human* need. The *rich* human being is simultaneously the human being *in need of* a totality of human life-activities—the man in whom his own realization exists as an inner necessity, as *need*."[115]

It is important to stress in the same context that the idea of the *communal mode of production and consumption*—which we have seen discussed by the "mature Marx" in considerable detail in his most important synthesizing works, including the *Grundrisse* and *Capital*—was clearly advocated by him already in his earliest system *in statu nascendi*. He characterized them as follows: "*communal activity and communal consumption*—i.e., activity and consumption which are manifested and *directly* confirmed in *real association* with other men—will occur wherever such a *direct expression of sociality* stems from the true character of the activity's content and is adequate to the nature of consumption."[116] This is the only viable overall horizon of the fundamental transformations through which the alienating conception of wealth can be consigned to the past. For only under the communal system can the orienting principle of *quality arising from human need* actually prevail.

No matter how much *relative* improvement is feasible under the rule of capital—and we know only too well how *little* has been achieved in terms of the world's *total* population by capital's ability for "heaping up" and "hoarding up" wealth on one side, and gruesome inequality and misery on the other, as the inescapable destiny of the overwhelming majority of humanity—there can be no *structurally viable* solution under the necessary practical premises and imperatives of fetishistic quantification. The completion of capital's ultimately destructive—and by implication also inevitably *self-destructive*—vicious circle, in the form of its ever more dominant *destructive production* in our time, as inseparable from the system's fully realized fetishistic quantifying logic, bears eloquent witness to this painful truth.

Another important manifestation of being theoretically imprisoned by capital's ubiquitously prevailing fetishism concerns the philosophical chimera of *subject-object identity*. This is a *strait-jacket* worn by even very great philosophers, like Hegel, who assume that they can get rid of the alienating and reifying actual separation of the subject from, and its opposition to, the object by positing their speculative *identity*. However, by doing that they can only get more tightly entangled in capital's strait-jacket, which they had willingly put on by identifying themselves with the system's vantage point. For in the real world the apparently insurmountable theoretical problem arises from the innermost determinations—and the necessary practice—of the capital system based on the *usurpation of the role of the subject* by depriving labour of the means of production, and thus *structurally preventing it* from asserting its legitimate *controlling functions* in the societal reproduction process.

The speculative philosophical solution consists in a totally unworkable attempt to eliminate the problem of *alienation in productive activity* itself by arbitrarily equating productive *objectification as such*—which is, and must always remain, the necessary manifestation and embodiment of human activity itself—with the historically created and likewise historically surmountable *capitalist alienation and expropriation* of the activity's products. Thus in actuality both the role of the subject and the objects produced by the real working subject are usurpatorily alienated and expropriated by capital. The only way to (imaginarily) "solve" this dual problem of alienating social practice in speculative philosophy, without changing anything at all in actuality, is by *positing the identity of subject and object* on the basis of the (far from equitable but fallaciously proclaimed) *identity of externalizing objectification* (inseparable from practical human activity by definition) and historically specific *alienation.*

The obvious alternative is the *restitution* of the real subject's autonomous controlling functions in production, together with the ability to determine the use to which the objects produced by him are put in society at large. In other words, it is a question of establishing the creative *unity* of the working subjects with the objective conditions of their *self-*

determined activity, rather than the invention of a fictitious—speculative—*identity* between the abstract *thought-entity: Subject* and the equally abstract/speculative *thought-entity: Object* (writ large or small). This is how Marx approaches the problem, insisting that

> man is not lost in his object only when the object becomes for him a *human* object or objective man. This is possible only when the object becomes for him a *social* object, he himself for himself a social being, just as society becomes a being for him in this object. On the one hand, therefore, it is only when the objective world becomes everywhere for man in society the world of man's essential powers—human reality, and for that reason the reality of his *own* essential powers—that all *objects* become for him the *objectification of himself,* become objects which confirm and realize his individuality, become *his* objects: that is, *man himself* becomes the object.[117]

Obviously, then, the *dialectical unity* of subject and object is a question of the historical determinateness and objective suitability of the conditions under which the appropriate relationship between the individuals, as real social individuals, and their society—capable of offering them the required scope for self-realization as rich social individuals—can be accomplished. Any attempt to posit the *identity* of subject and object is feasible only by abstracting from the actually existing and historically circumscribed social relations, making thereby also the concept of the individual most problematical.

At the same time it must be also stressed that social determinateness and the appropriate realization of individuality constitute a dialectical unity which cannot be distorted on either side. Marx is therefore anxious to underline that "What is to be avoided above all is the re-establishing of 'Society' as an abstraction *vis-à-vis* the individual. The individual *is the social being.*"[118] And he goes on to argue that "Man, much as he may therefore be a *particular* individual (and it is precisely his particularity which makes him an individual, and a real *individual* social being), is just as much the *totality*—the ideal totality—the subjective existence of thought and experienced society present for itself; just as he exists also in the real world as the awareness and the real enjoyment of social existence, and as a totality of human activity. Thinking and being are thus no doubt *distinct,* but at the same time they are in *unity* with each other."[119]

Naturally, the *distinctness* of the subject and object also in the overall material and cultural reproduction process must be clearly recognized without ambiguity, otherwise one is in danger of falling into the trap of the subject-object identity by default. But their relationship can make *substantive sense*—and neither a purely *formal*, nor a *speculative philosophical* sense could be appropriate in this respect—only if it is conceived, inseparably from the underlying *practical* social determinations, as constitutive of a dialectical *unity*. For both on the side of the subject (be that *individual* or *collective,* and indeed whether in a more general societal sense collective or specifically *communal)* and the object (e.g. the direct embodiment of some material productive activity or the enjoyment of an aesthetic object, like a work of art, by the individual) we are talking about the actuality of manifold social determinateness which cannot be abstracted from without wantonly emptying this important relationship itself of its defining content and meaning.

PLANNING OCCUPIES A MOST IMPORTANT PLACE among the categories of socialist theory. This is in sharp contrast to the capital system in which —due to the *centrifugal* inner determination of its productive and distributive microcosms—there is no real scope for planning in its full sense of the term. That sense is defined both as *consciously pursued comprehensive planning* of production and distribution, and at the same time as going well beyond the limitations of *technical/technological* coordination no matter how broadly based.

Naturally, the great thinkers who conceptualized the world from capital's vantage point realized that something *essential* was missing from their depiction of the established reproductive order without which it could not be sustained at all on a lasting basis, let alone qualify for being idealized as the one and only natural mode of humanity's social metabolic reproduction, as they declared it to be. Thus, as a striking but utterly mysterious afterthought, they introduced the idea of "the Invisible Hand" (Adam Smith), "the Commercial Spirit" (Kant), and "the Cunning of Reason" (Hegel).

Such a mysterious *supra-individual* entity, irrespective of its name, was supposed to achieve what in a non-antagonistically structured human society should be accomplished by freely determined *comprehensive planning*. And the projected supra-individual agency was supposed to fulfil the task of overall coordination and direction incomparably better, by definition, than the particular individuals could even dream about. For in the conceptions formulated from capital's vantage point two—*irreconcilable*—conditions had to be satisfied.

First, the *retention* of the political economist mythology of "civil society" (abstracted from the capitalist state), with its insoluble *individual* adversariality, quarrelsomeness and conflicts (as appropriate to Kant's "crooked timber" from which the particular individuals were supposed to have been made by Providence, nature-determined or Divine). Hence the particular individuals could not possibly be entrusted with the vital task of securing the orderly cohesion of reproductive activity on a societal scale without which the new economic order would fall to pieces.

And the second condition that had to be satisfied was the production of overall societal cohesion. This process was contradictorily posited in the form of reasserting what the thinkers in question considered to be the objective ontological determinations of insuperably conflictual "civil society." The imaginary solution to the insuperable conflictuality of civil society was offered by them in the way of transubstantiating the *negative* interchange of particularistic self-seeking adversariality as such into the *positive* benefits that were supposed to arise from the conflicts themselves for the *whole,* whereby in Hegel's words, thanks to a miraculous "dialectical" advance, *"subjective self-seeking* turns into a contribution to the satisfaction of the needs of *everyone else,"* as we have seen it above decreed by the great German philosopher. This kind of beneficial transmutation of the negative into the positive, to be realized in the postulated but never explained or demonstrated way, was celebrated by the thinkers who viewed the world from capital's standpoint as the *ideal* harmonization of the societal reproduction process in its entirety. Only a mysterious supra-individual agency—be that Adam Smith's "Invisible Hand," Kant's "Commercial Spirit" or Hegel's "Cunning of Reason"—could accomplish such *ideal reconciliation* of the *irreconcilable*.

Thus the projection of the supra-individual agency in place of the required social organ of *comprehensive planning,* as it would have to be instituted in reality by the freely associated *social* (and not isolated self-seeking) individuals, could create from the standpoint of political economy the *appearance* of solving the real problem. But even for creating that appearance only, it was necessary to misrepresent, first, the *fundamental social antagonism* of capitalist *class* society as the strictly *individual* conflictuality prevailing in eternalized "civil society." And second, it was also necessary to characterize the stipulated *object* of conflict itself over which the people had to confront each other as simply a matter of *individual enjoyment,* pertaining to the sphere of *consumption,* and thus *quantitatively* extendable—in Hegel's words to "everyone else." In this way the *class* determined and *structurally enforced hierarchical division of labour* —which constitutes the real ground of the capital system's irreconcilable and ultimately explosive fundamental antagonism—could be left at its place in society as before. And, paradoxically, this *dual* misrepresentation of the problem was to a remarkable extent justified, in the sense of being theoretically consistent.

It was theoretically consistent precisely as a dual distortion. For, from capital's vantage point, it was necessary to misrepresent, on the one hand, the real nature of insuperable *class* antagonism—deeply inherent in, and thus for its solution requiring the radical change of, the historically given *structural* framework of society—as purely *individual* conflicts in "civil society" (devised for the purpose), whose reconciliation would not call for any *structural change* at all in the really existing society; and on the other hand, it was also necessary to tendentiously depict the real object of conflict—the historical confrontation over two, incompatible, hegemonic alternative modes of *production,* as a straightforward matter of individual *consumption* whose magnitude could be enlarged through the readily quantifiable exchange-value of capital's self-expansionary production process. These two major aspects of the capital system's structural determinations were always closely interconnected. Thus opting for one from capital's vantage point, in tune with the absolutely necessary exclusion of any idea of structural change in the established mode of production, carried with it the requirement of embracing also the other: i.e., the confinement of all feasible remedial adjustments to the sphere of individual consumption. In this sense, there could be really no alternative way of conceptualizing the problems at stake from the standpoint of capital's political economy. For it would be inconceivable to institute in the actually existing world the required historic alternative—that is, the socially in the future unavoidable comprehensive planning of the reproduction process —without *qualitatively* overcoming on a sustainable basis the now *structurally* enforced hierarchical *division of labour* through a consciously manageable *organization of labour* in the communal organic system.

But even the mysterious supra-individual entity could not overcome the *post festum* character of planning: the only kind of planning feasible within the incurably fetishistic framework of capital's social metabolic control. For the *corrective functions* envisaged in that system, through the operation of the idealized market, must fail to qualify for the true sense of planning in two important ways. First, because they could only be *retroactive,* in response to perceived and—however reluctantly—"after the event" acknowledged miscalculations and failures. And second, because by the very nature of their retroactive modality they could only be *partial,* without any insight into the potentially far-reaching connections and ramifications of the acknowledged particular instances. Accordingly the necessary *overall foresight*—a vital defining characteristic of consciously pursued comprehensive planning in the proper sense of the term—could not play any role in it. For the necessary prerequisite for the realization of such a vital characteristic is the actual supersession of *adversariality* by not only overcoming under the historically given circumstances the established, necessarily disruptive, *vested interests,* but also by *preventing,* through the appropriate *structural change* in society, their reconstitution in the future. The political economist conception of the world, which *had to* idealize the adversariality of "egotistic" vested interests in their *individualistic* manifestations in "civil society," in order to be able to (more or less consciously) divert attention from, and thus "by proxy" legitimate and eternalize, capital's *structurally entrenched* vested interests of societal reproductive control, based on such class antagonism-producing vested interests, had no conceivable way of satisfying the conditions required for the realization of overall planning foresight even as a mysterious remedial afterthought. This explains also why even under the conditions of globally pursued monopolistic developments, irrespective of how large might be the transnational giant corporations brought into being through the irresistibly advancing concentration and centralization of capital, the pretended rationalizing solution of this fundamental defect of the capital system can only produce *partial* and largely technical/technological *post festum* "planning," without the proclaimed ability to remedy the underlying structural antagonisms.

Naturally, the genuine socialist planning process is unthinkable without overcoming the fetishism of commodity, with its perverse *quantification* of all human relations and activities. To be really meaningful, the criteria of socialist planning must be defined in *qualitative* terms, in the sense of not simply improving the productive viability of general economic processes but also directly enriching, in human terms, the life of the particular social individuals. This is the sense in which Marx was talking about the "rich human being" and "rich human need," in contrast to the fetishistic conception of wealth and poverty by political economy. For, as we have seen earlier, he insisted that "The *rich* human being is simultaneously the human being *in need of a totality of human life-activities*—the man in whom his own realization exists as an inner necessity, as *need*."[120]

This is why the communal system would have to define itself in terms of the exchange of *activities*, in direct opposition to the exchange of commodities under the rule of capital. For the fetishism of commodity prevails in capital's social metabolic order in such a way that commodities *superimpose* themselves on *need*, measuring and legitimating (or callously denying the legitimacy of) human need. This is what we are accustomed to as the normative horizon of our everyday life. The obvious alternative is to have the products themselves subjected to some meaningful criteria of evaluation on the basis of which they would be produced in response to real need, and above all in accordance with the individuals' basic need for *humanly fulfilling life-activity*. Since, however, such consideration cannot enter the framework of capitalist cost-accounting, because the organization and exercise of humanly fulfilling life-activity is an inherently *qualitative* concern (the judges of which can only be the social individuals themselves), we are not expected even to think about activities as belonging to the category of need. Naturally, even less are we expected to envisage the possibility of adopting the necessary practical measures through which we could reshape productive social intercourse on a *qualitative* basis, in harmony with the objectives which we, as freely associated producers, would set ourselves in order to gratify and further develop our genuine needs and realize our aspirations.

The important point in this respect is that if we define planning in this *qualitative* way, in its vital correlation to human need, as we must, it acquires a direct relevance in the life of every individual. For here we have a relationship of dialectical reciprocity between the general social and the individual dimension of planning. Neither of the two can work without the other. The reciprocity in question means that, on the one hand, in close consonance with the role which planning has to fulfil in the overall societal reproduction process, it simultaneously also challenges the individuals for the creation of a *meaningful* life of their own, to the highest possible degree, as real *subjects of their life-activity*. It challenges them to make sense of their own life as real *"authors"* of their own acts, in conjunction with the developing potentialities of their society of which they are themselves an integral and actively contributing part. And the reciprocity must prevail also in the other sense. For, only if the social individuals become real subjects of their life-activity and freely assume responsibility, as real authors, for their own acts in the overall social enterprise, only in that way can the general planning process lose its remoteness from the—no longer recalcitrant—particular individuals, who can fully identify themselves with the overall objectives and values of their society. In this way nothing could be further removed from the bureaucratic conception of planning, imposed on the individuals from above. On the contrary, through the dialectical reciprocity of qualitatively defined planning individual and social consciousness can really come together in the interest of positive human advancement. Indeed, this is how it becomes possible to constitute an alternative social metabolic order on a historically sustainable time scale. And that is what confers its true meaning on planning as a vital principle of the socialist enterprise.

MANY OF THE CATEGORIES OF SOCIALIST THEORY, envisaging a positive solution to humanity's apparently intractable problems, had a very long historical period of gestation. They have been advocated in some cases already thousands of years ago, including the idea of communal living, but prevented from getting anywhere near their possible realization;

partly by the missing conditions of the required productive development, and partly by the stubbornly persisting antagonisms of interchange across the overall trajectory of class societies. For the exploitation and domination of the overwhelming majority of the people by a small minority was not invented by capital. It only perfected a particular variety of structurally enforced economic, political and cultural domination, asserting itself in its general tendency on a global scale, in contrast to the more particularistic and far less efficient historical predecessors of the capital system.

This makes the challenge of viable socialist transformation that much more difficult. For partial improvements only, which leave the long established structural framework of inequality in its place, are woefully inadequate, as regularly happened in the move from one form of class society to another in the past. Nor is it feasible today to conveniently separate the "historical layers" of exploitative domination from one another, attending, in the vain hope of all-embracing success, only to the relatively recent ones through the chosen legal devices. We had to learn a very bitter lesson in that regard in the course of the twentieth century. For it proved to be totally insufficient to "expropriate the expropriators"—the private capitalists—by means of state-legislative measures in Soviet type postcapitalist societies, instituted for the announced objective of emancipating labour.

There can hardly be any doubt about it, the attainment of the highest level of productivity under the conditions of socialist development is necessary in order to satisfy human need denied on a massive scale in the course of history. Understandably, therefore, no matter how well-intentioned, any call for an equitable distribution of misery, at times sincerely advocated in the past, could only prove self-defeating. As forcefully underlined already in *The German Ideology*, "this development of productive forces . . . is an absolutely necessary practical premise, because without it privation, want is merely made general, and with want the struggle for necessities would begin again, and all the old filthy business would necessarily be restored."[121] Today, in contrast to the precarious conditions of the more remote past, sometimes naïvely idealized in utopian theories, the productive requirements of humanity's emancipation can be conquered. But they must be *conquered* by radically overcoming capital's wastefully and destructively articulated productive system before the now feasible potentialities can be turned into realities, fit for the purpose of emancipatory transformation.

At the dawn of the modern age, one of the historic aspirations pointing in the direction of a future socialist transformation was concerned with the question of productive activity itself. A most original and radical thinker of the sixteenth century, Paracelsus—one of Goethe's historical models of the "Faustian spirit"—wrote that "The proper way resides in work and action, in doing and producing; the perverse man does nothing."[122] According to him labour (Arbeit) had to be adopted as the ordering principle of society in general, to the extent of even confiscating the wealth of the idle rich, in order to compel them to lead a productive life.[123] However, the realization of such orienting principles always depends on the actual historical conditions and on the way in which the projected changes are sustainable in the overall framework of society. It was therefore by no means surprising that Marx sharply criticized the approach adopted by "crude and thoughtless communism"[124] to this problem. He pointed out that in such a crude approach "The category of *labour* is not done away with, but *extended to all men*. The relationship of *private property* persists as the relationship of the *community* to the *world of things*."[125] Thus the totally untenable postulate of "crude communism" was the retention of the alienating private property system while imagining to overcome it by extending the condition of labour to all men. In this way, self-contradictorily, "the community is only a community of *labour*, and an equality of *wages* paid out by the communal capital—the *community* as the universal capitalist. Both sides of the relationship are raised to an *imagined* universality—*labour* as a state in which every person is put, and *capital* as the acknowledged universality and power of the community."[126]

The extension of *productive activity* to all members of society is, of course, a vital principle of the socialist organization of society. But it could not be imagined as the imposition of *labour*—inherited from capital's mode of societal reproduction—with its *fetishistic/quantifying wage determinations from above,* even if positing the (never realized) "equality of wages." What was hopelessly missing from the conception of "crude and thoughtless communism" was the understanding of the *differentia specifica* of the actually given *historical* conditions under which the transformatory changes had to be made, and the need for the supersession of the antagonistic relations between capital and labour through the substantive *abolition* of private property under the circumstances, and not for its imaginary enhancement. These objective requirements were missing from the postulates of crude communism, and without them it was unthinkable to take the necessary steps towards the emancipation of labour in the only feasible *qualitative* way. For the only sense in which a —qualitatively different—conception of labour: as *self-determined productive activity,* can be extended (and should be extended) to all members of society, is the earlier quoted positive vision of the freely associated social individuals *"in need of a totality of human life-activities,"*[127] who would fulfil their autonomously determined tasks in community with each other on the basis of their *inner* necessity, their real *need.*

Equality is another category of fundamental socialist relevance with a very long period of historical gestation. Understandably, it is closely connected with the question of genuinely self-fulfilling productive activity in the life of the individuals. To be sure, it was originally conceived as *substantive* equality. For it was advocated as a type of human relationship suitable to significantly diminish discriminatory constraints and contradictions, thereby enriching the life of the individuals not only in material terms but also as a result of introducing a greater degree of fairness and justice in their interchanges with one another. Of course, there was also an obvious *class* aspect to these concerns, arguing in favour of the elimination of some pre-established and ossified measures and rules of subjection and subordination. It postulated the improvement of the general conditions of well being in society, thanks to a more enlightened and less conflict-torn management of its problems, in contrast to later *reversals* which, as a diametrical opposite, asserted that any attempt at spreading equality would unavoidably result in *levelling down* and thus bring with it the creation of *insuperable conflicts.*

The aprioristically disqualifying accusations which asserted the necessary connection between introducing a greater degree of substantive equality and the *"equitable distribution of misery"* were a typical manifestation of this line of approach, reflecting the actually existing relation of forces overwhelmingly on the side of the iniquitous established order. The brutal liquidation of François Babeuf's secret "Society of Equals" was also a clear indication of how negatively the fate of those pressing for substantive equality was sealed with the entrenchment of the new forms of inequality in the aftermath of the French Revolution. Capital's stabilized socioeconomic order, firmly securing the *structural subordination* of the subjected class of labour, could not offer scope for anything but the most restricted measures of strictly *formal* equality, confined to the legitimation of the *"contractual"* subjugation of the workers to the dominant material interests. This is how one of the great promises of the Enlightenment movement ended its days as a distant memory of a noble illusion.

However, this is by no means the end of the story itself. For with the appearance of organized labour on the historical stage, with its claims to be the carrier of a viable hegemonic alternative socioeconomic, political and cultural order, the issue of substantive equality has been reopened in a radically different way. It has been reopened in the form of asserting not the *equality of classes* but the necessity to put an end altogether to *class inequality as such* through the establishment of a *classless society*. Accordingly, the issue is defined in this revived form as most emphatically the advocacy of *substantive equality*. And this is not a *desideratum*. For the fact is that the envisaged socialist societal order is totally unworkable in any other way. In other words, the alternative in this respect is that either the idea of instituting a qualitatively different—classless—social metabolic order must be abandoned as an untenable illusion, just like the great illusions of the Enlightenment movement, or it must be practically articulated and firmly consolidated in all of its major aspects as a historically also in the long run sustainable society based on *substantive equality*.

THE REASONS FOR PRESENTING THE ISSUE in the form of this stark alternative are absolutely compelling. For the accusations levelled against those who maintain their concern with the realization of substantive equality—as hopeless "idealists" and "utopian dreamers" who are tied to the remnants of an Enlightenment illusion—are not just conveniently fashionable, even though they certainly are. There is a much more serious aspect to this kind of—behind the smiling face in fact most aggressive, and beneath the velvet glove iron fisted—critique. For, in its fallacious apologetics of the established order, it purports to be in no need of proving and substantiating its categorically dismissive position, assuming in its own favour that a vacuous disqualifying reference to an allegedly forever buried past (the unforgivably illusory Enlightenment movement) makes any proof utterly superfluous: a favourite methodological device in the service of justifying the unjustifiable.

In this way a vital terrain of practically most important theoretical contestation is ruled arbitrarily "out of bounds," on account of simply being connected with an intellectual tradition which in its time tried to genuinely respond to some major problems and grievances of the given social order, even if it was unable to do it without postulating its own illusions for solving them. The fact that the disqualified past—dismissed in the more or less visibly camouflaged interest of disqualifying the present —in truth belongs to the long *historical gestation* of a *socially irrepressible* concern, and that a legitimate critique of the Enlightenment should investigate *why* its solutions had to be in many ways illusory, due to the *underlying class determinations,* all that cannot be even mentioned. For what must be hidden from sight is the circumstance that the issue of equality itself concerns a strategically crucial orienting principle of the *necessary qualitative transformation* of the untenable established order, even if the imperative of that order's radical supersession, oriented by the principle of not formal but *substantive equality,* can only be spelled out at the present stage of historical development in the form of our stark alternative. For by aprioristically disqualifying all concern with equality they can easily do the same to all of the other seminal orienting principles of a sustainable socialist transformation of society closely linked to the requirements of substantive equality.

Redefining the fundamental conditions of the historically viable alternative mode of social metabolic reproduction in accordance with the principle of substantive equality is an essential part of the socialist strategy. For substantive equality is not just *one* of the many orienting principles of the socialist enterprise. It occupies a *key* position within the general categorial framework of labour's hegemonic alternative to the established societal reproductive order. For nearly all of the other vital orienting principles of socialist strategy can only acquire their *full meaning* in close conjunction with the requirement of substantive equality. Not in an *absolute* sense, of course, in that neither a *structural* primacy nor a *historical* antecedence could be asserted in favour of substantive equality as against the other important defining characteristics of socialist strategy, since we are concerned here with a set of dialectical interrelations and reciprocal determinations. Nevertheless, as we shall presently see, substantive equality occupies the position of *primus inter pares* (i.e. the position of the "first among equals") in this complex relationship of dialectical reciprocity, which is not only *compatible* with but also *required* by the historically unfolding, and reciprocally enriching, dialectical correlation in question. The other categorial orienting principles are not *less important* or *more negligible* but *more specific* and context-bound than substantive equality. To put it in more explicit terms, they all have a fairly direct connection with substantive equality, but not necessarily with each other, except through their complicated indirect mediations among themselves. This is why substantive equality can and must occupy the position of *primus inter pares* in an overall complex of strategic development from which *none* of the others can be omitted, nor indeed could they be even temporarily neglected for the sake of convenience.

Here are the principal classes in which the particular categories and orienting principles of the socialist strategic enterprise can be thematically related to each other, concerning: (1) the question of the established order's structurally insuperable *antagonisms,* and the hegemonic alternative way of organizing social metabolic reproduction; (2) the operating principles required for the realization of the historically sustainable form of *productive* activity in the hegemonic alternative order, and the type of *distribution* in harmony with that kind of societal reproduction; (3) the relationship between the categorial principles of *negation—vis-à-vis* capital's ruling social metabolic order—and the *inherently positive* articulation of the historic alternative; and (4) the categorial connection between the inherited, dominant *values* of society, together with the positive definition of the advocated alternatives, as well as the reassessment of the relationship between *individual and social consciousness,* including the thorny issue of "false consciousness." In all four classes the connection of the particular categories and orienting principles with substantive equality is very clear.

1. One of the most compelling reasons why labour's hegemonic alternative order is sustainable only on the basis of the institution and ongoing consolidation of substantive equality is because *adversar-*

iality—endemic to the antagonistically divided and structurally entrenched capital system of domination and subordination, assuming particularly destructive forms in our time—cannot be overcome in a lasting way without it. The *formal* devices of the societies even with the longest and most broadly diffused democratic tradition could achieve virtually nothing in this respect. On the contrary, in recent times they moved in the opposite direction, with gravely authoritarian curtailment of even the most basic constitutional and civil liberties on a growing scale. Evidently, the relationship not only between humanity and nature but also between states and nations, as well as among the particular individuals, must be *mediated* in all conceivable forms of society. Perilously for the future of humankind, the capital system is incapable of operating in any other way than through the imposition—whenever needed by the most violent means, including potentially catastrophic world wars—of *antagonistic forms and modalities of mediation* (through the hierarchical discriminatory class structure and through the force exercised by the capitalist state). Only on the basis of substantive equality is it possible to envisage the necessary *non-antagonistic* forms of mediation among human beings at all levels, in a historically sustainable way. It is also important to press in this context that what is at stake is not a question of abstract social determinations, capable of being imposed from above in the manner of the inherited forms of authoritarian decision making typical of capital's mode of social metabolic control. Since the decisions taken directly affect the life of *every particular individual,* non-antagonistic mediation, through their active participation in the vital material productive, political and cultural domain, is conceivable only on a—not fictitiously "tacit," vacuous formal, or arbitrarily manufactured—but meaningfully *consensual* basis. And that again underlines the relevance of substantive equality.

2. The historic challenge concerning the established mode of *production* and *societal reproduction* is clearly manifest in our time in relation to some major issues. In none of them could the underlying problems be conceptualized in generic social terms, because

they cannot be abstracted from the particular social *individuals,* with their *qualitative* needs and motivations, calling for appropriate solutions in the same sense. Since going into the details on these matters would take far too long, in the present context it is only possible to briefly enumerate them.[128] We have already seen in this regard one of the key operative principles of the socialist alternative, concerned with *planning* in the proper sense of the term, as opposed to its unviable *post festum* varieties under the now prevailing sociohistorical conditions. It is necessary to add to that vital concern some equally important issues directly connected with a number of socialist orienting principles that must become deeply rooted in order to supersede capital's wasteful reproductive order by labour's hegemonic alternative. These concerns can be recognized in the often unrealistically treated relationship between *scarcity* and *abundance,* as well as in the way in which the category of qualitatively defined real human *need* is tendentiously confused with capitalistically convenient *artificial appetites* which can be manipulatively imposed on the individuals in the service of commodity production. In the same context, it is also important to critically examine the valid criteria of really sustainable productive *economy,* inseparable from the meaningful and absolutely necessary demand for *economizing* (crucial also in relation to the question of overcoming scarcity), together with the long-standing socialist advocacy of managing the societal reproduction process in accordance with the qualitative criteria of *disposable time,* in contrast to capital's wasteful and irresponsible *self-expansionary* drive—blindly pursued no matter how dangerous the consequences of uncontrollable capital-expansion imposed on society in the name of quasi-mythical "beneficial growth"—and their relationship to the system's quantifying and necessarily constraining reified time-accountancy. Obviously, the successful operation of the required orienting principle of production and distribution in an advanced socialist order—"from each according to their *abilities,* to each according to their *needs*" —is inconceivable without the conscious acceptance and active promotion of substantive equality by the social individuals. But it should be equally clear that the *qualitative* definition and operation of *disposable time*—the potential source of the real (and not narrowly commodified) wealth of both the new social order in general and of the "rich social individuals" in its Marxian sense—has a dual sense. On the one hand, it means the total disposable time of society as a whole, rationally planned and allocated to the chosen purposes, instead of being dictated by the crude economic determinations of capital's exploitative pursuit of profitable minimal time. But the other sense of disposable time is no less important. It cannot be even imagined without the fully consensual contribution of their meaningful life-activity by the particular individuals, as discussed in the context of genuine planning. And a necessary condition of turning such potentialities into reality, of which so much else depends for making the alternative order historically sustainable, is again the conscious adoption of substantive equality by all concerned.

3. Naturally, the alternative order of society cannot be instituted without successfully *negating* in the real world capital's deeply entrenched mode of social metabolic reproduction. In that sense, *negation* is an essential part of the socialist enterprise under the prevailing historical circumstances. Indeed, in its immediate concerns it is not simply negation but, inevitably at the same time, *"the negation of the negation."* For the social adversary asserts its rule in the form of negating not only the actuality but even the most remote possibility of human emancipation. This is why the immediate task must be defined in socialist literature as "the negation of the negation." However, such a negative definition of the socialist challenge is very far from being able to fulfil the historic mandate in question, because it remains *in dependency* to what it tries to negate. In order to succeed in the envisaged historic sense, the socialist approach must define itself in *inherently positive* terms. Marx made this absolutely clear when he insisted that "Socialism is man's *positive self-consciousness,* no longer mediated through the annulment of religion, just as *real life* is man's positive reality, no longer mediated through the annulment of private proper-

ty."[129] A social order, remaining dependent on the object of its negation, no matter how justified in its original historic terms, cannot offer the required scope for the "rich human being" whose richness is said to arise from his meaningful life-activity "as an inner necessity, as *need"*: an inherently *positive* determination. For the negative definition of the social setting itself in which the individuals must act, on a continuing basis, would necessarily *prejudge* and *contradict*—through its own negativity—the *aims and objectives* which the social individuals are expected to *autonomously and freely* set themselves in an *open-ended* historical order. Moreover, also in general societal terms, the requirement of *non-antagonistic mediation* of humanity's relationship with the natural order, as well as the appropriate regulation of the *co-operative* interchanges of the particular social individuals among themselves, cannot be imagined in terms of the negation of the negation. The vital defining characteristic of the only viable mediating modality of the alternative historical order is *self-mediation.* But to postulate self-mediation in a negative way would be also a contradiction in terms. Naturally, on the basis of these important qualifying conditions it hardly needs adding that the orienting and operative principle of substantive equality is a necessary constituent of *socialism as humanity's "positive self-consciousness."*

4. The values necessarily inherited from capital's mode of social metabolic control, with its ferocious cultivation of whatever seems to accord with the system's practical imperative of structurally entrenched domination and subordination, are totally inadequate for the realization of the objectives of the socialist order. We could see earlier in which way and to what extent the once advocated ideals—like liberty, fraternity and equality, for instance—had to be completely emptied of their erstwhile content in the course of capital's descending phase of development. All connection with the Enlightenment tradition of the progressive bourgeoisie had to be, and actually has been, broken, and references to "liberty" and "democracy" today are cynically used in the service of oppressive, often even the most brutally violent, even if hypocritically pack-

aged, state political and genocidal military purposes. The deliberate cultivation and diffusion of false consciousness by the ruling ideology, thanks to its virtual monopoly of the means and devices of mass communication, greatly reinforced by the dominant practices of capital's fetishistic productive order, belongs to the same picture. Understandably, therefore, the radical alternative of the new historical order must be consistently articulated also in the domain of values. One of the principal requirements in this respect is that all of the advocated values, not only equality, have to emerge from actually unfolding social practice and be defined in *substantive* terms. It was a major characteristic of the conceptualizations of capital's reproductive order, even in its ascending phase of development, that—due to the system's ineradicable *class* divisions and contradictions—the substantive dimension was pushed into the background and the *formal* definition of the positive values was offered in its place. It is enough to remind ourselves of Kant's treatment of the question of *equality* in this respect.[130] Obviously, the value of *freedom* (or *liberty)* needs as much a substantive determination of its commendable nature in the socialist reproductive order as *equality*. The same goes for *solidarity, co-operation* and *responsibility,* to name only a few of the most important values in labour's hegemonic alternative order. All such concepts, in company with equality and freedom, could be reduced to their formalized skeleton, as they were in fact characteristically transfigured, in as much as they were advocated at all, even in the progressive capitalist past. They acquire their legitimacy in the socialist societal framework only if they are adopted as values and orienting principles in their genuine—and most important—substantive sense. Another vital aspect of this problem is that the value determinations of the socialist order cannot positively prevail unless individual and social consciousness are properly brought together in actual social practice. And that is possible only if the values in question can be autonomously realized, in their substantive reality, by the particular social individuals as freely associated producers. That is the only way to avoid the danger of "re-establishing 'Society' as an abstraction *vis-à-vis* the individual," to recall Marx's warning.

THE CATEGORIAL REFLECTION OF SOCIAL ANTAGONISM from the vantage point of capital was always problematical, and it has become progressively worse with the passing of time. Naturally, there were some powerful reasons for that. Thus, in any attempt to find enduring solutions to these issues, it is necessary to underline the key role of transformatory social practice. As we have seen in chapter 6, the dualisms and dichotomies of the post-Cartesian philosophical tradition have arisen from the soil of a determinate social practice, burdened with its insoluble problems. They were representative conceptualizations of deeply rooted *practical antinomies.* To think of theoretically resolving them, simply by means of the adoption of a different categorial framework, would be quite unreal. It is true, of course, that revolutionary practice is unthinkable without the contribution of revolutionary theory. Nevertheless, the primacy belongs to emancipatory practice itself. One cannot anticipate the solution of the difficult and in so many ways intertwined problems discussed in this section in any other way; without envisaging, that is, the institution of an alternative social order from which the *practical antinomies and contradictions* of capital's mode of societal reproduction are effectively removed.

8.6 Methodological Aspects of Mediation in an Epoch of Transition

With regard to method, *mediation* is both the theoretically and the practically most important category in our epoch of historical transition. There can be nothing surprising about that. Theoretically, because in view of the magnitude of the challenge we have to face, nothing can be successfully accomplished without an *intellectually coherent* and truly *comprehensive* conception of mediation. And practically, because it is unthinkable to institute in the established social order the required *qualitative* changes without adopting the appropriate forms of *practical mediation* that could make our inescapable mode of social metabolic reproduction—as *self-mediating* beings of *nature* who must secure even on the longest term basis their conditions of existence in a fully adequate interactive relationship with nature—historically viable in the future. Such qualitative changes are absolutely necessary because the existing order of societal reproduction, under the rule of capital, is rendered utterly unsustainable by the growing destructiveness of its deeply entrenched and ultimately explosive structural antagonisms.

In theoretical and political discourse conforming to the vantage point of capital in the descending phase of the system's development the question of mediation is as a rule trivialized. It tends to be reduced to an apologetic core of the concept, concerned with nothing more than the manipulative requirements of securing the perpetuation of the established relations. This is why the vitally important issue of mediation is defined as *"balancing"* the identified forces of potential or real conflict, in the interest of a projected *reconciliatory accommodation;* and even that concerned in its scope with strictly marginal detail, which would of course leave the *structural* determinations of the established order totally unchanged. What remains hidden in this kind of conception is the fact that the pretended rationality of "balancing" and "enlightened self-interested accommodation" conform to the crude reality of the pre-established, and on a continuing basis necessarily reimposed, *relation of forces* of capital's structurally entrenched hierarchical order of domination and subordination, and that, consequently, the idealized "consensual balancing" is a *sham* to which under capital's rule there can be *"no alternative,"* as it is at times even explicitly acknowledged.

In contrast to the structural apologetics of "balancing" and "accommodation," the question of real mediation in our historical epoch of transition can only be meaningfully defined as the *radical restructuring* of the established order as such, aimed at overcoming its structural antagonisms and the destructiveness arising from them. This is feasible only if the *historical subject* called upon to institute such transformation is really in control of the envisaged process of radical restructuring, as a genuine *self-mediating* and *self-controlling subject,* instead of being subjected to the fetishistic structural interests and determinations conceived from the vantage point of the capital system, including the postulated, and by definition insurmountable, all-embracing rules of the capitalist state within the confines of which all fictitiously "enlightened balancing and accommodation," nakedly at the cost of labour as the only viable alternative historical subject, must be accomplished.

All self-justifying conceptions of the capitalist state, even its most progressive varieties, like the political ideals of early liberalism, must postulate a nebulously defined (if defined at all) active subject at the apex of the state. Sometimes they do this by even openly admitting, as Hegel undoubtedly does so, as we have seen his words to this effect above,[131] that the Monarch at the apex of the idealized state has nothing much to do and decide on his own. They all need a nebulously defined commanding subject in order to impose through the state conceived in that way—by definition and in an *eternalized* form—a *separate authority* on the contesting parties, excluding thereby the possibility of the actually existing subordinate force gaining control of the ongoing historical process. And in a paradoxical sense worse than that. For the willing *personifications of capital* by no means could rightfully claim to be in control of the overall social and historical process. This is why even the greatest thinkers who conceptualize the world from capital's vantage point must resort to quasi-mythical explanatory schemes, like Adam Smith's "invisible hand" and Hegel's "Cunning of Reason."

Once, however, that kind of strategy is adopted, the concept of *mediation itself* becomes *ipso facto* emptied of its content in that the rather mysteriously stipulated authority nullifies the possibility of meaningful mediation by definitionally appropriating to itself the power of *decision making,* even if in Hegel's revealing words of admission the visible authority, like his Monarch, does not decide anything at all. Thus, within such a framework of aprioristically prejudged and utterly one-sided decision making, the process of "mediation"—irrespective of how much it might be idealized as "enlightened balancing"—can only be an empty ritual of pretended consensual *accommodation,* imposed by capital's structurally prevailing, ruthlessly hierarchical, material determinations and by the conveniently corresponding *"force of circumstance."* Significantly, by the time we reach the fully articulated parliamentary system, in its present-day variety, the accommodatory "consensual balancing and agreement" is *guaranteed* from the outset, with more or less open cynicism and hypocrisy, through the given machinery of conformist political decision making, ritualistically revered in the name of "democracy and liberty" to which in reality nothing more corresponds than the established "one party system with two right wings," in Gore Vidal's apt characterization.[132]

NATURALLY, CAPITAL'S SOCIAL ORDER is not without its *objective* system of mediations, even if the real nature of the prevailing modality of mediation is mystifyingly transformed—and *must be* mystifyingly transformed—in the theoretical images depicted and ideologically rationalized from the standpoint of the capital system itself. In fact no social formation ever had a more all-pervasive system of mediations than the socioeconomic and political order of capital, with its general tendency to imposing its material determinations and their cultural/ideological corollaries across the whole of the planet. Indeed, in a most important sense the constitution of capital's social order is identical to the emergence and consolidation of its unique system of inescapable objective mediations.

However, the intractable problem is that they are not simply *first order mediations*—without which human beings, as *self-mediating* beings of *nature,* could not secure at all their conditions of existence in a necessary and fully adequate interactive relationship with nature even in the most advanced form of society, as mentioned before—but *antagonistic second order mediations* which must be ruthlessly imposed on society in the interest of capital-accumulation and in the service of the capital system's ever-extended reproduction, no matter how destructive might be the consequences, including the potential destruction of humankind itself. Thus capital's *"universalizing tendency"* could not be more perilously *self-contradictory* in view of its ultimately untenable—that is, totally self-oriented, and under all conceivable historical circumstances nothing but crudely self-asserting/self-oriented—*antagonistic partiality.* At the same time, in order to be able to *eternalize* the prevailing socioeconomic and political order, as "the natural system of perfect liberty and justice" (Adam Smith), and even as "absolutely the end of history" (Hegel), as quoted already, the incurably *antagonistic* nature of the capital system's second order mediations *must be* mystifyingly transformed by the thinkers who adopt capital's standpoint into something not just tenable for a shorter or longer duration of time but into the insuperable *ideal,* fully in tune with the innermost requirements of Reason itself.

Already at a relatively early stage of development of bourgeois theory one of the most telling ways of trying to overcome the deficiencies of antagonistic second order mediations was a sharp separation of *"civil society"* from the *political state.* This separation was envisaged as a way of finding remedies to the material antagonisms of the individuals in so-called civil society through the postulated overarching rational reconciliatory functions of the state. However, the envisaged theoretical solution of simply assuming the claimed relationship between "civil society"—torn apart by its antagonisms—and the political state (which was supposed to overcome them, or at least to keep them indefinitely in balance), was extremely problematical, to put it mildly. The Hegelian conception occupies a prominent place in this respect.

The main deficiency of Hegel's approach to this issue was the role which he assigned to mediation in his theory of the relationship between the state and civil society. He realized that if the state was to fulfil the vital function of totalization and reconciliation attributed to it in his system, it had to be constituted as an *organic* entity. In that spirit he was asserting that "It is a prime concern of the state that a *middle class* should be developed, but this can be done only if the state is an organic unity, i.e., it can be done only by *giving authority to spheres of particular interests,* which are relatively independent, and by appointing an army of officials whose personal arbitrariness is broken against such authorised bodies." The trouble is, though, that the picture we are offered here is nothing but a speculative/idealized transubstantiation of the political state-formation of divided "civil society." A society that continues to maintain all the existing divisions and contradictions while stipulatively conjuring away their ultimate destructiveness. As Marx had put it in his comments appended to the lines just quoted from Hegel: "To be sure the people can appear as one class, the middle class, only in such an organic unity; but is something that keeps itself going by means of the *counterbalancing of privileges* an organic unity?"[133]

Thus the envisaged solution is even self-contradictory (defining "organicity" in terms of a perilously unstable "counterbalancing" of hostile centrifugal forces), not to mention its fictitious character which predicates a *permanent* remedy on the basis of an ever-intensifying conflictuality. In reality the modern political state was not constituted at all as an "organic unity" but, on the contrary, was imposed upon the *subordinate* classes of the *materially* already prevailing power relations of "civil society," in the preponderant (and not carefully "counterbalanced") interest of capital. Thus the Hegelian idea of "mediation" could only be a false mediation, motivated by the ideological needs of "reconciliation," "legitimation," and "rationalization." As Marx observes on the apologetic character of the Hegelian circularity of mediation speculatively prevailing in his "civil society" and the state:

> If civil classes as such are political classes, then the mediation is not needed; and if this mediation is needed, then the civil class is not political, and thus also not this mediation. . . . Here, then, we find one of Hegel's inconsistencies within his own way of reviewing things: and such *inconsistency* is an *accommodation.*[134]

Thus the Hegelian concept of mediation reveals itself as a sophisticated speculative reconstruction of the ahistorically assumed reconciliatory dualism between "civil society" and the state, and not a real mediation at all. As Marx puts it: "In general, Hegel conceives of the syllogism as middle term, a *mixtum compositum.* We can say that in his development of the rational syllogism all of the transcendence and mystical dualism of his system becomes apparent. The middle term is the wooden sword, the concealed opposition between universality and singularity."[135] And talking about the role assigned by Hegel to the relationship between the Monarch and the Estates of civil society Marx underlines the utterly fictitious and also self-contradictory character of the postulated mediation:

> The sovereign, then, had to be the middle term in the legislature between the executive and the Estates, and the Estates between him and civil society. How is he to mediate between what he himself needs as a mean lest his own existence becomes a one-sided extreme? Now the complete absurdity of these extremes, which interchangeably play now the part of the extreme and now the part of the mean, becomes apparent. . . .
>
> This is a kind of *mutual reconciliation society*. . . . It is like the lion in *A Midsummer Night's Dream* who exclaims: 'I am the lion, and I am not the lion, but Snug.' So here each extreme is sometimes the lion of opposition and sometimes the Snug of mediation. Hegel, who reduces this absurdity of mediation to its abstract logical, and hence pure and irreducible, expression, calls it at the same time the speculative mystery of logic, the rational relationship, the rational syllogism. *Actual extremes cannot be mediated* with each other precisely because they are actual extremes. But neither are they in need of mediation, because they are

> opposed in essence. They have nothing in common with one another; they neither need nor complement one another.[136]

Conceiving mediation as the self-serving instrumentality of a *"mutual reconciliation society"* hopelessly—but revealingly—misrepresents the actual state of affairs. For there is no *mutuality* at all in the actual, structurally established and enforced, strictly hierarchical power relationship that must remain permanent in capital's socioeconomic and political order for as long as such an antagonistic order—based on the materially established subordination and exploitation of labour—can survive. Moreover, the political dimension of this order is not a conveniently fictionalizable separate entity of "rational actuality" but an *integral* part of the system as a whole, with its ultimately unmanageable *irrationalist post festum modality* of social metabolic reproduction. It represents the overall command structure of a deeply integrated system through which the capitalist state can provide the *ultimate guarantee* for the perpetuation of the materially well established antagonistic power relations of domination and subordination, with *capital* and not the imaginarily *"mediating sovereign"* at its apex. In that way the capitalist state, inextricably intertwined with its antagonistic material base, can regulate under normal circumstances the overall political interchange of its various class constituents and politically *enforce* the system's primary determinations (including its legally codified material *property* relations), if needed even with the most violent means—in sharp contrast to the nebulous speculative postulate of insuperable and universally benevolent rationality—in the event of any major crisis.

It is precisely this relationship of structural domination and subordination that must be by mystification transformed and speculatively transubstantiated into an allegedly well and truly *"mediated"* ideal setup of "rational actuality" even in the greatest of all bourgeois theoretical conceptions, as we find it in Hegel. So that the actuality of the capital system's incurable *antagonistic mediations*—whose categorial reflections we have seen on the pages of the last section—should appear organically interrelated and perfectly mediated as well as fully balanced even in its minor conflictual details, removing thereby in the theoretical construct the signs of the deepening structural deficiencies and contradictions of the ultimately explosive socioeconomic and political order, in the interest of asserting its eternalizable rationality and material permanence as the insuperable system of "perfect liberty and justice." Accordingly, what must disappear without a trace through such mystifying theoretical transformation and self-contradictory speculative pseudo-mediation is the sobering fact that "*actual extremes cannot be mediated* with each other precisely because they are actual extremes."

The objective structural antagonism between capital and labour, as systemic alternatives to one another, is the most obvious and the most pressing example of that sobering fact. There can be no reconciliatory mediation between capital and labour, since they are in a potentially most unstable way—only for a determinate historical period—combined *actual extremes*. Capital is a fetishistic material force which can only *dominate* labour by ruthlessly enforcing—with all means at its disposal, including its state machinery—the objective imperatives of its self-expansionary drive. If it fails to do so, the capital system implodes. Thus rationally regulative human concerns and corresponding values must be a priori excluded from capital's self-expansionary calculations, excluding thereby the possibility of any mediatory concession to labour for *sharing* the role of control, which is grotesquely asserted in all mediatory mythology. At the same time, at the opposite pole of the now antagonistically mediated as well as materially enforced—and consequently in the longer run totally unsustainable—social metabolism, labour as the historic alternative to capital's blind self-expansionary societal reproduction cannot even begin to institute its qualitatively different mode of managing the required rational relationship to nature and among the individuals themselves. Attempting to do so—that is, attempting to incorporate, in the name of the stipulated reconciliatory "mediation" and accommodation, capital's *fetishistic irrationality* into labour's *consciously planned* mode of social metabolic reproduction, oriented by comprehensive foresight—could only be another version of the *absurdity* deplored by Marx in relation to Hegel.

It cannot be stressed enough, actual extremes cannot be mediated precisely because they are actual extremes. This is why the only feasible solution is the *radical structural change* of the established order, in terms of its innermost objective determinations, guided by the all-embracing objective of instituting a historically viable mode of social metabolic reproduction. It means the necessity of instituting a qualitatively different mode of societal reproduction, characterized by the *non-antagonistic mediation* between humanity and nature and among the freely cooperating social individuals themselves. And that can be achieved only by irreversibly overcoming capital's increasingly more destructive *second order mediations,* and not by a wishful reconciliatory tinkering with the constituents of the ruling order of which we have seen countless failed attempts in the past, irrespective of how outstanding might have been the thinkers who in their time advocated it, like Hegel.

THE STRUCTURAL INCOMPATIBILITY between labour's "new historic form" and capital's established order—an incompatibility which necessarily excludes the possibility of mediating and organically combining the two —presents a fundamental challenge in all fields, from the most elementary and direct material relations to the most mediated and comprehensive political and cultural interchanges of the social body. This means that a way must be found from the self-serving blind determinacy of capital's regulatory system—in which even the "personifications of capital" can only *obey* the objective material imperatives of their mode of expanded reproduction, even if such unconscious structural determinacy is idealized by them as the superior guiding force of the "invisible hand" and the ultimate ordering principle of the universe itself depicted as the "Cunning of Reason"—to a future modality of comprehensive reproductive rationality.

Thus the meaning of the necessary mediation in our epoch of transition is nothing mysterious, in conrast to the nebulous speculative transubstantiation of capital's structurally enforced material dictates (amounting in reality to the crude prevalence of *antagonistic mediation)* into a "consensual" balancing and universally self-interested accommodation. In other words, mediation in an epoch of transition can only be envisaged as the coherent elaboration and practical institution of the operative principles of societal interchange through which labour's hegemonic alternative to capital's antagonistic order—that is, the hegemonic alternative called "the new historic form," with its *comprehensive rationality* arising from the conscious determinations of its individual members—can sustain itself as a viable mode of social metabolic control.

The only viable and indefinitely sustainable mediation between humanity and nature and among the social individuals themselves, as the defining characteristic of the new historic form, is inconceivable without an *active social subject* who can *autonomously* intervene in the ongoing social process. In that sense, the mediation in question can acquire its proper meaning only if it is *self-mediation* of the social individuals who exercise their genuine *control* over the societal reproduction process as *freely associated real subjects* of their *comprehensively planned* action, together with the practical details of its implementation. That is, the concepts of *self-control, self-mediation,* and the *genuine autonomy* of the *consciously acting* real *historical subjects* all must go together if we wish to confer a tangible and viable meaning on the idea of mediation, in place of the speculative postulates which we have seen above, suitable only for obfuscating and idealizing the hierarchically enforced power relations of antagonistic mediation that rule the now established order. It is precisely this set of closely intertwined requirements of consciously self-assertive action, representing the genuine reproductive control exercised by the rationally self-mediating social subjects, that is—and *must be*—missing from capital's social order. This is why there could be no question of finding a solution to the pressing problems of our systemic crisis by an imaginary "reconciliatory mediation" of the established mode of social metabolic reproduction with the new historic form.

The growing destructiveness of the existing order is inseparable from capital's *fetishistic quantification:* the only conceivable modality of the capital system's reproductive practices. However, it is unthinkable to switch to a *qualitatively oriented* modality of societal reproduction, so as to overcome the contradictions of capital's escalating *destructive production*, without determining the targets as well as the forms of productive activity on the basis of the consciously assessed and legitimated *real needs* of the productively active human subjects. A qualitatively oriented mode of operation is feasible only in terms of a *genuine socialist accountancy* made possible through the self-determined allocation of their *disposable time* by the freely associated producers, in contrast to the wasteful *artificial appetites* that must be imposed upon society as a whole and upon the particular individuals because such appetites more or less automatically arise from the system's reified self-expansionary imperatives, in conjunction with the anachronistic but profitable exploitation of necessary labour time, whatever might be the human and ecological consequences.

The insurmountable problem for the established order is that only a real human subject, with its genuine needs and corresponding values, can offer a historically viable alternative to capital's fetishistic and destructive way of regulating the societal reproduction process. However, capital as the commanding force of reproductive interchange can never qualify for other than being a *usurping subject,* no matter how much it dominates through its objectively prevailing structural imperatives the social metabolic process. It is inevitably *parasitic on labour.* which is and must always remain the *real productive subject.*

Naturally, this is not a *symmetrical* relationship, since labour itself is by no means dependent on capital for its very existence, even if under determinate historical circumstances that may appear to be the case, as eagerly (but falsely) asserted by the ideologists of the capital system. By the same token, the unavoidable *false consciousness* of capital itself, with all of its potential and real negative consequences, is erected on the foundation of expropriating to itself the role of the historical subject—which it is capable of doing only in an extremely restricted sense, within the constraining strait-jacket of the fetishism of commodity—and therefore its strategic vision, concerning what might or might not be sustainable in the future is necessarily confined to what must be dictated by the interests and self-expansionary imperatives of commodity society. And while this kind of innermost structural determination is thoroughly compatible with a great productive (and reproductive) dynamism for a long historical period, it also carries with it the danger of catastrophic consequences once the objective conditions of historical development call for the *conscious and radical reassessment* of the road to follow. Especially when nothing less than the very survival of the human species is at stake.

Thus the radical incompatibility of the new historic form with the capital system's antagonistic mediations makes it amply clear that we are concerned with two *qualitatively* different historical conceptions. The fetishistic objectivity of capital's vantage point precludes the possibility of grasping the levers of a real, open-ended, historical movement, because the alienated actuality of the established structural hierarchy of domination and subordination, at the expense of labour as the real productive subject, cannot be challenged from capital's vantage point. Accordingly, in the theoretical images depicting the world from capital's standpoint the historically established system of *alienation* must be transformed into a *permanent* condition of human existence itself. In ideological rationalizations this is accomplished as a rule by means of the false identification of *objectivity in general* with the capitalistic *historical specificity of alienation.* And, of course, that freezes at the same time the system of capital's *antagonistic mediations* as *ontologically* insurmountable, nullifying thereby the possibility of instituting a historically viable alternative order of *non-antagonistic emancipatory mediations.*

We can see a clear example of this approach in Heidegger's mystifying characterization of the Marxian conception of history, presenting it with what seems to be a positive rejoinder and an unqualified approval. In truth, however, Heidegger's left-handed "praise" totally divests Marx's views of their critical substance. This is how Heidegger describes Marx's importance: "Because Marx, through his experience of the *alienation of modern man,* is aware of a *fundamental dimension of history,* the Marxist view of history is superior to all other views."[137] Naturally, Marx did not experience alienation as "the alienation of modern man," but as the alienation of man under the rule of capital. Nor did he look upon alienation as a "fundamental dimension of history," but as a vital issue of a given *phase* of history. By depicting Marx's historical conception in the way we find it transfigured in our quote, the Heideggerian mystification removes precisely the substance of the Marxian approach. For by identifying the alienation of labour, with all of its corollaries, as the strategically vital factor of a determinate and *surmountable phase* of historical development, which happens to assert itself for as long as the rule of capital can prevail, the founder of scientific socialism lays the stress on the necessity of *regaining control* over the historical process, insisting at the same time that this must be and can be done by *restituting* the power of control to the *real historical subject, labour.* This is what is made to disappear through Heidegger's identification of capitalist historical specificity (of which only the vacuously used word "modern" remains in his scheme of things) with "alienation as a fundamental dimension of history" conceived as a reified and ontologically inflated objectivity.

In the same vein as in Heidegger, as also in the conception of Jean Hyppolite, the historical specificity of alienation is mystifyingly transformed into an ontological absolute, decreed to be inseparable from human existence itself and from self-consciousness as such. He writes with direct reference to Marx's critique of Hegel's identification of alienation and objectification that "The author of the *Phenomenology of Mind*, of the *Encyclopaedia of the Philosophical Sciences*, and *The Philosophy of History,* did not confound the alienation of the human spirit in history with objectification without some valid reason . . . The fact that man, by objectifying himself in culture, in the State, in human work in general, at the same time alienates himself, makes himself other, and discovers in this objectification an *insurmountable otherness,* this is a *tension inseparable from existence itself . . . and from human self-consciousness.*"[138]

In this way, both in Heidegger and in Hyppolite, the road is blocked to any attempt that might be envisaged as engagement in an emancipatory intervention in the ongoing historical process. That process is said to be ruled by the "alienation of modern man" as the "fundamental dimension" of history itself. "Existence" is arbitrarily postulated as an inalterable ontological absolute, and its alienated/alienating manifestations therefore can be absolved from all possible blame as the "objectified but insurmountable" determinations of a—forever frozen—history. The antagonistic mediations of the established system of (allegedly "ontological") alienations must likewise forever prevail. Accordingly, there can be no question of a non-antagonistic order of mediations as a viable historical alternative. In other words, capital's alienated and reified second order mediations must be forever accepted as the absolutely insurmountable "fundamental dimension of history" into which human "existence" as such must be locked to the end of time. Notwithstanding its pretentious "deep existentialist" presentation, nothing could hammer home more crudely the inhuman propaganda of "there is no alternative" than its claimed identity to such speculatively and apologetically postulated "fundamental dimension of history."

HOWEVER, WITHOUT DRAWING A FIRM LINE of demarcation between alienation and objectification—not by romantically denying that alienation is a form of objectification but by clearly identifying the social and historical specificity of its character—the question of *restituting* the power of decision making to the real producing subject and thereby envisaging the *conscious control* of the historical process cannot be even raised, let alone turned into reality. For drawing that line of demarcation is not just one idea among many but an absolutely fundamental one.

This is well illustrated by Lukács's account, in 1967, of the great liberating effect exercised in his intellectual development when he had the opportunity to read in 1930, still in manuscript, Marx's at that time deciphered *Economic and Philosophic Manuscripts of 1844* in which that idea first appeared:

> I can still remember even today the overwhelming effect produced in me by Marx's statement that objectivity was the primary material attribute of all things and relations. . . . objectification is a natural means by which man masters the world and as such it can be either a positive or a negative fact. By contrast, alienation is a special variant of that activity that becomes operative in definite social conditions. This completely shattered the theoretical foundations of what had been the particular achievement of *History and Class Consciousness.* The book became wholly alien to me just as my earlier writings had become by 1918–19. It suddenly became clear to me that if I wished to give body to these new theoretical insights I would have to start again from scratch.[139]

This account is all the more important because many intellectuals, including Merleau-Ponty,[140] tried to use the author of *History and Class Consciousness*—in an attempt to disqualify the Marxian conception of history—against the major positive achievements of Lukács's post-1930 books, unthinkable without the radical turn in his philosophical orientation in the spirit of the necessary critical assessment of the relationship between alienation and objectification as described in our last quote. It is a measure of Lukács, as a man and as a thinker, that in 1930, with some world famous books behind him, like *Soul and Form, The Theory of the Novel,* and even *History and Class Consciousness,* he can actually "start from scratch" and carry his project to a rich conclusion under very difficult historical circumstances, when he must often write "in an Aesopic language," as he later puts it. Just as it is a measure of the unfolding crisis of the capital system that many important intellectuals—including

Maurice Merleau-Ponty[141]—do not hesitate to retreat from their once progressive stance and move in the opposite direction, whenever needed even directly contradicting their earlier position.

The point of the often contorted mystificatory attempts aimed at disqualifying the Marxian conception of history is that by undoing the necessary line of demarcation between alienation and objectification capital's alienated and reified second order mediations should be proclaimed to constitute the eternalized horizon of all social life. In this way, by glorifying at the same time the *usurping subject*, capital—irrespective of whether this is done explicitly or by implication—as the only conceivable controller of societal reproduction under the conditions appropriate to "modern man," we must also accept the fateful insuperability of the capital system as such, since it is said to be prescribed by alienation as nothing less weighty than the "fundamental dimension of history."

The Marxian conception of history, foreshadowing a necessary transition to a radically different system of—non-antagonistic—mediations, projects the outlines of a very different social metabolic order in which humanly fulfilling objectification is *extricated* from its alienated and reified integument, thanks to the comprehensive conscious foresight and action of the real historical subject of production, labour, oriented by *quality* based on human need, in contrast to *fetishistic quantification* insuperable under capital's rule. The reified objectivity blindly dominating capital's social metabolic order is eloquently described by Marx in relation to the overpowering role of money:

> If *money* is the bond binding me to *human* life, binding society to me, binding me and nature and man, is not money not the bond of all *bonds?* Can it not dissolve and bind all ties? It is the true *agent of divorce* as well as the true *binding agent*—the universal *galvano-chemical* power of society. . . . [F]rom imagination to life, from imagined being into real being. In effecting this mediation, money is the *truly creative* power. . . . Money, then, appears as this *overturning* power, both against the individual and against the bonds of society . . . Since money, as the existing and active concept of value confounds and exchanges all things, it is the general *confounding* and *compounding* of all things—the world upside down—the confounding and compounding of all natural and human qualities.[142]

If some people think that this characterization of the alienating role of money represents the "immature views of young Marx," they should think again. For they can find the same approach in Marx's *Capital* where he writes:

> With the possibility of holding and *storing up exchange-value* in the shape of a particular commodity, arises also the greed for gold. Along with the extension of circulation, increases the *power of money,* that absolutely social form of wealth ever ready for use. 'Gold is a wonderful thing! Whoever possesses it is lord of all he wants. By means of gold one can even get souls to Paradise.'[143] . . . Everything becomes saleable and buyable. The circulation becomes the great social retort into which everything is thrown, to come out again as a gold-crystal. Not even are the bones of saints, and still less are more delicate res sacrosanctae, extra commercium hominum able to withstand this *alchemy.* Just as every *qualitative* difference is *extinguished in money,* on its side, like the *radical leveller* that it is, does away with *all distinctions.* But money itself is a commodity, an external object, capable of becoming the private property of any individual. Thus *social power* becomes the *private power* of private persons. The ancients therefore denounced money as subversive of the economic and moral order of things. Modern society . . . greets gold as its Holy Grail, as the glittering incarnation of the very principle of its own life.[144]

Indeed, in a long footnote attached to the words "all distinctions" above, Marx incorporates in *Capital* even the lines he quoted on pages 137–8 of his *Economic and Philosophic Manuscripts of 1844* from Shakespeare's *Timon of Athens.*

Since capital's established social metabolic order, with its fetishistic system of ever more destructive second order mediations, is not sustainable, the unavoidable challenge is to institute in its place a qualitatively different and historically viable alternative. Money as the "Holy Grail" and the "life principle" of societal reproductive interchange, asserting its antagonistically mediating power as the "universal *galvano-chemical* power of society"—and is in that way imposed ubiquitously as the social power expropriated from the real producers by being turned into "the private power of private persons"—is devoid of all human consideration and can only lead to universal disaster through the assertion of its perverse *alchemy* under the conditions of the capital system's deepening structural crisis. The societal reproductive practice of storing up exchange-value in money—wantonly idealized and eternalized already in the philosophy of John Locke—is storing up the potentially most explosive antagonisms for the future. As the modality of fetishistic quantification *par excellence,* money is the tangible embodiment of the universally alienating capital system. It makes alienation inseparable from reified objectification by "extinguishing every qualitative difference." And, as we know only too well from painful historical experience, that favours the self-expansionary drive of capital for a long historical period. Until, that is, the system of capital's social metabolic reproduction collides with its own insurmountable structural limits as a result of its destructive encroachment on nature, undermining thereby the elementary conditions of human existence itself. This is the unvarnished reality of humankind's endangered *actual historical existence* today whose concept is strangely missing from "deep ontological" existentialism. For that kind of existentialism—which refuses to confront the dangers of actual human existence, even when those dangers become increasingly more obvious in our time—characteristically prefers to rivet objectification and alienation together in the interest of a pseudo-theoretical justification of its own defence of capital's fetishistic power as the permanent and "fundamental dimension of history."

Only the fully coherent and historically viable articulation of a system of *qualitatively oriented non-antagonistic mediations,* based on human needs necessarily repressed with utmost brutality by capital in structural crisis, can offer a way out of such contradictions.

IT IS ONE OF THE MOST PROBLEMATICAL ASPECTS of developments in philosophy and social theory in the twentieth century that *substantive* issues, together with their underlying value-determinations, tend to be transposed to what is supposed to be the only appropriate *meta-theoretical* level. That kind of shift is advocated, rather arbitrarily, in the name of "rigorous objectivity" and "value-neutrality" *(Wertfreiheit).* The production of readily formalizable "models," the repetitive and fashionable sloganizing about "paradigm shifts," leading absolutely nowhere, and the pursuit of self-referential and evasively self-contained methodological procedure tend to be idealized. At the same time, the engagement of intellectuals with problems that carry clearly identifiable practical implications is rejected, without any reasoning, by appending to such attempts what is meant to be an automatically disqualifying label, called "emotivism." The latter is decreed to be by definition incompatible with the requirements of rational philosophical discourse.

In one way or another all this is the manifestation of positivistic entrapment, with damaging implications and all too obvious negative consequences for the necessary emancipatory involvement of the intellectuals in the conflictually unfolding historical process. The self-defeating adoption of the institutionally well buttressed mythology of "value-neutrality," corresponding to the structurally (but by no means "value-neutrally") entrenched vantage point of capital's ruling order, is *self-defeating,* because it is *impossible* to realize that mythology in the actually existing, deeply antagonistic, world. In reality it means taking for granted, in the name of "supra-ideological" declarations, *conformity* to the fetishistic quantification and reification of the established order of social metabolic reproduction as the "value-neutral" measure and practical horizon of "*rigorous objectivity,*" disregarding the fact that capital's ruling order is incapable of separating the dehumanizing counter-value of *alienation* from its only feasible type of *objectification.* And all this is taking place at a time when the necessary institution of a humanly sustainable future depends on a *radical shift* to a fundamentally different, *qualitatively oriented,* mode of societal reproduction, consciously dedicated to overcoming the catastrophic *waste* that goes with the ever more prominent *destructive production* characteristic of the capital system in its historical phase of deepening structural crisis.

Accepting such a horizon, consciously or not, can only bring with it persistently evasive and more or less *ephemeral methodological postulates* as to the way of solving, with illusory "finality," the stubbornly recurring age-old philosophical problems, frequently characterizing them as "metaphysical," "conceptual" or "linguistic confusions." The embodiments of such methodological postulates range from *phenomenology* and *structuralism* to "analytic this" and "analytic that" (that is, not only to "linguistic philosophical analysis," which claimed at some point in quickly disappearing time to have realized *"the revolution* in philosophy," but even to the ludicrously navel-gazing and even more quickly imploding *"analytical Marxism"),* as well as to the monotonously generated "post-" labels, from *"post-structuralism"* and *"post-modernism"* to utterly vacuous *"post-Marxism."* Understandably, the self-righteous avoidance of commitment-demanding substantive issues and the values corresponding to them leads to the pursuit of *"meta-ethically"* oriented *"meta-theory."* Likewise, and again by no means surprisingly, the illusory "supra-ideological"—or "post-ideological"—engagement in *analysis for the sake of analysis* culminates in the practice of *methodology for the sake of methodology.*

In this way one of the most important figures of *linguistic philosophical analysis,* the Oxford-based English thinker, J. L. Austin, advocates as the universally valid methodological panacea for the production of general philosophical agreement—beyond all known and possible "metaphysical," "conceptual," and "linguistic confusions"—the confinement of discussion by all concerned to what could be "rationally" answered in terms of the question: *"What would one say when . . . ?"* He commends this linguistically oriented methodological principle in the interest of doing away with substantive comprehensive issues, so that we should not be called upon to provide any "concluding inference." This is how Austin argues his case: "We become obsessed with 'truth' when discussing statements, just as we become obsessed with 'freedom' when discussing conduct." Thus he advocates abandoning the discussion of problems like "freedom" and "truth," so as to concentrate, in their stead, on adverbs like "accidentally," "unwillingly," "inadvertently," because in that way "no concluding inference is required." Most curiously, however, in the next sentence Austin tells us: *"Like freedom, truth is a bare minimum or an illusory ideal."*[145] And nothing could have the character of a more concluding *assertion* than that, even if in Austin's paper on "Truth" just quoted it is totally devoid of any ground on the basis of which it could be considered a "concluding *inference.*" Far from being an inference, it is perhaps the "inadvertent" confession of an extreme sceptical, maybe even a heart-felt pessimistic, position held by the Oxford philosopher. Thus, paradoxically, Austin's methodological panacea can only make him fall into his own trap, ending up with a dogmatic assertion of the kind of substantive proposition which he firmly prescribed to avoid—and also proclaimed to be fully avoidable—with the help of his adverb-centered method of linguistic analytical philosophy.

As far as the inadvertently revealed but no doubt genuine substantive dimension of Austin's position is concerned, he invites his "rational" readers to be content (even if not happy) with the "bare minimum" and abandon the "illusory ideal." However, the trouble in this respect is that the advice given by Austin cannot be adopted as a general rule at a time of a profound historical crisis. The grave challenge of our time must be confronted somehow, and doing so requires a *practical intervention* in the unfolding sociohistorical developments, on the basis of some strategic conception or ideal appropriate to the situation. Nor should one gratuitously presume that all such conceptions or ideals are no more than *"illusory ideals."* I could hardly believe that Austin himself, despite his pronounced scepticism, would be capable of going as far as predicating the unavoidability (and absurdity) of that kind of fateful *"concluding assertion."* Nevertheless, the pessimistic implications of his methodological solution cannot be disregarded, precisely because the necessary call for the intellectuals' *practical involvement* is irremediably missing from the Oxford philosopher's approach.

The *structuralist* methodology for the sake of methodology does not fare any better in this respect than the self-referentially closed linguistic philosophical analysis for the sake of analysis. They also share the self-defeating remoteness of their conceptions from understanding the necessity of a socially tangible intervention of the intellectuals in the required sociohistorical transformations.

If in the case of Austin's linguistic analysis the pessimistic connotations appear only indirectly, in the conception of the most famous *structuralist* thinker, the French anthropologist Claude Lévi-Strauss, we are explicitly presented with the most gloomy form of pessimism. He paints an utterly desolate picture of the prospects of humanity's development for the future by declaring that

> Today the greater peril for humanity does not come from the activities of a *regime, a party, a group, or a class*. It comes from humanity itself in its entirety; a humanity which reveals itself to be its own worst enemy and, alas, at the same time, also the worst enemy of the rest of the creation. It

> is of this truth that one has to convince it, if there is to be any hope that one can save it.[146]

Reading these lines with some astonishment one could not avoid asking the questions: "But who was going to do the convincing and saving of humanity? What kind of vantage point could one adopt to stand outside humanity and castigate it as its own worst enemy, exempting at the same time the sociopolitical regimes, parties, groups, and classes of their responsibility? After all, when the Old Testament prophets thundered against sinful humanity, they claimed to have been ordered directly by God himself to do so. But now, where was to be found the social agency equal to the advocated task? How could one intervene in the actual process of transformation in order to counter the gloomily denounced trends of development, in the hope of realizing the desired objectives?" There was not even a faint hint in Lévi-Strauss's interview how to answer these questions.[147]

Thus, instead of a proper diagnosis of the social and historical forces at work in the deplored situation, together with *some* indication of what should and *could* be done in order to counter the catastrophic dangers, all we can receive from the leading figure of structuralism is a *jeremiad* devoid of any real frame of reference. Nor could this outcome be considered too surprising. For having programmatically broken the *dialectical* interrelationship between *structure and history,* by pushing aside the questions of the *historical dynamics* in order to postulate the viability of a self-contained *structuralist method,* the actually existing historical subjects—*antagonistically mediated* under the rule of capital—lose their reality, as well as the feasibility of overcoming their antagonisms in a historically sustainable way. It is totally vacuous to decree, as Lévi-Strauss does, that the grave structural crisis of our time has nothing to do with *"a regime, a party, a group, or a class."* But the avoidance of the substantive issues of our time in their sociohistorical specificity and dynamism, together with their underlying value-determinations—for the sake of a fictitious *"equidistancing"* of themselves by the thinkers in question from the rival social forces capable of deciding one way or another the outcome of the ongoing confrontations, as hegemonic alternatives to one another—can only produce jeremiads leading absolutely nowhere even in the case of an outstanding thinker like Claude Lévi-Strauss.

Sadly, also when we read the diagnosis offered by a major *post-structuralist* thinker, Michel Foucault, the picture is by no means more reassuring. He writes on the concluding pages of one of his important books, ending the whole book with the last four lines here quoted:

> In our day the fact that philosophy is still—and again—in the process of coming to an end, and the fact that in it perhaps, though even more outside and against it, in literature as well as in formal reflection, the question of language is being posed, *prove no doubt* that *man is in the process of disappearing*.[148]

> As the archaeology of our thought easily shows, man is an invention of recent date. And one perhaps nearing its end. If those arrangements were to disappear as they appeared . . . then one can certainly wager that man would be *erased like a face drawn in the sand at the edge of the sea.*[149]

All this may sound rather poetic (to some), but what is the ground on which we are supposed to take it seriously? Nothing more than a self-enclosed discourse on philosophy and language, with a categorical declaration that the author's assertions about the—highly debatable—elements of that discourse "*prove no doubt* that *man is in the process of disappearing*," although they *prove* nothing of the kind. But even if for the sake of argument we agree with Foucault about that danger, what are we supposed to do about it? Is this—or is there *at all*—a field of action opened up by the post-structuralist method of generalization, so as to *practically intervene* in the claimed process and counter the destructive forces to some degree at least? And what is the point of Foucault's desolate picture if a preconceived "no" is the answer to our question? How could one meaningfully proceed with the mandate of philosophy as an active contributory to a better future, whether through the direct investigation of the passionately long debated values in the fields of knowledge, religion, politics and aesthetics or on the more mediated terrain of methodology? Even with regard to the latter the critical *investigation of method* ever since Descartes was deeply concerned with improving the possibilities of a fruitful intervention of the people concerned in the ongoing societal reproduction process based on a sustainable relationship to nature.

Nothing could be, therefore, more distant from the horizon of the great French philosopher engaged in such an investigation than methodology for the sake of methodology. For Descartes insisted that the point of methodological doubt was to obtain *self-evident certainty,* insisting without the slightest ambiguity: "Not that in this [doubt] I imitated the *sceptics,* who doubt only that they may doubt and seek nothing beyond *uncertainty* itself; for on the contrary, *my design was singly to find ground of assurance,* and cast aside the loose earth and sand that I might reach the rock or the clay."[150] And, as we have seen above, when he was looking for philosophical certainty, Descartes strongly underlined the importance of making knowledge *practical* and useful in the great enterprise of the envisaged human control of nature by putting into relief that "I perceived it to be possible to arrive at *knowledge highly useful in life;* and in room of the speculative philosophy usually taught in the schools, to discover a *practical* [philosophy] by means of which . . . we might also apply them to all the uses to which they are adapted, and thus *render ourselves the lords and possessors of nature.*"[151]

This tradition is completely abandoned, even when in a methodologically transfigured way it is still referred to, as in the writings of Husserl. For on the crucial issue of the *practical intervention* of philosophy we find in Husserl the most rigid opposition between "the theoretical attitude" and "the practical." As, for instance, when he asserts that "The *theoretical attitude,* even though it too is a professional attitude, is *thoroughly unpractical.* Thus it is based on a deliberate *epoché* from *all practical interests,* and consequently even those of a higher level, that serve natural needs within the framework of a life's occupation governed by such practical interests."[152] This could be tragically self-defeating, as we saw it in the case of Husserl when he tried to counter in his Prague lecture the advancement of Nazi barbarism—which, due not simply to the consideration of some political danger but, more importantly, to his own proclaimed methodology of a "deliberate *epoché* from *all practical interests,*" he could not name by its proper name—with the certainly most unpractical generic postulate of the *"heroism of Reason."*

No one should simply blame the intellectuals who became entangled in the maze of these developments, offering us a more or less self-contained methodological discourse, with pessimistic messages or overtones, in opposition to the necessary practical engagement with the *major substantive issues* of our time. For the Cartesian programme of *"rendering ourselves the lords and possessors of nature"* had turned out to be realized in an extremely dangerous—indeed in a potentially catastrophic—form in the course of actual historical development.

To be sure, philosophy only contributed to that, consciously or not—even if ever more problematically in the descending phase of the capital system's global unfolding—but, of course, it was by no means the "prime mover" at the roots of such developments. The inescapable fact in that respect is that capital's mode of social metabolic reproduction is itself *structurally incapable* of establishing and maintaining a *historically sustainable* relationship of human beings to nature. For in its only feasible mode of fetishistic *objectification* capital is *structurally—and totally—incapable* of overcoming *alienation* in any one of its multiple dimensions, from the ruthless expropriation/alienation of productive activity and the concomitant callous negation of genuine human need, to the usurpatory denial of the power of *decision making,* not only in economics and politics but also in the field of culture, to the individuals who constitute the real historical subject, labour, as the possessor and potential realizer of creative human energy.

Capital under all circumstances must blindly assert and impose on society—as well as irremediably also on nature—the imperatives of its self-expansionary drive, no matter how *destructive* might be the consequences. This is why by the time we reach the present the once promising, or at least hopeful, Cartesian programme of *"rendering ourselves the lords and possessors of nature"* had to turn out to be translated into reality in an all too obvious *destructive* form, raising thereby the spectre and the real possibility of humanity's total annihilation.

But only its *possibility*. Nothing warrants the categorical assertion that today *"man is in the process of disappearing,"* nor indeed the equally pessimistic and "equidistancing" rhetorical flourish by Lévi-Strauss that "Today the greater peril for humanity does not come from the activities of a *regime, a party, a group, or a class.* It comes from humanity itself in its entirety; a humanity which reveals itself to be its own worst enemy and, alas, at the same time, also the worst enemy of the rest of the creation." The danger of destroying the conditions of human existence on this planet is undoubtedly very great. However, it is not caused by an abstract humanity but by a tangible—and historically transcendable—social force which *at present* controls our mode of societal reproduction.

This makes it all the more important of stressing the need for a renewed and intensely committed practical intervention in the ongoing historical process. The force bent on the destruction of the elementary conditions of human existence is not a mysterious "humanity" vacuously opposed by Lévi-Strauss to his list of active societal agents. For real humanity is made up of the "regimes, parties, groups and classes," as well as of the actually existing individuals—including the phenomenologist, structuralist, post-structuralist, post-modernist etc. intellectuals—who cannot distance themselves from the identified dangers without abdicating their responsibility.

The real culprit is the *overall controller* of our mode of social metabolic reproduction, capital, with its fetishistic and reified way of subjugating all dimensions of human life to its blind inner determinations and outward dictates. Capital exercises its control by absurdly transforming "the producer into the property of the product" and by structurally securing its own *all-embracing* modality of irrational self-expansionary drive through its system of *hierarchically* entrenched *antagonistic mediations*. Every aspect of this historically produced—and in our time increasingly destructive—force is clearly identifiable, including the *comprehensive* character and dominance of the established system of antagonistic mediations, requiring an appropriate comprehensive strategy and force to overcome it as the historically viable hegemonic alternative to capital's rule. The postmodernist's denunciation of "grand narratives" in favour of its own, by arbitrary definition self-justifying, "petits récits," is therefore in its nature self-defeating and mystificatory from start to finish, because it denies with its perverse apriorism the very idea of any meaningful comprehensive strategy, when the need for it could not be greater. But notwithstanding all such methodological ruses and evasions, the consistent elaboration and practical realization of an alternative system of *non-antagonistic mediations* remains an absolutely necessary requirement for a historically viable future.

THERE CAN BE NO ACCOMMODATING COMPROMISES between capital's ruling order and the *qualitatively different* alternative mode of social metabolic control feasible only through the establishment and consolidation of the "new historic form." Capital's long prevailing societal reproductive order constitutes a *comprehensive organic system,* notwithstanding its at first only partial or latent but ultimately all-embracing destructive antagonisms, managed in the course of actual historical development in the form of *antagonistic mediations*. Consequently on both counts—that is, both with regard to its necessarily all-embracing, *comprehensive* scope, and the *organic* (i.e., in its constituent parts reciprocally supporting and reinforcing) character of this mode of social metabolic reproduction—the capital system can only be historically superseded by a no less *comprehensive* and *organic* hegemonic alternative.

We have seen in the course of this study that the vital *practical premises*—corresponding to the fundamental *structural determinations*—of the capital system had to be, and actually have been, *internalized,* with undeniable consistency in ideological as well as in methodological terms, by even the greatest thinkers of the bourgeoisie. For in actuality it was quite unthinkable to sustain the system without even a single one of them for any length of time.

The great thinkers of the bourgeoisie took for granted the *fundamental practical premises* of their system in their *combined totality,* as a *set of deeply interconnected determinations.* To name only the most important of these practical premises—which must remain in force for as long as capital's logic is enabled to prevail—they are:

1. the radical divorce of the *means and material of production* from living labour;

2. the assignment of all of the important *directing and decision making functions* in the established productive and reproductive order to the *personifications of capital;*

3. the regulation of the social metabolic interchange between human beings and nature and among the individuals themselves on the basis of capital's *second order mediations;* and

4. the determination and management of the *all-embracing political command structure* of society in the form of the capitalist state, under the mystifying primacy of the *material base*.

Naturally, in view of the fact that these fundamental practical premises of the capital system constitute a set of *closely interlocking* determinations, they cannot be abandoned *selectively*, Nor can they be practically transcended by a rival force *partially*. The total failure of all *reformist* attempts in the twentieth century, and the humiliating abandonment of any idea of significant reform by the political parties which originally defined themselves—as their *raison d'être*—in terms of such reforms, proclaimed by them to be leading *in due course* through the political strategy of "evolutionary socialism" and its fictitious "progressive taxation" to the programmatically announced radically different kind of society, have provided ample proof for the utter futility and the ultimate bad faith of all such attempts.

The principal reason why all such "reforms" *had to fail* was their confinement to the *structurally prejudged* framework of capital's self-serving and inalterable practical premises. Thus the announced reforms were no reforms at all in the sense that they would point even minimally in the direction of a different social order. They were, on the contrary, the necessary *partial*—and even in that way *"in due course"* profitably undoable —*conjunctural corrective devices* instituted for the perpetuation of capital's socioeconomic and political order. Roosevelt's "New Deal" was in this sense no more than the conjuncturally required—strictly partial and temporary—response by a more enlightened capitalist to the crippling aftermath of capital's "World Economic Crisis of 1929–33." Likewise, the institution of the "Welfare State" in a handful of capitalistically most privileged countries after the Second World War, and this time in a more mystifying form by some labourite parties, was strictly conjunctural, despite all social democratic mythology to the contrary. Not only because such reform had to be confined from the start (which turned out to be also the finish) to an extremely limited number of countries in capital's global pecking order, but also because the reformist panacea of the "Welfare State" as such, instead of spreading everywhere else, as disingenuously propagandized earlier, had to be humiliatingly abandoned—parallel to the unfolding of capital's structural crisis all over the world—even in those few countries where it was instituted for a while.

As regards capital's necessary practical premises of operation were concerned, nothing happened to rectify the structurally entrenched and safeguarded "radical divorce of the *means and material of production* from living labour." The post-Second World War *"nationalizations"* in Britain, for instance, could achieve nothing more than the deceptively claimed "socialist" transfer of some *capitalistically bankrupt* key sectors of the economy, from coal mining and gas as well as electricity production all the way to the vital transport services, to *general taxation,* so as to be fraudulently *re-privatized* later, once they have become profitable again through the injection of huge public funds. At the same time the *false consciousness* with which extricating bankrupt capital from its plight was presented to the public, as "gaining control over the commanding heights of the economy"—in Prime Minister Harold Wilson's notorious words—could only demonstrate the utter failure of the "political arm" of the once promising labour movement.

The fact that the present "New Labour" government is rather shy about using the term "nationalization" about its recent bailing out, with massive public funds, the totally bankrupt banking and mortgage company which happens to be called, with unintended irony, *"The Northern Rock,"* should not deceive anybody about the real character of the operation in question; i.e., the more or less fraudulent rescue-operation of a major capitalist firm, in the interest of hiding that beneath the *tip of the iceberg* there lurks the menacing iceberg of the banking business in general. Nor should anybody imagine that this kind of operation is pursued because the government in Britain is administered by a party which at times, when it finds doing so politically convenient, still calls itself *"socialist."* For the same type of rescue-operation is taking place—on a much larger scale, with incomparably bigger icebergs under the surface of the water—in George W. Bush's United States of America itself, which by no stretch of the imagination could be called "socialist" even by the most extreme "neo-liberal/neo-con" apologists of the global capital system. What is absolutely excluded is that capital should be able to yield the power it continues to gain by maintaining the "radical divorce of the *means and material of production* from living labour" as one of the pivotal practical premises of its control of the established social metabolic order. Yielding in that way would mean to *consent* to the meaningful *socialization* of the means and material of production, instead of its vacuous and reversible *"nationalization."* And that is inconceivable. For genuine socialization could not be accomplished as a *partial* measure, in view of its necessary *structural* interconnections. It could only be undertaken as a radical project of fundamental *systemic* transformation, with its *qualitatively* defined *comprehensive* ramifications in all domains of human activity. Capital's still far from exhausted modality of managing even the present kind of crisis, with giant icebergs multiplying across the sea, offers the practicable strategy of the capitalist state itself "nationalizing" the totally bankrupt "sub-prime" and other mortgage institutions, and leasing the houses back to the repossessed individuals, in the interest of saving, for as long as in that way it remains feasible, the bankrupt banks themselves. For, obviously, the banks and mortgage companies cannot themselves profitably occupy the vast numbers of houses which they are now ruthlessly *repossessing* on a dangerously growing scale. And thus, when in the event of a further extension of this crisis the state might become the ultimate mortgage company, without abandoning the fundamental modality of the *economically regulated extraction* of surplus labour as surplus value —a distinct possibility under the conditions of massive private capitalist default; and of course that could be in the future a type of potential state intervention which by no means would have to be confined to the domain of housing—then we could really give a tangible meaning to the often misused term of *"state capitalism."* But even that would in no way extricate the capital system itself from its deepening structural crisis.

The other three insurmountable practical premises of the capital system mentioned above are no less forcefully imposed on the overwhelming majority of human beings in our society than the first. Thus the practical imperative dictating with categorical exclusiveness the assignment of all of the important *directing and decision making functions* to the *personifications of capital* in the established productive and reproductive order must prevail even under some surprisingly modified historical circumstances. This is what we had to witness in the postcapitalist capital system after the successful encirclement and isolation of the 1917 Russian Revolution by Western capitalism and the ensuing stabilization of the Soviet type reproductive order under Stalin. Naturally, Marx could not even dream about the bewildering new variety of the personifications of capital which succeeded in imposing itself as the highly bureaucratized overall controller of the postrevolutionary Soviet system for seven decades of real or claimed emergency. Indeed, it would be extremely hasty and foolish to conclude even today that the Soviet type personifications of capital constituted the last possible variety of the antagonistic way of controlling the social metabolism inherited from capital's long established reproductive system even in the event of some significantly changing historical circumstances. It all depends on the *depth* of the unfolding crisis and on the nature—whether all-embracing or partial—of the strategies undertaken for historically overcoming the established social metabolic order in which capital exercises its controlling functions through its *necessary personifications*, as a *usurping subject*.

The same goes for the regulation of the social metabolic interchange between human beings and nature and among the individuals themselves on the basis of capital's antagonistic and alienating *second order mediations*. The latter constitute a perversely *interlocking* system of material and institutional reifications—the uncontrollable conversion of social relations into things and the alienated/objectified things themselves into opaquely overpowering social relations—which in their ultimate implications foreshadow the destruction of nature (and of course the human individuals with it) in the interest of the fetishistic domination of self-expansionary *quantity* over *quality* that could meaningfully arise from *genuine human need*. We have seen in chapter 4 above that even the greatest synthesis of bourgeois philosophy, the Hegelian system, could not escape the gravitational pull of these fetishistic determinations. Instead, Hegel ended up with the glorification of alienating objectivity and all-pervasive quantification in his conceptualization of "measure" as the unexplained, yet from strictly individual conflictuality mysteriously emerging —and apologetically unchallengeable—"convention" that was destined to prevail with unproblematical universality in the established order. Tellingly, this view could be complemented in the Hegelian vision only by the reconciliatory function of his principle of "negativity as self-transcending contradiction" which was speculatively postulated by the German philosopher to preserve forever the ruling order in its claimed "rational actuality." Thus the antagonistic second order mediations of the capital system could continue to superimpose themselves through their self-propelling determinations and alienated imperatives on the primary mediations between human beings and nature that must take place in essential productive activity. Naturally, when in the course of development this fetishistic way of regulating the societal reproduction process becomes *historically anachronistic,* due to the dangerous advancement of *destructive production* in place of "productive destruction," the only "corrective" response compatible with the systemic determinations and inalterable practical premises of capital is the *intensification* of its alienating self-expansionary practices, and thereby the hastening of destruction. The interlocking set of antagonistic second order mediations—which must prevail at all cost, as the hierarchically entrenched and safeguarded structural foundation of the whole system—offer truly *no alternative* to the personifications of capital.

As to the determination and management of the *all-embracing political command structure* of society in the form of the capitalist state, under the mystifying primacy of the *material base*, its importance is enormous. This is so notwithstanding the misconceptions formulated on the ground of very different motivations. They range from Adam Smith's rather naïve suggestion of minimal state involvement, at a time of aggressive colonial expansion, all the way to the cynical and hypocritical neoliberal ideology of *"rolling back the boundaries of the state."* And the latter is invented, of course, against the background of the greatest ever state support given to private capitalism not only in the form of all kinds of material subsidies, including massive research funds, as well as the blatant rescue-operations directly benefitting some huge bankrupt enterprises in the world of finance and industry, but also the fraudulent near-astronomical sums transferred to the military-industrial complex on a continuing basis for the purpose of its economically destructive operations and even for its large scale genocidal wars. Moreover, the mystificatory primacy of the material base in capital's reproductive order over its historically created state formations makes it extremely difficult to properly assess—in terms of the synthesizing visions of the particular thinkers conceived as a rule in a greatly exaggerated and even idealized form—what the state, as the comprehensive political command structure of capital is actually capable of accomplishing, or not, as the case might be. This is so even in the theories of the greatest bourgeois philosophers, like Hegel. Nothing illustrates that better than his critique of the Liberal state which hopelessly misses its target, as we have seen above. For Hegel could not submit the Liberal state formation to the required critical scrutiny for the simple reason that his own conception *shared* with the Liberal approach the same substantive ground. As the exploitative beneficiary of capital's structurally antagonist order Liberalism could have nothing whatsoever to do with the *substantive* ("empirical") requirements of making the *general will* effectively prevail in all domains of social life. And that was true also of the role assigned by Hegel himself to the state, as indirectly even admitted by him. Their differences were secondary and rather superficial with regard to "the rule of the many" in Liberalism against which Hegel complained. For what the Liberal state formation in actuality perpetrated, as clearly demonstrated by our historical chronicles, was only the continuing rule of the *plurality of capitals*—switching intermittently from *some* of its strictly mandated personifications to *others*—against the *structurally subordinate class of labour*. Liberalism could never conceivably intend the practical embodiment of the ideal principles of Rousseau's General Will into its state legislative framework. Its appeal to the idea of governing in the form of the "Many" served very limited *electoral* purposes. They were never oriented even in theory, let alone in the political practice of Liberalism, so as to be directed toward altering in any tangible way the Liberal state, including in its social democratic versions. While talking about "pluralism," they succeeed only in *totally disenfranchising* the working classes through their deceptively routinized consensual switch from one *pseudo-alternative* to the other.[153] Another, in its positive implications much more important, aspect of the mystifying primacy of the material base over the political dimension of capital's rule in society—directly relevant to the formulation of viable socialist strategies—is that we should not expect too much of what even the most radical political intervention, in the form of the *political* and not the multidimensional *social revolution* advocated by Marx, can accomplish on its own within the domain of state legislative practices. The control of the *juridical* domain is of course the necessary first step on the road to a far-reaching *qualitative* social transformation. But it should not be allowed to be turned conveniently to the inherited and new personifications of capital,[154] into a new variant of wishfully adopted *juridical illusion*. Also in that respect it would be tragic not to be able to learn from the painful experience of the past.

Evidently, the character of all of the fundamental practical premises here surveyed is both *substantive* and *comprehensive,* as much in and by themselves taken one by one as in their combined totality of reciprocally sustaining and reinforcing determinations of capital's *organic system.* Accordingly, they must be countered by a set of no less *substantive and comprehensive* operative principles and determinations, but this time in the only viable form of the social individuals' *autonomous and conscious,* critical as well as self-critical, deliberations aimed at the strategic elaboration of the required *non-antagonistic mediations* of the new historic form. That is the only feasible way of superseding on a lasting basis capital's ever more destructive social metabolic order by the *positively sustainable* hegemonic alternative of the *socialist organic system.* For only by successfully asserting its principles as a constantly self-renewing societal reproduction can the socialist hegemonic alternative acquire—and maintain—its profound historical legitimacy.

THE QUESTION OF HISTORICALLY SUSTAINABLE TRANSITION to a radically different form of social metabolic control is not an *abstract theoretical postulate.* On the contrary, it is *historically most determinate*, calling for the elaboration and practical institution of a viable system of non-antagonistic mediations. Indeed the question of non-antagonistic mediations arises from the actually existing and pressing *global international* context for the first time ever in history in this no longer *postponable* way, under the weight of the ruling reproductive order's grave contradictions.

In this respect it is enough to think of capital's incurable vicious circle between *waste* and *scarcity*—that is: the constant reproduction of scarcity on an increasing scale through the multiplication of waste while denying the satisfaction of even their elementary human needs for billions of people—as our fairly obvious starting point. To envisage overcoming that vicious circle in the foreseeable future is not a wishful postulate but a vital *necessity.* However, it is quite impossible to introduce the required changes to that effect within the necessary constraints of the established order. For the capital system—due to the inseparability of its mode of objectification from the alienating imperative of its cancerously imposed self-expansion on society through the reified multiplication of *exchange-value,* at the expense of humanly meaningful *use-value*—is structurally incapable of *economizing* on the basis of *qualitative* considerations rooted in human need. Yet, only the latter would allow the expansion of society's productive powers simultaneously to the rational control of waste, so as to consign in that way our fetishistic reproduction of scarcity to the past. Accordingly, only a *coherently planned and pursued economizing mode* of production can be considered viable in the future: a condition impossible to realize for as long as the capital system's antagonistic second order mediations continue to regulate our mode of social metabolic reproduction.

When we compare the defining characteristics of the established historic order with the envisaged "new historic form" we are confronted by the insuperable *radical incompatibilities* between the two. The denial of those incompatibilities—in the service of unprincipled reformist accommodation—could only be self-defeating, as we know from the past. Acknowledging the vital need for the creation of a system of non-antagonistic mediations should not mean at all the watering down of the concept of mediation in the customary sense of "balancing." For in the case of attempting the envisaged reconciliatory balancing of the two would have to be accomplished between two radically different social and historical orders: a blatant *contradiction in terms.* Thus, our vitally necessary point of departure can only be the *radical principled negation* of capital's destructive societal reproductive order. But precisely because we are concerned with a *principled* negation of the substantive defining characteristics of the existent, the new historic form cannot be satisfied with the *"negation of the negation"* only. Its historical legitimacy depends on the successful institution of a long-term viable reproductive alternative in its own substantive positive terms, in place of the now prevailing modality of antagonistic second order mediations.

To be sure, it is politically much easier to advocate to follow "the line of least resistance" for the sake of some hoped for gains than the required radical alternative under the relation of forces in organizational terms still overwhelmingly in capital's favour, especially in the light of the disheartening failure of the Soviet type postcapitalist historical experience.

However, the obtainable gains are by now at best partial and temporary, if not altogether illusory, in view of the deepening structural crisis of the system. This is demonstrated not only by the eruption of major industrial and financial turbulence, as well as through the gravely deteriorating ecological conditions of our planet, but even through the constant engagement in grotesquely rationalized military adventures by the global hegemonic imperialism of the U.S. and its subservient allies. Accordingly, there can be no significant improvement in the fortunes of the socialist movement until the need for engaging in a substantively oriented principled negation of the capital system as an all-embracing mode of social metabolic control is consciously adopted on an appropriate scale as the necessary strategy for the future.

In this respect the principled negation of the capital system carries with it also the rejection of the derailing misconception that the elaboration of the non-antagonistic mode of mediation means a mediation *between* the still dominant societal reproductive system, notwithstanding its destructive antagonisms, and the advocated new historic form. That could only lead to a blind alley.

The real mediation in question is not what is feasible *between* the two qualitatively opposed historic orders but *within* the domain of the necessary *hegemonic alternative* to capital's historically no longer tenable domination over humanity's relationship to nature and over the particular social individuals themselves. And that kind of crucially important mediation is not concerned with some more or less remotely envisioned *future* but with the *now unfolding historical process.* It is directly relevant to the practical constitution of the modalities and organizational prerequisites of action in which the objective and subjective conditions for the realization of the necessary substantive values, as well as the corresponding forms of historically sustainable reproductive interchanges among human beings, can be instituted and consolidated as the *historically viable hegemonic alternative* to capital's antagonistic second order mediations. In other words, it is concerned with consciously *articulating* the non-antagonistic reproductive interchanges of a qualitatively different societal order as both the clearly identified *objective* or *destination* to be reached and the *compass* of the emancipatory journey undertaken already in and through the now unfolding historical process. In that sense the consciously pursued *radical principled work* for overcoming the antagonisms of the existing order is inseparably negative *and positive* at the same time. That is the only proper meaning we can give to *radical* which cannot afford to remain tied to an—ultimately unsustainable—purely negative posture. Especially when what is at stake is the question of a historically viable hegemonic alternative. It is therefore by no means surprising that Marx defined socialism as "man's *positive self-consciousness.*"[155]

In the interpersonal relations of the social individuals non-antagonistic mediation means their genuine co-operative engagement in activity with the consciously chosen purpose of solving some problems, or indeed of resolving some disputes that might arise in their relations. What makes the contrast of this type of consciously regulated interchange very clear in comparison to the now dominant modality of antagonistic mediations is that the projected solution of the problems themselves that must be faced within the framework of a system of non-antagonistic mediations cannot be allowed to be consolidated and perpetuated as *structurally entrenched vested interests*. In the ongoing historical course of constituting the new modality of non-antagonistic mediations the inherited vested interests must be radically superseded through sustained *co-operative* action, securing at the same time the objective and subjective conditions for preventing their reconstitution.

The prevalence of vested interests happen to be the dominant modality of our existing relations of societal reproduction under the rule of capital. Hierarchically secured and safeguarded class interests and determinations *necessarily prejudge* these matters—inevitably in favour of the stronger party—well before the question of "mediation" or "balancing" can even arise, making often a complete mockery (or a vacuous ritual) of the undertaken "problem-solving" procedure. With regard to all of the matters of truly overriding importance from the vantage point of the now dominant social metabolic order, concerning the structural imperative of reasserting the established *power relations* upon which the given societal reproduction process is grounded, it all boils down to the *enforcement* of the objective power relations required by the continued functioning of the system, by whatever means. That is to say, to enforce them with the help of cultural/ideological devices, provided that they work under the prevailing circumstances in tune with the all-important systemic requirements, or through the exercise of *naked force* (and even the imposition of extreme *repressive violence)*, when the conditions call for it. The latter vary from the need for enacting inside a particular country some more or less long lasting *states of emergency,* in the event of a major crisis, all the way to waging even world wars of genocidal proportion against other states. This is why the normality of the capital system is inconceivable without its formally varied but in substantive terms always forcefully imposed sets of antagonistic second order mediations.

Here we can also see that the question of mediation is not a matter of philosophical postulates or speculative projections. It is deeply concerned with objective determinations and with the corresponding forces and agencies of societal reproductive action. This is the case whether we have in mind the antagonistic mediations involved in capital's social metabolic procedures, or those of its hegemonic alternative in the process of their principled articulation through the unfolding historical process. The crucial question with regard to the institution of a historically viable social metabolic order is the replacement of capital's antagonistic second order mediations between humankind and nature and among the individuals themselves by a qualitatively different alternative, from the fetishistically quantifying exchange relations of commodity society to the quintessentially alienated power of overall decision making by the state. That is possible only by strategically redefining and practically reconstituting—in accordance with the most developed historical conditions and productive attainments actually or potentially available to the people involved—the *primary modalities* of creative interchange between humanity and nature: by removing the capital system's encrusted and antagonistically perpetuated layers of *second order mediations over the necessary primary mediations* from the social body.

Naturally, that requires also the return of the *real subject* of history to its rightful place of control of the societal reproduction process in place of the usurping subject. For inasmuch as the now established mode of social metabolic control is inconceivable without the earlier mentioned *vested interests* and without the usurping subject of history: the "personification of capital," in any one of its feasible varieties—not simply as the conscious beneficiary of those vested interests but, above all, as the privileged controller of the means and material of production and the *willing enforcer* of the *objective imperative* of self-expansionary accumulation and accumulatory self-expansion—only the real subject of history can carry out its productive and creative functions without appropriating to itself the structurally prevailing and grossly discriminatory vested interests with which we are all too familiar. Indeed, only a social subject constituted on the basis of consciously defined and coherently articulated, as well as in that form always maintained, *substantive equality,* only that kind of subject is capable of asserting its historical mandate by instituting the required alternative forms of non-antagonistic societal mediation.

As mentioned earlier,[156] historically sustainable mediation is feasible only as the *self-mediation* of an active social subject; one capable of *autonomously* intervening in the ongoing process of transformation in accordance with its own coherent design. This is why it was stressed that the seminally important concepts of *self-control, self-mediation,* and the genuine *autonomy* of the *consciously* acting real historical subject all must go together in order to be able to give a tangible meaning to the idea of the long term sustainable mediation required in our historical predicament. It was also stressed throughout this study that not only *equality* but all of the values required for sustaining this conception need to be defined in *substantive* terms. This must be done in sharp contrast to the characteristic reorientation of the capital system in its descending phase of development. For that regressive reorientation of the capital system completely emptied all of the positive values—from "liberty" and "fraternity" to "democracy" and "equality"—of their once advocated content, in the interest of making *counter-value* effectively prevail, as we had the opportunity to see before. At the same time the ruling ideology was preaching the opposite of what was being practised (and continues to be practised), disingenuously idealizing the ruling order on account of the vacuous institutional virtues of *"formal universality"* while deceptively enforcing in every possible way the destructive self-expansionary *partiality* of capital's *antagonistic second order mediations.*

A PARADIGM EXAMPLE OF THIS MYSTIFICATION is the operation of the liberal state—to name only the most progressive variety of overall political control feasible under the rule of capital. The insuperable systemic requirement in this respect is the *radical exclusion of the masses* from the substantive decision making process. In the activities of direct material reproduction this is perfectly accomplished by the *economic compulsion* to which the working people are subjected, as wedded to the legally safeguarded exclusive property of the means and material of production by the personifications of capital, enabling them to exercise the "authoritarianism of the workshop" in accord with their vested interests. In the political domain, however, there is no such forcibly pre-established—and indeed by the infamous historical process of "primitive accumulation" most brutally instituted—equivalent to the structurally secured hierarchical power relations of permanent class domination and subordination through which the capital system, in its primary economic reproductive modality, defines itself. On the contrary, the deliberately cultivated mythology of "democracy" and "liberty," together with the easily manipulated machinery of "free elections," would seem to point in the opposite direction, stipulating "the rule by the Many" by which even a philosophical genius like Hegel could be so pathetically deceived, even if by no means independently of his own ideological interests, as we have seen above.

Naturally, the feudal absolutist state had to be consigned to the past through the ascending phase of capital's development. For it was clearly incompatible with the new relations of class domination and subordination, although, significantly, the most extreme forms of authoritarian and dictatorial power enforcement have been retained by capital for its intermittent states of emergency. But irrespective of that, even the normal varieties of capital's state formations remained always most problematical with regard to the structurally entrenched alienation of the power of substantive decision making from the overwhelming majority of the people. The great masses of the people received only *formal* rights (like putting a piece of paper into the ballot box once in four or five years) whose hoped for impact could be nullified without any difficulty by the actual functioning of the state even without the institution of its states of emergency. Thus the liberal state, by "democratically" confining the political decision making process to the selected *few,* despite calling them *"the Many"* (in the interest of mystification), in actuality excludes the masses *by definition* from the effective decision making process. At the same time it makes a *virtue* out of the adopted procedure of institutionalized exclusion by conferring the noble sounding but utterly dubious title of

"*Representative Government*"—which is supposed to be fully matching the claimed ideals of "liberty" and "democracy"—on the underlying real determination of decision making. Naturally, the unvarnished truth of the matter is that neither *the many,* nor the *obedient few,* but the *structural imperatives* of capital determine the outcome of overall decision making. For capital, as the *extra-parliamentary force par excellence,* totally dominates from *outside*—and consequently (thanks to the "realistic" acknowledgement of the compelling *practical premises of the political system itself* by the consensually participating parties in awe to capital's societal power directly embodied in the countless material reproductive units of the social metabolism)—no less from the *inside* as well, the narrowly institutionalized, customarily formal/rubber-stamping, political decision making also in its *liberal parliamentary* variety, including of course the social democratic states.

This is why the intermittent switch from liberal democracy to authoritarian forms of political rule presents no real problem to the personifications of capital. Max Weber, who (thanks to his spurious mythology of "value-neutrality," *Wertfreiheit*) is an idol of liberalism and of its strictly self-serving "democracy," is a very good case in point. Lukács reminded us of the fact that

> Like the English or French, Weber thought, the Germans could become a 'master race' only in a democracy. Hence for the sake of attaining Germany's imperial aims, a democratization had to take place internally and go as far as was indispensable to the realization of these aims.[157]

As to what Max Weber actually meant by "internal democratization," fully in tune with his liberal credentials serving the interests of an imperialist German "master race," Lukács also quoted a conversation that took place after the First World War between Weber and the extreme right wing figure, General Ludendorff, Hindenburg's Chief of Staff and one of Hitler's earliest champions. These were Weber's words, as reported not by some hostile critic but by his widow, Marianne Weber:

> In democracy the people elect as its leader a man it trusts. Then the man elected says, 'Now hold your tongues and obey!' Neither the people nor

> the parties may contradict him . . . Afterwards it is for the people to judge —if the leader has erred, then away to the gallows with him.[158]

And Lukács rightly added: "It is not surprising that Ludendorff said to this: 'I like the sound of such a democracy!' Thus Weber's idea of democracy lapsed into a Bonapartist Caesarism."[159]

These are not corrigible aberrations, to be redressed by reasoned argument—that is, by "the politics of the understanding" which Merleau-Ponty mythically opposed in his *Adentures of the Dialetic* to Marx and Marxism in the name of Max Weber's "heroic liberalism." Correctives in this respect can only be concerned with partial, circumstance-bound considerations, and not with the core interests and orientation of the liberal state formation. In that partial sense Weber's advocacy of "internal democracy" as the pathway to the hoped for success of the competing German imperialist "master race," on the model of the then still highly successful English and French imperialisms,[160] pointed only to differences in historical circumstances whose attempted "rectification" later by Hitler—pioneeringly and revealingly admired by Ludendorff—took the form of the Second World War, and not "the politics of the understanding." The important point is that the radical exclusion of the masses from the power of substantive decision making—to be exercised if possible without generating too much conflict—is an *absolute requirement* of the capital system. It is instituted in the best practicable way precisely by the liberal state formation which reserves the much more unstable forms of its direct authoritarian political rule—a prospect always on its ultimate horizon—for its more or less long lasting, but in principle transient, states of emergency. This absolute requirement of radical exclusion had to be always maintained at all levels of capital's structurally entrenched hierarchical system of decision making, from the direct material reproductive units to the highest levels of the state legislature, because the *antagonistic second order mediations* of capital could not possibly prevail without it. The idea of managing the material reproductive units of the system on the basis of the "*authoritarianism of the workshop,*" as capital's established mode of social metabolic control must always do, and at the same time running the overall command structure of political decision making in the sharpest possible contrast to it, in full agreement with the substantive principles of genuine democracy *"by the people and for the people,"* could only be considered a blatant absurdity.

THE GREAT CHALLENGE FOR THE FUTURE is to redress all this in the interest of realizing the only historically viable mode of substantive decision making by the social body as a whole. For, obviously, the institution of a *non-antagonistic mode of mediation* is inconceivable for as long as the great masses of the people are radically excluded from all meaningful—which in this context equals substantive—decision making. The practice of strictly *formal* involvement by the people in electoral rituals—not to forget the fact that also that kind of involvement is categorically denied to them in the intervening four or five years, even if not with the cynical openness of Max Weber's "Now hold your tongues and obey!"—is a very poor substitute for the requirements of substantive decision making.

To be sure, the "new historic form" is unthinkable without the exercise of substantive decision making by the freely associated producers as a truly co-operative social body. It is equally unthinkable, contrary to reformist fantasies, to obtain such power of substantive decision making by the great masses of the people as a concession generously conferred upon them by the willing personifications of capital. They must *conquer* it "by themselves for themselves" with the help of the development of the necessary *organizational forms* through which their most radical intervention in the unfolding historical process becomes possible. This is why Marx insisted from the very beginning that without the development of *"communist mass consciousness"* the great historic challenge directly affecting the prospects of humanity's survival[161] cannot be met. And this is how he judged the importance of communist consciousness on a mass scale:

> Communism is for us not a state of affairs which is to be established, an *ideal* to which reality will have to adjust itself. We call communism the *real* movement which abolishes the present state of things.[162]
>
> Both for the production on a *mass scale* of this *communist consciousness,* and for the success of the cause itself, the alteration of men on a *mass scale* is necessary, an alteration which can only take place in a *practical move-*

> *ment, a revolution:* the revolution is necessary, therefore, not only because the ruling class cannot be overthrown in any other way, but also because the class overthrowing it can only in a revolution succeed in *ridding itself* of all the muck of ages and become *fitted to found society anew.*[163]

As we know, due to the historical circumstances of an extreme authoritarian regime ruling in Tsarist Russia at the time of Lenin, prior to the revolution of October 1917, his party had to be constituted as a vanguardist type of political organization capable of surviving and extending its influence under the most severe conditions of clandestinity. And also later, when Gramsci had to redefine his conception of the party, as spelled out in his work on "The Modern Prince" in Mussolini's jail, the relation of forces prevailing in Fascist Italy—and later also in Nazi Germany—made it again extremely difficult to envisage the formation of a revolutionary political organization oriented toward the Marxian strategic view of developing "communist mass consciousness." Moreover, thinking of what had actually happened in the more recent past to both the Leninist party in Russia and to Gramsci's party in Italy, it is hard to avoid the conclusion that the Marxian programme "for the production on a mass scale of communist consciousness" remains a great challenge for the future. Indeed, to make matters even worse in that regard, among several of the small radical groups which try to remain faithful to the idea of a revolutionary transformation, despite the bitter disappointments of the past, there is a tendency to dismiss, with sectarian inwardness, the programme of constituting a mass socialist movement as inadmissible "populism" and "spontaneism." Thus, much remains to be clarified and redressed also on that score. For it would be very naïve to imagine that the required system of non-antagonistic mediations could be instituted and successfully maintained as the new historic form's hegemonic alternative to the destructiveness of the established order without the most active involvement of the great masses of the people. It should be constantly kept in mind in this respect that "Modern universal intercourse cannot be controlled by individuals, unless it is controlled by all."[164]

The final point to be made is that when we think of the vital *substantive values* required for the qualitatively different system of non-antagonistic mediations, in conjunction with *real equality,* the importance of *sol-*

idarity comes to the fore. Inevitably, in view of the acute dangers of our present conditions, it has to assume the form of *international solidarity,* as the necessary orienting principle and operative framework for the positive interchange by the freely associated social individuals among themselves in a globally intertwined reproductive order. The nation-states were always an integral part of capital's antagonistic system of mediations, regularly colliding with each other in the most destructive way, with particular gravity in the two world wars of the twentieth century. It is one of the great historic failures of capital as a system of social metabolic control that —in direct contradiction to its inexorable drive toward global economic integration—it could not bring into being on the political plane the state of the capital system as a whole. It could only offer a *ruthless substitute* for it in the form of *modern imperialist supremacy* from the last third of the nineteenth century. And that had to result in the most unstable domination, always at the cost of monumental devastation, foreshadowing in the event of yet another global conflagration the total destruction of humankind. The much propagandized process of "globalization" in our time did not—and cannot—resolve any of the underlying fateful antagonisms of the long established iniquitous system of nation states. The now aggressively promoted capitalist globalization under U.S. hegemony is only another ultimately doomed attempt at superimposing the "*state of the capital system as such*" on the rest of the world,[165] without any endeavour to solve the historically generated and persistent grave national iniquities and grievances. Only the successful institution and maintenance of the non-antagonistic system of mediations, as the hegemonic alternative of the new historic form to capital's now ruling order, can show a way out of these perilous antagonisms. For such antagonisms cannot be overcome without the fully equitable interrelationship of substantive solidarity among the freely associated social individuals, as well as of their countries, in the form of their genuine international solidarity capable of positively confronting the failures of the past. That is the only historically sustainable prospect for the future.

NOTES

1. Marx, *A Contribution to the Critique of Political Economy,* Lawrence & Wishart, London, 1971, p. 21.
2. Marx talks in this respect about "an absolutely necessary practical premise, because without it privation, *want* is merely made general, and with *want* the struggle for necessities would begin again, and all the old filthy business would necessarily be restored." Marx and Engels, *Collected Works,* vol. 5, Lawrence and Wishart, London, 1975, p. 49.
3. Marx, *A Contribution to the Critique of Political Economy,* p. 21.
4. Karl Marx and Frederick Engels, "Theses on Feuerbach," *Collected Works*, vol. 5, Lawrence and Wishart, London, 1975, No. 3.
5. Marx and Engels, *Collected Works*, vol. 5, p. 52.
6. Ibid.
7. Ibid., p. 87.
8. See my book, *Marx's Theory of Alienation,* first published by The Merlin Press, in London, in 1970.
9. For a more detailed discussion of these problems see chapter 4 of my book, *Beyond Capital,* The Merlin Press, London, 1995; especially pages 108–118 and 132–141.
10. Marx, *A Contribution to the Critique of Political Economy*, p. 20.
11. Ibid., p. 21.
12. Adam Smith, *The Wealth of Nations,* Adam and Charles Black, Edinburgh, 1863, p. 273.
13. Hegel, *Philosophy of Right,* Clarendon Press, Oxford, 1942, p. 222. There is even a touch of cynicism with regard to the actual destructive functions of the "ethical state," including the idealization of its wars, when—scoffing at Kant's wishful projection of "eternal peace"—he concludes that "corruption in nations would be the product of prolonged, let alone 'perpetual' peace." Ibid., p. 210.
14. John Stuart Mill, *Principles of Political Economy,* Longmans, Green, and Co., London, 1923, pp. 199–200.
15. Marx, *Grundrisse,* Penguin Books, Harmondsworth, 1973, pp. 832–3.
16. Marx's concluding 11th Thesis on Feuerbach.
17. Marx, *Grundrisse,* p. 172.
18. Ibid., pp. 171–2.

19. This is where we can see the relevance of Marx's sharp critique of John Stuart Mill's undialectical opposition of the two.
20. Ibid., pp. 83–4.
21. Marx describes the process of capital's centralization as the expropriation of many capitalists by the few, underlining at the same time also the far-reaching implications of this process for the socialization of production on a global scale. This is how he puts it: "This expropriation is accomplished by the action of the immanent laws of capitalist production itself, by the *centralization of capital.* One capitalist always kills many. Hand in hand with this centralization, or this expropriation of many capitalists by few, develop, on an ever-extending scale, the *cooperative* form of the labour process, the conscious technical application of science, the methodical cultivation of the soil, the transformation of the instruments of labour into instruments of labour only usable in common, the economizing of all means of production by their use as the means of production of combined, socialized labour, the entanglement of all peoples in the net of the *world market,* and with this, the *international* character of the capitalistic regime." *Capital,* vol. 1, Foreign Languages Publishing House, Moscow, 1959, p. 763.
22. Marx, *Grundrisse.,* p. 108.
23. As Marx puts it on page 171 of the *Grundrisse:* "The communal character of production would make the product into a communal, general product from the outset. The exchange which originally takes place in production—which would not be an exchange of exchange values but of *activities,*—determined by *communal needs and communal purposes*—would from the outset include the participation of the individuals in the *communal world of products.*"
24. Marx, *Economic and Philosophical Manuscripts of 1844*, Lawrence & Wishart, London, 1959, pp. 162–3. Marx's emphases.
25. Ibid., pp. 152–3. Marx's emphases.
26. Ibid., pp. 149–50. Marx's emphases.
27. Marx, "Second Thesis on Feuerbach," Marx's emphases.
28. Hegel, *The Science of Logic,* George Allen & Unwin, London, 1929, vol. 1, p. 40.
29. Marx, *Letter to Engels,* 25 March 1868.
30. Hegel, *Logic: Part One of the Encyclopaedia of the Philosophical Sciences* (from this point on abbreviated as Hegel, *Logic),* Clarendon Press, Oxford,

1975, p. 8.

31. Ibid., p. 10.

32. Ibid., p. 20.

33. Hegel's *Philosophy of History*, Dover Publications Inc., New York, 1956, p. 43.

34. Ibid., p. 44.

35. Ibid.

36. Hegel, *Logic*, p. 275.

37. Ibid., pp. 276–7.

38. Marx, *A Contribution to the Critique of Political Economy*, p. 21.

39. Hegel, *The Phenomenology of Mind*, George Allen & Unwin, London, 1949, p. 129.

40. Hegel's *Philosophy of History*, p. 103.

41. Ibid., p. 457.

42. Hegel, *Logic*, pp. 272–3.

43. Marx and Engels, *Collected Works*, vol. 5, p. 48.

44. Ibid., pp. 47–8.

45. Ibid., p. 43. Marx's emphases.

46. Ibid., p. 42.

47. Ibid., p. 28. Marx's emphases.

48. Marx and Engels, *Collected Works*, vol. 5, p. 92.

49. Marx, *Economic and Philosophical Manuscripts of 1844*, pp. 110–11. Marx's emphases.

50. Marx and Engels, *Collected Works*, p. 35.

51. Ibid., p. 41.

52. Lukács, *History and Class Consciousness*, The Merlin Press, London, 1971, p. 217.

53. He summed up his criticism in the extensive Preface he wrote in 1967 to the new edition of *History and Class Consciousness*.

54. First published by Gallimard in Paris in 1955.

55. Lukács, *History and Class Consciousness*, p. 199.

56. The interested reader can find a detailed discussion of Lukács's *History and Class Consciousness* in several chapters of my book: *Beyond Capital*.

57. Marx, *Pre-capitalist Economic Formations*, Lawrence and Wishart, London, 1964, pp. 85–7. In the Penguin edition of the *Grundrisse*, pp. 488–90.

58. Hegel, *The Phenomenology of Mind*, p. 145.

59. Ibid., pp. 142–5.
60. Marx, *Capital,* vol. 1, p. 72.
61. Ibid., p. 73.
62. Ibid., p. 75.
63. Ibid., p. 80.
64. Marx, *A Contribution to the Critique of Political Economy,* p. 20.
65. Marx, *Capital,* vol. 1, p. 81.
66. It is enough to remember in this respect the reactionary use to which Hayek puts the work of Adam Smith in his crusading writings, like *The Road to Serfdom.*
67. Marx, *Capital,* vol. 1, pp. 80–81.
68. Ibid., p. 92.
69. Ibid., pp. 92–3.
70. See Marx's Introduction to the *Grundrisse.*
71. Marx, *Capital,* vol. 1, p. 86.
72. Ibid., pp. 87–8.
73. Marx, *Grundrisse,* pp. 277–8.
74. Ibid., p. 277.
75. Ibid., p. 278.
76. Ibid. Edward Gibbon Wakefield (1796–1862) is author of *A View of the Art of Colonization, with Present Reference to the British Empire*, London, 1849. He proposed that the government should reserve land in the colonies and put a higher price on it than prevailed in the open market.
77. Marx, *Economic Works: 1861–1864, Collected Works*, vol. 34, Lawrence and Wishart, London, 1975, p. 109. Marx's emphases.
78. Ibid., p. 429.
79. Adam Smith, *The Wealth of Nations,* p. 273.
80. Marx, *Economic and Philosophical Manuscripts of 1844*, p. 152. Marx's emphases.
81. Marx, *Capital,* vol. 1, p. 81.
82. Marx, *Grundrisse,* pp. 105–6.
83. Henry Home (Lord Kames), *Loose Hints upon Education, chiefly concerning the Culture of the Heart,* Edinburgh & London, 1781, p. 284.
84. Ibid., p. 257.
85. Marx stressed in this regard that "It was an immense step forward for Adam Smith to throw out every limiting specification of wealth-creating

activity—not only manufacturing, or commercial or agricultural labour, but one as well as the other, labour in general. . . . As a rule, the most general abstractions arise only in the midst of the richest possible concrete development, where one thing appears as common to many, to all. Then it ceases to be thinkable in a particular form alone. . . . Indifference towards specific labours corresponds to a form of society in which individuals can with ease transfer from one to another, and where the specific kind is a matter of chance for them, hence of indifference. Not only the category, labour, but labour in reality has here become the means of creating wealth in general, and has ceased to be organically linked with particular individuals in any specific form." Marx, *Grundrisse,* p.104.

86. Marx and Engels, *Collected Works*, vol. 11, pp. 106–7.

87. As an article on a conference in Beijing reported recently in *Monthly Review,* some Chinese participants argued that "When a State Owned Enterprise is turned into a joint stock corporation with many shareholders, it represents socialization of ownership as Marx and Engels described it, since ownership goes from a single owner to a large number of owners [among others, this was stated by someone from the Central Party School]. If State Owned Enterprises are turned into joint stock corporations and the employees are given some shares of the stock, then this would achieve 'Marx's objective of private property.' In dealing with the State Owned Enterprises, we must follow 'international norms' and establish a 'modern property rights system'. [As in the Soviet Union and Eastern Europe at the end of the 1980s, the terms in quotes were euphemisms for capitalist norms and capitalist property rights.] Enterprises can be efficient in our socialist market economy only if they are privately owned. [This statement, voiced by several people, comes directly from Western 'neoclassical' economic theory.]" David Kotz, "The State of Official Marxism in China Today," *Monthly Review,* vol. 59, No. 4, September 2007, pp. 60–61.

88. Marx, *Gundrisse,* p. 512,

89. Ibid. p. 303. Marx's emphases. The socialist writings referred to by Marx are John Gray, *The Social System* (p. 36), and J.F. Bray, *Labour's Wrongs* (pp. 157–76).

90. Marx, *Economic Works: 1861–64, Collected Works*, vol. 34, p. 422. Marx's emphases.

91. See in particular Sections 17.2 ("Socialism in One Country"), 17.3 ("The

Failure of De-Stalinization and the Collapse of Really Existing Socialism"), and 17.4 ("The Attempted Switch from Political to Economic Extraction of Surplus-Labour: 'Glasnost' and 'Perestroika' without the People") of *Beyond Capital,* pages 622–672, in English.

92. See, for instance, the writings of Ricardo Antunes—including *Adeus ao trabalho?* (Cortez, São Paulo, 1995) and *Os sentidos do trabalho* (Boitempo, São Paulo, 1999)—in this respect.

93. Vadim Medvedev, "The Ideology of Perestroika," in *Perestroika Annual,* vol. 2, edited by Abel Aganbegyan, Futura/Macdonald, London, 1989, p. 32.

94. Marx, *Grundrisse,* p. 172.

95. Marx, *Grundrisse,* p. 105.

96. For a comprehensive survey and assessment of Utilitarianism see Catherine Audard (editor), *Anthologie historique et critique de l'utilitarisme,* Presses Universitaires de France, Paris, 1999, vol 1: "Jeremy Bentham et ses précurseurs, 1711–1832," 340 pages; vol. 2: "L'utilitarisme victorien, John Stuart Mill, Henry Sidgwick et G. E. Moore," 278 pages; vol 3: "Thèmes et débats de l'utilitarisme contemporaine," 371 pages.

97. The post-Second World War promises for significantly improving the painfully iniquitous conditions of existence by the overwhelming majority of the people even in the handful of the most privileged capitalist countries through the loudly propagandized but never seriously implemented beneficial redistributionary policies of the "Welfare State" turned out to be utterly hollow. To quote the critical words of a former leader of the Canadian New Democratic Party: "At a time when the average family income [in Canada] has actually dropped by $4,000 (between 1989 and 1996 for families with children over eighteen) and that of the richest 10 per cent has escalated to 314 times the bottom 10 per cent, there is Alice-in-Wonderland talk of social cohesion. . . . There are now many in Anglo-American countries who use 'community' and 'cohesion' the way neo-conservatives once co-opted 'family values', fine phrases that can disguise or gloss over brutalizing inequality." Edward Broadbent, "Ten Propositions about Equality and Democracy," in *Democratic Equality: What Went Wrong?,* edited by Edward Broadbent, University of Toronto Press, Toronto, 2001, pp. 10–11.

98. Kant, "Theory and Practice: Concerning the Common Saying: This May Be True in Theory but Does Not Apply to Practice," in Carl J. Friedrich

(ed.), *Immanuel Kant's Moral and Political Writings,* Random House, New York, 1949, pp. 417–8.

99. See his book: *Full Employment in a Free Society,* 2nd. edition, Unwin Hyman, London, 1960.

100. The last two quotations are taken from Marx and Engels, *Manifesto of the Communist Party,* in Marx and Engels, *Selected Works,* Foreign Languages Publishing House, Moscow, 1958, vol. 1, p. 37.

101. Ibid., p. 39.

102. Marx, *Grundrisse,* pp. 92–94.

103. Ibid., p. 270.

104. For a detailed discussion of these problems see "The Activation of Capital's Absolute Limits," chapter 5 of my book: *Beyond Capital,* pp. 142–253.

105. John Locke's "Memorandum on the Reform of the Poor Law," discussed in chapter 6 above, despite its utmost brutality and cruelty, represented a more advanced stage of capital's development, when—thanks to colonial expansion as well as to the expanding manufacture—there was a considerably greater potential demand for the "labouring poor" to be productively absorbed, alive, than in the age of Henry VIII. Hence the measure of "extermination/execution" could be more sparingly used, even if the alternatives recommended by Locke—children in compulsory work-houses above the age of *three,* and offending "beggars" being turned into slaves, with their ears clipped off, and branded on their forehead, as well as transported to the colonies, etc.—were by no means cheerful liberal devices.

106. As Hegel insisted, "with firmly established laws, and a settled organization of the State, what is left to the sole arbitration of the monarch is, in point of substance, no great matter. It is certainly a very fortunate circumstance for a nation, when a sovereign of noble character falls to its lot; yet in a great state even this is of small moment, since its strength lies in the Reason incorporated in it." Hegel, *Philosophy of History,* p. 456.

107. See in this respect Harry Magdoff's classic books: *The Age of Imperialism: The Economics of U.S. Foreign Policy,* Monthly Review Press, New York, 1969, and *Imperialism: From the Colonial Age to the Present,* Monthly Review Press, New York, 1978, and an equally illuminating book, co-authored by Paul Baran and P. M. Sweezy: *Monopoly Capital,* Monthly Review Press, New York, 1966.

108. Like: Saddam Hussein's "weapons of mass destruction are ready to be launched against the West in forty-five minutes," as debated and accepted (not with one but with both eyes closed) in Tony Blair's British Parliament.

109. Marx, *Economic and Philosophic Manuscripts of 1844,* p. 129. Marx's emphases.

110. Naturally, the capitalists and the workers internalize the established order's self-expansionary imperative in very different ways. If they did not do so, they could not be carriers of opposed, but historically in principle sustainable, hegemonic alternatives in their confrontations. Nevertheless, there is also a common feature in their conflicts. It is the false appearance of merely individualistic vicissitudes against the reality of objective determinations. On capital's side, in tune with the *centrifugal* character of the system's microcosms, it is the necessity of conflicts pursued among particular capitalists for the purpose of gaining *relative advantage* to themselves as more viable capitalists than their capitalist competitors. For they must secure their position in the overall social reproductive order on a basis whose real measure is the *longer term* success, as *structurally viable* productive units, in their fundamental antagonistic confrontation with the hegemonic alternative class. In other words, the struggle for *relative advantage* among the particular capitalists is pursued in the final analysis for the fundamental purpose of securing and safeguarding *absolute advantage* and *permanent domination* of the capitalist class over labour. This is why the ideologically projected postulate of undivided class solidarity among the totality of the personifications of capital belongs to the realm of fairy tales, and must remain there also in the future.

On the other hand, the conflicts among the workers themselves are inherent in the conditions under which they have to confront the organized power of capital and secure to themselves work as more or less *isolated individuals*. Marx acknowledged this by stressing that "Competition separates individuals from one another, not only the bourgeois but *still more the workers,* in spite of the fact that it *brings them together*. . . . Hence every *organized power* standing over against these isolated individuals, who live in conditions daily reproducing this isolation, can only be overcome after *long struggles*. To demand the opposite would be tantamount to demanding that *competition* should not exist in this definite epoch of history, or that the individuals should *banish from their mind* conditions over which *in their isolation* they have no control." (Marx and Engels, *Collected Works*, vol. 5, p. 75.) Evidently, therefore, the miserly competitive success obtained by the individual workers against other workers, due to the internalization, at the given time, of their conditions of structural subordination to productively successful capital, has nothing to do with some nature-determined, ineradicable *egotism*, as the "civil society" theories suggest. It is a problematical but understandable response to the power of capital which could not be overcome without the workers' *conscious organization* in pursuit of not minor competitive advantage but for the institution of their own alternative reproductive order: a fundamental challenge. Thus, what appears to be an inherently egotistic characteristic in the workers' behaviour is not a self-originating *causal* determination. On the contrary, it is the *consequence* of their structurally imposed domination by the historically changeable capital system.

111. Locke, *Two Treatises of Civil Government,* Book I, paragraph 45.
112. He argued that "Find out something that hath the use and value of money amongst his neighbours, you shall see the same man will begin to enlarge his possessions." Ibid., Book I, paragraph 49.
113. Ibid., Book I, paragraph 50.
114. Ibid., Book II, paragraph 119.
115. Marx, *Economic and Philosophic Manuscripts of 1844,* pp. 111–2. Marx's emphases.
116. Ibid., p. 104.
117. Ibid., p. 107. Marx's emphases.
118. Ibid., p. 104. Marx's emphases.
119. Ibid., p. 105. Marx's emphases.
120. Marx, *Economic and Philosophic Manuscripts of 1844,* pp. 111–2.
121. Marx and Engels, *Collected Works*, vol. 5, p. 49.
122. Paracelsus, *Selected Writings,* Routledge & Kegan Paul, London, 1851, p. 176.
123. Paracelsus, *Leben und Lebensweisheit in Selbstzeugnissen,* Reclam Verlag, Leipzig, 1956, p. 134.
124. Marx, *Economic and Philosophic Manuscripts of 1844,* p. 99.
125. Ibid.
126. Ibid. Marx's emphases.
127. Marx, *Economic and Philosophic Manuscripts of 1844,* pp. 111–2.
128. I have discussed these problems in considerable detail in my book: *O*

desafio e o fardo do tempo historico, Boitempo Editorial, São Paulo, 2007; and *The Challenge and Burden of Historical Time,* Monthly Review Press, New York, 2008. See in particular chapter 6: "Economic Theory and Politics—Beyond Capital" (pp. 163–180) and chapter 9: "Socialism in the Twenty-first Century" (pp. 235–342), in English.

129. Marx, *Economic and Philosophic Manuscripts of 1844,* p. 114. Marx's emphases.
130. See Kant, "Theory and Practice: Concerning the Common Saying: This May Be True in Theory but Does Not Apply to Practice," in Carl J. Friedrich (ed.), *Immanuel Kant's Moral and Political Writings,* Random House, New York, 1949, pp. 417–8, quoted above, on page 297.
131. See the passage quoted from page 456 of Hegel's *Philosophy of History.*
132. See a detailed discussion of this problem in "The Structural Crisis of Politics," in chapter 10 of my book: *O desafio e o fardo do tempo historico,* Boitempo Editorial, São Paulo, 2007, pp. 347–364; in English: *The Challenge and Burden of Historical Time,* Monthly Review Press, New York, 2008. See also "Alternative to Parliamentarism: Unifying the Material Reproductive and the Political Sphere," section 7 of chapter 9 of the same book, pp. 276–293.
133. Marx, *Critique of Hegel's Philosophy of Right,* Cambridge Universiy Press, 1970, p. 54.
134. Ibid., p. 96.
135. Ibid., p. 85.
136. Ibid., pp. 88–9.
137. See Irving Fetscher, *Marxismusstudien,* in *Soviet Survey,* No. 33, July-September 1960, p. 88.
138. Jean Hyppolite, *Études sur Marx et Hegel,* Librairie Marcel Rivière & Cie., Paris, 1955, p. 101.
139. Lukács, *History and Class Consciousness,* p. xxxvi.
140. See the much celebrated book by Maurice Merleau-Ponty, *Les aventures de la dialectique,* Gallimard, Paris, 1955.
141. See a fully documented discussion of his retreat in "Merleau-Ponty and the 'League of Abandoned Hope' " on pages 161–167 of my book: *The Power of Ideology*, Harvester/Wheatsheaf, London, 1988.
142. Marx, *Economic and Philosophic Manuscripts of 1844,* pp. 139–41. Marx's emphases.

143. Columbus in his letter from Jamaica, 1503.
144. Marx, *Capital,* vol. 1, pp. 131–3.
145. J. L. Austin, *Philosophical Papers,* Clarendon Press, Oxford, 1961, p. 98.
146. "Plus loin avec Claude Lévi-Strauss," an extensive interview in *L'Express,* No. 1027, 15–21 March 1971, p. 66.
147. István Mészáros, *The Power of Ideology,* p. 54.
148. Michel Foucault, *The Order of Things,* Tavistock Publications, London, 1970, p. 385.
149. Ibid., p.387.
150. Descartes, *A Discourse on Method,* Everyman Edition, Dent and Sons, London, 1957, p. XVI.
151. Descartes, ibid., p. 49.
152. *Philosophy and the Crisis of European Man,* in Husserl, *Phenomenology and the Crisis of Philosophy,* Harper & Row, New York, 1965, p. 168.
153. To consummate fully the total disenfranchising of the working classes, the ultimate logic of the parliamentary "two party" system (i.e., the now existing "one party with two right wings") is the formation of capital's automatically self-justifying *"national unity governments"* in the event of a major electoral deadlock. Germany already produced a good example of it after the defeat of the social democratic chancellor, Schroeder. The further deepening of capital's systemic crisis could turn this form of "parliamentary democracy" into the—conjuncturally prevailing—general rule.
154. It is important to remember here that while in March and April 1917 Lenin was still advocating "a state *without* a standing army, *without* a police opposed to the people, *without* an officialdom placed above the people" (Lenin, *Collected Works,* vol. 24, p. 49, Lenin's emphases), and proposed to "organize and arm *all* the poor, exploited sections of the population in order that *they themselves should constitute* these organs of state power" (ibid., vol. 23, p. 326, Lenin's emphases), later, however, his views significantly changed under the conditions of a grave state of emergency. The extent to which the newly created state organs were structurally conditioned by the old state were clearly acknowledged by Lenin in these words: "We took over the old machinery of the state, and *that was our misfortune.* Very often this machinery operates against us. In 1917, after we seized power, the government officials sabotaged us. This frightened us very much and we pleaded: 'Please come back'. They all came back but that was our

misfortune. We now have a vast army of government employees, but lack sufficiently educated forces to exercise real control over them. In practice it often happens that here at the top, where we exercise *political power*, the machine functions somehow; but down below government employees have *arbitrary control* and they often exercise it in such a way as to counteract our measures. At the top, we have, I don't know how many, but at all events, I think, no more than a few thousand, at the outside several tens of thousands of our own people. Down below, however, there are hundreds of thousands of old officials whom we got from the Tsar and from bourgeois society and who, partly deliberately and partly unwittingly, work against us." (Ibid., vol. 33, pp. 428–9.) As we all know, the situation had become much worse as time went by, parallel to the extension of arbitrary control also at the top of the state through Stalin's consolidation of power whose danger was perceived by Lenin, and even clearly stated in his famous "Testament," but to no avail.

155. Marx, *Economic and Philosophic Manuscripts of 1844,* p. 114. Marx's emphases.
156. See page 342 above.
157. Lukács, *The Destruction of Reason,* Merlin Press, London, 1980, p. 609.
158. Marianne Weber, *Max Weber, ein Lebensbild,* Tübingen, 1926, p. 665. Quoted by Lukács on p. 610 of *The Destruction of Reason.*
159. Ibid.
160. And now, of course, also U.S. imperialism which retains "internal democracy" and "liberty" as its far from negligible points of reference, notwithstanding all of their attempted, so far still partial, violations, while unhesitatingly practising very different principles abroad.
161. See the passage quoted in 7 of chapter 8, where Marx stressed that, in view of capital's growing destructiveness, nothing less than "merely to safeguard their very existence" is now at stake for the individuals. Marx and Engels, *Collected Works*, vol. 5, p. 87.
162. Ibid., p. 49. Emphases in the original.
163. Ibid., pp. 52–3.
165. We should never disregard Democratic President Clinton's earlier quoted assertion that "there is only one necessary nation, the United States of America."

Index